The Mongols at China's Edge

WORLD SOCIAL CHANGE
Series Editor: Mark Selden

FORTHCOMING TITLES

The Mongols at China's Edge

History and the Politics of National Unity

Uradyn E. Bulag

ROWMAN & LITTLEFIELD PUBLISHERS, INC.
Lanham • Boulder • New York • Oxford

ROWMAN & LITTLEFIELD PUBLISHERS, INC.

Published in the United States of America
by Rowman & Littlefield Publishers, Inc.
An imprint of the Rowman & Littlefield Publishing Group
4720 Boston Way, Lanham, Maryland 20706
www.rowmanlittlefield.com

12 Hid's Copse Road, Cumnor Hill, Oxford OX2 9JJ, England

British Library Cataloging in Publication Information Available

Library of Congress Cataloging-in-Publication Data

Bulag, Uradyn Erden.
    The Mongols at China's edge: history and the politics of national
unity / Uradyn E. Bulag.
        p.   cm. — (World social change)
    Includes bibliographical references and index.
    ISBN 0-7425-1143-X (alk. paper) — ISBN 0-7425-1144-8 (pbk. : alk. paper)
    1. Inner Mongolia (China)—Politics and government.   I. Title.   II. Series.
DS793.M7 B95   2002
951'.77—dc21   2002001193

Printed in the United States of America

♾ ™ The paper used in this publication meets the minimum requirements of American
National Standard for Information Services—Permanence of Paper for Printed Library
Materials, ANSI/NISO Z39.48-1992.

Contents

Illustrations

Acknowledgments

On not a few occasions during my fieldwork in Inner Mongolia I encountered people who prepared notes, rather than orally telling me what they knew, to make sure they did not "mislead" this "young man with a bright future" by saying something in violation of the Party's nationality policies. They tried to protect me from writing something politically incorrect, thereby destroying my own "future." Their fears are not unfounded. Many showed their wounds, the prints of past injustices for merely being Mongol. They gave me the sincerest advice—don't touch the nationality question! Their weak, trembling advice is deafening. I appreciate the time and words of many of my compatriots who provided a clear vision of the Mongol ethnopolitics in China and the dilemmas of their articulation or lack thereof. The 2000 summer trip to Inner Mongolia proved challenging, as all their warnings proved true. But this was also a rewarding two-month stay, because, for the first time in over ten years after I had left Inner Mongolia, I had the opportunity to spend extended time with my parents and relatives. I listened to the detailed explanation from my parents and in-laws, who have a deeper faith in the horoscope determining one's fate than they do in temporal political and cultural contexts: "This is your year; it goes against you. But next year everything will be fine."

This book is thus written with my mind and heart. It combines cool-minded analysis and emotional passion; it contains my relenting sighs and my self-acknowledged limitations. There have been ups and downs in writing this book. My former mentor Caroline Humphrey has encouraged me to get above the immediate entanglement and see this as a valuable contribution to both the people and the profession I deeply love. I owe this profession to my education under her tutelage, and I gratefully thank her for maintaining an active interest in my work, long after her professional responsibility ended. She read and commented on various versions of all the chapters with her usual acuity.

I am fortunate to have met Mark Selden, whose breadth of knowledge of Chinese, Japanese, and Vietnamese societies and whose sense of justice—whose relentless effort to unveil injustice, political or otherwise—do not stop impressing and inspiring me. He has been patient to my complaints concerning the emotional difficulty for a native Mongol to write about his own society and my threat to drop my Mongol studies once and for all. He encouraged me to submit the manuscript to the series he edits and has edited several versions of these chapters, pruning many a weed. It would not have attained its present shape without his superb editorship combined with deep academic knowledge.

I want to express my gratitude and respect to Susan McEachern, vice president and executive editor for Area Studies and Geography at Rowman & Littlefield Publishing Group, for her enthusiastic support and for steering the manuscript through the process of publication with understanding and patience.

I have also benefited a great detail from exchanging ideas with Pan Jiao, professor of anthropology at the Central University of Nationalities in Beijing. His profound knowledge of theories and histories of nationalism and ethnicity in China is a constant source of inspiration. He has read all the chapters, some several times, over the last few years, constantly challenging me to come to terms with the imbrication of class and ethnicity in socialist China. I also thank Luisa Schein, Allen Chun, Liu Xiaoyuan, and Wurlig Bao for offering critical readings on some chapters.

I owe the completion of this book to my wife, Lan Mei, who has accompanied me since 1990, sharing my trauma and pleasure of writing the first book about Mongolia and then this one. She has been through every phase of my mental movement, my joy and frustration. And when I threaten to relax or even quit, she snaps back: "If you dare."

This book was initiated when I was a research fellow of the Leverhulme Foundation and research fellow of Corpus Christi College (1995–1998), my good old Cambridge college, which also funded my M. Phil. and Ph.D. studies in Cambridge. It was in that three-year period that I completed my first book, *Nationalism and Hybridity in Mongolia* (Oxford 1998), and earlier versions of some chapters in this book. Here I want to extend my sincere gratitude to both the Leverhulme Foundation and Corpus Christi College. The project was then brought to the United States in September 1998 when I took up the assistant professorship in anthropology at Hunter College of the City University of New York. I must say that the three years' experience of teaching has been no less rewarding. My colleagues at Hunter College and the Graduate School have been helpful and caring, assisting my integration into the new community and directing me to new research funding opportunities. One chapter in the book was read in early 1998 as part of my job interview, and another in 2000 as an entrée into the Graduate Center as a faculty member. I have tested some of my ideas on my anthropologist colleagues Susan Lees and Gerald Creed, Chinese historian colleague Rick Belsky, and Asian-American studies colleague Peter Kwong. I have received two CUNY fellowships, which, while intended for other research, were helpful in allowing me to visit Harvard Yenching libraries in the summer of 1999.

Early versions of three chapters have been published elsewhere. Chapter 3 was published in *Cultural Studies* 14:3 (2000), and chapter 7 in *Central Asian Survey* 17:1 (1998) (see www.tandf.co.uk for journals published by Taylor & Francis). Chapter 6 was published in *China Journal* 42 (July 1999). I thank the journals for allowing them to be republished here. The current versions are, however, substantially different in scope and content, incorporating additional research, and thus are substantially revised.

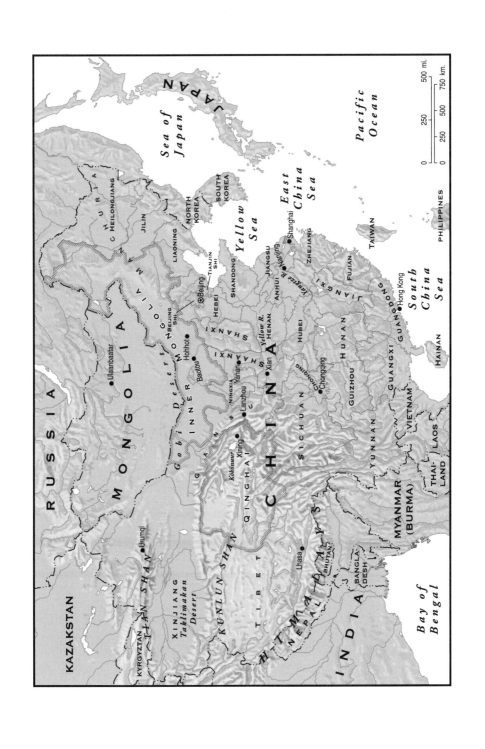

1

𝄞

By Way of Introduction: *Minzu Tuanjie* and Its Discontents

This book represents an effort to understand the multifaceted Mongol experience in China, past and present, and through it, to highlight broader issues pertaining to the Mongols and other peoples on China's vast borders. It particularly seeks to cast light on the development and praxis of the concept of minority nationalities in the People's Republic of China in the context of the politics of national unity, *minzu tuanjie*. Above all, this book explores from diverse angles the moral and political implications and contradictions of minzu tuanjie in a socialist regime.

Rather than assuming totalitarian power on the part of the Chinese Communist Party, I have explored some of the intricate relations between socialism and nationalism that produce both resistance and complicity and the moral dilemmas that have confronted Mongols and Chinese in negotiating nationality issues. Thus the book does not privilege the Mongols as a colonized ethnic minority with "authentic" voices challenging "power." Instead, the text is a conscious exploration of blurred boundaries—geographic, conceptual, and ideological— offering an analysis of the complex modern history of the Mongols, nationalism and communism, and ethnic relations in terms of land tenure, class struggle, tribal and regional antagonism, as well as the state's nationality policy.

I have written this book with several questions in mind. First, to understand the characteristics of Chinese national unity, an ideology framed to define Chinese–minority relations and encapsulated in the expression "minzu tuanjie." Such a unity is premised on the unity of diverse groups, many of which had been antagonistic to one another throughout history, but now find themselves in the territorial confines of China through various processes. Chinese political, cultural, and historiographical discourse represents them as conscious or thinking subjects who fought together to achieve the present Chinese national form. Sec-

1

ond, there are questions pertaining to Mongolian nationalism and communism. The Inner Mongolian Autonomous Region emerged in 1947 as a product of cooperation between Mongol communists, led by Ulanhu and the Chinese Communist Party (CCP); Mongols played a significant role in the CCP victory in the civil war that brought the Party to power. How do Mongol nationalism and socialism configure in a China that is also nationalistic and communist in its own right? Third, given that Mongols constitute a tiny minority not only of the Chinese population but even of the population of the Inner Mongolia Autonomous Region, how can they legitimately exercise their rights of self-government as the titular nationality in their historic homeland? Fourth, Mongols in China do not live in isolation from the Mongol world; they constitute part of a transnational community, one with historical, cultural, and genealogical bonds with Mongols in Mongolia. This, then, raises a moral and political question about the extent to which the struggle for Mongol cultural integrity and reproduction in China and Mongol aspirations to achieve legitimacy as citizens come into conflict with a demand for authenticity in a wider Mongolian community. Finally, should we treat Mongols as a "category" or as a "community"? If a community is imagined as sovereign and limited, we should ask not only about its "national belonging" (i.e., belonging to a larger national, yet culturally antagonistic, state), but also about the integrity and morality of the culture of the community in the process of achieving or losing that "belonging."

Some of the previously mentioned issues haunted me while I researched my previous book, and they continue to resonate with me as I write this one. Whereas *Nationalism and Hybridity in Mongolia* (Bulag 1998) records the sense of displacement and predicament of Inner Mongols in the wider Mongol world, this book represents my continued effort to comprehend the historical process by which Mongols have sought to survive as Mongols in China.

MONGOLS AT CHINA'S EDGE

Inner Mongolia presents a paradox for understanding contemporary ethnopolitics in China. Unlike Tibet and Xinjiang, whose ethnonationalist movements have attracted great attention, inviting speculation concerning a direct ethnic challenge to the communist regime and even anticipating a Soviet-style scenario of national disintegration, Mongols apparently no longer exhibit such an independent spirit. Whatever its cultural and ethnic links with the Republic of Mongolia on its northern border, Inner Mongolia appears a quiet backwater. Indeed, this state of Inner Mongolia is often presented as a possible fate for Tibet and Xinjiang, as Inner Mongolia is considered a model of the CCP solving of its nationality questions. This may be manifest in the very name the Chinese government wants the world at large to call Inner Mongolia: *Nei Monggol*, a hybridized name combining Chinese word *Nei* (Inner) with *Monggol*, the classical

Mongolian spelling for "Mongol." This vulgarized hybridity displays a certain poetic authenticity of the Mongolness, while simultaneously denoting its political belonging.

The light weight that Inner Mongolia carries in China's ethnopolitics poses interesting questions, not least because, in recent decades, it has been ignored in comparison with Tibet and Xinjiang. Minorities in the southwest, especially in Yunnan province, have moreover attracted much Western anthropological gaze, by virtue of their purported peacefulness and colorfulness, as well as their ascending importance in Chinese exhibitions celebrating the nation's colorful ethnic and cultural diversity. Mongols thus have been doubly sidelined in both China and in Western academia: They are neither "dangerous" nor "colorful." How, then, did the Mongols manage to come to such a pass? Indeed, the very question requires a study, if only to shed light on the great disjuncture between the historical image of Mongols as the most ferocious world conquerors and their current "peacefulness" or "sheepishness."

For those with historical knowledge of the Mongols, the link of Mongols with China—in a unitary state without Mongol domination—also poses a conundrum. It is difficult to reconcile the fact that Mongols constitute an absolute minority in China's Inner Mongolia Autonomous Region, while enjoying nominal status as its titular rulers. Given the historical conflicts between Mongols and Chinese, often with Mongols conquering or pillaging China, how do such historical memories figure in the development and maintenance of the Mongols as a national minority in a multinational state having Chinese as its core? Above all, what justifies China's "ownership" of Inner Mongolia within the territorial and moral confines of China, which Mongols have trespassed historically and geographically, as testified by the existence, however tenuous, of the independent Republic of Mongolia and other Mongol republics in Russia, such as the Buryat and Kalmyk republics? These issues open up further questions of Mongols in China; about Chinese approaches to ethnic management, ideological, cultural, and physical; as well as about how, when, and why Mongols in China have been imagined.

Modern nation-states have many ways of managing their diversity, aiming to cohere diverse and often conflicting groups into a unitary whole. Ironically, nation-states usually deny such a constructivist effort, often going to great lengths to "naturalize" the belonging of different groups to the nation, thereby seeking to achieve a seamless entity to defy any challenges. Narrating the Mongols into a naturalized, but also a subordinate, group internal to China since antiquity, in terms of power and civilization, has been the task of many a contemporary Chinese historian. But this naturalization has never been easy. Until the early twentieth century, Mongols exhibited great strength vis-à-vis the Chinese. Indeed, in the thirteenth and fourteenth centuries, the Chinese experienced the iron rule of the Mongols, as did many other peoples across Eurasia. It may not be an exaggeration to claim that the very consciousness of Chineseness has been shaped by the nomadic Others in Inner Asia, represented by the Xiongnu, Mongols, and Manchu—thus constituting a unique ethnoscape, civilization versus barbarism, from the Chinese perspective. This worldview persisted until the late nineteenth century, when the new European "barbarians" replaced steppe "barbarians" as the predominant threat to China. Viewed historically, the Mongol–Chinese conflict cannot be explained in terms of *minzu*, or nationality politics, in a territorially and ideologically enclosed Chinese nation-state.

In the thirteenth century, Mongol military engagement ranged across the length and breadth of Eurasia, including the Middle East and parts of western Europe. In this vast setting—belying pundits' typical, one-sided prediction that barbarians are inevitably attracted to Chinese civilization and are culturally uplifted (*wenhua*), hence becoming Chinese—Mongols demonstrated a spirit that frustrated Chinese civilizational discourse. Even when Mongol rulers were eventually subjected to alien cultural influences as they dismounted in order to rule their subjects, they chose not Chinese Confucianism but Islam and Buddhism. Eventually, those who embraced Islam formed separate nations (e.g., the Kazakhs), while those who accepted Buddhism retained their Mongol identity, genealogically linked with Chinggis Khan. This tendency was apparent even in the Mongol Yuan, a dynasty of conquest that the Chinese now claim as their own and that is presented as proof of China's ownership of Mongols—indeed, this example is sometimes used to justify Mongol sovereign appropriation of Tibet on behalf of China. Mongols, far from succumbing to Chinese culture, in fact exerted considerable influence upon the Chinese—so much so that the first emperor of the Ming dynasty, Zhu Yuanzhang, in November 1367 and in February 1368 repeated edicts designed to cleanse Mongol cultural traces from among the Chinese. He complained that many Chinese had Mongol names, spoke Mongol, wore Mongol clothes, and "have forgotten the surname of their ancestors, and in contrast have turned to the barbarian caitiff's animal names, and consider them honorable titles. They use the names of the Yuan for their personal advantage" (quoted in Serruys 1959: 162). It is of more than idle interest that Zhu Yuanzhang raised the clarion call to "expel the barbarian, and restore China" (*quzhu dalu, huifu zhonghua*), a slogan echoed in 1905 when Chinese nationalists attempted to overthrow the Qing dynasty. It is apparent that if nationalism is defined as a discursive, as well as an institutional, ethnic boundary-setting ideology and practice (cf. Duara 1996), Ming China, established in 1368, was already a full-blown nation-state. Indeed, Ming ideals inspired later Chinese nationalists to overthrow the Qing and establish the Republic of China (Zhonghua Minguo), with its capital in Nanjing, the Ming capital.

The continued Mongol–Chinese and steppe people–Chinese confrontations after the Yuan—later monumentalized in the Ming Great Wall—point to the clash of two value systems. Although the term "civilizational clashes" is much denounced in contemporary progressive circles, and I am far from ready to accept Samuel Huntington's advocacy of such a notion to define a post–Cold War

global context, the persistent Mongol–Chinese confrontation had wide ramifications that might well be termed "civilizational." This conflict of core values is
arguably the most fundamental binary division of humanity, between nomadic
and sedentary, as Deleuze and Guattari so elegantly argue. They lament that
"[h]istory is always written from the sedentary point of view and in the name of
State apparatus, at least a possible one, even when the topic is nomads. What is
lacking is a Nomadology, the opposite of a history" (1987: 23).

Much of the sedentary world history demonizes Mongols. Mongols invariably
represent the devilish Other, to Europeans no less than to Chinese. As far as the
Europeans are concerned, the Mongol conquest not only conjured up dread in
the form of the Yellow Peril, the Scourge of God, or the Mongol Horde, but also,
thanks to Marco Polo's account, it caused a new fascination with the Orient that
became one inspiration for world exploration. As Edward Said notes, "There has
been some important recent work on the background of Biblical scholarship to
the rise of what I have called modern Orientalism. The best and the most illumi-
natingly relevant is E. S. Shaffer's impressive '*Khubla Khan' and the Fall of Jerusa-
lem*, an indispensable study of the origins of Romanticism, and the intellectual
activity underpinning a great deal of what goes on in Coleridge, Browning, and
George Eliot" (1978: 18). This romanticism later gave way to racism, as Mongols,
with their allegedly characteristic slanted eyes and blue birth spots, came to represent the paragon of the yellow race, which would be honored after the Mongols—Mongoloid. Mongols are also supposed to be mentally handicapped, hence
the term "Mongol" for Down's syndrome (cf. Stuart 1997). Mongols figure prominently in Marx's formulation of "oriental despotism" and the "Asiatic Mode of
Production" that allegedly made Asia, especially India, stagnant and that
required England to "fulfill a double mission in India: one destructive, the other
regenerating—the annihilation of the Asiatic society, and the laying of the
material foundations of Western society in Asia" (quoted in Said 1978: 154).
What is interesting is that Karl Wittfogel (1957), an anticommunist warrior,
used the Mongols and the concept of "oriental despotism" as a weapon against
communism and Marxism. Mongols, in his rendering, apparently contributed to
the intransigence of Soviet totalitarianism.

Until very recently, in China there has been little romanticization of the
nomads. The nomads ultimately represented a barrier to the expansion of Chinese civilization. The Great Wall, although not originally built to shield against
nomadic power, came to symbolize the national defense of Chinese civilization
against barbarian invasion (Waldron 1990). In juxtaposition to this "defense"
against nomadic Mongols, the Chinese, in the early twentieth century—in a
more romantic and yet racist mood of pan-Asianism—appropriated Chinggis
Khan as a Chinese hero, prompting the iconoclastic Chinese writer Lu Xun to
comment sarcastically in 1934,

> When I was a kid, I knew that China, after "Pangu opening up the heaven and the
> earth," had three emperors and five kings, . . . Song dynasty, Yuan dynasty, Ming

dynasty, and "Our Great Qing." At the age of 20 I then heard that "our" Chinggis
Khan conquered Europe, and it was "our" most glorious era. Only when I reached 25
did I learn that the so-called "our" most glorious era was nothing but when Mongols
conquered China. We became lackeys. And not until August this year, because I
read three books about Mongol history to check some stories, did I realize that Mongol conquest of "Russia," invasion of Hungary and Austria preceded their conquest
of the whole of China, and Chinggis Khan at that time was not yet our Khan.
Rather the Russians had longer credentials for being enslaved, and it is they who
should say, "Our Chinggis Khan conquered China, and it was our most glorious
era." (Lu Xun 1981: 631–32)

At the turn of the twenty-first century, numerous books and movies about Chinggis Khan are being churned out in China, often with a logo, "The Only Chinese to defeat the Europeans." Mongols, or rather their history and their
quintessential heroes, have fought for the Chinese—wholeheartedly, it seems.

This greatness of Mongols, in its positive or negative and Chinese or Western
representations, is today often divorced from the historical path through which
Mongols came down. In the seventeenth century, Mongols lost their preroga-
tives to another power, the Manchus. Mongols became a junior partner in
founding the Qing and enjoyed more privileged status vis-à-vis the Chinese
within this Manchu empire. The Qing empire experience, however, proved devastating in its consequences. Qing territorial reorganization of the Mongols into
mutually exclusive but loyal subjects to the Qing court fundamentally undermined the Mongol potential to rise as a great power once again under a new
leadership. On the more positive side, the Qing territorial designation and
encouragement of Tibetan Buddhism gave rise to a new Mongol historical and
cultural consciousness. Above all, it inculcated a territorial consciousness that
had ramifications for not only an internal tribal boundary, but also a boundary
with China—the latter thanks to the Qing policy of segregating Mongols from
Chinese in order to preserve Mongol pristine prowess. The consequence of this
Qing experience resonates strongly today, for not only do Mongols remain split
along the line of Inner and Outer Mongolia, the latter becoming an independent
state as soon as the Qing collapsed in 1911, but Inner Mongolia was colonized
by Chinese warlords and subsequently came under Chinese Republican administration.

The transition from an empire to a nation-state is never an easy one, especially for China. Louisa Schein succinctly outlines the two nationalisms China
embraces: "They can be referred to as Han nationalism and Chinese nationalism. Han nationalism was concerned with boundaries between peoples within
the shifting territory of the Chinese polity, specifically between Han and those
they designated as 'barbarians.' Chinese nationalism rose in response to inci-
dences of foreign imperialist aggression that prompted a unifying within the
physical boundary of China against the outside" (2000: 108). Here, we have a

problem, almost a dialectical one. Han nationalism originally targeted Manchus and Mongols, who for hundreds of years had been China's historic enemies. How, then, can Manchus, Mongols, and other non-Chinese peoples be accommodated as equal national siblings in unity against a racial imperialism from without? This dialectical conundrum is fascinating, especially when those now styled as minority nationalities persistently refuse to be confined to this newly imagined sinocentric community. To what extent is Chinese nationalism civic, as opposed to a primordial Han nationalism?

These are particularly pertinent questions regarding Mongols. Their incorporation into China was not a smooth one, by virtue of the fact that Outer Mongolia—the other half of the Mongolian geobody—became independent, allegedly with the assistance of Russian imperialists. Inner Mongolia, because of its geographical proximity to China's political centers, ultimately failed to win independence or unification with Outer Mongolia—not without a fight, of course. Much of the first half of the twentieth century witnessed the Inner Mongols languishing under Chinese colonialism, which erased Inner Mongolia as an entity, dividing the area under several Chinese provinces, at various times including Gansu, Ningxia, Suiyuan, Chahar, Rehe, Jilin, Liaoning, and Heilongjiang. Inner Mongolia experienced massive militarized Chinese immigration, leading to the opening up of Mongol grassland for Chinese agricultural development. Various attempts were made for Inner Mongolian independence from China or for unification with the Mongolian People's Republic, even resorting to collaboration with the Japanese, in the hope for deliverance from Chinese rule. A Mongol communist movement eventually succeeded in collaborating with the Chinese Communist Party, entering strategic alliances against the Japanese and the National Chinese government, in exchange for CCP support of an Inner Mongolian autonomy consistent with the proclaimed communist goals of colonial liberation.

An Inner Mongolia Autonomous Region under Chinese communist aegis was founded on May 1, 1947, two and a half years before the founding of the People's Republic of China. It expanded its territory, dismantling Chinese provinces built on Inner Mongolian territory, and only in 1956 took the shape that we know today. Ironically, Mongols were made the titular nationality of the autonomous region, but as early as 1947 they became an absolute minority in their own homeland, with a ratio of one Mongol to five Chinese.

History thus poses profound questions, questions somewhat different from those related to Tibet and Xinjiang and perhaps to other minorities in the southwest. How does the Inner Mongolia Autonomous Region, which was founded as a demonstration of the communist spirit of national equality, configure in the two nationalisms that China embraces? How do Mongols, especially communist Mongols, explain their path until today to prove the resolution of their own "nationality question"? How are the historical memories and cultural differences of Mongols and Chinese mediated in a socialist, but also nationalist, regime?

Above all, what is the future for the Mongols in China, when the nation increasingly abandons its socialist veneer and promotes a more virulent nationalism that centers on the discourse of minzu tuanjie (national unity) and *minzu fenlie* (national splitism)? This book attempts to answer some, if not all, of these questions.

MINZU TUANJIE AND ITS DISCONTENTS

The People's Republic of China, a state founded in October 1949 on the premise of a radical communist vision of building a new society for the emancipation of all humanity, ironically defined itself as a unitary but multinational state (*tongyi de duo minzu guojia*), based on the Qing imperial geographical domain. Such a nation-building principle has set the stage for the clash between two contradictory phenomena: the desire on the part of the state to promote and enforce unity, homogenizing the nationscape; and the desire of each minority nationality to preserve distinctive cultural and social characteristics and which may or may not wish to remain within a "unitary" Chinese state. In what ways are such tensions in China different or similar to those in other nation-states? It is no exaggeration to say that no single state in the world entirely meets the condition of a nation-state, which, according to Ernest Gellner (1983), must make the boundaries of the nation and the state congruent. But since nation-states are the only legitimate territorial organizations recognized in the current world order, congruency of the boundaries of nation and state is nonetheless the ideal for any nation-state to achieve. This is especially ironic for Europe and North America, the wellsprings of nationalism, because they have been torn between the nationalist ideal and the multicultural or multiracial reality. Since the 1960s the civil rights struggle and myriad other conflicts in those countries may be characterized as striving to enlarge the discursive space of the nation, dislodging the monopoly of the nation by bourgeois elites, and redefining the terms of citizenship so that the "fragments" of the nation—ethnic, racial, gender, religious and class, among others—can be accommodated and represented in the nation without discrimination. Many of these countries now strive to achieve a new model of diversity— multiculturalism. To be sure, the struggle for minority rights is far from complete, and repression and discrimination take various overt and covert forms. Moreover, struggle for multiculturalism may be as much a struggle for recognition and rights by marginal groups as it is an elite effort to "manage" tensions within the nation. Nevertheless, the contours and discourses of nationalism and diversity have experienced subtle and far-reaching changes in these societies.

In contrast to these multicultural countries, China confronts a different set of problems of diversity. Like the former Soviet Union, China consists of a mosaic of many territorial nationalities whose historic homelands have been incorporated into the modern Chinese state and whose positions have been transformed from being sovereign or semi-sovereign people on China's periphery to minority nationalities. And yet these minorities, instead of being organized in a federation as in the former Soviet Union—thereby recognizing and giving corporate expression to their intrinsic national integrity—have been made an integral part of a unitary Chinese nation and granted limited powers of regional autonomy. This is not to understate the ways and extent to which the Soviet Union suppressed autonomous expressions of nationalities, culturally and politically. Here I only want to note that while both the former Soviet republics and the Chinese autonomous regions were imbricated within a system dominated by Russians and Chinese, the different state-making principles and strategies and the differential nature of demographic disparity had different consequences.

A legitimate question is whether the regional autonomy granted to national minorities in China encourages a sense of separate nationhood for Mongols or contributed to the integration of Mongols into the Chinese state. This question echoes recent debates among Sovietologists regarding the effect of Soviet nationality policy in destroying the Soviet Union. Yuri Slezkine (1996), for instance, criticizes Soviet policies of what he calls "compensatory 'nation-building' " for fostering localism and nationalism that eventually brought down the Soviet Union. Francine Hirsch (2000), on the other hand—in my view, more accurately—argues that for Soviet policymakers, colonization and "making nations" went hand in hand, through a process of what she calls double assimilation—the assimilation of diverse peoples into official nationality categories and the assimilation of nationally categorized groups into an all-union political, economic, and ideational whole. This is a participatory and multifaceted process: "as new dominant nationalities and national minorities used a common vocabulary and standardized administrative procedures to fight for resources and assert their rights, they also become increasingly anchored in the Soviet state and society" (Hirsch 2000: 225).

China's autonomous regions, somewhat like the ethnoterritorial republics in the Soviet Union, gave rise to "expectations of belonging," in which titular nationalities have a sense that they "own" the autonomous territorial units. But whereas the Soviet republics institutionalized that ownership, and the problem derived from the fact that "the nationalities 'possessed' their respective territorial republics rather than being constituted by them" (Brubaker 1996: 46), in China there is an additional dimension. This centers on the fact that the emphasis on "unity," backed up by overwhelming Chinese majority population (not only nationally, but in most instances even within the putative autonomous regions), together with the power of the state and army, renders unattainable or suspect any promise of national minority "autonomy."

Perhaps the most distinctive characteristic of contemporary Chinese nation-building is the framing of the concept minzu, which denotes both a nation and an ethnic group. Minzu (nationality) is part and parcel of Chinese nation-state building, which is marked by what Michel Foucault has called governmentality—the application of techniques of surveillance and control to a whole range of institutions of a political economy and moral community (cf. Burchell et al. 1991). China's minzu-building project can be understood as a boundary-producing project predicated on the Chinese notion of genealogy and Stalin's four criteria defining nationality: common territory, common economy, common language, and common psychological make-up (Stalin's lexicon for "culture").

In determining the ethnicity of a group, one criterion may play a larger role than another, depending on the group's cultural proximity to the Chinese. In the case of the Mongols, for example, the mode of production, including the nature of economic enterprise and class structures, pivotal in the Marxist binary thesis of base and superstructure, has been deemed by both Mongols and Chinese of primary importance in demarcating Mongols from Chinese. Pastoralism, an economic practice adapted to the ecology of the grasslands and dating back to antiquity, became the ultimate cultural symbol defining the core of Mongol identity. The minzu-building project is simultaneously a purifying process, designed to make ethnic traits congruent with the qualities said to define Mongolness. In this process, other economic activities, such as agriculture, although long practiced by a large proportion of the Mongol population, including pastoralists, came to be associated with memories of Chinese colonization and thus was seen by Mongols as alien to Mongolness.

Chinese minzu management has a propensity to reify ethnic consciousness along lines specified in the minzu-building project. Minzu building is not just a state project; it is also, in this and many other instances, one that is embraced in diverse ways by the minzu subjects or fractions thereof. These amount to colonizing operations within a majoritarian Chinese society that is simultaneously colonizing minorities. The socialist "subjects," like *funü* (women) (Barlow 1994) or "*nongmin*" (peasantry) (Cohen 1993), constitute the constituencies for special citizen-forming projects that create categories that energize certain elements while suppressing others. Resistance and complicity of these groups with the state may produce a range of outcomes, including patronage and affirmative action, but also, alternatively, heavy-handed discrimination and even massacre.

Scholars, especially anthropologists, have documented some of the ways in which ethnicity and ethnic nationalism emerged with China's modern mode of governance, particularly classification and categorization of the citizens of China into 56 minzu or nationalities, which are further divided into two blocks, the majority Han and 55 ethnic minorities. In this new image of a multicultural China, the 56 being an invention of the People's Republic, we see ethnicity or perhaps deeply rooted manifestations of ethnicity working dialogically with the state's signifying machinery (Gladney 1991; Harrell 1995b; Litzinger 2000; Schein 2000). We also glimpse the potential for ethnic minority conflict and challenges to the Chinese state. These researches depart from an earlier historical and political science approach that viewed China as a nationalizing and assimilating regime (Dreyer 1976; Herberer 1989; Mackerras 1994).

So we have a theoretical and practical impasse, between China's universalizing or nationalizing tendency and its particularizing practice. The latter tendency has caused alarm among China's leaders and outside analysts, especially following the collapse of the Soviet Union, when the Soviet national-territorial delimitation demonstrated its efficacy in serving as foundations for new nation-states.

Such alarmism is not confined to China. In much of today's world there is an outcry against the rise of a new "tribalism" that either brings down a multinational state or demands the right to express ethnic identities. Primordial ethno-nationalism, which is another name for the new tribalism, is pitted against the merits of a civic empire. There is thus nostalgia in many quarters for "national unity" and repeated denunciation of any continued struggle for ethnonational liberation as "racism" wedded to primordialism. In progressive scholarly circles, the controversies are often couched in terms of civic nationalism versus ethnic nationalism or citizenship versus ethnic rights (cf. Couture et al. 1998; Kymlicka and Norman 2000).

Eric Hobsbawm, for instance, sees no value in post-1945 nationalisms, treating all of them as regressive, as "ethnic." Nationalism today, in his view, no longer contributes to "nation-building" in any progressive sense. "It is no longer, as it were, a global political program, as it may be said to have been in the nineteenth and earlier twentieth centuries. It is at most a complicating factor, or a catalyst for other developments" (1990: 181). Similarly, most postcolonial scholarship treats all nationalisms, even anticolonial nationalisms, as elite bourgeois nationalist ideologies. Tim Brennan observes of the Western criticism of nationalism in Third World countries that Western critics have shown a "conveniently European lapse of memory" (1990: 57). Praising early European nationalism as modernizing, unifying, and democratizing, they denounce Third World nationalisms as reactionary, anarchic, and irrational. "The terms of nationalism have from the European perspective apparently reversed. Not freedom from tyranny, but the embodiment of tyranny. The question is: how much is this new perspective a result of owning, rather than suffering, an empire? That is, can't it be said that the recoiling from nationalism is also partly due to the challenge of the rising national movements of the developing world?" asks Brennan forcefully (1990: 57). Here, I do not mean to endorse ethnic nationalism, but, following Brennan, only propose to question this unabashed "lapse of memory" as applied to the Chinese context.

With regard to China, I argue, these two perspectives are as much a reflection of Western intellectual paradigm shift in studies of ethnicity and nationalism as a reflection of Chinese authorities' shifting attitude toward minorities. International scholars widely recognized Chinese minority policies as assimilationist during the 1960s and 1970s, but it is often debated whether China still openly practices such a policy today. Does this mean that the Chinese regime has given up its assimilationist ambitions in favor of a more tolerant approach, granting greater autonomy to its minorities, or is it rather a strategic adjustment for its own survival? Is China a minzu-builder or a minzu-destroyer? Are these indeed mutually exclusive? How should we understand the condition of the minorities and their assertion of difference, as well as the regime's repeated denunciation of so-called national splitism (*minzu fenlie zhuyi*), even within the new official ideology of multiculturalism (*duoyuan wenhua*) as advocated by China's preeminent anthropologist Fei Xiaotong (1989)? What is minzu tuanjie, a banner that has been hoisted high in recent decades?

Important dimensions of the Chinese management of diversity are embodied in a unique expression, "minzu tuanjie," which can mean both "national unity" and "amity between nationalities" (minzu). One can visualize minzu tuanjie in diverse forms. Casual visitors to a frontier minority region cannot but be struck by the contrived friendship between nationalities that is officially trumpeted on every important occasion and even on a daily basis. To demonstrate certain contemporary dimensions of minzu tuanjie, let us journey to Hohhot, the capital city of Inner Mongolia. At the turn of the twenty-first century Hohhot is a bustling city, with a motorway interchange popularly nicknamed "Xinjiapo" (a Mandarin version of Singapore, but in this context, meaning "newly added hill," a pun deriding its uselessness), running through the middle of town. It carries few cars, blocks large sections of road, and destroys the businesses along the street below, through which it has been built, much like the thruways through some American cities. In the middle of "City-Heart Park," in front of the landmark Inner Mongolian Museum, with its flying horse facing south toward China (rather than toward the North, the trope for the Republic of Mongolia, hence "national splitism"), a gigantic billboard towers over the square, depicting Party General-Secretary Jiang Zemin overseeing a line of joyous Chinese, Mongols, and other minorities in Inner Mongolia and admonishing them to unite in order to build a more beautiful Inner Mongolia. The Inner Mongolia Museum displays an exhibition of minzu tuanjie that was mounted in 1997 on the occasion of Inner Mongolia's fiftieth anniversary. It chronicles the friendship of the Mongols and Chinese and their common effort to build a prosperous Inner Mongolia and China. The foundation for these achievements is said to have been laid by Ulanhu, a communist who was Inner Mongolia's paramount leader and China's highest ranking minority official from 1947 to 1966, and who served as China's vice president in the 1980s.

As the chapters in this book demonstrate, minzu tuanjie is a hegemonic management device to maneuver in the context of China's diversity. It is also a way to talk about nationality relationships, a statement about the state's desire to achieve its goal—that is, the homogenization of the Chinese nationscape. Gramsci's notion of hegemony is generally understood as political and cultural domination and popular acceptance of ideologies of domination. William Rose-

1.1. Jiang Zemin Overseeing *Minzu Tuanjie* in Hohhot (2000)

berry, extending Gramsci, suggests that we "explore hegemony not as a finished and monolithic ideological formation but as a problematic, contested, political *process* of domination and struggle (1996: 77, original emphasis). He further argues that formations of particular regional, religious, ethnic, national, or class communities and identities involve languages of contention and opposition to other groups that vie for dominance. We can examine minzu tuanjie as such a two-way process of community and contention in a situation whose outcomes are not predetermined.

Minzu tuanjie as a trope for national unity is often set against an antithesis—minzu fenlie (national splitism or secessionism). It is based on the premise that tuanjie ("unity") is a guarantee of stability, whereas fenlie ("split") leads to instability and disorder. Thus, there is always a power relation imbedded in minzu tuanjie—that is, insofar as it is meant to uphold the welfare of a wider community at the expense of a smaller one, tuanjie implies a coercive unity. As a reaction to "splitism," we can understand minzu tuanjie as the state's hegemonic *and* contentious rhetoric.

Let me state at the risk of reification that there are two basic positions, one represented by the state and the other by national minorities. If, from the national minority point of view, their demand for greater autonomy is under-

1.2.   The Inner Mongolian Museum with a Horse atop, Galloping Southward (2000)

stood as a plea for acceptance of a more diverse China, one that grants equality
to minorities, guaranteeing their cultural dignity and difference, the counterar-
gument from the majoritarian state is that such demands threaten minzu tuanjie
and are in effect minzu fenlie. The subtext is that the demand for greater autonomy and rights is either the demand of a handful (*yi xiao zuo*) of reactionaries of
a minzu, or it is instigated by the imperialists in order to undermine China's
sovereignty.

It is interesting to note here that while the majoritarian state refuses to reify
minorities as unitary autonomy-seeking agents by insisting on the diverse interests within them, the Chinese national community is always set against a devilish imperialist Other, which is in fact no less than the rest of humanity. And
then, of course, the best interests of the national minorities are said to lie in
upholding minzu tuanjie and resolutely fighting against minzu fenlie, instigated
from within and without. Under such sloganeering and "policymaking," draco-
nian measures may be taken to punish minzu fenlie elements in the name of
patriotism. Minzu tuanjie is thus not only a fait accompli masqueraded as the
best possible human condition, a basic human desire (for stability and harmony),
but also a magic wand to stave off all challenges. Minority demands for autonomy
are thus simultaneously rendered perverse, futile, and jeopardizing (to use

Hirschman's [1991] insightful phrases), both to the minority and to the Chinese nation.

As noted previously, the Chinese state is fond of portraying national unity, with all nationalities basking in the happy moment with the "leader," be it Mao Zedong, Deng Xiaoping, or Jiang Zemin. The language used for all these incarnations of minzu tuanjie invariably expresses "familial" relationships, in which the various minority nationalities are younger siblings of the elder brother Chinese. But what has been glossed over in these happy and familial slogans and exhibits? And what are the historical processes that have led to the representation of Inner Mongolia as a hospitable land, welcoming friends from near and far? In front of the Hohhot municipality building stands a gigantic statue of a Mongol woman-cum-hostess holding a ritual scarf and a wine cup in her "left" hand (ritually incorrect) to welcome guests—Chinese guests, of course. This is ironic in a city in which the Chinese population is 90 percent of the total. Anthropologist William Jankowiak (1993) calls Hohhot a "Chinese City," perhaps rightly so.

The huge gap between official ideology and social and political reality is characteristic of many multinational and polyethnic states, in which official ideology regularly invokes harmony regardless of the extent of oppression of nationalities. Michael Herzfeld writes that "the formal operations of national states depend on coexistence—usually inconvenient, always uneasy—with various realizations of cultural intimacy . . . a government may try to co-opt the language of intimacy for its utilitarian ends of commanding loyalty under what seem to be the most unpropitious conditions. Indeed, in the face of globalizing processes, defensive domesticity can acquire a persuasive appeal" (1997: 4). The transnational Mongols are thus domesticated through minzu tuanjie, the poetics of which being often literally expressed in physical intimacy, in the marital union, monumentalized in the statues and exhibits of Huhanye and Wang Zhaojun, an ancient Xiongnu emperor and a Han dynasty courtier sent to marry him in order to secure peace for the Han dynasty, memorialized in suburban Hohhot. Chinese national unity is expressed in an "irresistible romance" between Mongols, purportedly the metaphorical and genealogical descendants of the Xiongnu, and Chinese (Sommer 1990; see chapter 3; for a recent reincarnation of the theme in the international arena, see the film *Crouching Tiger, Hidden Dragon*).

Minzu tuanjie can perhaps be understood as an official nationalism. " 'Official nationalisms,' " writes Benedict Anderson, "can best be understood as a means of combining naturalization with retention of dynastic power, in particular over the huge polyglot domains accumulated since the Middle Ages, or to put it another way, for stretching the short, tight skin of the nation over the gigantic body of the empire" (1991: 86). According to Anderson, official nationalisms seek to weld two opposing political orders, one national and another imperial or dynastic. What is more interesting, while nationalism developed out of empires, official nationalism "developed after and in reaction to" nationalist movements. Therefore, official nationalism, which initially recognizes diversity, seeks to defuse the centrifugal tendency of that diversity by imposing a uniform culture, as in the case of Magyarization of Slovaks in Hungary or Japanization of Koreans under colonial rule. Similarly, in the case of China, we observe attempts at sinicization of all the groups that happen to fall within the territorial confines of the People's Republic, which combines the imperial and national political orders in one. Such an official nationalism, Anderson contends, constitutes a kind of "imperialism" to the peripheral peoples it embraces.

Here I find Stevan Harrell's discussion of sinicization germane. In "The Role of the Periphery in Chinese Nationalism" (1999), Harrell identifies the imperialist dimension of Chinese official nationalism in relation to the peripheral national minorities. He examines two processes of inclusion of the peripheries in Chinese discourse. In addition to providing justification for "the *faits accompli* of *Realpolitik*," Chinese nationalism also sets itself the task of including the peripheral territories and peoples of Mongolia, Tibet, and Xinjiang. "Without the criteria of inclusion for those areas that during the Qing were in the middle ground of the scale of literization, and are now among the peripheries to be included in the integral nation," writes Harrell, "the nationalist projects so important to all Chinese governments in the 20th century somehow lose their vital force" (1999: 138–39). Twentieth-century Chinese state nationalism is thus energized by its desire to incorporate the peripheral areas into the Chinese nation, and various criteria have been designed to stretch the short, tight skin of the "Chinese" nation over the gigantic body of the empire, which constitutes many different groups with diverse cultures, by means of cultural, linguistic, genealogical, racial, historical, and political appeals to loyalty. All these appeals are to identify common ground for a Chinese nation that can be simultaneously unified and defended against "foreigners."

Where, then, is the place for national minorities in a regime of official nationalism-cum-imperialism or minzu tuanjie? Can there be a "minority discourse" as endorsed by most postcolonial scholars? "Minority discourse," according to Homi Bhabha, the doyen of postcoloniality, "acknowledges the status of national culture—and the people—as a contentious, performative space" (1994b: 157). This formulation takes national culture and the people as moral authority and looks to the postcolonial struggle for the rights of the fragments of the nation (Chatterjee 1993) to rescue "History" from the nation (Duara 1995). Similarly, attempts to dislodge the patriarchal monopoly of the nation, as many feminist scholars contend, are predicated on the goodness of the national culture or the people, lending them a moral authority. But what is the "national culture" and who are "the people" in China?

As noted previously, in recent years Chinese ethnicity has become a legitimate field of academic inquiry. Not only are minorities seen as constructed by the state, but the hitherto unchallenged "Chinese" is also increasingly perceived as a category that is constructed. Specialists increasingly use the indigenous ethnonym "Han," rather than "Chinese," to denote the majority nationality in

China. Historians of the Qing empire trace the emergence of the term "Han ethnic identity" to the Qing classificatory system, which divided the population into Manchu, Mongol, Tibetan, Han, and Huizi (Millward 1998; Crossley 1990, 1999; Elliott 2001). According to Dru Gladney (1991), Han as an ethnic category was invented by Sun Zhongshan in the early years of the twentieth century for the purpose of rallying Chinese nationalism to unify the broadest possible support against the Manchus, who then ruled China. Of course, the canopy of "Han" disguises a plethora of identities, such as Hakka, Minnan, Cantonese, and other groups, who now begin to reassert their identity yet have no place within the category of the fifty-six nationalities. Emily Honig's study of the Subei people in Shanghai indicates the fluidity of term "the Han," arguing compellingly that "native place identity may become the basis of identities and relationships that are as ethnic in the context of China as African American, Italian American, or Chicano identities are ethnic in the United States" (1996: 143). Edward Friedman (1995) raised the scenario of a split between North China and South China, due to increasing economic, cultural, and political disparity caused by the introduction of the market economy, thereby pointing to the instrumentality, rather than the primordialism, of the Han. This is corroborated by the emergence of Taiwanese identity based on Minnanese and Hakka hybridized with the Taiwan aboriginals, in contrast and often in opposition to the Han, the latter the umbrella term now used to designate the mainland Chinese (*waishengren*) (Ren 1996).

This awareness of the multiple ethnicitites concealed within the rubric Han allows one to highlight the asymmetrical power relations of "ethnicity" in various local contexts. It is also an intervention that seeks to rescue the Han from the Chinese state (*Zhongguo*), reserving the latter as a term to convey a civic supra-ethnic domain. This is hardly a unique situation but rather is characteristic of many national states struggling to maintain unity in the midst of cultural diversity and ethnic conflict. The equation of Hindu and India—for example, in understanding the meaning of India—is critical for grasping the dynamics that led to the partition of India and continues to reverberate half a century later, defying efforts to accommodate non-Hindu minorities, notably a large Muslim population and many groups that the Indian state classifies as tribes (Ludden 1996: 4–8). In the Soviet Union, a neutral nonethnic term, "Soviet people," was used to defuse Russification, but it could not prevent the break-up of the Soviet Union. In order to foster a nonethnic civic federation of post-Soviet Russia, an ethnically neutral term, "Rossia" (instead of Russia), has been suggested (Balzer 1999; Tishkov 1997). In this sense, the use of Han, instead of "Chinese," is part of the search for solutions to China's nationality problems.

However, I remain unconvinced of the civic dimension of the term "Chinese" (Zhongguo, Zhonghua), for centuries of historical baggage cannot be defined away simply by separation of ethnic Han from nonethnic Chinese. In fact, the notion of Chinese Nation (Zhonghua Minzu) as an inclusive concept presumes the "Han" as its core and is deeply inflected by racism. As the early nationalist debates for naming the post-Qing new Republic "Zhonghua Minguo" indicate, the name was a combination of a republican ideal with the restoration of "Zhonghua" as opposed to *Dalu*, the barbarians. According to Shen Sung-chiao (1997), even the inclusivist notion of *Da Minzu Zhuyi*, or "Great Nationalism," as advocated by Liang Qichao and later adopted by Sun Zhongshan, which embraced the unity of Han, Manchu, Mongol, Tibetans, and Muslims (*wuzu gonghe*), centered on the assimilation (*tonghua*) of other nationalities into the Han. It should be further noted that so-called China, also known as the Middle Kingdom (Zhongguo), was never an official name. The two Chinese states that exist today, despite their ideological differences, both call themselves Zhonghua: Zhonghua Minguo (the Republic of China) and Zhonghua Renmin Gongheguo (the People's Republic of China). The Middle (Zhong) is always hyphenated with "Hua," a term reserved exclusively for the Han. It is this inseparability of Han or Hua from "China" that makes minority identification with China so ambivalent or difficult. In English, we can write Han Chinese, but it is impossible to hyphenate other nationalities with Chinese. Mongol Chinese or Tibetan Chinese are impossibilities (cf. Gladney 1991 and Lipman 1996 for discussions of hyphenating Muslims with Chinese; see chapter 5 for the hyphenated Daur-Mongol identity). In this book I will continue to use the English word *Chinese* to designate the "Han" in contrast to Mongol—mindful, though, of the tensions, as well as of the peculiarly constructed concept of "Han."

Ethnic or cultural diversity in China is rather different from multicultural Euro-America and even from the former Soviet Union, and these differences—historical, institutional, and cultural—account for different responses from minority peoples to the state and vice versa. Perhaps it is useful to make a distinction between a multinational state and a polyethnic state, as Will Kymlicka (1995) argues. Kymlicka distinguishes two broad patterns of cultural diversity that are related to the history of nation-building. "In the first instance, cultural diversity arises from the incorporation of previously self-governing, territorially concentrated cultures into a larger state." He calls the incorporated cultures "national minorities." "In the second case, cultural diversity arises from individual and familial immigration." He calls the loose associations into which such immigrants often coalesce "ethnic groups." This distinction is important, for the two kinds of groups are likely to have different aspirations and expectations pertaining to the state. Whereas national minorities "typically wish to maintain themselves as distinct societies alongside the majority culture, and demand various forms of autonomy or self-government to ensure their survival as distinct societies," ethnic groups "typically wish to integrate into the larger society, and to be accepted as full members of it" (1995: 10–11). These two are, of course, ideal types. Nonterritorial groups, like Jews everywhere and Turks in Germany, may also wish to preserve significant elements of their culture, even as they seek to claim citizenship, and (some) may wish to assimilate as well.

In China, most of the pertinent groups are territorial "national minorities," although they have long been associated with China. It is indisputable that the long history of China's nation-building and the incorporation of far-flung groups such as Mongols, Uygurs, and Tibetans by the time of the Republic of China (1912–1949) or earlier make them "national minorities." Indeed, the CCP's notion of minzu for nationalities contains an explicit dimension of territoriality and political autonomy. Instead of thinking only in terms of the state's benevolence in granting territorial homeland to the newly classified minorities, however, I would also argue that it is the historic struggles for independence on the part of non-Chinese nationalities such as Mongols that resulted in different levels of territorially based administrative autonomous units (see chapters 4 and 5). Of course, the ethnic picture is more complex than presented here. Some minzus, such as the Hui, are scattered all over China, although some also live in compact communities like the Ningxia Hui Autonomous Region. And others, such as Hakka, Cantonese, or Minnanese, by virtue of distinct historical and cultural features, might qualify for non-Chinese identity, but they have not been designated as nationalities or minzu. While some groups number tens of millions, others such as Orochon number only several thousand. Nevertheless, historical and political processes determine that where national minorities form compact territorial communities, especially along China's borderlands, the Chinese state has relentlessly encouraged settlement by Chinese migrants so as to outnumber the native populations. This achieves two purposes simultaneously: "integration" of the frontier regions into China and a release of population pressures in agrarian China. China's frontiers have been conquered by outright military occupation, as in the case of Tibet and Xinjiang, or combined with communist ideological unity and promises for territorial autonomy, as in the Inner Mongolian case.

In a multinational state like China (as distinct from a polyethnic state), in which "the core nation is understood as the legitimate 'owner' of the state, which is conceived as the state *of* and *for* the core nation," (Brubaker 1996: 5, original emphasis) and in which national minorities may have their own tangible or imaginary homelands outside the nationalizing state, the struggle cannot always take the form of a "minority discourse." In the case of minzu tuanjie and minzu fenlie, the national state's moral authority has repeatedly been called into question. This has not only been done by the Mongols, Tibetans, and Uygurs who have challenged the Chinese national state at various times during the twentieth century, with varying degrees of intensity, but also by the Chinese state's repeated denunciations, tarring demands for equality and autonomy with the brush of external imperialism.

In this regard, Edward Said's (1979, 1997) study of Zionism and the Palestinian question is instructive. He discusses the Palestinian question in relation to the narratives of Zionism, tracing what he calls the self-consciousness of Palestinian experience to the first Zionist settlements of the 1880s. He studies Zionism's contradictory lineage—the colonial provenance of Zionism's emancipatory ideals; inversions of the roles of oppressors and victims, militarists and refugees as manifested in the baffling displacements of the Palestinians. And yet any social criticism of the Jews in the West is invariably equated with anti-Semitism, leading to invocation of Jewish suffering in history. Thus, Said underlines the global and colonial dimensions of the Palestinian question. The imbrication of colonization and emancipation in Zionism escapes the "national" attempt to see it as an "internal affair."

Similarly, the Chinese communist emancipatory ideal often blends with Chinese racism. The international dimension of the Mongols, Tibetans, and Uygurs and their geopolitical location at the borderlands of China suggest the reason for the intensity of Chinese sloganeering of minzu tuanjie and minzu fenlie. National unity is most vulnerable precisely at the borderlands. "Borders," write Donnan and Wilson, "are signs of the sovereignty and domain of the state, and are markers of the peaceful or hostile relations between a state and its neighbors" (1999: 15). The territoriality of the geopolitical borderlands sets them apart from the similar tropes used in postmodernist scholarship that celebrate border crossings (Gupta and Ferguson 1992). However, fragmented identities and hybridity produced at the borderlands are not always happy, nor are they necessarily signs of liberation in a new synthesis, as Gupta and Ferguson contend. Rather, hybrids produced by competing national power contentions may often give rise to a cultural, moral, and political predicament (Bulag 1998; Donnan and Wilson 1999: 39–40). Hybrids at the geopolitical borderlands are people upon whose bodies and consciousness national states map their power, often in contradictory or antagonistic ways.

Recognizing the diverse historical, political, cultural, and territorial aspects of the Mongols, Tibetans, and Uygurs would allow us to identify some of their aspirations, which may be distinct not only from one another but particularly from those of other nonterritorially based groups. It is quite apparent that without this distinction, implementation of strategies supportive of the interests of one type of group can be detrimental to the interests of another. In other words, some international academics or human rights activists seeking to intervene on behalf of "ethnic minorities," assuming that their best interests lie in integration through gaining equality, might seriously misread the goals of "national minorities," whose attitude to the state may be far more ambivalent. This is not to say that national minorities do not fight for equality and justice within a national state. Rather, I argue that if a particular national minority manifests characteristics of "ethnic group" aspiration, wishing "to integrate into the larger society and to be accepted as full members of it," we should seek to understand the mechanisms and processes of this outcome, as I attempt to do throughout this book with respect to the Mongols. Nor does it mean that Mongols do not aspire to get along with other nationalities, including the Chinese. Indeed, their version of minzu tuanjie calls for amity between different nationalities, based on equality and respect for differences.

Minzu highlights central contradictions of Chinese socialist nation-building. Minzu is to be constructed for the ultimate purpose of its destruction—that is, the destruction of differences among the minzu will pave the way for the elimination of minzu as policy. Having made its contribution to Chinese national unity and economic development, its mission is complete. Although the state's leading propaganda journal on minorities still retains its original Chinese name, *Minzu Tuanjie*, it is notable that in 1995 the English translation was changed from "Nationality Unity" to "Ethnic Unity," "ethnic" connoting more of a nonpolitical, cultural character. The Chinese state has devoted substantial resources to build up minzu regional autonomy and solidify it through affirmative action, while at the same time busying itself by devoting commensurate energy to "solving the nationality problem" (*jiejue minzu wenti*) in ways that ultimately assume assimilating minorities into the Chinese Nation, politically and culturally.

Deng Xiaoping's reform project, and that advanced by his successor Jiang Zemin, promotes a multiculturalism that constitutes not socialist subjects but *Chinese* subjects. Minorities are evaluated by meritocratic criteria—in other words, their service and contribution to the Chinese Nation. Unlike the worker subject who is forever dreaming of resuming center stage or attaining some kind of autonomy from the state, but who nevertheless constitutes the national citizenry (if at present a powerless "national citizenry" facing unemployment), minority minzu has only two options for the time being: it becomes a foil to the Chinese national state, displayed in the human zoo theme park to illustrate China's colorful image of minzu tuanjie, or it becomes the antithesis of the Chinese, serving to unite the Chinese, as reflected in the denunciation and suppression of minority minzu fenlie of recent years.

This condition gives rise to conflicting strategies on the part of different national minorities, some emphasizing individual rights, some collective rights, and yet others opting to "exit," in Hirschman's sense (1970). What characterizes the Mongol situation is that these strategies are often simultaneously pursued by different sections of the Mongol population. The tricky question is how Mongol demands to fulfill the promise of minzu tuanjie, in the form of equality and diversity, as well as amity among different minzu, ineluctably intertwine with the Chinese state's version of minzu tuanjie for homogeneity in the service of national unity. We may even pose a futuristic question, however remote and quixotic it may appear: How can we construct an ethnopolitics in which democracy, civil rights, representation, and equality need not hinge on the moral authority of the "Chinese Nation"?

A PREVIEW OF THE CHAPTERS

In contrast with many studies that are mainly concerned with "cultural politics" such as ethnic identity and/or ethnic representation, this book locates the Mongols in the complex geopolitics and historical trajectory of Inner Asia and relations involving China, Mongolia, and the Soviet Union. This is informed by my personal sense of the history of the Mongols—that is, the process of Mongol integration into the modern Chinese polity and the development of the Mongols as an ethnic minority from a national minority. In many instances, it is in dialogue with scholars dealing with issues of national integration, federalism, modernity, gender, ethnicity, and class. It offers critical analyses of the imbrication of notions of liberation, class and ethnicity, the hazardous maintenance of ethnic boundaries mired in socialist notions of universalism and particularism, as well as ethnic resistance, complicity, and morality.

The two chapters in part I analyze forms and processes of Chinese national unity in the *longue durée* of Chinese history, examining ritual and sexuality as materials for constructing "unity." I follow Said's suggestion that powerful ideas like Zionism need to be examined historically in two ways: "1. *Genealogically*, in order that their provenance, their kinship and descent, their affiliation both with other ideas and with political institutions may be deconstructed; and 2. as practical systems for *accumulation* (of power, land, ideological legitimacy) and *displacement* (of people, other ideas, prior legitimacy)" (1997: 16, original emphasis). This approach challenges the seamless Chinese master narrative of uninterrupted flow of unity by exploring its bricolage, whereby the older discourse of conquest, kinship, and sexuality was first abandoned, then recovered, modified, and inscribed in new forms.

Challenging the current literature on Chinese state-building, nationalist discourse, and the demise of the federalist movement in the early twentieth century, which characteristically posits the "local" versus the "national," chapter 2 introduces an ethnic dimension to the discussion by examining the genealogy of the cult of Kökönuur Lake. The Mongols discussed here are not Mongols in Inner Mongolia but nearby in today's Qinghai province—yet the historical processes of their integration into the Chinese polity mirrors that of Inner Mongolia. What started out as a political ritual of the Manchu colonial state in the eighteenth century was gradually transformed through various historical stages, from a means of controlling the Mongols and Tibetans into a festival celebrating the unity of all Chinese nationalities in the struggle against imperialist Japanese. In the process, the colonial content of the ritual was mysteriously phased out in favor of modernist and nationalist ideas of national unity and equality. This chapter shows that the choreographed public spectacles are not mere window dressing for the brutality of an emerging national state but are themselves the site of power par excellence, wherein the policies and decisions of the state are enacted. If a nation is an imagined community, then its imagined form is rendered visible in such national festivals.

Chapter 3 departs from conventional approaches that see Chinese nationality policy purely as assimilationism, to look at the cultural process that underscores the production of ethnic subjectivity. Taking issue with the recent anthropological "gaze" at sexuality and minority that focuses on the contemporary Chinese discourse of feminization and eroticization of ethnic minorities, the chapter examines the inverse of this course—that is, the self-feminization on the part of Chinese and masculinization of nomadic peoples, a discourse built on an ancient institution called *heqin* (peace marriage), wherein Chinese princesses or court women were married out to Inner Asian nomadic peoples. I focus on the "naturalizing" tendency of Chinese Confucians and communists in their imagination and management of ethnic relations in terms of marriage between Chinese and minorities. The chapter examines the procession of historical reconstructions of an ancient Chinese court woman, Wang Zhaojun, married to a Xiongnu ruler in a heqin pact two thousand years ago. Zhaojun remains alive and vivid until now, reincarnated in various forms—first as a femme fatale with a political mission of subjugating nomads, then as a site to demarcate the ethnic boundary between "civilized" Chinese and "barbarian" nomads, and recently as a symbol that promotes national unity. I examine how Chinese kinship systems have evolved in relation to non-Chinese peoples over centuries, from a system of alliance wherein women perform important diplomatic functions to a unilineal system that domesticates women. At each historical juncture of China's crisis with neighboring Inner Asians, Chinese intellectuals, in their "anxiety to serve" their overlords or regimes, have invoked Wang Zhaojun. I argue that Chinese patriotism or nationalism vis-à-vis non-Chinese peoples on the Inner Asian frontiers has been configured historically along kinship and gender lines. I explore this historiography in the complex history of interactions between Chinese and Inner Asian peoples and analyze the discursive formation of the Chinese concept of national unity in the twentieth century.

The incorporation of the Mongols in the socialist Chinese state was premised on the cooperation of Mongolian communists with the Chinese Communist Party. What visions did Mongol communists have for the future of the Mongols in China? What were the bases for cooperation and coexistence? The chapters in part II explore two issues: class and ethnicity in socialist China as manifest in the land reform and problems of writing Mongolian "revolutionary" history in a multinational communist Chinese state.

Through a historical ethnography exploring the imbrication of class and ethnicity in socialist China, chapter 4 studies multinational socialism as a variant of colonialism, with its contradictory ramifications of universalism and particularism. The "colonial" cultural politics of socialism are examined in Inner Mongolia, the northern frontier of China, where the historical formation of social class and ethnic relationship defies any clear-cut dichotomy of colonizer and colonized. In the first half of the twentieth century, Inner Mongolia was colonized by Chinese warlords. Yet at the same time, the majority of the Chinese population in Inner Mongolia consisted of poor Chinese peasants leasing Mongol land. Nonetheless, the Mongols won limited ethnic autonomy within China in 1947 by applying Leninist colonial liberation ideology, defining the Mongols as a collective group that had been colonized by the Chinese.

However, socialist ideology premised on class analysis during the land reform targeted many Mongols as class enemies, thereby justifying the redistribution of Mongol land among the Chinese majority in Inner Mongolia. The ensuing ethnic violence forced Inner Mongolia's Mongol leaders, who were both agents of the Chinese Communist Party and representatives of the Mongolian nationality, to devise and press for an explicit nationality policy to defend the ethnic rights of Mongols and thus the autonomy of Inner Mongolia. In the early 1960s this deployment of ethnic principle amid China's class struggle campaign came to be interpreted as betrayal of the socialist principle and of China as a nation, setting the stage for collective Chinese violence against the Mongols during the Cultural Revolution. The chapter suggests that instead of a sterile debate of subaltern representation, which often reflects the scholar's own "position" devoid of social context, a historical ethnography may better illustrate historical contingencies of the interplay of ethnicity and class in the practice of subalternity in socialist China.

Mongols in China are one of the few national minorities that participated significantly in the communist revolution that helped establish both the Inner Mongolia Autonomous Region and the People's Republic of China. Chapter 5 examines the interface of communism and nationalism and the complexities of the process of writing an Inner Mongolian revolutionary history that records the trajectory of the road to victory and the birth of a socialist Mongolian nationality. I argue that communist revolutionary "ethnohistory" is a field of power relations that justifies the raison d'être of the political status of a nationality in a socialist state. Inherent in writing such a history is the tension between a particular ethnonational history and the larger universal history of China.

This chapter explores the difficulty of Mongolian historiographical efforts to demarcate the boundary of their revolution within the Chinese communist revolution and the challenge in doing so in a multinational Inner Mongolia, where Mongols are dominated by Chinese and in turn dominate other smaller minorities such as the Daur. Once self-identified as a Mongol subgroup with a new appellation, "Daur-Mongol," during the Republican period, Daur political and intellectual leaders played a prominent role in the Mongolian nationalist movement in the 1920s and 1930s. Their recognition as a separate nationality in the 1950s caused difficulty in incorporating "Daur-Mongol" revolutionaries into Mongolian revolutionary history, because of their newly attained autonomy from Mongol identity, or in Daur history, because of their prior struggle for the "Mongolian" cause. In post-Mao China, in an effort to elevate their diminished political status, Daur intellectuals reappropriated "their" revolutionary ancestors by arguing for their simultaneous "contributions" to the Daur, Mongolian, and Chinese revolutionary causes and to the founding of the Inner Mongolia Autonomous Region, thereby challenging the Mongolian revolutionary historiographical monopoly. The Daur struggle for recognition has led to a historiographical modus operandi—a de-ethnicized, China-focused, "Inner Mongolian

Revolutionary History," which reflects the ethnic power configuration in the northern frontier of China.

Communism and nationalism are never pure ideologies but are mired in political machinations of various sorts. One of the central features of Inner Mongolian ethnopolitics was the centrality of Ulanhu in all struggles from the 1940s to the 1980s. The chapters in part III examine Mongol exemplars invented and deployed by Ulanhu and the posthumous apotheosis of Ulanhu, for both the Chinese state and the Mongols, but for different reasons and purposes. They discuss representation of Mongols and problems of ethnic and socialist morality.

Chapter 6 explores inter- and intra-ethnic morality in socialist China by examining the changing narratives of the parable "Little Heroic Sisters of the Grassland," initially produced in the early 1960s. It shows that the two Mongol little sister models were created by Mongol officials in an effort to resist the mounting class struggle waged by Mao Zedong. However, the construction of a Mongol self-representation was complicated by socialist morality. The chapter suggests, therefore, that instead of being romanticized, resistance should be seen as a diagnostic of power within the society concerned. The parable was quickly caught up in Chinese and Mongol counterclaims that evoked conflicts over ethnicity and class. As recently revealed, the Chinese proletarian-cum-savior turned out to be an opportunist, whereas the real person behind the character of the Mongol sheep rustler-cum-class enemy eventually won recognition as the actual savior of the two little sisters. Nonetheless, because of the continued value of this parable for some Mongol elites, the rehabilitation of the "sheep-rustler" after the Cultural Revolution was tortuous. Examining the twists and turns of the story and the changing fortunes of the historical figures involved, the chapter explores the moral constraints on the maintenance of ethnic boundaries within the Chinese socialist regime of truth.

The final chapter considers the rise of the posthumous cult of Ulanhu in the form of constructing a huge mausoleum and defining him as a great state leader who fought for the unity of the Chinese nation—an effort carried out by Mongols and the Chinese state, but for different purposes. Through examining the historical context of the rise of the cult, and the variegated and conflicting evaluations of Ulanhu's achievements and failures by the Mongols, as well as the Chinese state, it is argued that Mongol participation in defining the cult does not mean an obeisance to power. Rather, it demonstrates that the use value of hegemony to the subordinate, as well as to the powerful, constitutes a platform of ritual interaction in Inner Mongolia. The chapter reveals how a communist cadre has been turned into an ethnic and a national hero simultaneously. The nostalgia for Ulanhu, at a time of economic uncertainty, social anomie, and, above all, ethnic unrest after the Tiananmen Square incident and the collapse of the Soviet Union, invested in him a mystique of being a representative of loyalty and an upholder of national sovereignty. Ulanhu provides a contradictory point of reference, legitimating the state's penetration and consolidation of the frontier and exercise of direct power, as well as the Mongols' resistance to further incursions on their autonomy.

A new page of ethnicity is unfolding right before our eyes. But while we look forward to new manifestations of ethnicity in an increasingly globalized China, we also need to look back and examine how we have reached this state. That is what this book sets out to do in the case of the Mongols at China's edge.

PART I

PRODUCING AND REPRODUCING NATIONAL UNITY

2

Ritualizing National Unity: Modernity at the Edge of China

Twentieth-century China has all the characteristics of an empire with multiple territorially based ethnic minorities, yet it also claims to be a national-state struggling to achieve unity. The tension between "multiple" and "one" in China can be best exemplified in the ambiguity of the phrase "minzu tuanjie." It means both amity between nationalities and national unity. Minzu tuanjie is a ubiquitous and dominant discourse in twentieth-century China that aims to regulate ethnic relations in the attempt to create a seamless Chinese Nation (Zhonghua Minzu) within the territorial and moral confines of China—a cultural and racial identity constantly in flux—in opposition to non-"Chinese." With fifty-six formally recognized "nationalities" (minzu) since the 1950s and 1960s, some of whom were at various times "alien" rulers of China and/or large areas of Eurasia, the People's Republic faces the task of not only "imagining" but also "managing" its diverse populations. It has not been hesitant in deploying administrative and military measures to secure the "unity" that it considers essential to that end. But physical coercion has been accompanied by other devices to make the new order of "national unity" palatable. One such device is teleological "History." National history is especially important, for it has the potential to lend an aura of authenticity to sovereignty and unity, conveying (paradoxically) a sense of both linear evolution and timelessness (Duara 1998) to disguise any forged or contrived elements of a nation-building project. But this aura of authenticity must be supplemented with an "aura of descent" (Keyes 1981) to demonstrate that the socialization of the disparate ethnic groups was not just in abstract History but also was rooted in concrete kinship bonds. Modern nationalism thus aspires to build coherence or unity among diverse populations; each would have to be cooked to blend or melt in the national "pot," as it were. I discuss the kinship dimension of minzu tuanjie in chapter 3. This chapter mainly concerns the "nation form" China has taken, whereby unity is made visible, manifest, and public. And this nation form, I contend, is best seen in the rituals and ceremonies of minzu tuanjie that emerged in the 1920s through the 1940s, when China had five officially recognized nationalities: Chinese, Manchu, Mongols, Tibetans, and Muslims.

Ritual has often been regarded as integral to the Chinese or even the entire "Asian" concept of power.[1] Given the centrality of "ritual" to politics in Asia, and its perceived characteristics of generating social solidarity, it is not surprising that "ritual" has been taken on board to shed light on Chinese social, cultural, or national integration. A number of scholars have explored how certain deities and their cults in China performed this function. All of them note the attempt of the state to control the cult and the response of the worshipers at various levels of Chinese administrative hierarchy. Watson, in his study of "Tian Hou" (alias Mazu), a deity worshiped in south China and Taiwan, writes that "the Chinese state intervened in local cults in subtle ways to impose a kind of unity on regional and local-level cults" (1985: 293). This state intervention not only resulted in a "surprisingly high degree of uniformity" of the cult, but also made sure that the zealous devotion of local elites in building temples for Tian Hou expressed their desire "to join the mainstream of Chinese culture" (1985: 317).

James Hevia provides a fascinating account of the controversy over the Manchu guest ritual. Although not overtly concerned about national or cultural integration, he falls in the same camp of looking at the Manchu polity as primarily a ritual polity (1995: 29–56). In describing the Manchu model of galactic polity, or what he calls "a multitude of lords," the Manchu at least initially built multiple centers and conducted different rituals, following customs that were adapted to the subjects of the ritual action.[2]

In my view, the idea of the ritual polity sheds as much light as it obscures on the political process, especially in a multiethnic empire like the Qing. The state, in this analysis, performed rituals saturated in the elite's self-satisfaction that lower subjects would thereby look at them with awe and obedience, or sometimes, in fear that they might not. Of course, all politics involves rituals, including those of modern Western societies (Kertzer 1988). However, Lucian Pye would go as far as to contrast the Asian concept of power with the Western one: "Although Asians have traditionally tended to crave stronger authority, their politics until recent times has not been directed toward policy choices and implementation. They want authority, but they have less interest in policies" (Pye and Pye 1985: 38). Such a moralistic approach largely divorces the prerogative of ritual from power asymmetry or conquest or other means of governance that preceded and accompanied the rituals.[3] Indeed, for such an approach to be meaningful, the power of ritual depends on cultural homogeneity, or at least the subject's ritual action would have to share certain cultural norms if the ritual is to have the desired effect.[4] Then what happens if different cultures or even different civilizations perform their integration on the ritual platform?

In this chapter I hope to show the paradoxical nature of the Chinese polity by exploring the rise and fall of the cult of the Kökönuur Lake[5] and its political role in controlling Mongol and Tibetan nomads in the Qing dynasty. The ritual associated with the cult involved submission and obeisance, sustained by the threat of violence. In the Republican period, in an interesting paradigm shift, we see the role of the lake ritual turning from a political institution to a symbolic representation of China's "multiethnic" characteristics. The celebration of minzu tuanjie became a constant theme in the first half of the twentieth century, somehow enacted in the crucible of worshiping the Kökönuur Lake, characterizing modernity, ethnicity, and national integration at the edge of China.

ESTABLISHING THE GOD OF KÖKÖNUUR: THE MYTHOLOGY OF CONQUEST

Kökönuur, or Qinghai in Chinese, although never under "Chinese" jurisdiction until the eighteenth century, had nonetheless long constituted an important part of the Chinese imaginary geographical cosmology. For much of China's history, until the Qing conquest, the Kökönuur Lake was called Xihai or West Sea. It was one of the four cardinal "seas"—that is, the East Sea, North Sea, South Sea, and West Sea—defining the symbolic boundary of the Middle Kingdom. It was worshiped not by holding rituals at lakeside, but from the suburbs of the capital city, a system known as *yaoji* (sacrifice from a distance). The lake was constantly metamorphosed, bearing changing titles representative of the Chinese spiritual bureaucracy. For example, in the Tang dynasty the Kökönuur Lake was granted the title *Guang Run Gong* (Moisture-Spreading Duke) (in 751), and in the Song dynasty the duke was promoted to king, and two more characters were added to the original title, which became *Tong Sheng Guang Run Wang* (Efficacious Moisture-Spreading King) (in 1041).[6]

The tradition of granting titles to deities is an ancient Chinese tradition, dating at least from the Zhou dynasty (Zhang 1993). Hansen claims that such a title-granting tradition experienced a resurgence in the southern Song dynasty in response to military weakness: "besieged by non-Han peoples in the north, it instituted more and more comprehensive policies to recognize the achievements of local gods" (1990: 9). The lake's promotion in title in the Song dynasty was probably due to a concern for the increased power of the Xixia (Tangut) state dominating the region, if we follow Hansen's theory.

However, the Qing Dynasty ushered in a new tradition: the lake deity was no longer personified. The new Kökönuur cult became a monument to mark the Manchu victory over the Mongols in establishing Manchu hegemony in Tibet and adjacent regions. The control over Tibet was significant, as the religious loyalty to Tibetan Buddhism, represented by the Dalai Lama, remained central to whether Manchu conquest of the Mongols could be consolidated. Tibet was then under the rule of the Hoshut, a tribe belonging to the Oirad, or Western Mongolian Confederation. Throughout the Manchu conquest of Inner Mongolia and expansion to Inner Asia, the Hoshut stayed neutral, by maintaining links and paying tribute to both the Manchu and their rival Jungar Mongols. After establishing tributary relations between Hoshut Mongols and the Qing in the mid-seventeenth century, sacrifice to the God of the lake was made an important event, as the Qing deemed it the physical completion of the four cardinal points of the Middle Kingdom. Following Chinese ritual convention, the Qing sent ritual envoys to make sacrifices to the "West Sea" and sometimes assembled the relatively submissive Hoshut Mongols to pass on to them royal gifts and to exhort them to live in peace with the Qing. However, such a sacrifice did not become an institution for local rule until the conquest of the Hoshut Mongols in 1724, when a "miracle" occurred.

The murder of Mongol Lazan Khan of Tibet by the Jungar expedition army in 1717 finally brought an end to the seven-decade-long Hoshut Mongol domination of Tibet.[7] The Hoshut Mongols proved no match for either the Manchu or the Jungar Mongols in the race to control Tibet and the Dalai Lama. In ostensible alliance with the Hoshut, the Manchu annihilated the Jungar expedition forces. But instead of returning Tibet to the Hoshut, the Manchu reorganized the Hoshut, conferring titles, gerrymandering the Mongol hierarchy, and cultivating pro-Manchu elements. The unruly behavior of the arrogant Qing garrison army in Xining was the last straw for the independence-minded Mongol warriors. Lobsandanjin, the most senior chief of the Hoshut Mongols, after the loss of Tibet to the Qing, challenged the Qing in 1722, taking advantage of the Kangxi emperor's death. His challenge was supported by local Tibetans, Buddhist monasteries, and, most important, the Jungar Mongols, the latter being regarded as the most powerful contender for supremacy in Inner Asia. Lobsandanjin assembled his troops at Chagaan Tolgoi,[8] which is close to the lake of Kökönuur, and proclaimed himself the "Ochir Khan" (Thunderbolt Khan). He ordered the revival of indigenous titles and the abolishing of the titles given by the Qing, such as *wang, beile, or beise* (Wei 1965, vol. 3). He also announced his intent to unite with the Jungar against the Qing.

The Hoshut rebellion posed a great threat to the Qing, for the control of the Dalai Lama was key to controlling all the Mongols who were his ardent worshipers. In order to cut off the link between Lobsandanjin and the Jungar Mongols, the Qing in 1723 sent the Sichuan and Shaanxi governor-general Nian Genyao and the Sichuan provincial commander-in-chief Yue Zhongqi. Yue Zhongqi, a veteran Chinese general with extensive experience in campaigning against Tibetans, commanded 6,000 Chinese troops. In hot pursuit in the second lunar month of 1724, Yue's army penetrated into the Nar Sar (a.k.a. Ri Yue, in Chinese) mountains, passing the Daotang river, and finally crushed the main force of Lobsandanjin, while capturing Lobsandanjin's mother and sister. Lobsandanjin fled to Jungaria. Immediately after the victory, Yue reported to the emperor the following miracle:

> [Yue Zhongqi] defeated Arabtanombu at Har River, after pursuing for a whole night. Both men and horses were exhausted from thirst, and no water could be found anywhere. Yue Zhongqi, ordered to dig into earth to seek water, unexpectedly found a spring. So he reported to the court that "the Qinghai God showed efficacy" (*Qinghai Shen Xianling*). (Wei 1965, vol. 3)

The text indicates that Yue apparently attributed his victory not to his excellent leadership, but to the miracle of the spring, which helped him and his army. This was as much modesty as flattery to the Qing, indicating that the Way (*dao*), symbolized by this miracle, favored the Qing.

The Qing court commended Yue's outstanding military victory over the Kökönuur Mongols, promoting him to the rank of *sandeng gong* (third-ranking duke).[9] In 1725 he was promoted to the post of governor-general of Sichuan and Shaanxi and granted the title *taizi shaofu* (tutor to the heir-apparent) (Yi 1990). In the following year, the court formally granted a royal investiture to the lake God, giving it the title *lingxian xuanwei Qinghai zhi shen* ("The god of Qinghai which manifests efficacy and shows might"), and instructed that sacrifices be made to it. The title was inscribed in Manchu, Chinese, and Mongolian on a tablet. A new tradition of the cult of Kökönuur was born to mark the Qing victory over the Mongols.

But why did Yue use the term *Qinghai zhi shen* (the God of Qinghai)? It turns out that in 1723, immediately after Lobsandanjin's rebellion broke out, the Qing court had already granted the title *Qinghai lingxian daxie zhi zunshen* ("the holy God of Qinghai, the great water, which shows efficacy") to the lake (Wang Donghai 1992). It is probable that the Qing court hoped the lake God would show efficacy by assisting in their suppression of the Mongols. And Yue's earnestly pretentious report pandered perfectly to the Yongzheng emperor's expectation. The Qing court's change of the title to *lingxian xuanwei Qinghai zhi shen* ("The God of Qinghai which manifests efficacy and shows might") in 1726, in response to Yue's report, was not a small one. The God was supposed to have shifted its allegiance or supernatural support from the Mongols to the Manchus. Note also that the lake no longer bore titles of duke or king, but became *shen* or *zunshen*—God or Holy God.

The conquest of the Hoshut Mongols meant that the worship of the Kökönuur Lake deity no longer required *yaoji* (worship from a distance). Rather, the new title was accompanied by the establishment of a new ritual institution, whereby "imperial officials were sent, tablets written, a title given, and a temple built for it" on the spot (*qian guan zhiji, yen xie bei er zhi feng hao*)[10] (Wei 1965, vol. 3).

The emperor also personally wrote a eulogy, repeating the story of the miracle, "In the former time, thanks to the bravery of the celestial army, it showed efficacy. A spring gushed out so spectacularly that it startled the Shule River. . . . I attribute this to the efficacy of the God, and hereby praise it with felicitations" (quoted in Mi 1993: 214). He further instructed that the sacrifice be included in the imperial sacrificial system (*sidian*).

The Qing granting of a title to the Kökönuur Lake deity does not mean that the emperor "recognized the power of the local people, and yet relegated them to subordinate roles," as Hansen argued for the Song dynasty (1990: 80). The God was now on the imperial Qing side, rather than that of the recalcitrant Mongols.

The granting of titles in accordance with the degree of "efficacy" of a cult, measured by its achievements, posed a moral dilemma for rulers. Confucian ideology posits a kingly virtue, or *de*, that alone has the moral power that can govern subjects: "if the prince is a genuine man of virtue, then all officials, fathers, and husbands will perforce follow his example" (quoted in Rawski 1998: 230). The ritual importance of such a virtue has recently drawn enormous attention from cultural historians studying Manchu court rituals (Farquhar 1978; Hevia 1994, 1995; Zito 1984, 1997; and Rawski 1998). These scholars take note of the multiple roles taken by the emperor to represent himself to differently structured subject populations in the empire—Confucian monarch, khan of khans, Buddhist reincarnation, and so on. In this recognition of the rule of virtue, James Hevia observed that "Qing rulers were fundamentally concerned with claims about the proper way of constituting supreme lordship in a world made up of a multitude of lords and multiple centers of power. Ritual techniques established cosmo-moral dominion, while extending Qing rulership spatially and temporally" (1995: 55). In this understanding, the subjective power of the subjects or "multitude of lords" was explicitly recognized, and the emperor became vulnerable, as he had to "present" himself to his lesser lords. Insightful as this analysis may be, it has neglected discussion of the notion of *ling* (efficacy) of cults or shrines in establishing that supreme rulership.

Rawski discussed briefly the notion of ling in rituals for rain and noted the moral dilemma: "In ancient Confucian thought *de* is in itself sufficient to produce the correct social order. Incorporation of popular deities into the state religion should not be needed. *That it occurred was an implicit recognition of the chimerical nature of rule by virtue alone—and a reflection of the realpolitik dictating imperial action*" (1998: 230, emphasis added). Rawski did not elaborate on the realpolitik but noticed the general tendency in Qing royal historiography of gradual reduction of ling, or silence concerning ling, and the increasing emphasis upon virtue. The Kökönuur cult was an extension of the rain ritual to celebration of conquest; it was a celebration of both the efficacy of heavenly power and kingly virtue. The result of such a combination was amply shown when, on the occasion of worshiping the lake, Mongol singers were also enjoined to celebrate their submission joyfully, as their "lake worshiping song" indicated:

The auspicious first day of the year of the tiger
marked the promotion to the title of Wang,[11]
and the accompanying nobles of various ranks also received promotions.
How magnificent the majestic-looking tiger seal in your right hand!
How awe-inspiring the 60 volumes of laws in your left hand!
The overflowing kumiss in the silver bowl is the nectar offered to you,
and the fast steed with silver shoes is your expeditionary mount.
The ginger mule is the mount of the Xining superintendent,
and the dark gray mules belong to his retinue.
By beautiful Kökönuur Lake stand six large tents
where officials and chiefs gather together to hold the rite to worship the lake.
May our good fortune be according to our wish!
May the lake God bless us! (quoted in Mi 1993: 214)

COLONIZING THE MONGOLS: THE CULT OF THE KÖKÖNUUR GOD AND THE INSTITUTION OF ASSEMBLY

I started this chapter by insisting that ritual power be analyzed in association with the wider political structure. In the fanfare of the previously mentioned ritual we see elaborate policy implementation directed toward the conquered Mongols. Insofar as the Kökönuur cult was a state ritual by which to rule the conquered Mongols, we need to understand the nature of the Qing rule as "colonial." Recent scholarship (Wong 1997; Perdue 1998; Di Cosmo 1998; and Heuschert 1998) challenges the assumption of colonialism as only a European enterprise, by looking at the remarkably "modernist" measures taken by the Qing to rule the vast empire. Measures included fixing boundaries, mapping territories, prohibition of population flow through administrative and legal controls, taxation, surveillance, and so on. These authors are unanimous in recognizing that the Qing was particularly successful in integrating the far-flung regions within the imperial state. But this body of scholarship needs to be connected to the cultural and historical study of Qing rituals by scholars such as Rawski, Hevia, and Zito. They should not be two exclusionary zones. We should thus, in light of the song quoted earlier, look at both the ritual and the realpolitik aspects and examine what Bernard Cohn (1983) called "representing authority."

As with any colonial regime, the conquest of the Kökönuur Mongols was followed by the classification and reorganization of the Mongol political structure. This was facilitated by information about them, which was obtained through extensive research conducted by the Li Fan Yuan, set up by the Manchus specifically to administer the Mongols and later expanded to rule non-Manchu and non-Chinese peoples.[12] Following the Inner Mongolian example, the Kökönuur Mongols were subject to strict military control, in accordance with regulations and laws imposed on them. Nian Genyao, the governor-general in charge of the campaign against the Mongols, promulgated "Thirteen Articles for Settling the Qinghai Affair" (*Qinghai shanhou shiyi shisan tiao*) and "Twelve Articles for Controlling Qinghai" (*jinyue Qinghai shi'er shi*) in 1724. As a result, in 1725 the Kökönuur Mongols were divided into two wings and twenty-nine banners.[13] Each banner was headed by nobles, chosen and made hereditary by the Manchu court, with salaries paid by the Qing court. A banner was further divided according to *sum* (*zuo* in Chinese), each *sum* constituting one hundred households, very much like the Chinese household registration *baojia* system (see Dutton 1988). These banners were allocated pastureland, and their members were strictly prohibited from crossing borders. Unauthorized communication between them was also forbidden. The assembly was convened and supervised by the Xining *banshi dachen* (superintendent) (a.k.a. Qinghai *banshi dachen*). The Hoshut leaders were stripped of their indigenous titles. Interestingly, for the ritual assembly, they were to elect a ritual chief, who was, however, different from the *chuulgan darga* (league governor) elsewhere in Inner Mongolia.[14] Meanwhile, the Kökönuur banner princes would have to participate in a rotational system called *nian ban* (annual attendance duty)—that is, to appear at the Qing court to pay tribute to the emperor and report on their duties. The attendance was compulsory. Failure to attend would incur punishment—in the case of a banner prince, a fine of three years' salary. The purpose of such audiences was "to inculcate awe and veneration in the heart" (*xing sheng jing wei*) among the Mongol nobles (Yuan 1991: 299–303).[15]

Meanwhile, monasteries were tightly controlled, as the number of monastic cells was restricted to a maximum of two hundred and the total number of monks in a monastery to three hundred. Far from being deferent to Tibetan Buddhism and its hierarchs, as Hevia claims, the Qing rulers did not hesitate to execute the leading lamas who supported the Mongol rebellion. The Qing used both *en* (grace) and *wei* (awe), punishing the recalcitrant, awarding the submissive. Elaborate measures were undertaken to exercise political surveillance on monasteries, so that they could no longer become the focus of resistance against the Qing. Moreover, the monk community became divorced from lay support; their livelihood was to be provided by the Qing local administrations. Further measures were adopted to demarcate boundaries between Kökönuur Mongolian banners and the territory under the jurisdiction of the Xining Fu, or prefectural government, where numerous border garrison troops were stationed and fortresses built. A buffer zone was established between the two, where Chinese criminals and peasants were sent to engage in agriculture. Tibetans were also separated from Mongols. Here we see a glimpse of the developing Manchu colonial regime that formalized and rationalized the structures of political authority and protocol of both the indigenous populations and their relations with the Qing state.

The conquered and colonized Kökönuur Mongols were administered by a governor called the *zongli qinghai menggu fanzi shiwu dachen*[16] ("Superintendent in Total Charge of Qinghai Mongolian and Tibetan [Barbarian] Affairs"), and an office was set up in 1725 in Xining. His job was to run the day-to-day affairs of the Mongols, supervise their annual assembly, and decide on their tribute-bearing annual visit to the imperial court in Beijing.

The effect of Qing colonial rule was soon felt by the Mongols to be too hard to bear. The cost of the annual assembly became such a burden[17] to Mongols that, after a while, some simply refused to attend. In the ninth year of Yongzheng (1731), one banner prince, Norbu, moved out of his allocated pastureland and refused to come to the assembly. Several more banners moved beyond the Yellow River, farther from the Xining power control (Zhecang 1994: 1–3). This was regarded as betrayal of the benevolence of the emperor. As a result, the Qing made a new law called *Fanli Tiaokuan* ("Articles of the Barbarian Code") in 1733, which stipulated, inter alia, that the annual assembly be conducted on the fifteenth day of the seventh lunar month and be attended by all Mongol banner ruling princes on the east bank of the Kökönuur Lake. The assembly must be supervised by an imperial envoy and must not be held privately. Severe administrative and financial penalties were imposed on those who failed to attend in person (Chen and Xu 1992: 64). Subsequently, the assembly was turned into a court to judge violators of the rules (Zhecang 1994). Mu Shouqi commented on the atmosphere of the assembly thus: "Nobody would dare talk about politics. The ritual rules were really strict, indeed one could only say that it was immensely fortunate for the descendants of the Yuan dynasty that they managed to keep their racial identity until today" (1970, vol. 8).

A compromise was eventually reached to reduce the burden on the Mongols. In 1763 it was decided that the assembly would be held once every three years. The Qing imperial history *Qing Shi Lu* ("Veritable History") noted: "Upon investigation, it was found that the assembly in Xining was originally held once a year, but because of the petitions of the military governor and monks, it was changed to once every two years. Since the Kökönuur pastures are remote from the assembly site, change to once every three years would harm nothing, but it would certainly save a lot of return fares for the Mongols." It was decided then that "in the year of the assembly that is to be held once every three years, the list of vice-presidents of one of the Six Boards, deputy military governor, imperial body-guards, and Qianqinmen guards, should be prepared and reported; patiently wait to be dispatched by the emperor. Travel swiftly by relay to Xining. Start from Xining, order the brigade-general and superintendent of the region to allocate award gifts, banquets and silk, etc. as needed by the assembly, and dispatch an army to escort (the envoy)" (*Da Qing Gaozong Chun Huangdi Shilu* 1964, section 680).

The sources do not indicate whether a lake-worshiping ritual was held on the occasion of the government assembly. Since assembling was prohibited without supervision by the imperial envoy, and each banner was segregated from the others, it is highly unlikely that the Kökönuur Mongols had any opportunity to hold a ritual together. However, ten years later, in 1773, at the suggestion of the new imperial Xining superintendent, Mitai, the Qing Board of Rites decreed a sacrifice to the Kökönuur Lake deity in conformity to that attributed to Four Great Seas (Xining Fu Xuzhi, vol. 9). Da Qing Huidian ("The Statutes of the Great Qing") records the rite thus: "The efficacy manifesting, might-demonstrating Qinghai God is offered sacrifices at the city of Xining, Gansu. Sacrifices would be made every autumn. In the year of assembly, an envoy is dispatched for the sacrifice. Sheep offerings are made. After offering incense, a eulogy is read. Make three presentations to receive the God, then send off the God. The officiator and his assistants each perform three prostrations and nine koutous" (quoted in Qinghai 1987: 192).[18]

This seems to be the start of the overlapping of the lake worship ritual with the assembly (both held in autumn). It should be noted that the ritual (but not the assembly) was held once a year. As the previous ritual manual indicates, in the interval years between assemblies, sacrifice to the lake deity was made in Xining city, very possibly in the manner of yaoji by the Xining superintendent and his subordinates, rather than by Mongols. And only in the year of assembly would an imperial envoy be sent to the lake.

In this new arrangement the lake worship ritual was held a day before the assembly. After the ritual, Mongol nobles would attend a reception held in the nearby Dunkher monastery. A banquet would be thrown by the imperial envoy. On the occasion, the imperial envoy would first read out the imperial edict and then sort out disputes and affairs between Mongol banners. The disputes would be judged by the envoy, and he would also decide on the matter of tributes and visit of the Hoshut Mongol princes to the capital. Gifts from the emperor and court would also be distributed on this occasion (Qinghai 1987: 192).

It is abundantly clear that the lake ritual was instrumental and was held for political purposes.[19] The Manchus used the Kökönuur God to assemble the Mongols and used the congregation or assembly to demonstrate the rules of the emperor. As shown, originally the lake ritual was almost entirely a Confucian one, celebrating the Manchu conquest, and was held separately from the Mongolian assembly. After the Mongols became restive, some refusing to attend the assembly, a new tradition combining the lake-worshiping ritual and the assembly was designed to assemble Mongols through the lake deity. Refusing to come to such a ritual would mean defying the supernatural spirit, which no religious-minded Mongol would dare.

RITUALIZING ETHNIC HARMONY? INCORPORATING THE TIBETANS IN THE RITUAL COMMUNITY

The conquest of the Mongols led to a different kind of ethnopolitics in the region. While earlier the Mongols dominated the Tibetans, now the two groups were segregated and both were brought under the Manchu polity. The Tibetans, like the Mongols, were also allocated pastures and were prohibited from traversing fixed boundaries. The Manchu colonial divide-and-rule policy pivoted on fixation of pasture, ensuring stability. What the Manchus did not intend, however, was a different kind of politics involving conflict between the Tibetans and Mongols. In mediating this ethnic conflict, the Kökönuur God was also extensively deployed.

In the aftermath of the Manchu conquest of the Mongols, Tibetans thought that the Manchus were supporting the Mongols; they felt disadvantaged by the fact that they had been given less fertile land south of the Yellow River, while the Mongols were allowed to continue to occupy the fertile pastureland around the Kökönuur Lake. These Tibetans had earlier lived around the lake but were pushed out by the Mongols, who were invited there by the fifth Dalai Lama in the sixteenth century. From the mid-eighteenth century onward, the weakness of the Mongols encouraged the Tibetans to cross the Yellow River to occupy Mongol pasturelands. A massive migration took place, leading to protracted conflicts and wars between Tibetans and Mongols. In the early nineteenth century, 23 of the 24 Mongol banners were perennially raided by the Tibetans, and more than 10,000 Mongol refugees were scattered and reduced to beggary. The Tibetan expansion was initially encouraged by the Manchu court as a tactic to reduce Mongol power. However, the unruly Tibetans began to not only raid Mongols, but also to raid Tibetan envoys or Mongol pilgrims from and to Lhasa, and sometimes even the Qing garrison army came under attack. By 1821, 23 out of 25 local Tibetan tribes had crossed the river and pushed into Mongol territory. Tibetan expansion violated the Qing rule prohibiting crossing boundaries (see Qinghai 1987).

The fifty-sixth year of Qianlong, or 1791, saw Manchu policy shift from an anti-Mongol to a pro-Mongol one. In that year, Sharabtili, a Mongol banner prince, was killed in one of the Tibetan raids. To better control the Tibetans, the Qing transferred Tibetans who had earlier been ruled by the Guide and Xunhua administrations to the jurisdiction of the Xining superintendent (Zhecang 1994: 17). Since the Tibetans directly threatened Qing frontier law and order, the emperor and the imperial superintendent repeatedly criticized Mongol princes for their failure to stand up to Tibetan bullying (Zhecang 1994: 19).

In one of the worst battles between Mongols and Tibetans in 1798–1799, the lake God temple was razed and the tablet overturned. That the temple was burned by Tibetans really puzzled the Manchus, as one imperial superintendent reported: "In my view, the Tibetan barbarians, although wild, . . . still believe in the deity and Buddha. What would overturning the tablet benefit them? There must be some other reason." Extensive investigation was made into this incident, but nothing could be found (Zhecang 1994: 21). Since the Mongols lost their pastureland around the lake, in 1804 (the ninth year of Jiaqing), the Xining superintendent Durja removed the tablet to Chagaan Tolgoi, a snow-capped mountain, the original site at which Hoshut Mongols had assembled (twenty-five kilometers east of the lake). "Every year long distance sacrifices were made to the lake (*yaosi*), but the attempt to build a temple fell through" (Heng Jin, quoted in Mi 1993: 210). The previous description reveals the serious decline of Mongol power, and the assembly and lake sacrifices practically lost their function.

In 1822, in response to increasing aggression from the Tibetans, the Qing finally decided to take military action to force the Tibetans back to their originally allocated pastureland—that is, south of the Yellow River. But as soon as the Qing army completed the mission and went back, Tibetans again crossed the river into Mongol territory. Later in 1822, Nayanceng, the governor-general of Shaanxi and Gansu, was sent as an imperial envoy to Xining to handle the "Tibetan case." Nayanceng brought in more military garrisons, reorganizing and sending back the Tibetans, and all were sent back to the south of the Yellow River. In order to "protect" the Mongols against Tibetan raids, Nayanceng built a fortress in Chagaan Tolgoi, stationing one thousand Qing troops there. Meanwhile, in view of the real economic difficulty of the Tibetans in the less fertile and crowded pasture, a few Tibetan groups were allowed to settle in the lake region (see Qinghai 1987; Zhecang 1994).

In 1831, as peace was gradually restored, Heng Jin, the new Xining superintendent, felt the need to revive the lake ritual by building a new temple at Chagaan Tolgoi and placing the tablet inside the temple.[20] The construction of the temple was completed the following year, and after that, the ritual no longer had to be conducted in open air but took place inside a properly built temple, something the Confucian-minded officials felt was especially important for the dignity of the empire, as the Kökönuur Lake was so important for the ritual construction of the symbolic boundary of the imperial domain. In the new lake ritual, nobles of the Tibetan groups newly settled into the former Mongol territory were also incorporated, and the ritual was held once a year under the supervision of an imperial envoy. With a struggle lasting over one hundred years and at enormous human cost, the Tibetans had finally won their right to settle around the lake. In 1858 the Qing court legalized the Tibetans' position and demarcated their pastureland around the Kökönuur Lake. Paradoxically, access to better pasture meant coming under more strict control, through incorporation into the ritual and administrative realm.

The ritual incorporation of the Tibetans did not signify that they were conquered. Rather, it was, in fact, an admission that the Qing could not force the Tibetans back to where they "should" be. The Tibetans fought their way into the ritual realm. In this case, the lake ritual had its geographic limitation. The lake God governed the immediate land adjacent to the lake, and it was supposed to be ethnicity-blind. Now that the Mongols and Tibetans occupied the lake region together, it became impossible to hold the ritual and political assembly separately for the Mongols and the Tibetans; to do so would suggest that the God differentiated among ethnic groups. Nevertheless, common assembly did not mean that they were all the same. Indeed, precisely because they were different, they had to be made to come together, and only by submitting to one God could they be governed and their conflicts be mediated effectively by the imperial envoy. In the Manchu ritualized colonial pecking order, the Tibetan nobles, because of their late arrival, ranked lower than the Mongol nobles. In the assembly, Mongol nobles were seated, while Tibetans had to remain standing.[21]

The incorporation of the Tibetans into the ritual was followed by their containment in their newly allocated special pastures. Their victory in gaining the territory was bought at the price of losing their right of freedom of movement. Yet at the same time, they gained "protection," as the Mongols did from the Manchus. The Mongols' victimization by the Tibetans was largely due to their military ineffectiveness, a product of the fact that they had been tied by Manchu law. Had they been allowed to form alliances freely, they might have been able to form a formidable force and perhaps defeat the Tibetans and even challenge the Manchus, as they had earlier. Fragmentation meant that they could no longer do so. For if they formed any collective alliance, they would invite direct retaliation from the Qing army. Their weakness and fragmentation, the very result of the Qing system, meant that they surrendered their self-defense to the Qing.[22] The Qing, in turn, was obliged, by its own law and morality, to protect the Mongols. The Tibetans' collective attempt to move across the Yellow River, although into the enemy (Mongols were made the enemy to both Tibetans and Manchus) territory, had to be stopped and punished by the Qing government. Interestingly, the Qing then had to support its enemy—the Mongols—to attack its ally, the Tibetans.

My concern here is as much with the imperial Qing efforts to secure law and order as it is with the emergence of a new kind of community. And this was a Kökönuur Lake ritual community, which regulated the behavior of Mongols and Tibetans. Their ethnic relations were mediated, now, through worshiping the same lake God. In this process, we can also see that the ritual rules became less coercive as a means to ensure the submission of the Mongols but more restrictive as a means to ensure harmony between Mongols and Tibetans. There was a subtle shift into something cultural, fully blossoming in the Republican period, a celebration of "minzu tuanjie."

A CHANGE OF MASTERS:
FROM THE MANCHUS TO THE MUSLIMS

Over one hundred years of war greatly reduced the strength of both Mongols and Tibetans, giving way to more powerful contenders, the Hui Muslims. A major anti-Qing Muslim rebellion in the second half of the nineteenth century clashed not only with the Qing army, but also with Mongols and Tibetans. The lake temple itself seemed to have been left at the mercy of nature, as it soon collapsed. During the reign of the Guangxu emperor, the ritual was held in tents. Perhaps, in order to summon the power of the Kökönuur God to help the Manchus suppress the Muslim rebellion, in 1877, the third year of Guangxu, the Qing court blessed the lake temple with a hanging horizontal board inscribed with four characters, *wei jing he huang* ("mightily pacify the Huanghe and Huangshui regions"), and a new temple was built just outside the west gate of Xining fortress. The board was hung on the temple that was to be used for spring and autumn sacrifices to be made by officials at every level of administration in Xining (Mi 1993: 211). We can clearly see that as the troublemakers shifted from Mongols and Tibetans to the Muslims, the God of Kökönuur would also be deployed more frequently to suppress the Muslims. The long-term Qing ritual investment into Mongol and Tibetan affairs also paid off: Mongols and Tibetans stood steadfastly on the side of the Qing to suppress the Muslims. So grateful was the Qing that the court rewarded some meritorious Mongol princes by increasing their salaries (Mi 1993: 216). But the Mongol and Tibetan support for the Qing also incurred heavy losses in their confrontation with the Muslim rebels. Kumbum monastery was severely damaged in the war.

With much of the Kökönuur region in ruins, it was 1902 before the ritual for Mongols and Tibetans was resumed. By then, the Muslim rebellion had been largely quelled. In 1907 Qing Shu, the Xining superintendent, decided to build a temple on the side of the lake. The original stone tablet was moved into the temple. But that seemed more to mark the end of Qing rule than its reassertion. Very soon, the strategic geopolitics of the region, with its link to the wider international politics, the ambition of the Muslims to make the region their sphere of influence, and the desire of the newly founded Republican government to establish a unified political system throughout China made the region politically significant. Subsequently, the Kökönuur Lake sacrifice was deeply implicated in the struggle between the central government and local Muslim power.

Let us now turn to the Muslims, who began to assert their authority in the region and to replace the Manchus as masters of the Mongols and Tibetans. Although not defeated by the Qing army, some Muslim rebel leaders shrewdly surrendered and vowed to serve the Qing. As a result, the Muslims in the Gansu and Kökönuur regions emerged as an organized military power, serving the imperial court and fighting against the anti-Manchu Chinese revolutionaries toward the turn of the twentieth century (Lipman 1984, 1997). Kökönuur, which was earlier a separate administrative region ruled by the Ministry of Colonial Affairs of the Qing Government, was made a special region within Gansu province—Qinghai, the Chinese translation of Kökönuur.

The 1911 Qing abdication upset the entire political system of administration of non-Chinese peoples, leaving the Qinghai or Kökönuur region in Muslim hands. Outer Mongolian independence in 1911 was perhaps the most unsettling event for those seeking to preserve the original borders of the Qing empire. In 1913 Outer Mongolia and Tibet recognized each other's independence. This was followed by an Outer Mongolian military expedition into Inner Mongolia and the British renaming of Qinghai as New Tibet. These developments made untenable the position of the local Muslim military leader Ma Qi, who had obtained his position through supporting the Manchu imperial house against his fellow Muslims. In this light, his official position had to be revalidated, either by declaring independence or by seeking recognition from the new Republican government. As neither a Buddhist Mongol nor a Tibetan, he was unable to join the Mongolian or Tibetan movement for independence; in effect, he had to submit to the Republican government to secure political recognition of his authority in the region. This meant that instead of supporting the Manchus to suppress the Republicans as he had done earlier, Ma Qi had to join the Republicans to demonstrate his ability to control or contain this looming wider international situation. Crucially, he turned to the Kökönuur Lake ritual to reconstruct the local political hierarchy.

This he carried out masterfully. In September 1913, Ma Qi, who had just been promoted to brigade-general of Xining, started to take advantage of the chaos in the political transition. Although it was not within his formal authority to deal with Mongols and Tibetans in Qinghai, Ma Qi established relations with Lian Xing,[23] formerly the prefect of Xining, now retitled *Qinghai Banshi Zhangguan* (superintendent for Qinghai affairs). Together, they officiated at the annual autumn lake ritual by gathering together Mongolian and Tibetan nobles at the lake God temple, on the second day of the tenth lunar month, 1913. Clearly reversing roles as a result of power changes, Ma Qi took the role of imperial envoy in the ritual by distributing brocades, brick teas, and sheep and by showering the Mongols and Tibetans with profuse encouragement. Remarkably, the old tablet inscribed "Long, Long, Long Live the reigning Emperor" was replaced with "Long Live the Republic of China" (Chen Bangyan 1981: 65). After the ritual, Ma Qi immediately sent a telegram to Yuan Shikai, the new president of China, saying that he had "invoked the virtuous ideas of the Center [to the Mongols and Tibetans], held the ritual, together with princes and dukes, and informed them all of the aim of the Republic." And he also promised to "lead his subordinates and follow [Yuan Shikai]" (Qinghai 1987: 268).

In a tricky maneuver, Ma Qi forced the Mongol and Tibetan nobles to support his bid for the title of the Qinghai Mongolian Tibetan Pacification Commissioner. After bribing the new governor-general, Zhang Binghua, Ma Qi even managed to have Lian Xing arrested, and he took the title of *Xining Banshi Zhangguan* in 1914. That he got this job appears to be partly related to the 1913 Outer Mongolian expedition into Inner Mongolia (Chen Binyuan 1986: 20). Apparently, the Mongolian invasion sent a shock wave to Gansu, as the Gansu provincial government reportedly had planned an expedition to Kulun (Khüree, or present-day Ulaanbaatar, the capital of Mongolia). It was feared that "Qinghai Mongols might be instigated to respond to Outer Mongolia. Then, the entire situation of the Northwest would become unthinkable" (Mu 1970). It seems, however, that his appointment also had something to do with the perceived threat from the British. The official appointment text stated that the new Chinese Central government had long been concerned about this danger and, as a preventive measure, appointed Ma Qi to the position, since he was known to be familiar with Tibetan affairs and also spoke Tibetan (Mu 1970).

Ma Qi's skill in combining military might and political tactics was evident in the description of the ritual conducted by him. There was "heavy and stern army protection and a lavish banquet. After the ritual, everybody (Mongol and Tibetan nobles) was happy and told each other that the Chinese government still existed. Therefore they recognized the Republic and sent representatives (to Lanzhou) to present Tibetan rugs, etc. [as gifts]" (Mu 1970).

There is little evidence to indicate that Ma Qi brought any innovations to the ritual itself, apart from changing the tablet. Despite his allegiance to the Republican regime, Ma himself was hardly a convinced revolutionary. For Mongols and Tibetans, what changed was not the political system, but the ruler, a ruler who was not effectively linked to the National government and one who wanted to maintain autonomy from the Center. Controlling the Tibetans and Mongols on behalf of the Center was the crucial way to maintain his power. Therefore, Ma Qi pandered to the Mongol and Tibetan imagination by sending to the lake ritual fake Qing imperial edicts and an imperial seal wrapped in yellow silk. Mongols and Tibetans continued to koutou three times until 1927. Yet we can see a new ethnic order. There were now two powers, Muslims and Chinese, whose positions vis-à-vis the Mongols and Tibetans were ritually distinguished as masters, one regional, the other national. This triangular relationship in the new "national order of things" (to use Malkki's phrase, 1995) under the Chinese Nationalist government was to be sorted out, often ritually in the Kökönuur worship.

MODERNITY AT THE EDGE: MUSLIM "FEUDAL" RULE AND MINZU TUANJIE THROUGH THE KÖKÖNUUR CULT

The Muslim rise in Gansu in the early decades of the twentieth century was symptomatic of a new kind of polity emerging in China. The center was very much weakened as a result of the prolonged death agony of the Qing and the subsequent Chinese nationalist revolution. Indeed, in the effort to overthrow Manchu rule, provincial autonomy was made an alternative polity designed to save China. In recent years, scholars, in a new turn of postcolonial critique of Chinese nationalism, moved to defend provincial autonomy which was ultimately replaced by a rhetoric of national unity and centralization. This theoretical intervention allowed us to see some positive value in the provincial movement, which, in much of the rhetoric of Chinese historiography, both nationalist and communist, was denounced as divisive warlord politics detrimental to China's unity and peace. This new critique concentrated overwhelmingly on Sun Zhongshan's relationship with Chen Junmin, a Guangdong warlord (Duara 1995; Fitzgerald 1996). Duara argues, for instance, that investment of negative meaning to the term *fengjian* truncated the possibility of a regional autonomy advocated by provinces. What is missing in this discussion is the relationship between the discourse of provincial federalism and the discourse of ethnic autonomy. Furthermore, what has not been explored was the continued warlord dominance of China's ethnic frontiers. Such warlordism was condoned, at times through the politics of identity, as a means of preserving Chinese territorial unity.

The Hui Muslim domination in Gansu and Qinghai provides another dimension of fengjian. By virtue of their adroit participation in the Chinese nationalist revolution, the Hui managed to maintain their autonomy. Jonathan Lipman (1997) provides an insightful discussion of several prominent Hui leaders, celebrating their hybridity by combining Chineseness and Muslimness. But what Lipman neglects is their relations not with the Chinese, but with other minorities under their rule. I argue that Muslim domination did not hinge just on demonstrating their "progressive" fealty to China, but, more important, on their ability to assure Tibetan and Mongol loyalty to China. Lipman's discussion of Muslim identity politics was more complex than Duara's and Fitzgerald's one-dimensional discussion. And yet the unconditional praise for their "alternative" model for China glosses over the backyard of their own domain. The remainder of this chapter will demonstrate that the desire of the Chinese Center and the Chinese to penetrate into Qinghai or the Northwestern ethnic frontier—not only for the sake of Chinese unity, but also because the Northwest became the pivot of the very survival of the Chinese nation—and the Muslim ability to maintain autonomy in the region was one important factor in the outcome. Modernity introduced a number of new ideologies, such as unity and equality. Curiously, the Muslim discourse of national unity and that of the Chinese central government converged on the common ground of the Kökönuur Lake ritual. The ritual offers us the possibility of gazing into the new Chinese "Nation Form."

Ma Qi's domination of the Kökönuur Mongols and Tibetans continued without external checks until 1926, when the Guominjun (Citizen Army) forces of Feng Yuxiang, the Christian general, pushed into Gansu. Liu Yufeng, an anti-Muslim Chinese general, was appointed governor of Gansu province in June 1927. Although Ma Qi was made a member of the provincial committee, Muslim power was at an all-time low. The national government's new civilizing mission was also to bring education to the region, specifically to educate the Mongols, Tibetans, and Muslims as Chinese citizens. Education, more than anything else, became the touchstone for penetration of the Center into Mongol and Tibetan areas.

Ma Hetian,[24] a newly appointed commissioner of the Education Bureau of the new Gansu government, was dispatched to tour Qinghai and inspect its education situation in September and October 1927. Accompanied by Ma Qi, he attended and officiated at the 1927 lake sacrificial ritual. (Apparently, the Chinese control of the provincial government did not entirely deprive Ma Qi of accessing the Mongols and Tibetans.) Ma Hetian radically reformed many of the contents of the ritual to reflect Chinese modernist and nationalist ideologies. Since he was an important witness to, and participant in, the event, let us see his account in more detail.[25]

At the lake temple, he was welcomed by several dozen Mongol princes and Tibetan nobles. At 7 A.M., he and the Mongol princes and Tibetan nobles were ushered to the temple to offer their sacrifices. The temple was on a high slope. It had a gate and a main hall. On top of the gate was a horizontal tablet inscribed with the characters *Haishen Miao* ("Sea God Temple"). In front of the main hall was a tablet inscribed with *qinghai shengjin* ("The Marvelous Scene of Qinghai"). Texts on the pole supporting the temple indicated that the temple was built in the thirty-third year of Guangxu (i.e., 1907) by Qing Shu, the imperial envoy and deputy governor-general mentioned previously. Because of a shortage of wood and stone, it took Qing Shu three years to complete the construction. The temple had a dozen small rooms. In front of the temple were two walls in ruin. The smaller was said to have been the site of the old temple, and the larger that of the fortress built by Nayanceng around 1822.

In the middle of the temple was a stone tablet inscribed with *lingxian qinghai zhi shen* ("the God of Qinghai, which manifests efficacy and shows might"), in front of which were offered vegetables, fruits, and sweets. On the left-hand side was a whole boiled sheep; on the right-hand side was a whole boiled cow. A fake imperial edict wrapped in yellow brocade was conspicuously displayed on the table. When Ma Hetian gave instructions to remove this latter, Ma Qi, who accompanied him, explained that the reason for keeping it was that "the Mongols and Tibetans very much revered such things. If removed, it might have some adverse effect. So, our soldiers carried fake seals and fake edicts from Xining, only to cater to the reverence of the Mongols and Tibetans." The sacrifice was held outside the main hall. Three offerings were made. Ma Hetian prohibited the three koutous; instead he suggested using three bows, the new body language associated with the Republican era.

On the following day, at the congregation of Mongol and Tibetan princes and nobles in the nearby Dunkher monastery, Ma distributed numerous gifts and presented portraits of Sun Zhongshan, the founding father of the Republic. Ma made a speech, first explaining Sun's Three People's Principles (*sanmin zhuyi*), emphasizing the point that every nationality be completely liberated and made equal. After denouncing the Manchu Qing's repressive and obscurantist policies, he promised that the Gansu provincial government was committed to opening up the frontier region and supporting the Mongolian and Tibetan nationalities. He urged them to pursue education by sending their children to schools. After his speech, he was astonished to find Mongols and Tibetans carelessly stuffing meat, yellow brocade–wrapped gifts, and the Sun Zhongshan portraits together into their dirty bags. This only led to his further determination to educate these coarse barbarians (Ma Hetian 1932). As is clear, Ma Hetian's attitude toward the ritual was unabashedly instrumentalist. The ritual was to serve as a means to disseminate the ideology of the new Chinese Nationalist regime. It was a civilizing mission.[26] By changing the content and slightly modifying the form, Ma Hetian sought to effectively bring the Mongols and Tibetans under the sovereignty of the new China through this ritual.

Unification of China under Jiang Jieshi's Nationalist Party (GMD) forces in late 1927 found Feng Yuxiang deputy commissioner of the Administrative Yuan. On September 5, 1928, under his encouragement, Qinghai was made independent of Gansu, from which was also created Ningxia province. In the new Qinghai provincial committee under Feng Yuxiang's control, the local Muslim strongmen did not have much of a role.

But the situation turned better for the Muslims in October 1929, when civil war between Jiang Jieshi and the combined force of Feng Yuxiang and Yan Xishan, a warlord of Shanxi province, absorbed most of Feng's army, thus leaving Qinghai to the local Muslim leaders. Ma Qi was appointed provisional provincial chairman. Due to a disastrous famine, 1929–1930 turned out to be bad for the Northwest, so supporting Feng's large army was a tremendous burden for the local Hui and Chinese. Making an astute political judgment, Ma Qi and his Muslim supporters purged the Feng clique and declared allegiance to Jiang Jieshi. According to Li Shijun (1987), in 1930, as war intensified in the eastern front, Jiang Jieshi encouraged local Hui and Chinese forces to reclaim local autonomy from Feng, raising the slogans *Gan Ren Zhi Gan* ("Gansu to be ruled by Gansu people") and *Quzhu Guominjun* ("Drive out the Citizenship Army") (1987: 83). By switching allegiance from supporting Feng Yuxiang to supporting the victorious Jiang, Ma Qi gained tremendous political capital. In July 1931 he was appointed chairman of Qinghai province, and his second son, Ma Bufang, was made the commander of the new ninth division of the National Army. In this maneuver, Ningxia, Gansu, and Qinghai provinces all came under Muslim rule. It thus became clear that the Muslims emphasized not their Muslim identity, but their loyalty to the new government. It is especially interesting to read Lipman's comment on the political astuteness of another Muslim leader, Ma Fuxiang:

Building on three years of gradual approach to the Guomindang, Ma Fuxiang broke openly with Feng Yuxiang, using nationalistic rhetoric to justify a new alliance with Jiang Jieshi. All warlords traded in these sentiments of "for the people" and "unify the nation" to justify their militarism, but this new sloganeering, however superficial, had special significance when it came from a Muslim. For Muslims, even more than non-Muslims, this explicit nationalism contrasted with dynastic loyalty, Islamic isolationism, and Gansu regionalism and meant the end of the imperial era—a new stage in the slow, murky dawning of the polyethnic Chinese nation-state. (1997: 175)

The Muslim power concentration coincided with further complications in international relations. In 1931 Japan invaded Manchuria and started to penetrate into Inner Mongolia in the following year. Meanwhile, a dispute in Kham between the chief of Beri and the Nyarang led a Tibetan army to clash with the Chinese troops of the Sichuan warlord Liu Wenhui. Soon, another monastic dispute occurred in Nangchen, near Jyekundo; again Tibetan troops were dispatched from Chamdo to Nangchen. These frontier crises would inevitably invite the Center's intervention, and for a GMD government that just lost Manchuria, the backyard turmoil must be resolutely brought under the Center's control before it was too late. Conversely, the Center's preparations for intervention ultimately threatened Muslim power and de facto autonomy.

According to Chen Binyuan (1986), Ma Bufang, Ma Qi's second son and a new player in regional politics, saw in this an excellent opportunity to elevate his personal reputation and, at the same time, to prevent Jiang's central army from entering Qinghai, as Jiang was increasingly concerned about Muslim power in the northwest of China. Ma secretly ordered his subordinate Ma Biao to provoke the Tibetan army, and the resulting monastic dispute soon escalated into a bloody Tibet–Qinghai war (Chen 1986: 46). Although Jiang Jieshi was annoyed at Ma Bufang and started to suspect him, fearing that he might one day become Feng Yuxiang the second (Chen 1986: 46), Ma did succeed in enhancing his own prestige by whipping up patriotism among the Chinese population. According to H. E. Richardson, the Tibetan military operation in Sichuan and Qinghai was suspected by the Chinese of British intrigues.

> The Nationalist Press, although far from the scene of action and from any reliable source of information, at once launched out into the frantic anti-British propaganda which was almost automatic whenever the Tibetans got the better of the Chinese. British trained troops with British officers were alleged to have established themselves in Chamdo; and charges of British instigation of the Tibetans were hurled about. (Richardson 1984: 134)

The acceleration of this local dispute into an international intrigue quickly transformed the ideological and nationalist landscape in Qinghai. Suddenly, the attitude of the Mongols and Tibetans, who were intimately related to wider Tibetan and Mongolian politics, was deemed crucial. Qinghai came to be seen as a terribly unruly place. This was no longer a mere local affair; the new provincial chairman Ma Ling, who was Ma Qi's younger brother, asked the Administrative Yuan for solutions. Meanwhile, the Mongolian-Tibetan Affairs Commission[27] in Nanjing also sent a petition to the Administrative Yuan, asking it to allocate funds to send an envoy to officiate at the lake worship ritual. The petition read:

Should the lake ritual be neglected for long like this, it is feared that the Mongolian and Tibetan nationalities may forget the existence of the central government; the prospect is extremely worrying. At the moment when the nation is in trouble, and when the Tibetan army invades Qinghai, it is most appropriate to dispatch a special envoy in a simple manner to go and inspect (the region); the inspection would not only disseminate the state's policies and ideology and consolidate the centripetal tendency of the frontier peoples, but also inspect and explore the local customs, so that the [new] political system may be conveniently implemented. (Qinghai 1987: 345–46)

From this petition, we can see the significance of the ritual in the eyes of Chinese officials. In 1932, the GMD central government sent Chen Jinxiu, a member of the Mongolian-Tibetan Affairs Commission, as the special sacrificial envoy and a junior official Pu Jian as his assistant. They brought with them numerous propaganda materials, portraits of the GMD government leaders, and gifts to Mongolian and Tibetan leaders. Somehow, they were delayed on the way and missed the ritual date. Although I do not want to read conspiracy in this delay on the part of the Muslims, pending further documentary evidence, the delay gave Ma Ling the opportunity to officiate at the ritual instead, on behalf of the Center. There is little available description of this ritual, but we do know that upon his belated arrival, Chen Jinxiu and the Qinghai government threw a party to entertain Living Buddhas, Mongol and Tibetan secular leaders in Xining, where Chen told them how much the central government was "attentive to Mongols and Tibetans." As a result, Mongol and Tibetan religious and secular leaders had to show that they were grateful to the central government's "cherishing" (*huairou*) and accepted its "propitiation" (*fuwei*). Led by a high-ranking Tibetan lama, Minjur Hutagt, they issued a joint circular telegram to the central government, "swearing to unite all hearts into one thereafter, obey the central order, obey the local government, and become the shield to support the internal pacification [by the central government] and oppose external threats [from the Japanese]" (Qinghai 1987: 346–47).

It was apparent that Ma Ling and Ma Bufang successfully offset Jiang Jieshi's attempt to undermine Muslim domination by making the Mongols and Tibetans an issue of patriotism, and the more the latter seemed to pose trouble for the unity of China, the more the Ma family promoted its own patriotism and the greater its reason for preserving the legitimacy of its rule over the province. I submit that the 1932 ritual was, therefore, in effect a political coup instigated by Ma Ling and Ma Bufang. It was to their advantage to play the Mongol and Tibetan card, thus sidelining the real issue of Qinghai—that is, the GMD drive for national integration against regional "feudalism." The lake ritual now became a means of publicity, a political yardstick against which to measure the political and ethnic instability in the region. Ma Ling and Ma Bufang were more than happy to welcome the ritual envoy from the GMD government to officiate at the sacrifice.

In this contentious politics, the Mas simultaneously remained firmly committed to the central government and kept the central government at arm's length. However, Muslim local power had many ideological foes, plus ethnic enemies. In 1936–1937 the Red Army's northwestward military expedition to link up with Soviet forces in Xinjiang was routed by Ma Bufang's forces.[28] Ma tortured and enslaved numerous Red Army POWs, distributing hundreds of female soldiers to his subordinates as wives and concubines (Dong 1995). That Ma carried out this atrocity even after the Xi'an incident, which resulted in the second GMD-CCP alliance against the Japanese invasion, enabled the CCP to whip up an ideological campaign by calling the Qinghai army *Ma Jia Jun*—that is, Ma Family army, which had a clear negative "feudal" connotation. This labeling put enormous pressure on Ma Bufang, who had to defend himself in the press and send a report to the Military Committee of the central government, stating that his army was part of the "national army, people's power." The victimized Mongol and Tibetan students from Qinghai also carried out a relentless campaign in Nanjing, the national capital, accusing Ma of imposing feudal rule in Qinghai. This public opinion forced Ma Bufang to offer to resign from his acting chairmanship of the province and commander of the Second Army in December 1936. Perhaps in consideration of his defeat of Jiang's archenemy, the communist Red Army, Jiang could not but seek to placate him. He sent his personal envoy, Xiao Zhiping, to Xining to appease Ma Bufang in April 1937. In a dramatic episode, the *Qinghai Daily* published an editorial entitled "Welcome Xiao Zhiping to Placate (*xuanfu*) Qinghai," to the embarrassment of both the envoy and Ma Bufang. Xiao immediately demanded that it be corrected to *weiwen* (expressing sympathy and/or appreciation). Ma Bufang told the editor of the *Qinghai Daily*, "People say that I expand my personal force, so [the envoy came to] pacify [me]. Now that [the envoy said 'weiwen,'] then it should be 'weiwen'" (Chen 1986: 142–43). In the modernist and nationalist China in the first half of this century, to be called "feudal" not only meant delayed evolution in terms of political culture, but also posed the risk of being "pacified" by the civilizing center, thereby losing political autonomy in Chinese-dominated Nationalist China.

Jiang's continued concern over Ma family rule, and the key position of Northwest China in China's strategic survival in the anti-Japanese war, suggested that control of the Northwest, especially Qinghai, was of great importance. To ensure the continued commitment of Ma Bufang to the anti-Japanese cause, and to pacify the Mongols and Tibetans, Jiang Jieshi sent Zhu Shaoliang, the commander of the No. 8 War Zone that encompassed the Northwest, to officiate at the lake worship ritual in 1939, which was said to be the largest ever held in the history of the Kökönuur cult.

The occasion provided an excellent opportunity for Ma Bufang to demonstrate his political skill. He had to convince Zhu Shaoliang that he was simultaneously absolutely loyal and at the same time absolutely in control of the Mongols and Tibetans. Still more, he wanted to show that all nationalities (minzu) in Qinghai were united (tuanjie). Indeed, the success of the 1939 sacrificial ritual was to determine Ma Bufang's political future.

The Mongols and Tibetans would not let him down, for Ma Bufang had already eliminated the autonomy of the Qinghai Mongols and Tibetans and organized them into the Qinghai local administrative baojia system in 1938. In 1937 Ma Bufang had set up a Mongolian-Tibetan middle school and made himself the principal! His slogans were: "Enhance Mongolian and Tibetan Cultures, Develop Mongolian and Tibetan Education, Train Mongolian and Tibetan Intellectuals" (Cairenjia 1983: 125). He ordered Mongol and Tibetan nobles to send their children to the school. Some of these young people, after a short training, were assigned to work as secretaries and so forth, in various governmental offices in Xining. They were in fact hostages (1983: 125; Chen 1986: 256).

According to Chen Bangyan (1981), who was involved in preparing the ritual, Ma Bufang asked Mongol and Tibetan nobles to come to the preparation in advance, bringing good horses, sheep, and other valuable local products as gifts to Zhu. In order to make Zhu's travel comfortable, several hundred laborers were drafted to build roads day and night. The ritual site, which was located on the side of the Qunguojiala Lake to the northeast of the Kökönuur Lake (Zhu et al. 1994: 139), was beautifully decorated with eight new Mongolian-style yurts and over one hundred ordinary tents. A gigantic earthen ritual platform large enough for ten thousand people was also built. In front of the platform facing the Kökönuur Lake was built a small one-meter-high platform, upon which was placed the tablet inscribed *Lingxian Qinghai zhi shen* ("The God of Qinghai, which manifests efficacy"). The following was also placed on the platform: 1 yak, 2 sheep, 1 *hadag* (ritual scarf), 2 red candles, numerous incense sticks, some silver bowls with milk tea, fried oat flower, butter, various crops, dried fruits, and candies, 32 types in all. In front of the small platform were 2 large burning bonfires (Zhu et al. 1994: 139–40). On the fourteenth day of the seventh lunar month (August 30, 1939), when Zhu and Ma and their protégés approached the lakeside, Mongol and Tibetan nobles welcomed them from a distance of one kilometer away from the lake. Gancha *Qianhu* (leader of 1,000 households), a Tibetan noble, and a close ally of Ma Bufang, offered ceremonial scarves to Zhu and Ma on behalf of the Mongol and Tibetan nobles (Chen 1981).

Zhou Kaiqing (1968: 73), another witness to the event, recorded that the procedure was as follows: (1) All stand silently; (2) ritual officiator is seated; (3) music; (4) sing national anthem; (5) three bows to the GMD flag and the portrait of Sun Zhongshan; (6) ritual officiator reads out Sun Zhongshan's will; (7) offering: (a) offering incense, (b) offering silk, (c) offering sacrificial text, (d) reading sacrificial text, (e) all bowing three times to the lake god, (f) *wang* (gazes at the lake) and *liao* (burns fireworks), and (g) finish. Zhu Shukui et al. (1994: 140) noted that after burning fireworks, many soldiers at the lakeside fired cannons, and some soldiers on two sheep-skin boats fired guns toward the sky. Then, as soon as it was announced that the ceremony was "over," people rushed to the platform to snatch up the ritual offerings, believing they would be blessed. Meanwhile, some people threw live cows and sheep into the lake, and some threw silver or copper collars or even jewelry into the lake. Some also tossed bottles filled with money and grain and wrapped in ritual scarves into the lake for blessing.

The eulogy delivered by Zhu Shaoliang on behalf of Jiang Jieshi was a modification of the set eulogy, adapted to reflect China's current need for racial and national liberation:

> The virtuous god and the mountain and water are situated right at the western cardinal point. . . . The Japanese barbarians have invaded China, and we organize expeditions to punish them. The [Kökönuur] God blesses us silently and our prowess prevails. The rolling ripples cleanse flaws and filth, and the lost land is to be recovered. [The state] will be strongly fortified, and the sun and moon will shine again. At this moment of offering pure sacrifices, [we] have prepared sacrifices with reverence. The sea [lake] looks as if it was preparing to accept the fragrance of this sacrifice. Please deign to accept this, my sacrifice. (Quoted in Zhou 1968: 73–74)

Zhu's personal speech also betrayed his real intention in these succinct words: "Sincerely unite, and obey orders" (Qinghai 1987: 347). Here, interestingly, the efficacy of the Kökönuur God was no longer to suppress the Mongols, but to help all members of the newly imagined community Zhonghua Minzu (Chinese Nation) to resist the Japanese barbarians. Zhou Kaiqing made an interesting comment: "Sacrificing to the Lake today (1939) no longer means merely a grand ritual ceremony, but is a manifestation of the unity of all the nationalities of our country" (1968: 72).

After the lake ritual the assembly was held. What is striking was the elaborate gift exchanges during the assembly between the central delegation and the local Mongol and Tibetan dignitaries. Moreover, more people were included in the ritual realm in order to show unity of all nationalities in China. According to Zhu et al. (1994), participants included 8 Living Buddhas, 22 Mongolian princes, 22 Tibetan *qianhu* (leaders of 1,000 households), 109 Tibetan *baihu* (leaders of 100 households), 59 Mongolian *jangin* (leaders of *sum*, a unit below banner), 13 monk officials, 193 Mongols, 1,593 Tibetans, plus numerous Kazakh, Hui, and Chinese people, guests, and mounted soldiers, totaling about 2,000 people.

Let us see how much Zhu Shaoliang gave to the 52 Mongol and Tibetan princes and Living Buddhas: 104 pieces of brocade, 52 caps, 52 sacks of rice, 104 sheep, 208 packs of tea, 52 kilos of biscuits, 26 kilos of candies, and 52 silver handkerchiefs. Mongols and Tibetans of lower ranks received their due as well. In addition, 1,800 ordinary participants also received 60 sacks of flour, 1,852 packs of tea, 900 kilos of alcohol, 210 sheep, and 53 sacks of rice.[29] In return, according to Chen Bangyan (1981: 67–68), a representative of Mongol and Tibetan princes and leaders presented a ritual scarf and conducted what was considered the most respectful "wine offering" ritual to Zhu Shaoliang. In addition, three hundred fine horses, as well as precious local produce, were presented. Ironically, however, Ma Bufang kept the fine horses for his own cavalry and sent some poor ones to Zhu!

Cultivation of Mongol and Tibetan loyalty and celebration of sincere Chinese national unity (*zhonghua minzu jingchen tuanjie*) was also conducted one day before the lake ritual and the day after the assembly. Xin Hua, an eyewitness, recalled,

> On the night of the 15th of the seventh lunar month, the bright moon shone white, and the lake and sky had the same color. Songs and dances were performed under the moon light. First, Kazakh herdsmen from Xinjiang danced a bear dance, they jumped up and down, accompanied by music, rather interesting. This was followed by long sleeved Tibetan women who sang and danced.[30] Their music was exhilarating, the meaning of the song is roughly this: How great the Qinghai Lake; Qinghai looks like an ocean; ripples flow away but they have no edges; the wind blows and the grass bends; fine guests from near and afar, now gather together." (Quoted in Zhu et al. 1994: 142)

Mongol or Tibetan women may have provided some pleasures to the bored Chinese and Hui dignitaries, thus fostering another kind of "national unity." Zhou Kaiqing was rather carried away by the wonderful festival mood that night, as he stated: "Several dozen beautifully dressed Mongol and Tibetan women gathered in front of the tent of chairman Ma and sang and danced. . . . This scene which reflects the sincere unity of our Chinese Nation . . . was a beautiful interlude in the lake worship ritual" (1968: 74–75).

It would be preposterous to suggest that the numerically few and militarily powerless Mongols and Tibetans in Kökönuur could make any difference to the anti-Japanese war. But their symbolic significance for both the GMD central government and the Ma local government was great. Mongol and Tibetan nobles did not disappoint Ma Bufang. Since their children were kept hostage, ostensibly working at the side of Ma Bufang, the nobles issued a joint telegram to the central government that they would follow the national government and obey Ma Bufang. Their forced loyalty ultimately saved Ma Bufang's political career (Chen 1986: 211–14). And it was in their use value for Ma Bufang that we discern the significance of the Mongols and Tibetans. Not only the Mongols and Tibetans, but indeed all ethnic groups in the province were incorporated in this ritual community. A Chinese official, Xue Wenbo, who attended the 1943 ceremony, was deeply moved by Ma Bufang's sincerity in mediating ethnic conflict. After learning from fellow travelers that Ma Qi had allowed the Tibetans to join the ritual in the past, and Ma Bufang allowed the Kazakhs to join the ritual this time, Xue exclaimed,

In the past, the Mongols and Tibetans were divided as lords and slaves, but the two chairmen [Ma Qi and Ma Bufang], insisting on the principle of equality of all nationalities in our country, corrected the absurdity and astutely reformed it, which is really a perceptive measure greatly significant for the frontiers. Better still, in September when cattle and sheep are plump, people cheerful, making the lake worship ritual is really a celebration, analogous to the Mid-Autumn Festival in agricultural society, celebrating the harvest. The nomadic nationalities can now all rejoice without division in land and region. (Xue 1943: 53)

From the Chinese government's point of view, not only the Mongol and Tibetan but also the Hui Muslim culture was targeted for assimilation. The Chinese central government tacitly supported Ma Bufang's repression of Mongols and Tibetans, allowing Ma to destroy numerous Buddhist monasteries, to carry out seven genocidal expeditions into the Golog region and kill thousands of Tibetans (Chen 1986: 217–43). Yet the Chinese government would also use Mongol and Tibetan dissent to check the Ma regime. Dorji, a Kökönuur Mongol politician, recalled that when he was working for Ma Bufang as deputy director of the office of the 2 Kökönuur Mongolian leagues and 29 banners in Xining in 1947, he was in charge of nominating 11 Mongolian representatives for the National Congress and other legislative bodies in Nanjing. Ma Bufang tried to send two Chinese as Mongolian representatives. Dorji was sacked from his post because of his protest at this deception, but he sent a secret telegram through the GMD's Youth League Qinghai branch to the Mongolian and Tibetan Affairs Commission. Mongols from other provinces there were outraged. He then managed to sneak out of Xining to Lanzhou, where he met the Gansu province chairman, Guo Jijiao. Guo welcomed him as a Qinghai Mongolian representative of the National Congress and reported their meeting in the *Gansu Daily* the following day. Dorji noted, not without irony:

That the Gansu Province government chairman Guo Jijiao rendered such warm support to me was actually mockery at Ma Bufang. I was really flattered by the unbelievable and unexpected attention given by Guo to such a small figure as me. But careful thinking allowed me to see what's behind it. At the time, Ma Bufang was arrogant and domineering. His ambition to dominate the Northwest had incurred Jiang Jieshi's suspicion and he was on the lookout. Gansu certainly felt greatly threatened, so Guo could not be unconcerned. (Dorji 1984: 91–92)

This incident showed an interesting triangular relationship in the frontier, and it tells us much about the process of national integration. In other words, when Muslim leaders attacked Mongols and Tibetans for showing separatist tendencies, the GMD supported the Muslims. When victimized Mongols and Tibetans used the national media to condemn Ma's feudal family rule in Qinghai, the government moved against the Muslim leaders. The poor Mongols and Tibetans were caught up in this two-way struggle, and their plight was dramatized in the politically orchestrated lake ritual, used by both the central government and the local Muslim government for their own separate and overlapping purposes.

Finally, Ma Bufang's alienation of the Mongols and Tibetans exacted a toll on him. In 1949 the Chinese People's Liberation Army pushed toward Lanzhou, launching a fierce military sweep to eliminate Muslim power. Ma Bufang ordered the Mongols and Tibetans under his control to organize militia and deploy them to Lanzhou to resist the PLA. It was August 1949; on the fifteenth day of the seventh lunar month, the last Kökönuur Lake ritual was held. Sources available do not reveal who attended the ritual, but it was clearly a moment of mobilization: Mongols and Tibetans were poised to fight for Ma Bufang. Unfortunately for Ma Bufang, Wang Benba, a Kökönuur Mongol politician who had traveled widely in China, serving as the Kökönuur Mongols' representative in Xining and Chongqing at various stages of his political career, participated in the lake ritual and lobbied the Mongol and Tibetan nobles not to fight for the GMD, identifying Ma Bufang's army as the doomed Chinese nationalist force: "The GMD is as good as dead; the momentum of the Communist Party and the PLA for liberating the whole country is unstoppable, why do you send kids with hunting guns only to be killed?" (Kang 1989: 155). Thus unceremoniously ended the historic Kökönuur ritual, its political mission at an end.

The new Communist China had much more powerful control of Qinghai, so the Kökönuur God was no longer needed, or, may we say, the jurisdiction of the God was considered too limited? The new God was "invincible Mao Zedong Thought" and the People's Liberation Army. In November 1949, two months after the "liberation" of Xining, the victorious army and the new provincial government of Qinghai decided to organize "The United Friendship Festival of the Qinghai People," scheduled for January 1950 in Xining. It was a ritual of another conquering force, this time ostensibly one that came not as a conqueror, but as a liberator, as a unifier. The ritualized festival was touted as "an unprecedented grand ceremony of the great unity of the people of all nationalities, having great political and historical significance" (Zhang and Yao 1984: 53).

The festival was not just a symbolic fanfare; it was also the first official occasion to "select" representatives of various minzu, according to the new pecking order. It laid out new China's "nationality policies" for unity and equality of all nationalities. It mobilized all the peoples to eliminate bandit opposition to the new regime. Various levels of government were set up to conduct population census, eliminate "bad people," encourage repentance, and make merit by working for the new regime. Indeed, a whole series of activities fundamentally restructured Qinghai into a "unity." In the festival, the province's Party, government, and army leaders spoke, exhorting people to "get united" to support the new regime and the PLA. In return, several Mongolian, Tibetan, Hui, Salar, Tu, Chinese, and Buddhist monk representatives made speeches, unanimously swearing to support all the calls by Qinghai's new rulers. On the final day of the festival, 30,000 people gathered in the military training ground, and sixty-five different kinds of cannons fired into the air, demonstrating the might of new China (Zhang and Yao 1984).

History turned a new page for Kökönuur and China, a page that would be inscribed with further fanfare of minzu tuanjie, one with further twists of charm and brutality.

CONCLUSION:
NATIONAL INTEGRATION FROM THE EDGE

We can reach different conclusions on the basis of the preceding detailed histori-cal account. This political history of the cult of Kökönuur Lake should give us pause in thinking about nation-building in China and its culture. What started out as a symbolic and political ritual of the Manchu colonial state was gradually transformed through various historical stages, from a means of controlling the Mongols and Tibetans, into a festival celebrating the unity of all Chinese nationalities in the struggle against imperialist Japanese. In this process, the colonial content of the ritual was mysteriously phased out in favor of modernist and nationalist ideas of national unity and equality. This chapter has sought to show that the choreographed public spectacles must not be seen as mere window dressing for the brutality of an emerging national state, but are themselves the site of power par excellence, where the policies and decisions of the state are enacted. If a nation is an imagined community, then its imagined form is ren-dered visible in such national festivals. Furthermore, as Anderson argues, "Nationalism has to be understood by aligning it, not with self-consciously held political ideologies, but with the large cultural systems that preceded it, out of which—as well as against which—it came into being" (1991: 19). But the state form emerged prior to the national form. Balibar argues that national formation must be seen in the intricate relations between hierarchically organized "core" and "periphery," and "every modern nation is a product of colonization: it has always been to some degree colonized or colonizing, and sometimes both at the same time" (1991: 89). The nation form is never a predictable linear develop-ment. Seen in this way, multiculturalism in the *one* Chinese Nation, as expressed in the ambiguity of "amity between nationalities" or "National Unity," must then be understood in terms of a mysterious process of national integration.

Such national integration is certainly volatile, as we see in our Kökönuur case. Ritual, insofar as it provides a forum for worshiping the society or state in the Durkheimian sense, works largely in a tribal setting. For the multinational Qing dynasty, rituals were also a means to assemble and rule the colonized. The sym-bolic and the military threats were stuffed down the throat simultaneously. How-ever, this formulation is too simple to explain the processes of integration, wrought with compliance and defiance. Pomeranz (1997) proposed a notion of ritual imitation, following the lead of, but departing from, scholars like Bin Wong (1997) and Duara (1988). Premodern China could be understood as having universally accepted moral maxims as legitimating ideology accessible to both emperors and the lowest subjects of the empire, or a "cultural nexus of power" that "incorporate[d] even communities in which nobody was well-versed in classical culture into a culturally defined 'China' and [made] people feel a part of that larger entity" (Pomeranz 1997: 8). China, then, consisted of, according to Pomeranz, hierarchically imagined communities. But he noted that such ritual might entail as much stabilization or integration, as "it can also threaten the identities of higher elites, and imitation of forms with altered content can seem like dangerous misappropriation of both earthly and cosmic authority" (1997: 9). What this formulation implies is a particularly modernist polity, one that is inherently unstable. But this instability does not presume disintegration, for communities and individuals made reference to the same moral maxims. This model is particularly useful in explaining Muslim local authority and Chinese central authority in their perpetual struggles for autonomy and unity. In ritual interaction, central authority might not have penetrated physically into Qinghai, yet it certainly did ideologically. But what is threatening, from the central government's point of view, was precisely the Muslim ritual imitation that can successfully offset the need for other ethnically or regionally dominant representatives.

Pomeranz is short of formulating a theory of state-building and nation-building from the bottom up, although the model differs significantly from the state-building literature, especially the contributions by Duara and Fitzgerald. In their analysis of Chinese nationalist discourse and the demise of the federalist movement, they posit the "local" as authentic, whereas the "national" is viewed as alien and artificial. Hence their own intellectual resistance on behalf of the "subaltern" federalists. In a recent anthropological study, David Nugent criticizes precisely this kind of scholarship:

> In seeking to explain how the artificial has been made to appear natural in the making of national cultures, analysts have had recourse predominantly to Gramscian notions of cultural hegemony, and Foucauldian arguments concerning institutional practices and technologies of power. . . . Analysts may differ in which theory of "naturalizing the artificial" they draw on to explain how states nationalize their populations, but they share the assumption that some such form of "mystification" is essential to the making of national cultures. (1997: 9)

He argues in his study of Peru that "things modern," such as the concepts of democracy, citizenship, private property, individual rights, and protections initiated from the national center, were welcomed enthusiastically as liberating and empowering by the subaltern, who were in direct conflict with regional elites.

It was only because these subaltern groups embraced the national community—to the point of risking their lives in an armed uprising against the ruling landed elite—that the central government was able to establish any real institutional presence in the region. Only after the local population reimagined itself in modern form and actively sought out the institutions of the nation-state, then was the state able to initiate the individualizing, homogenizing, institutional practices discussed at length in the literature on the making of national cultures. (1997: 12)

Whereas in the Peruvian case the aristocrats were always opposed to the state, the frontier Chinese warlords were solicited by the modernizing Chinese state to act as its agents to expand the Chinese state into far-flung frontier regions. Provincialism in China before 1949 was often manifested in warlordism, which aimed to maintain "autonomy" by controlling and suppressing minorities in the name of the expanding state. Therefore, the frontier minorities' response to such provincial domination, which was often brutally imposed, was frequently two-fold: either to look outside of China for international principles of national liberation and national equality, as in the case of some parts of Outer Mongolia and Tibet, or appeal to the Chinese state, inviting the modernizing power, a power with some humanist heart, as in the case of Tibetans in Kham and Mongols in Qinghai and Inner Mongolia.

Wenbin Peng, in a recent study of the provincial and ethnic narratives in the former Xikang province, noted that the Tibetan autonomous movements and their clashes with the frontier Chinese warlords must not be seen as "accidental, or isolated events," but were political events "orchestrated by goals, calculations, and organization." "They were 'basically the anti-Liu Wenhui campaigns' couched in the appeal of 'Kham for the Khampa,' supported by (albeit tacitly at times) the 'Center' striving to curtail provincialism and Tibetan Nationalist expansions in Kham, and operated upon ties of native place, as well as of ethnicity" (2000). It should be added, based on his ethnographic discussion, that the Kham Tibetan leaders worked for and with the Chinese government, each using the other, aiming to abolish Xikang provincial warlordism, for different purposes: the Khampa to exercise their self-rule, the Chinese state to expand into the local area. Interestingly, in Inner Mongolia, Mongol communists were drawn to the Chinese Communist Party for its promises of ethnic equality and freedom. The integration of Inner Mongolia was enacted precisely through the conflicting and overlapping agendas of the Mongols and the Chinese state. Only after Inner Mongolia became a part of Communist China were individualizing, homogenizing, and institutional practices initiated, which then led to further rounds of despair and resistance, again appealing to the state (see chapters 5, 6, and 7).

We should not be perplexed by this "pro-modern" sentiment that led to further national integration, nor should we ignore the importance of this phenomenon. It was, argues Nugent in the case of Peru, but equally applicable to our case study, "a historically emergent phenomenon whose specific nature was contingent upon a complex field of interacting forces, from those within the local, to those emanating more properly from the national arena, to those from beyond the territorial boundaries of the state" (1997: 13).

NOTES

1. Lucian Pye, in his survey of Asian concepts of power, delineated two approaches to power: "One was the Sinic approach, which asserted an ethical-moral socio-political order; the other, used in many of the Southeast Asian cultures, conceived of ritualized power in relation to a cosmic order ruled ultimately by otherworldly forces" (1985: 40). The latter approach may be characterized by what Clifford Geertz described as the "theater state," with regard to Bali (1980), and Stanley Tambiah's "galactic polity," for the South and Southeast Asian states (1976).

2. He attributed too much power to lords, without defining what he meant by them. The so-called lords, in the Mongol case, would be *wang*, or princes, mostly Chinggisids. These people were given the title not because of their relative power leverage against the Qing, but because of their servitude and meritorious services during the Manchu conquest. Those lords who resisted did not survive. The rebellious Chakhar and the Tumed, for example, were stripped of their Chinggisid leaders.

3. These scholars have paid too much attention to Confucian values, i.e., social relationships or indeed what the Chinese call *ren zhi* ("rule of man"), but ignored other institutions such as the state and territorial organizations, which would fall into the realm of *fa zhi* (rule of law). It seems as though the Chinese polity was almost entirely "concerned not with government through regulation, but with self-government through the concept of *Li*" (Dutton 1988: 203). In a criticism that may be equally applicable to the foregoing approaches to ritual as power, Dutton (1988, 1992) rightly criticized the tendency in sinology of putting too much emphasis on the Confucian value of kinship. He argued that family and lineage are certainly central to the Confucian state, which sees them as morally good and politically useful, but unchecked kinship may also become the center of resistance to the state. The state certainly would not encourage that to happen and designed the household registration systems (baojia) so that "the useful remained just that" (1988: 209). Therefore, all families and clans had to be under close surveillance. In his view, "despite the fact that familialism was the cornerstone of the Chinese social system, and enjoyed privileges accordingly, it is no exaggeration to conclude that there is a strong counter-familial element in most, if not all, of the traditional pro-imperial polices, procedures, techniques and decrees of local government" (1988: 209).

4. Duara, in a more nuanced analysis of how the Manchu state power appropriated the Guandi cult and thus promoted uniformity throughout China, suggests that the secret may be attributed to what he calls "superscription of symbols" by various dynastic powers. Guandi (c.e. 162–220) was a hero of the period of the Three Kingdoms, later apotheosized. Over centuries, there were various versions of Guandi, which are, in Duara's view, "simultaneously continuous and discontinuous" (1988: 778). Duara argues, like anthropologists such as Victor Turner, that a symbol has multiple meanings, conveying different things to different people. Duara's theory has a historicist edge, capable of explaining

different versions of a myth linked in a semantic chain. He argues that the mode of super-scription makes a symbol ambiguous and multifarious and involves a higher political power imposing its meanings, in addition to those already there. Duara's point is to show that superscription was an arena "in which subordinate groups . . . were able to mobilize the hegemonic image to their own considerable benefit but also one where dominant and subaltern groups could draw on each other's images for their own purposes" (Duara 1988: 791).

5. Kökönuur, or Qinghai, is in the territory of today's Qinghai province of China. It is 4,583 sq. km in size, the largest saltwater lake in China.

6. *Wen Xian Tong Kao,* vol. 83, jiaoshe section 16.

7. The Hoshut Mongols came to dominate Tibet and the Kökönuur region in the early seventeenth century amid turmoil throughout Inner Asia, as the Manchus started their conquest of Mongolia, and Gelugpa Buddhism, led by the Dalai Lamas, began to be threatened by the Tibetan kings and their Mongol allies. Tsogt Taiji, a Halh Mongol prince hostile to Gelugpa Buddhism, fled to the Kökönuur region, posing a severe threat to the very survival of Gelugpa Buddhism. Invited by the fifth Dalai Lama, Gushri Khan, a personal friend and classmate of the Dalai, led his Hoshut Mongols into Tibet and elim-inated opposition to Gelugpa Buddhism. But instead of returning to Jungaria, Gushri Khan established his overlordship in Tibet in 1642, dividing Tibet into two domains for the Dalai Lama and the Panchen Lama and reserving Kökönuur for eight of his ten sons, who led the bulk of the Hoshut themselves. Lazan Khan was Gushri Khan's grandson. See Lee (1979) for this part of history.

8. The governance of the Kökönuur Mongols was markedly different from the Tibetan court, still preserving the tradition of assembly (*huraltai*). According to Mi Yizhi (1993: 131–32), the fixed site for the Kökönuur Mongolian assembly was at Chagaan Tolgoi, which is sixty-five kilometers west of Xining. The participants in the assembly were eight princes (*taiji*) of the Hoshut. The head of the eight princes was called Hung Taiji, or crown prince, who was responsible for supporting the Hoshut Khan (i.e., the King of Tibet).

9. Nian Genyao was awarded the title *yideng gong* (first-ranking duke).

10. The lake deity was specifically known as *Long Shen,* "dragon deity," and the temple was called *Longshen Miao.*

11. This appears to refer to the year 1696 (year of the tiger), when Jashi Baatar was granted the title *qing wang* by the Qing court.

12. *Li Fan Yuan* (Ministry of Colonial Affairs) was preceded by *Menggu Yamen* (Mon-golian Office), set up in 1631. The name was changed to *Li Fan Yuan* in 1638. Within it were three schools for training scholars in Mongolian studies, Tibetan studies, and Oirat studies (Yuan 1991: 287–93). See also Chia 1993, Di Cosmo 1998, and Heuschert 1998.

13. Not all of them were Hoshut banners. The Hoshut constituted 21 banners, while the other 8 banners were comprised of 4 Torgut banners, 2 Joros (Jungar) banners, 1 Khal-kha banner, and 1 Hoid banner.

14. For security reasons, the Kökönuur assembly would not be chaired by the elected ritual leader—rather, by the Qinghai superintendent, personally. It was not until 1823 that the Kökönuur Mongols were divided into two leagues, and each was appointed a league leader and a deputy (cf. Yuan 1991: 279).

15. The Kangxi emperor once remarked, after squashing the rebellion of Wu Sangui

in Yunnan: "The governors and generals of the frontier have been holding military power far too long. If they had come to have audiences, then they would have developed awe and veneration. Take Wu Sangui for instance. Although he was sincere and loyal, yet since he did not come to the court for long, he gradually developed arrogance" (Ma and Ma 1994: 146). Consequently, the Qing decided that not only frontier generals and governors, but also Buddhist leaders such as the Dalai Lamas and the Panchen Lamas, as well as Mongol princes, would have to come to the court regularly.

16. The complete title is *qianchai banli qinghai menggu fanzi shiwu dachen*; in short, *xining banshi dachen*, or *qinghai banshi dachen*. The office is habitually called *Qinghai yamen* or *tusi yamen*. The institution ended in the first year of the Republic of China. The superintendents were all Manchu or Mongol (non-Hoshut Mongol) officials. The rank is similar to *zongdu*, or governor-general. The office (*yamen*) where the superintendent was supposed to live and work was not set up until the tenth year of Qianlong, i.e., 1745 (Gu 1992).

17. For example, one *zasag* (ruling) prince called Lamonch complained in 1731 that his banner had to provide 8,000 sheep, 700 horses, and 300 troops, each of whom had to prepare three good horses (Zhecang 1994: 2). These livestock were for both consumption and taxation.

18. This ritual is similar to the grand sacrifice of the Qing. See Zito (1984, 1997).

19. C. K. Yang, in his book on Chinese religion, mentions a similar ritual community in south China. "In Chou time the altar of *she chi* (gods of earth and grain) was universally the sacred symbol of the political community of the feudal state, worshiped by the ruling house in every kingdom. In Han times (206 B.C.E.–C.E. 220), the *she*, or the altar of earth, was universally found in all counties, villages, towns, and neighborhoods, and it became the ceremonial ground for a large variety of community activities such as the swearing of a local official into office, praying for rain, taking a public vow, or praying for blessing" (1961: 98). A 1923 gazetteer noted the function of the gods of earth and grain: "Officials who are skilled in government *use the gods to assemble the people, and use the congregation to demonstrate the rules*" (quoted in Yang 1961: 99, emphasis original).

20. Heng wrote an article to record the event, "Xiujian haishen miao bei ji," which was printed in *Xining Fu Xuzhi*, vol. 9.

21. The Tibetans were offered seats only in 1932, when they became an important element in the national concern. It was also a reflection of the new ideology of "nationality equality." In the new seating order, Mongols were to sit on the left (junior) side and the Tibetans on the right (senior) side (cf. Hanguan Quejia n.d.: 103).

22. Territorial fixation and administrative fragmentation of the Mongols had the most devastating consequences for a nomadic people. The usual explanation for Mongol power decline focuses on Buddhism, whose otherworldly ethics was said to have led to the decline of their warrior prowess. That this is not a plausible explanation can perhaps be seen in the ferocity of the Buddhist Tibetan attacks on Mongols, or indeed the power demonstrated by Buddhist Gushri Khan, who, in order to defend Gelugpa Buddhism, eliminated Chogt Taiji and the Tibetan opposition. The Jungar Mongols, who staged the strongest opposition to the Manchu, were indeed Buddhist fundamentalists. My argument is that once made immobile and fragmented, a Mongol tribe became defenseless. The damage done by Tibetans on Mongols was not due to a massive armed assault; rather, it was due to a mobile guerrilla type of harassment, driving off livestock and kidnapping

children. When made immobile and fragmented, even when strongly encouraged by the Manchus to arm themselves and strike at the Tibetans, Mongols felt unable to do so. Although one may say that the ritual brought them all together, I would argue that they came in explicitly hierarchical (read vertical) relations with the Center, rather than horizontal relations among themselves. The cult of the Kökönuur, as part of the wider institutions of government, performed an effective role in reducing Mongol power.

23. The new policy of the Qing Dynasty, implemented in 1902, seemed to have changed the tradition that the lake sacrificial ritual be conducted by an imperial envoy. The Xining superintendent started to officiate the sacrifice, assisted by Mongol and Tibetan nobles (Chen 1981: 64).

24. Ma Hetian (Ma Ho-t'ien) is well known to students of Mongolian studies. His memoir on his official tour of the newly founded Mongolian People's Republic was translated and published in English (Ma 1949).

25. He went to Chagan Cheng, which was named after Chagaan Tolgoi. Ma wrote that in 1723, Lobsandanjin lured his tribes for an assembly there. He saw debris of the fortress built by Nayanceng, the governor-general of Shaanxi-Gansu-Ningxia, and said that it was abandoned in the sixth year of Xianfeng. From atop the fortress, he saw the lake clearly, although it was still about twenty-five kilometers away. Once Mongol land, it was now occupied by around one thousand households of a Tibetan tribe called Gombol.

26. See Steven Harrell's (1995b) introduction for his analysis of the civilizing mission of various groups: missionaries, GMD, and CCP in China.

27. The Commission was the Republican Chinese version of the *Li Fan Yuan* (Ministry of Colonial Affairs).

28. Between October 1936 and May 1937, the Western Route Army (Xilujun) of the CCP-led Red Army, numbering 21,800, was almost completely exterminated by Ma Bufang's troops in the Gansu Corridor. The CCP attributed the defeat to one of its discredited leaders, Zhang Guotao, and also regarded it as a loss of face. The survivors were long treated with discrimination by the CCP after their victory in 1949. Until 1983, the survivors were regarded as "traitors," "deserters," "turncoats," etc. (Dong 1995).

29. After Qinghai province was founded in 1928, the Republican government allocated 15,000 yuan for annual expenditure for sacrificial items and presents. In 1939, however, the Republican government paid 500,000 yuan to Qinghai for the purpose of preparing presents for Mongol and Tibetan leaders. Zhu Shaoliang personally donated over 10,000 yuan. In addition, the Qinghai provincial government allocated 300,000 yuan.

30. Chinese eyewitnesses would never fail to observe what they regarded as the fascinating erotic behavior of flirtatious Mongol women, as Xue Wenbo observed during the 1943 ritual: "Young Mongol women started dancing, they danced while singing, and no sooner had they slowly approached guests than would they suddenly offer alcohol. The women loved to make mischief; the audience also focused their eyes on the women's intention in the first few seconds; nobody knew who would be the target. So the targeted persons were often caught unprepared. They would be stunned. And their embarrassed expression amused everybody tremendously" (quoted in Zhu et al. 1994: 142).

3

飞

Naturalizing National Unity: Political Romance and the Chinese Nation

In recent years, Western scholarship on Chinese ethnicity has moved from the prediction of eventual "assimilation" or "integration" of ethnic minorities into the majority Chinese to an analysis of identity politics that suggests that ethnic minorities, far from being "assimilated," have actually been reified or even "invented." This paradigmatic change stems from an understanding of the Chinese ethnic polity as a hierarchical representational polity of majority domination of the minorities. Key to this refiguration of ethnicity in China is the introduction of notions of gender and sexuality in understanding power relations among ethnic groups. In this genre, heavily borrowing from the postcolonial studies literature that emanated from Edward Said's *Orientalism* (1978), the focus has been the exoticization, feminization, and eroticization of minorities by the majority Chinese in their cultural representation. The Chinese discourse toward minorities is thus characterized as orientalist or "internal orientalist" (Gladney 1994; Litzinger 2000; McLaren 1994; Millward 1994; Schein 2000; and Zhang Yingjin 1997), and the majority Chinese are said to have subjugated minorities and remained "on top," as it were. Central to their analysis is the Chinese male sexual encounter with, or sexual fantasy of, minority women, often in a "colonial" setting of minority regions. In her perceptive discussion of "internal orientalism," Schein argues that "those othered in dominant representation may simultaneously be considered an integral part of their representers' people or nation" (2000: 106).

However, this feminization of the minority thesis is premised on asymmetrical "illicit" sexual relations between majority Chinese men and ethnic minority women, eschewing any discourse of "kinship" or reproduction. In other words, too much emphasis has been put on these "unnatural" or "unethical" relations, and scholars have failed to examine the "naturalizing" effects of gender representation. As Doris Sommer argues, it is not in sexuality per se that the truth is lodged, but in how productive it is (1991). In making numerical majority the basis for determining who would stay "on top," such an approach ignores the long history of China's interaction with its Inner Asian neighbors and, specifically, the fact that more often than not, numerically small, but militarily strong, so-called barbarians conquered and ruled the Chinese, often for protracted periods, as in the case of the Mongols and Manchus.[1] Although such conquest is no longer possible in the modern world, its historical legacy has a lingering effect.

Emma Jinhua Teng, in her study of Ming and Qing Chinese travel writing about indigenous women in Taiwan, alerted us to the asymmetrical Chinese gendered imagination of southern and northern "barbarians." In both literary and historical sources, the Chinese tended to feminize the south but masculinize the northern frontier:

> These gendered stereotypes were influenced by several factors: the existence of matrilineal customs among southern "barbarians"; the association of northern "barbarians" with warfare; theories of the environmental determinism of human character (the environment of the north being rugged and that of the south being wet and fertile); and the relative strength of the expansionist northern dynasties vis-à-vis the over-refined and declining southern dynasties during the Six Dynasties era. These stereotypes were further developed in Tang literary treatments of the northern frontiers and the southern borderlands. The emasculation of the southern male was in part a result of the general feminization of the region. The feminization of southern peoples and the masculinization of northern peoples served to center the ideal Han self of the "central plains" as a normative identity. (1998: 362–63)

Although lending historicism to this gendered imagination, Teng did not go into the northern frontier and discuss the Chinese "masculinization" of Inner Asians, nor did she discuss what this "northern" dimension might imply for the "centrality" of the Chinese in terms of their sense of cultural and national integrity, especially what it meant for the Chinese understanding of ethnic relations today. I argue that China's contemporary imagination of its minzu tuanjie (national unity/amity between nationalities) is largely derived from the symbolic and institutional logic of its historical relations with Inner Asians, a rich historical repertoire that provided much of the rhetorical demarcation of its identity and civilization throughout China's history. This chapter is thus not about the "minority" response to Chinese gendered imagination, but about the "Chinese" response to the "masculine" Inner Asians in the form of self-feminization and male anxiety. A new world of Chinese morality, identity, and consciousness unfolds as we go toward the northern frontier. And crucially, this self-feminization and its associated reproductive discourse inform much about the contemporary Chinese imagination, particularly its idea of national unity as a kind of "gender regime," which consists of a gendered division of labor, a gendered structure of power, and a structure of cathexis. As I argued in the previous chapter, minzu tuanjie discursively constitutes a Chinese "nation form." Likewise, our study of gender and ethnicity must explore the emotional and moral world of a nation that struggles to reinvent itself from the past, from an empire to a nation.

Let me provide here a brief prelude to what I will argue in detail. The Chinese discourse of national unity is gendered; it is predicated on an invocation of an ancient institution called *heqin* (peace-marriage) in which ancient Chinese princesses or disposable court women were married to "barbarian" chiefs, thereby achieving sovereignty over their contemporary descendants—minorities. Here we have a reverse feminization, by the Chinese of themselves, often harking back to some seemingly authentic history. This feminization of the Chinese is reflected not only in historical discourse but also in artistic and literary representation. Together, this represents the "official" Chinese discourse. A genealogical examination of the discourse of gendered national unity is indispensable should we ever hope to understand this political project.

In recent decades, there has been a high profile use of heqin as a claim for sovereignty over almost all the leading minorities in China. In 1959, immediately after the Tibetan rebellion, Tang dynasty Princess Wencheng's marriage to the Tibetan King Srongtsan Gampo was explicitly used by "Marxist" Chinese historians to demonstrate sovereignty claims over Tibet and the spread of allegedly superior Chinese culture, including Buddhism, to the Tibetans. It appeared that the mere marital union was sufficient proof of Tibetan "subordination" to, or "unity" with, the Tang (China) to satisfy contemporary Chinese conceptions of "sovereignty."

In Inner Mongolia, there are reportedly more than a dozen Wang Zhaojun tombs, said to bury a woman from the Han dynasty harem married to a Xiongnu (a.k.a. Hunnu or Hun) emperor (*shanyu*), Huhanye, a union said to have secured sixty years' peace between the Han and Xiongnu. The one officially recognized by the Chinese state in the southern suburb of Hohhot, the capital of Inner Mongolia, has become a symbol of minzu tuanjie between Mongols and Chinese, for this particular Xiongnu emperor was alleged to have recognized the "sovereignty" of the Han. Although the actual genetic or cultural links between the Mongols and the Xiongnu remain unclear, the fact that the Mongols came to live in what was once a Xiongnu land, and that the legendary tomb is conveniently located in Inner Mongolia, appears to be sufficient to "prove" Chinese sovereignty over the Mongols before they had ever acquired such an autonym themselves.

The significance of this kinship symbolism must not be lost in its farce. There were quite a few heqin relations between Chinese in Han or Tang dynasties with some other peoples that are now classified as "minorities," such as the Uyghurs in Xinjiang and Yi in southwestern China. These ancient marital unions are now invoked to prove "conquest" as much as "unity." The celebration of national unity has been monumentalized; today, newly built statues of Chinese princesses and "minority" kings or chiefs stand prominently in key cities of minority autonomous regions. Movies, TV series, novels, and poems about heqin abound.

This chapter is thus an attempt to understand power in the People's Republic, imbedded in a teleological imagination of minzu tuanjie and referencing of heqin in the service of nation-building. It is about the discourse of kinship, but not of the actual interethnic marriages, although the latter have been taken as an index to measure the degree of the formation of an integrated Chinese Nation, as sociologist Ma Rong and anthropologist Zhou Xin continue to advocate (Ma and Zhou 1999). After analytically tracing the genealogy of heqin and the changing Chinese attitudes to it over two millennia, I discuss the extensive use of the heqin motif in the People's Republic to shore up minzu tuanjie.

The central concern that compels me to undertake this investigation is the significance of the fact that loyalty, sovereignty, or unity in socialist China has to be secured through invocation of ancient corporal unions. Given all the propaganda of China's civilizational and ideological capacity, such an emphasis on biological unity is only too glaringly farcical. But this farce must not be lightly dismissed, for it is ubiquitous and overwhelming. As Brackette F. Williams argues, "when social classification meets hierarchy, their union is made possible by myths that fold social space back on itself to naturalize power differences that are legitimated in particular representations of the historicity of kin substance. . . . Classification of social types are situated in an ideology of power and reproductive distribution which must be all-inclusive" (1995: 201). "Natural" here is understood not only in the sense of hegemony numbing the mind, but in referencing biological reproduction. The integration or assimilation of various nationalities into the unity of the Chinese Nation may well be predicated upon the reproductive distribution of the "kin substance" through the "peace marriage" of Chinese princesses to "barbarian" chiefs, or the discourse thereof.

THE CHANGING RELATIONSHIP BETWEEN CHINA AND INNER ASIA: FROM ALLIANCE TO DESCENT/DISSENT

Historical Inner Asia and China can best be characterized as two distinct polities: until the twentieth century, marriage alliance was an important feature of the Inner Asian polity, whereby various tribes were linked to the ruler. Mongols and Manchus were perhaps the paragons of this system. China, on the other hand, was based on morality, juridical, examination, and other mechanisms, wherein kinship plays little role in connecting the emperor to the localities (Rawski 1991, 1996; Ho 1998; Humphrey 1992). I argue that this distinction, although useful and interesting, has perhaps led to the relative neglect of the study of heqin (peace marriage) between royal families of opposing regimes as a device regulating relations between China and Inner Asia. In Western literature, heqin is discussed in terms of military strategy and is equated with failure, weakness of China, as a contrived device to appease the "barbarians" (Waldron 1990).

Interestingly, when we examine the flow of elite women from the Han dynasty to Inner Asia, we gain a different picture of China and its culture. This flow of elite women and their role in relation to the "barbarians" provided the site of a tension wherein was lodged the eternal saga of China: beautiful women, Confucian civilization, and Chinese ethnicity.

The heqin system should be seen as a marriage alliance used for "international" or, more precisely, "interstate" relations in China and Inner Asia. While marriage alliance as part of exogamous institutions was not alien to Chinese, "heqin," or peace marriage, as a special interstate institution, was first introduced by the Xiongnu shanyu Modun in relation to the Han dynasty. In 200 B.C.E., fresh from victory in unifying China and founding the Han dynasty, Han Gaodi, the first emperor of the Han, launched an expedition to wipe out once and for all the menacing nomadic Xiongnu, which had built a powerful empire almost simultaneously with the Qin dynasty, but which, unlike the short-lived Qin, would last over six hundred years. Yet arrogance led to disaster; Han Gaodi's 300,000-strong army was ambushed and trapped by the Xiongnu army of 400,000 cavalry for seven days and nights in a major battle. Miraculously, his aides negotiated his release by accepting Modun's proposal to marry a daughter of the Han emperor and the Han to pay an enormous amount as tribute to the Xiongnu. It was both humiliation and exploitation to the Han, but they had to agree to it. Han Gaodi sent a woman from the royal family (*zongshinü*) instead of his own daughter, without telling Modun. Nonetheless, since this was the first time that a powerful Inner Asian state forced the Han to accept such a marriage, the Han side had to justify it on cultural grounds to make it more palatable. In their masterful rendition, giving a royal princess to the Xiongnu was turned into a Han initiative. This stratagem was clearly spelled out by Liu Ching [Jing], a leading advisor to the Han emperor—"whereby in time Mo-tun's [Modun] descendants can be made subjects of the Han":

> If you could see your way clear to send your eldest daughter by the empress to be the consort of Mo-tun, accompanied by a generous dowry and presents, then Mo-tun, knowing that a daughter of the emperor and empress of the Han must be generously provided for, would with barbarian cunning receive her well and make her his legitimate consort and, if she had a son, he would make him heir apparent. . . .As long as Mo-tun is alive he will always be your son-in-law, and when he dies your grandson by your daughter will succeed him as Shan-yü. And who ever heard of a grandson trying to treat his grandfather as an equal? Thus your soldiers need fight no battles, and yet the Hsiung-nu will gradually become your subjects. (Watson, trans., 1961: 289)

This scheme should not be dismissed as kinship fantasy. Rather, we should emphasize that it was a revolutionary design that extended the native Chinese kinship system to "interstate" relations, albeit at Xiongnu, not Han, initiative. This cultural scheme enabled the Han dynasty to take the initiative, that is, voluntarily send a princess (i.e., if the enemy was strong, a high-status woman was sent; otherwise, a woman with low status was sent but crowned with a title of princess). It is clear that during the Han dynasty, princesses or nominal princesses were seen as an important sexual resource that could be put to political purposes. What we can also glean from this is that the Chinese task of conquest (if not civilizing) was intended to be fulfilled by means of women's sexuality, and loyalty was to be obtained not through cultivation of mind and spirit, but primarily through the exchange of women—that is, through reproduction.

We need to explain this one-way flow of Chinese women to "barbarians" from a kinship point of view, rather than purely from the perspective of military and political power. Chinese kinship during the Han and Tang appears to have been a patriarchal system, based on exogamous alliance.[2] The Xiongnu, or by extension the Inner Asian system, was similarly patriarchal, but they practiced a stricter clan system of levirate. Alliance, as in heqin, did not prescribe deference to the mother's brothers; rather, a married woman must serve her husband's clan, and she had no rights to divorce or remarriage outside her husband's clan. She could, however, marry her husband's brother or his male heir not borne by her. Sima Qian, the grand historian, wrote with disdain in his celebrated *Shiji* that the Xiongnu's "only concern is self-advantage, and they know nothing of propriety or righteousness (Watson, trans., 1961: 155). He further noted, "On the death of his father, a son will marry his step mother, when brothers die, the remaining brothers will take the widows for their own wives" (Watson, trans., 1961: 156).

Levirate marked one of the fundamental differences between the Han and Xiongnu, and indeed "barbarity" and civilization were distinguished more at this kinship level than anything else. This seemingly obnoxious levirate system posed strong ethical problems to the Chinese in their heqin stratagem, producing some sagas of death. In 133 B.C.E., Wudi launched a massive assault on the Xiongnu. He then terminated the heqin with the Xiongnu for the first time but sent envoys to seek alliances with others in the western region (*xiyu*) to attack the Xiongnu from the western flank. In 105 B.C.E., Han Wudi sent Xijun, the daughter of Liu Jian, the king of Diandu, a member of the Han royal clan, to marry the king of Wusun.[3] Unfortunately, apparently unable to either understand her mission or to appreciate the life there, Xijun was said to have written the following poem:

> My folk have wedded me
>   Across heaven's span,
> Into a far country,
>   To a Turkish Khan.

> A black tent is our hall,
>   With felt for party wall:
> Flesh is our nutriment,
>   And cheese for condiment.
> So homesick here—would I
>   From this lothly band
> Like the Brown Swan might fly
>   To my native land! (In Turner, trans., 1976: 45)

Apparently, the king of Wusun was old, and there was little communication between them because of language and age difference. The Wusun king, appreciating his own physical incapacity, remarried her to his eldest son by a different wife.

Xijun died soon afterward (in 105 B.C.E.). In order to strengthen the alliance, Han Wudi sent Jieyou, the granddaughter of Liu Rong, the king of Chu, in replacement. Princess Jieyou was more open-minded and resourceful than her predecessor. True to her name, which means "dispelling worries," she married three kings of Wusun successively, attempting to murder Kuang Wang, one of her husbands, who defied the Han. She not only managed to order Wusun to fight against the Xiongnu for the Han, but put Wusun under Han rule. This was an ultimate success of the heqin. With mission accomplished, she returned triumphantly to Chang'an, the Han capital, in 51 B.C.E.

By 33 B.C.E. the Xiongnu shanyu Huhanye, a loser in the Xiongnu civil war and the Xiongnu war with Han and their allies, Wusun, finally made peace with the Han by proposing to marry a Han princess (which the Chinese source termed "willing to be 'son-in-law' " to Han). From the Han point of view, he was the first ever Xiongnu shanyu to *submit* to the Han; the significance was too great to be lost, yet his very act of submission devalued him, so the Han emperor Yuandi, rather than send a "princess," offered him a woman called Wang Zhaojun, a member of his 3,000-strong harem who had never seen the emperor. She was, however, also afflicted emotionally by the levirate. After Huhanye's death, she expressed her desire to "return to the Han." But she was advised to "follow their custom." She then married three generations of Xiongnu shanyus successively, giving birth to one son and two daughters, all of whom had important leadership roles among the Xiongnu. No major problems developed along the border between the Xiongnu and Han for about sixty years.

As we see, levirate was culturally offensive to the Chinese at that time, but it did not deter Han rulers from tolerating it or even encouraging it for military or political expediency. For the ultimate objective of this "peace marriage" was the reproduction of later generations who could be placed in the hierarchical kinship network of the Han. In other words, we may say that civilizing the "barbarians" was as much a military conquest as a kinship union.

The Chinese had a mixed record of success in heqin practice. It appears likely that overuse of heqin during the Tang was ultimately responsible for a backlash against it later. Tang emperors established marital relations with many Central Asian leaders by marrying off their own daughters or female members of the royal family. The marriage of Princess Wencheng to the Tibetan King Srongtsan Gampo in 640, now often used by today's Chinese historians to demonstrate the surrender of Tibetan sovereignty to China, took place during this period. Heqin was developed into a full-blown institution to manage interstate affairs. In many ways, Tang was a cosmopolitan society. Confucianism was openly challenged by Buddhism. There were many non-Chinese in the capital, who were not necessarily "assimilated." Many Inner Asians were accepted and allowed to serve the Tang, in light of their marital relations with the royal family. Women enjoyed relatively more freedom than in previous or later dynasties, and the women of the royal families were particularly powerful and willful. Heqin was seen as an effective means of controlling the neighboring states and tribes.

A turning point that shook the foundation of the Tang was the An Lushan rebellion in 755. In putting down the rebellion, the much weakened Tang court requested the help of the nomadic Uighur, whose Khan was married to a Tang princess. The Uyghur Khan, in 757, humiliated the Tang heir apparent by whipping to death several of his advisers, a punishment for the failure of the Tang heir apparent to pay homage to the Khan. To add to Tang woes, Srongtsan Gampo's successors in Tibet never stopped raiding China. In late 760, the Tibetans swept into Chang'an, the Tang capital, and during the two weeks they remained in the city, they not only looted and burned, but "as a puppet emperor, the Tibetans chose an aged brother of the Chinese princess who had been married off to the Tibetan king fifty years earlier" (Dalby 1979: 569). This was Princess Jincheng, who had married the Tibetan king Megasthom in 707.

The Uyghur and Tibetan attacks fundamentally undermined Chinese confidence in kinship politics. The Tang suffered humiliation, not at the hands of total "barbarians," but at the hands of their sons-in-law or sister's husbands or sons! This was a virtual counterkinship revolution. The result was also to call into question the extent to which corporeal union could substitute for "civilization." Once bitten, twice shy. After the Tang (907), heqin was never conducted by any "Chinese" dynasty. Heqin as an Inner Asian institution was practiced by the Mongols and Manchus in their respective empires, but neither group established any institutionalized marriage alliance with the Chinese.

Historians and historically minded anthropologists have noted that the transition from Tang to Song coincided with the change of Chinese kinship "from alliance to descent," to the "modern" social forms—corporate lineages. This means that marriage alliances ceased to be a strategy of social mobility (Watson 1982: 617–19). James Watson argues that "lineages and related social forms (ancestral halls, focal graves, corporate estates, modern surnames) emerged as a consequence of an ideological transformation among the national elite. Some historians would have it that lineages and other corporations based on descent were consciously constructed, from the social debris of the post-Tang collapse, to serve the political goals of scholar-bureaucrats" (1982: 618). The "national elite" in the Song dynasty were leading scholar-officials such as Chen Yi, Sima Guang, and Zhu Xi, who propagated a revival of the ancient *zong fa* descent system, revival of the classical rites of ancestor worship (cf. Chun 1996). I argue that this ritual fundamentalism, called neo-Confucianism, can best be understood in light of the kinship debacle in the "international" arena and the problems it brought to China. This was not just an attempt to define kinship organization; it was also an attempt to define Chineseness. The core ideology of this new ritualism is an adage from the *Zuo Zhuan*, a book compiled around 300 B.C.E.: *Fei wo zu lei, qi xing bi yi* ("The hearts of those who are not of our race [*zu*] must be different"). The idea is further clarified by a phrase from the same book: "People do not sacrifice to those who are not of the same tsu [*zu*], and the gods do not savor the fragrance of sacrifices from those who are not of the same nature [*lei*]" (in van der Sprenkel 1962: 152).

This neo-Confucian "cultural revolution" forever removed heqin from the Chinese political repertoire in dealing with Inner Asian peoples—forever until the second half of the twentieth century. Indeed, the Song dynasty would be willing to pay more tribute, rather than send women to the Liao (Tao 1988). The kinship dimension of neo-Confucianism did not affect the Mongols or the Manchus, who continued to practice marriage alliance, though not with the Chinese. For the Chinese in Song and after, shoring up Confucian values would be predicated on domesticating women, keeping them for the Chinese themselves. China, by Song times, had attained a unique "national identity," if we follow Verdery's argument: "a national identity may be defined and protected by sequestering or defending 'our' women from the allegedly insatiable sexuality of other nations' men" (1994: 228). Let us then examine this modernity and nationalism of the Chinese through this jealous "protection" of one lowly Chinese court woman, Wang Zhaojun, originally considered ugly and disposable.

DOMESTICATING WANG ZHAOJUN: MALE ANXIETY AND THE DEPLOYMENT OF SEXUALITY AND ETHNICITY IN THE SERVICE OF CHINA

I have alluded to using "nation" and "nationalism" to describe Chinese and Inner Asian peoples and their relationships. Prasenjit Duara insists that the Song demonstrated most clearly an "ethnic nation" (1996: 35). Duara rightly argues that "every cultural practice is a potential boundary marking a community":

When a master narrative of descent/dissent seeks to define and mobilize a community, it usually does so by privileging a particular cultural practice (or a set of such practices) as the constitutive principle of the community—such as language, religion or common historical experience—thereby heightening the self-consciousness of this community in relation to those around. What occurs, then, is a hardening of boundaries. Not only do communities with hard boundaries privilege their differences, they tend to develop an intolerance and suspicion toward the adoption of the other's practices and strive to distinguish, in some way or the other, practices that they share. Thus, communities with hard boundaries *will* the differences between them. (1996: 49)

It is particularly important to analyze the role of narrative of the descent/dissent in marking the boundary of the Chinese from the Inner Asians. This can be most fruitfully achieved by examining the literary representation of heqin and especially that of Wang Zhaojun. Wang Zhaojun, the hapless woman sent in marriage to Huhanye, is arguably the most heavily and continuously written-about woman in Chinese history. Interestingly, almost all of those writings are by Chinese men.

The earliest record of Wang Zhaojun appeared in *Han Shu, Xiongnu Zhuan*, which mentioned that Huhanye shanyu came to the court in the first year of Jing Nin (33 B.C.E.), when "Shanyu himself stated that he was willing to become a son-in-law of the Han. Emperor Yuandi then granted him from his seraglio Wang Qiang, known as Zhaojun, a girl from a good family." A satisfied shanyu was said to have sworn to stop his aggression against China, thereby introducing peace. After Huhanye's death, Wang Zhaojun was said to have married his successor, giving birth to two daughters. From this matter-of-fact account grew much more complicated accounts in later generations and centuries.

But as heqin was used extensively in Han and Tang literary representations, Wang Zhaojun's representation received most attention and was repeatedly used by the literati to express their opposition to appeasing the "barbarians." In fact, the seed for this literary representation was already planted in *Qin Cao* ("Principle of the Lute"), written by Cai Yong (b. 133–d. 192), an anti-heqin official who lived toward the end of the Eastern Han period, a period of enormous turmoil. This was not long after the death of Zhaojun, and the threat of nomads was by no means over. In this piece, Wang Zhaojun was one of the many women in the Han harem. For five or six years she did not attract the emperor's attention. The disappointed Wang Zhaojun then neglected her appearance, "she would not 'prettify' her face with cosmetics, so that every time Emperor Yüan went to the seraglio, he would pass her by" (Eoyang 1982: 7). When Huhanye's emissary came to the Chinese court to pay his respects, the emperor Yuan decided to give a woman from his seraglio to reward his loyalty. Wang Zhaojun then dressed herself up and volunteered. Her beauty was revealed for the first time only when she presented herself before the "barbarian," and only then did the emperor appreciate that beauty and regret his negligence, but he could not retract his offer in front of the emissary. Thus Zhaojun's decision to volunteer her services as a result of her grudge against the emperor's lack of appreciation of her beauty became the central theme that caught the imagination of the literati.

What is interesting is that Cai Yong ventured into Wang Zhaojun's life with the Xiongnu, where she was said to have been miserable and homesick. The most interesting part is the end of her story:

> Chao-chün (Zhaojun) had a son called Shih-wei. When the Shan-yü died, the son Shih-wei succeeded him. Now, among the barbarians, when the father dies, one takes the mother to wife. Chao-chün asked Shih-wei: "*Are you Chinese or barbarian?*" Shih-wei replied: *"I am more barbarian."* Chao-chün thereupon swallowed poison, and committed suicide. The Shan-yü erected a tomb for her. In the steppes, where the grass is white and withered, this tumulus alone is green. (In Eoyang 1982: 20, emphasis added)

This account evokes a clear sense of "patriotism." "Away from the palace, in this wasteland," she became homesick or what we might call "patriotic": "Chao-chün regretted that the emperor had not appreciated her. Her mind was troubled; and her thoughts were of home" (Eoyang 1982: 19). Ethnicity was highlighted by the incest motif. Clearly, levirate here defined whether one was Chinese or "barbarian." For Cai Yong, informed by the Confucian kinship ethic, marrying one's mother was the greatest crime against humanity. Perhaps, in order to drive home his point, Cai Yong deliberately arranged a marriage between Zhaojun and her own son. Under his pen, the irreconcilable moral conflict finally pushed her to commit suicide rather than be insulted.

What emerged strongly from this piece is the notion of exile, reflecting the dilemma between a beauty unappreciated by the Han emperor, hence voluntarily departing to the Xiongnuland, and yet in the "wasteland," longing for the homeland, finding life and customs there repugnant. The dilemma could only be resolved by death.

But this death was not entirely the product of frustration toward the Han emperor for desertion or punishment; rather, the emperor must be exonerated of all blame. One way to achieve this was to portray Zhaojun's marriage as a result of the strength of the Xiongnu and weakness of the Han. For instance, a poem about Wang Zhaojun by Shi Cun during the Western Jin dynasty (268–316) states that "The Xiongnu rose in power and proposed marriage to the Han" (Lin and Ma 1994: 61). His poem, written in Zhaojun's voice, is deeply prejudiced against the Xiongnu, preaching incompatibility of the marriage in fundamental terms:

> I was born a girl of the Han family
> but married to the court of Shanyu.
> Before the farewell poem was finished
> The guards already raised their flags for departure.
> (In Lin and Ma 1994: 62)

So great was her grief that the five inner organs were hurt. And she was said to scorn the Xiongnu title *Inji* (empress), saying, "It is not glorious despite its nobility." Incest was again introduced:

> Father and son insulted me,
> I gradually felt aghast.
> It's difficult to commit suicide,
> I could only beg to live in silence.
> How tedious is such a life.
> The accumulated thought annoys me.
> I wish to rely on the wings of a flying swan,
> and fly on it in a long journey.
> But the swan ignores me,
> it stands there hesitating.
> Once a jade in a box,
> Now a crystal on a pile of feces.
> The morning flower is not worth admiration,
> I am willing to be with the autumn grass.
> I wish to tell later generations:
> It is unkind to be married far away.
> (In Lin and Ma 1994: 62).

Ultimately, heqin was denounced, implying that one should not marry afar, especially to an alien. The undesirability of heqin was blamed on the strength of the Xiongnu, and the incompatibility of the marriage rested on the fact that the Xiongnu were aliens, thus marrying among them would be soiling a beautiful jade on a pile of feces. As time went by, literati frustration grew, but, unable to blame the emperor whom they aspired to serve, they had to scapegoat an internal enemy, in addition to emphasizing the incompatibility of the Xiongnu "barbarians." From the *Xijin Zaji* ("Sundry Accounts of the Western Capital"), written in the third century, we see the effort to shield the emperor from blame, finding a scapegoat in a painter, Mao Yanshou, symbolizing the corrupt official, and later those who preached heqin appeasement:

> Since there were many women in the harem of Emperor Yuan [r. 48–33 B.C.E.], he didn't have a chance to see them regularly. So he had painters do their portraits, and on consulting the portraits he would summon women to his bed. The court ladies all bribed the painters, some giving as much as a hundred thousand taels, and at the very least offering no less than fifty thousand. Lady Wang alone refused to pay a bribe, and as a result she did not get to see the Emperor.
>
> The Xiong-nu came to court seeking a beautiful woman to be the Khan's bride. Thereupon His Majesty consulted the portraits and chose Wang Zhao-jun to go. When she was leaving, he summoned her to an audience. Her features were the loveliest in all the harem; she was quick in her replies and graceful in her bearing. The Emperor regretted it, but her name had already been decided on. The Emperor had repeatedly commended her to the foreigners, so he couldn't make an exchange.
>
> He then made a thorough investigation of what had happened, and the painters were all beheaded in the marketplace, and the vast fortunes of their households were all confiscated.
>
> Among the painters was Mao Yan-shou of Du-Ling; in drawing the human form,

he always captured the true image of beauty, ugliness, youth, and age. Chen Chang of An-ling and Liu Bai and Gong Kuan of Xin-feng were all skilled in catching the moving cattle, horses, and birds in flight, but in the beauty of the human form they were not equal to Mao Yan-shou. Yang Wang of Xia-du was a skilled painter, particularly in the use of color; Fan Yu was also good at using colors. On the same day they were all beheaded in the marketplace. Thereafter, painters were rather scarce in the capital. (Birch 1965: 306–7)

The central achievement of this piece was to establish Wang Zhaojun as a beauty and a wise and witty one. Her beauty and wit were perhaps commonplace among the Chinese, but they gained special significance only when Zhaojun was about to be married to an alien. The emperor's fury and regret were directed at Mao Yanshou and other famous painters in the capital, who were scapegoated for the emperor's own lack of appreciation of special beauty and talent. This story inspired the best Chinese writers and poets, including Li Bai, Du Fu, Bai Juyi, Ouyang Xiu, Su Shi, and Wang Anshi, for centuries to come. In some literary pieces, by virtue of being a beauty unappreciated by the emperor until the last moment because of the failure of the painter, Zhaojun became the representative of loyalist scholar literati and Mao Yanshou, a paragon of corrupt officials who cheated the emperor, hence a "traitor."

Although new motifs were added, something was also dropped—that is, her life in Xiongnuland, and especially the fact that she had children with the Xiongnu leaders. This is rightly noted by Eugene Eoyang, in discussing the characteristics of the Zhaojun literature in the fifth and sixth centuries:

The segment recording the fact that she bore children after leaving the Han palace—whether by the chieftain or his successor, whether one boy (as in the Ch'in Ts'ao version), two boys (as in the Hou Han-shu version) or two girls (as in the Hanshu version)—this is totally omitted. Somehow the image of a domesticated Chinese woman bearing her barbarian captor's offspring proves inconvenient in more romanticized renditions. It is clear that the major reference in most allusions in poetry, including those by women in the early sixth century, will stress her continuing sorrow, the treachery of the court-artist, Mao Yen-shou, with nary a mention of Wang Chao-chün's miscegenetic offspring. (1982: 9)

These changing literary representations of Zhaojun as a victim of either Xiongnu aggression or corrupt Chinese "traitor" officials were part of the intellectual movement brewing at the height of the heqin system, trying to define the moral and ethnic boundary of the Chinese in the face of increasingly powerful "barbarian" influence in China. For the increasingly inward-looking Chinese literati, the prototype of Zhaojun as a willing volunteer was no longer easy to stomach. Indeed, the ambiguity built into the story gave ample room for manipulation and imagination, serving both anti-heqin and pro-heqin camps. These were the fact that Zhaojun's marriage brought about peace with the Xiongnu and that she voluntarily departed from the harem because of her grudges against the emperor, both pointing to tensions in Chinese society: the role of men defending the state and female chastity to her "husband" (and her state). This tension is vividly expressed by a hostile poem written by Rong Yu during the late Tang period, after the An Lushan incident:

> In the blue history of the Han House
> the most misguided policy was *heqin*.
> The state is dependent on the wise lord,
> but the safety relies on woman!
> How can you send the jade like beauty
> to settle the war dust raised by the Barbarian?
> There are bones thousands of years old
> But who are the reliable ministers? (Lin and Ma 1994: 105)

The extraordinary fact was that all these poems and stories were written by men[4] and, indeed, not ordinary men! Literature was a two-edged sword of descent/dissent, not only expressing different "descent" from the Xiongnu, but also a "dissent" against the emperor and against corrupt officials. Momentum was building, from a simple lackluster story in an official history to one filled with emotion, involving tears and death. Before we examine the transformation in the Song and afterward, we need to tackle this interesting phenomenon of men expressing their anxiety through a hapless woman. We need to understand this male feminine tradition better before we can appreciate the enormous emotional investment of Chinese men in Wang Zhaojun.

Shuhui Yang suggests that when we look at Chinese gender relations, we should not treat them as binary opposition, but rather in terms of yin-yang principle. Inspired by Julia Kristeva's understanding of femininity in terms of social positionality, "that which is marginalized by the patriarchal symbolic order" (quoted in Yang 1998: 110), Yang is able to suggest that politically marginalized men in China are often presented as feminine or yin. He finds this most eloquently expressed in the doctrine of the "three bonds" (*san'gang*) put forward by Dong Zhongshu (ca. 179–ca. 104 B.C.E.), one of the most influential Confucian theoreticians: "the relationships between ruler and subject, father and son, husband and wife, are all derived from the principle of the yin and yang. The ruler is yang, the subject yin; the father is yang, the son yin; the husband is yang, the wife yin" (Yang 1998: 112). In this scheme, a man of the literati class might be yin or yang simultaneously: yin in relation to the ruler or the center of political power or father, but yang in relation to his wife and children. "When in a yin position vis-à-vis some higher authority, it is reasonable to assume that a man might sometimes identify with women who are perpetually in a yin position." But because of the relationality of the yin-yang paradigm, yang does not necessarily represent moral authority; rather, what is emphasized is the harmonious balance of yin and yang. The imbalance may thus enable the yin to take moral position to redress it. "In the eyes of a *yin* figure, especially when he/she feels unfairly put into an inferior position by those with power, moral superiority may belong to those marginalized or *yin*. It is largely the moral superiority or sense of justice assumed by the yin figure that explains his/her developing a subversive attitude toward yang figures, or what yang represents" (Yang 1998: 115). Yang further theorizes that with centralization of the Chinese polity in the warring states and especially the Han period, the chances for the literati to choose their own masters radically diminished, thus leaving the literati in a perpetual state of precariousness and marginality, or what he calls "anxiety of service":

> This anxiety was often expressed allegorically through a woman's voice or through the representation of a woman in relation to her love or husband. We frequently see the analogy drawn between a deserted or neglected wife and a frustrated scholar whose talents and inner worth go unrecognized and unappreciated by the sovereign. (1998: 118)

Yang's theory has much to offer in explaining the literati's obsession with Wang Zhaojun and especially in representing her alleged tragedy. But we can go further than Yang's two dimensional treatment of yin-yang cycling and locate the dilemma of the male literati in situations of "national" crisis. Indeed, although initially poignantly resentful and showing independence, their "anxiety of service" was enhanced by experiences of exile in the "wasteland," making them long all the more for the homeland. Their "anxiety of service" ended up in their competing for "our" women with the "barbarians."

More "feminine" literature by men would appear during the Song dynasty, which was under intense military threat from northern peoples. In these poems or lyrics, "we do not 'see' the physical attributes of these women but simply 'overhear' the musings of their hearts, the lyricism of their declarations of love. They sing openly of their excitement, joy, and grief" (Fong 1994: 111). Such a representation of women in Chinese poetry, "constructs the poetic paradigm of a female image subordinated to the [male] gaze and the play of desire" (1994: 114). Interestingly, much of this literature was about woman warriors, such as Yang family women generals and Hua Mulan. However, according to Louise Edwards, rather than seeing them rebelling against restraints imposed upon their sex by patriarchal society, these tales have been read then and since as exemplifying the virtues of patriotism and filial piety: "In the tale of Fourth Sister Lin another important feature of the women warrior emerges. She shames the menfolk by the depth of loyalty and devotion to her patriarch. The woman warrior is thereby a moral mirror for the degenerating menfolk. When the women are more moral than the men a strong condemnation of the depths of depravity into which society has sunk is implied" (1994: 103).

The Song dynasty saw a radical redefinition of manhood and womanhood.

Both of these ideals should be understood in terms of their Chineseness. Ebrey captures this nicely:

> It has long been noted that the Sung period marked a general shift in ideals of manhood toward the literatus. This cultural shift was manifested on many levels, from increased use of sedan chairs, to fads for collecting antiques and delicate porcelains, to a decline in the popularity of hunting. The model literatus could be elegant, bookish, contemplative, or artistic, but did not need to be strong, quick, or physically dominating. The popularity of the literatus ideal undoubtedly owed much to the spread of printing, the expansion of education, the triumph of the examination system for recruitment to office, and the revival of Confucianism. *It also, I suspect, was influenced by the international situation. For Sung men in the ruling elite to cultivate the image of the refined literatus accentuated the contrast between the Chinese and their northern rivals, the Turks, Khitan, Jurchen, and Mongols, all much more martial types. Tacitly asserting the superiority of the literary way of life was thus a way of asserting the superiority of Chinese over non-Chinese culture.* (1993: 33, emphasis added)

All these factors had to do with the emergent neo-Confucianism that enshrined extreme gender inequality in the emphasis on descent. The redefined gender relations confined women to the home and barred them from the outside world. One could argue that the tradition of women's footbinding established during the Song was the most physically poetic expression of gender relations as a result of the "international situation." Dorothy Ko (1997) argues that we must not treat footbinding as simply mutilation of women's bodies, as many have come to understand it from today's perspective, for it was in fact an honored practice throughout much of its history. Footbinding was a sign of civility! The bound feet marked the ethnicity of the Chinese, creating a moral and physical boundary that separated the "barbarians" from the civilized Chinese.

In parallel with the emergence of female footbinding there appeared corresponding changes in the literary representation of Zhaojun. In the earlier literature, Zhaojun committed suicide in Xiongnuland because of the deemed ethical impropriety of levirate. In the new and more dramatic representation during and after the Song, she would drown herself in the river before even setting foot in Xiongnuland. Through this representation, Zhaojun became a loyal and chaste woman, sacrificing her life to her "husband," the emperor, thereby inviting comparison with Qu Yuan (ca. 343–278 B.C.E.), the most famous loyalist in Chinese history. Qu Yuan's drowning was alluded to in a poem by one of China's most renowned loyalists, Wen Tianxiang, an anti-Mongol Chinese national hero:

> Minfei's (Zhaojun's) horse stands alone on the steppe,
> There flows the fish belly boat at the edge of the river.
> Who will help revenge this new score?
> The old dream is difficult to realize. (Lin and Ma 1994: 110)

A new "chaste woman" whose feet were "bound" was the theme that was fully developed in *Han Gong Qiu* ("The Autumn in the Palace of Han"), a drama written by Ma Zhiyuan, during the Mongol Yuan dynasty. Ma's drama was important, for it had a lasting influence on later dramatists (see Besio 1997). The form of drama developed in the Yuan under the Mongols was highly popular; its audience was not just literati, but ordinary illiterate people. Dramas substituted for history. It was a literature of resistance against foreign conquest, par excellence.

Let us have a closer look at the drama. In this drama, Ma Zhiyuan depicted a belated romance between Zhaojun and Emperor Yuan, delayed because of the treachery by the court painter Mao Yanshou. Mao was no longer an ordinary painter but had a rank of *zhong dafu* (counselor), thus elevating his weight as a paragon of treason. Emperor Yuan was very reluctant to give Zhaojun to the Xiongnu emperor, but the prime minister insisted that the emperor must surrender his love for the sake of the dynasty, reiterating: "There have been instances enough since ancient times of nations failing because of beautiful women" (Liu, trans., 1972: 212). However, Zhaojun's loyalty is seen in her act of leaving behind her clothes in the Han palace before departure, lamenting, using a poem by Li Bai, the preeminent Tang poet:

> Today a woman of the Palace of Han,
> Tomorrow a wife in the land of Hu.
> How shall I endure [to wear the robes from my lord],
> To enhance my beauty for another! (Liu, trans., 1972: 215)

Her loyalty and commitment of chastity to the emperor were fulfilled when at Black Dragon River, the boundary between the two countries, she drowned herself in the river, after uttering: "Emperor of Han, this life of mine is ended. I shall await you in the life to come" (Liu, trans., 1972: 219).

What distinguished this drama from earlier representations of Zhaojun was clearly the romance. It was a romance between the emperor of the Han and his "wife," which, because of both "barbarian" strength and internal traitorous acts, turned into a tragedy. It was as much a celebration of Zhaojun's chastity and loyalty as a condemnation of internal treason or appeasement toward the "barbarians." According to Ann-Marie H. K. Hsiung, in this play, "Wang Zhaojun has shown positive characteristics of strength and control over her own destiny. Through her decision to commit suicide, she has given dignity and meaning to her life, instead of being a puppet controlled by external circumstances, though the dignity and meaning she has evoked are directed toward the values and ends which only make sense in a patriarchal world view" (1996: 69). But the imbrication of Chinese ethnicity and sexuality is at the heart of the matter, as Kimberly Besio rightly notes, arguing that the legend "held a specific cultural meaning as a site upon which succeeding generations could inscribe ideals about female virtue and Han cultural identity" (1997: 256).

元曲選 圖 漢宮秋 一 中華書局聚

沉黑江明妃青塚恨

倣趙千里筆

3.1. Wang Zhaojun Committing Suicide on Her Way to Xiongnu (*Yuan Qu Xuan* [*Sibu Beiyao*, vol. 341]. Shanghai: Zhonghua Shuju, 1936)

There were literally hundreds of poems, dramas, and novels written about Wang Zhaojun during the Ming and Qing period. As printing technology improved, romantic novels became commercialized for mass consumption, thus further popularizing the "tragedy" of Wang Zhaojun (cf. Xue 1992).

There is no space to review this literature here, but we should pause and ask one simple question: Why, for two thousand years, has a lowly woman attracted so much attention, some sympathetic, some scornful, whereas more noble princesses were ignored? Chinese Marxist "materialist" historians often write in very unhistoricist ways, attributing interest in Zhaojun to class differences: the lower one's class status, the more sympathy one's tragedy would evoke (cf. Lin and Ma 1994). But the trouble is that those who lament her fate were almost all high-class Chinese elite males, and there were plenty of other lower-class women in China's history. In my view, the enigma lies not in her class background, but in her status as a potential "wife" of the emperor and the Han emperor's reluctant "surrender" of his "wife," either to pacify the enemy or as a ruse to win submission of a dangerous foe. Indeed, the irony is that our earliest, and presumably most authoritative, source suggests that she was one of a thousand in the harem and never even slept with the emperor, not to speak of marrying him. Zhaojun's "married" status, albeit loosely defined, ultimately contravened the Confucian ethic of loyalty whereby the wife must be loyal to her husband in life or death. In ethnic politics, women's sexuality is often politicized to demarcate the ethnic boundary. It is domesticated to serve the male at home but not the enemy. A national endogamy had been advocated after the late Han period and then enacted after the Song dynasty. Seen through the lens of this ideology, we can better appreciate the view held by Confucians that Emperor Yuan's sending his "wife" constituted a "national" humiliation, whatever goodwill or strategic genius lay behind it. Embodying this ultimate shame, the legend of Zhaojun defined who is Chinese and who is not. The moral and ethnic rectitude of the Chinese must be repeatedly fleshed out by Zhaojun's tears, her flying back home in the form of a sparrow, leaving her "Han" clothes behind, committing suicide when confronted with the levirate, or, best of all, drowning herself in the river that demarcated the "barbarian" domain from that of the "civilized" Han.

UNBINDING WANG ZHAOJUN'S FEET AND HER SEXUALITY DURING THE REPUBLICAN ERA

Historians have long lauded the Qing ability to legitimate its rule over a vast multiethnic empire, as noted in chapter 2. While the Qing emperors wholeheartedly embraced Confucianism, presenting themselves as Confucian sage kings, in biological fundamentals the Qing royal family prohibited intermarriage with civilian Chinese, while encouraging formation of extensive marital relations with Mongols and Chinese bannermen (Hanjun) (Rawski 1991). Millward mentions one exception to this rule: Qianlong's taking as a concubine a Uyghur woman of the Makhadumzada Khoja clan. The reasons for this kind of political exogamy were both political and cultural. Millward asks an interesting question about the legitimacy of Chinese nationalism: "A particular problem was how a Han nationalism, defined to a great degree in racist, anti-Manchu terms, could justify retaining the former imperial holdings in non-Han areas and including the non-Han occupants of these former territories within a Han-dominated state" (1994: 446). The Han Chinese, Millward argues, having none of the resources of legitimacy enjoyed by the Qing, sought to "justify maintenance of the former Qing borders on the basis of Western principles of nationalism, as they understood and adapted them" (1994: 445). And this nationalism was to "define away the minorities." However, as discussed in chapter 2, Chinese nationalist rhetoric of doing away with the minorities to form a Chinese Nation had to face the hard reality of survival in a multiethnic world, and ritualizing *minzu tuanjie* as a device to solicit minorities for the common cause had the effect of reifying ethnic differences. We can further discuss this ethnopolitics through reproductive sexuality. We may ask, if the national minorities could now be taken as organic but lower parts of the Chinese Nation, how would this be reflected in sexual discourse? And how would Wang Zhaojun figure in this changed relationship?

One characteristic of the early Republican years was sexual revolution. Female chastity and loyalty to patriarchy were targets of the May Fourth iconoclasts, who lambasted Confucianism, the pillar of Chinese society, by introducing the concepts of liberty and democracy. Confucianism was attacked for its ethical and moral teachings then held responsible for China's decline. Women's chastity was seen as the very embodiment of that Confucian value, and women's liberation could not be envisaged without freeing them physically by loosening their bound feet and encouraging them to flee the hellish Confucian "family" system to go out into the "society." But in parallel with this class-oriented vision that attempted to undermine Confucianism was another equally strong passion for making Confucianism the very core of the Chinese Nation. It is interesting to note that during this period, two major works emerged with regard to Wang Zhaojun, and that they broadly represented the two complementary visions of a new Chinese Nation.

Guo Moruo, who would become one of the standard-bearers of communist literature and Mao Zedong's acolyte, wrote a play entitled *Wang Zhaojun* in 1923. The play presented Zhaojun as a tragic heroine who was enslaved to serve the emperor. This service was portrayed, like countless other May Fourth representations of "family," as illegitimate, virtually to the point of being cannibalistic. The freedom of Zhaojun could only be enacted by her fleeing this hellish family, and it was made possible by the Xiongnu emperor's courtship. In a break with all earlier accounts, Zhaojun found happiness in this opportunity to get out into "society." Xiongnu was an unknown world to her, but in it she was to explore and find her own value. The play offered a dramatic presentation of the conflict between individualism and Confucian familialism. In this representation, the Xiongnu represented the superior alternative. It was imagined as a land of freedom, free from all the enslavement of Confucianism, the ultimate enemy of freedom.

"Nationalism" was not the explicit operating principle here, nor was ethnicity consciously invoked. Nonetheless, examination of the social context within which the play was written is revealing. The 1920s were a period of explosive nationalism. China was afflicted with warlord conflicts and imperialist aggression. The liberal vision of sexual liberation and the search for democracy and freedom were also deeply implicated in the national salvation movements of the era. The slogan "going out to society," or "going to the people" "gradually became a clarion call among the intellectuals in the 1920s as more young Chinese became worried that their own country was being torn apart by internal strife and imperialist aggression," writes Hung (1985: 11). The rural areas became, in the imagination of many radical youths, a place where they could "save" China. We should also note that during this period, the "society" to which modern Zhaojun aspired to go was Inner Mongolia, which, although already within the Chinese Republic, was a site of Chinese warlord fighting, and the nominal independent Outer Mongolia, the only Qing territory lost, was the target of the Chinese nationalist battle cry for "recovering." We can thus safely say that Guo Moruo's iconoclastic criticism of the Chinese tradition was predicated precisely on a vision of going to the far-flung areas, not only through military conquest but through a marriage, an exploration for freedom. That was where China's future lay. We may also suggest that Guo Moruo's *Wang Zhaojun* became what Sommer (1991) calls "foundational" literature for Chinese national unity, a unity through marriage or romance.

In 1929, Wang Tonglin (1993) wrote an important academic study of heqin. He offered an encomium to heqin, praising its contributions to the new Chinese mixed-race ideology, its "function" being to facilitate the "melting of races" (*ronghua zhongzu*). In fact, he did not even mention the fig leaf Zhonghua Minzu (Chinese Nation) so widely propagated at the time but unabashedly claimed that "among China's 400 million people, the Han race-lineage (*zu*) constitutes over 95%, and most of them are mixtures of Manchu, Mongol, Hui, Tibetan, Miao and other foreign nationalities" (1993: 41). All the "barbarians" that existed throughout Chinese history were said to have been assimilated (*tonghua*) to the Han race-lineage, and one of the reasons for this "Han" expansion was interethnic marriage. It is interesting to note his glorification of the Han race-lineage:

> Since time immemorial, China has been a great Eastern country; the territory within its boundary is a great plain, so the Han *minzu* who emerged there were far-sighted, unbiased, unjealous; they treated all other nationalities with sympathy,

conferred upon them complete equality in law, politics, economy and education, without any differentiation of treatment. As for all those foreigners who lived mixed with the Han, most of them had freedom in marriage, belief, production and repro-duction, and after one century or several, one hundred years or several decades, they voluntarily or passively assimilated into the Han. Once the Han encountered other race-lineages, whether culturally or militarily, whether victorious or defeated, they could always absorb the other race-lineages' bone and blood, absorbing them into the Han system. (1993: 41)

In this way, heqin was removed from the negative moralistic system of Confu-cianism, including its concepts of female chastity, but was vested with the pro-gressive notion of contributing to the transformation of other nationalities into "Han." The author proposed an interesting theory that any group that had not "married" with the Chinese was left out of Chinese sovereignty.

> The *heqin* policy was usually limited to those militarily powerful countries, but not those culturally advanced countries; usually nomadic *minzu*, but not agricultural *minzu*; and limited to northwestern tribes (*buluo*), but not various southeastern countries; limited to Manchu, Mongol, Hui, Tibetan and Miao *zu*, but not other *minzu*. India, Japan, Korea, Xinluo, Bohai and Zhancheng, their cultural level being far superior to that of Xiongnu and Turkish countries, did not enter into marital relations with China. It was limited to close neighboring countries, but not to those living across oceans or other countries; Rome and Dashi existed at the time of the Han and Tang dynasties, and were great countries in the West, but China did not enter into marital relations with them. (Wang Tonglin 1993: 44)

So what is the problem? The author concluded by saying: "That Han and Tang did not establish marriage with culturally advanced countries was a histori-cal pity; had China established marital relations with great eastern and southern countries, there would have been huge changes in the cultures of China and the Eastern Ocean (Dongyang, i.e., Japan), and the results would undoubtedly have been progress" (1993: 46). But "progress," in Wang's language, was a code word for becoming Chinese. What must not be lost in this grandiose talk of the great-ness of Chinese ability to assimilate other nationalities is Wang's view that it was the magical and perhaps virile Chinese blood that did the trick through ancient marital union or heqin.

These two complementary views of the Chinese Nation are indicative of the two radical visions of China: one in terms of nationalism and racism and the other in terms of freedom and liberty. What is striking is that both of these lofty ideals were expressed through Wang Zhaojun or through other ancient Chinese women and the institution of heqin. In recent years, China scholars have drawn attention to representations of women in nationalist discourse in Republican China. Lydia Liu, for example, in examining Xiao Hong's novel entitled *The Field of Life and Death* (1935), discusses the tension between national liberation and women's liberation. In Chinese nationalist representation, women's victim-ization under the Japanese, such as rape, is used to "eroticize China's plight. In such a signifying practice, the female body is ultimately displaced by national-ism, whose discourse denies the specificity of female experience by giving larger symbolic meanings to the signifier of rape: namely, China itself is being violated by the Japanese rapist" (Liu 1994: 44). Xiao Hong's novel challenged precisely this nationalist signification, by insisting upon treating women in their own right, whose suffering and victimization required their liberation. Xiao Hong, as a woman writer, was caught in the dilemma of having to face two enemies rather than one: these were imperialism and patriarchy. In this dilemma, female resis-tance to imperialism is precisely the moment of subjugation to patriarchy that claims priority over national subjects. Liu thus recognizes the central importance of women subjects in the patriarchal nationalist project: women and their bodies are sites where the essence of a nation is being defined.

Prasenjit Duara (1998) similarly discusses women and nationalist patriarchy. He argues that early Chinese nationalists of various hues imagined a unitary national community for their objective, but such a unity in their narratives was as much a preexisting unity as a future goal. "Thus the unchanging unity of the nation over time, its timelessness, has to be marked by signs of its authenticity. The authenticity of this originary unity is demonstrated and guaranteed by the values of the pure, the honorable, the good, and the spiritual which the nation supposedly embodies" (Duara 1998: 290). The embodiment of nationalist authenticity is woman—her body and spirit—"a very significant site upon which regimes and elite in China responsible for charting the destiny of the nation have sought to locate the unchanging essence and moral purity of the nation" (Duara 1998: 296).

However, these writings, feminist in their true spirit, are guided by their "resis-tance" to an inward-looking patriarchy. Women, in their writings, have become passive victims of patriarchy, something to be protected: keeping them pure and good, free from being violated. "It is their passivity, their being spoken for, that represents the political meaning of their gender" (Duara 1998: 301). This may well be so, but while they were rendered passive in relation to the patriarchal national power and "protected" from "racial" enemies, they could also be invested with hypersexuality and unleashed to "love" (that is, to tame) ethnic minorities, as we have seen in the case of Guo Moruo's play and Wang Tonglin's discussion and will see in the socialist period to which I now turn.

FROM TRAGEDY TO COMEDY: PRINCESS WENCHENG AND WANG ZHAOJUN AS DEFENDERS OF SOCIALIST CHINESE SOVEREIGNTY

Literary discourse, as noted previously, is an important weapon in the political arsenal in national and social movements. Meng Yue rightly points to the role of literature in socialist China: "As a singularly important type of writing, literature generated a mutually implicated dynamic between state discourses and civic, private, and cultural life. Not only did literature reproduce state policies and bring them into civic or private cultural contexts, it also shaped the national conception of what constituted Chinese social 'reality' " (1993: 118). The power of literature to replicate social reality was further enhanced by injecting heavy doses of history. Literature—or more precisely, historical drama—was so important, and sometimes so threatening to the state, that thousands of Chinese writers were purged or jailed for what they wrote, and the Cultural Revolution was partially triggered by the conflict in the literary realm.

Literature, for precisely these reasons, has naturally been important to managing ethnic relations in socialist China. The People's Republic was established as a multinational state (*duo minzu guojia*), predicated on denouncing the Zhonghua Minzu of the Chinese Nationalist version as Han chauvinism. The years 1949 to 1957 marked the first phase of China's implementation of this vision, identifying nationalities and designating autonomous territories. But as in all other areas in China, something went terribly wrong with the ethnic situation. The anti-rightist movement launched by Mao in 1957 signaled a radical departure in nationality policy. In the field of political economy, Chinese critics of Mao's "leftist" impulse were labeled rightists and were harangued and persecuted. In the field of ethnic relations, China began to denounce alleged local nationalists for excessive demands for equality and autonomy. China then intensified its integration drive by raising aloft the slogan "minzu tuanjie," a tone set by Zhou Enlai in the Qingdao Nationality Affairs Conference in July 1957. This was clearly an implementation of Mao Zedong's February 1957 treatise on the correct handling of China's increasingly complex "contradictions" so as to consolidate the power of the Party. Mao claimed that "the unification of our country, the unity of our people and the unity of our various nationalities—these are the basic guarantees for the sure triumph of our cause" (Mao 1977: 384). In 1957 the Party published its first journal on nationality affairs and called it *Minzu Tuanjie*. But this integration drive in the sphere of "democratic reform" provoked the Tibetan rebellion in early March 1959.

Let us examine the intellectual response to these two events, the debacle of the Great Leap Forward and the ethnic unrest represented by the Tibetan uprising. One of the most important means for intellectuals to express their views was in historical plays, which had become hugely popular in the 1950s. China's leading historians and dramatists were initially engaged in a battle, either to support or to criticize Mao for the failure of the Great Leap Forward, using historical allegory. For example, Guo Moruo's *Cai Wenji* and *Wu Zetian* were supportive of Mao, while Wu Han's *Hai Rui Dismissed from Office* and Tian Han's *Guan Hanqing*, in providing heroic portrayals of Confucian loyal resistance, were critical of Mao (cf. Wagner 1990). The power of the plays lay in their innuendo concerning their time.

What I am interested in is the relationship between Guo Moruo (the "national poet" and the president of the Chinese Academy of Social Sciences) and Tian Han (the author of China's national anthem and head of the Drama-tist's Association), as well as the relationships among intellectuals and dissent, gender, and ethnic minorities. Guo's *Cai Wenji* (1959) was, according to Wagner (1990), a direct response to Tian Han's *Guan Hanqing* (1959). *Guan Hanqing* was a limited criticism, through the voice of a woman, Dou E, of the injustice done by some officials during the Mongol Yuan dynasty; thus, by innuendo, it was a criticism of Mao and his corrupt officials. Guo's heroine, Cai Wenji, learned to praise Cao Cao, a ruler of Wei during the Three Kingdoms period and by extension, Chairman Mao (Wagner 1990: 247–50). The play was intended to rehabilitate Cao Cao, who had been denounced throughout Chinese history as a paragon of treacherous pretenders. Cao Cao was praised as a first-rate politician who restored stability in the late Han period, paving the road for eventual unifi-cation of China under the western Jin dynasty and eliminating the nomadic threat from the northern borderlands; as a military strategist who defeated his challengers and as a gifted poet who befriended many literary figures in his time—all traits shared by Mao. In so doing, Guo was helping Mao Zedong, legiti-mating his rule of China, ethically and historically.

But it is interesting that Guo Moruo, in order to elevate Cao Cao's prestige, resorted to arranging for Cao to "save" Cai Wenji, a Han woman, from the "bar-barian" Xiongnu. The play centered around Cai Wenji, a gifted female writer, during the civil war in the late Han, who fled to the Xiongnu. In the play, Cai's son, whose name was unknown in historical sources, was given the name Yituzhi-yashi, the name of Wang Zhaojun's son, "to sufficiently demonstrate Cai Wenji's cherishing the memory of Wang Zhaojun" (Guo 1959: 1).

Historical sources do not say that Cai Wenji "married" the Xiongnu prince Zuo Xian, but it appears that she had two children while she remained in Xiong-nuland when Cao Cao bought her back from the Xiongnu. Despite this historical obscurity, Guo depicted Cai Wenji as Prince Zuo Xian's "wife," captured when she was eighteen years old (1959: 33). Guo used various phrases to reveal Prince Zuo Xian as an ambitious Xiongnu prince, a Xiongnu "nationalist," who had a fantasy of reliving the glory of Modun shanyu, who humiliated the first Han emperor, Gaodi. And Guo presumably considered such a marriage illegitimate, for he writes that since Cai was "captured" as a "slave," she must return to Han, thanks to Cao Cao's appreciation of her talent. In a series of intrigues, Prince Zuo Xian was even persuaded by the Chinese envoy Dong Si to remark that allowing Cai to return to the Han was more "meaningful" than her staying among the Xiongnu, and he knelt down and handed over his knife to Dong Si, swearing: "I have been carrying this knife for ten years, and I have fought count-less battles, and killed countless people. I offer this knife to you! I swear to you: from now on, I will be peaceful and friendly to the Han dynasty forever!" (Guo 1959: 18–19). Wagner perceptively comments, "In Guo Moruo's play, Cai Wenji returns home to Central China, leaving her husband and children. In his effort to deal with his own return from Japan in 1937 to join in Mao's enterprise, Guo ended up writing a chauvinist plot, because the Huns (Xiongnu), in contempo-

rary parlance, were 'national minorities,' and therefore life among them would
be quite acceptable for an educated Chinese woman" (1990: 85).

This comment is, however, only partially correct. Under Guo's pen, Prince
Zuo Xian's loyalty to the Han was suspect. His death had to be arranged, and he
died in the play. After his death, not only was Cai to be remarried to Dong Si,
but the two "children" also "returned" to Han upon Prince Zuo Xian's own
instruction in his deathbed (Guo 1959: 81). The play ended in comedy; everyone in the court was happy, with the two *hu er* ("barbarian children") of Cai
Wenji, shouting, "Long Live Prince Wei!" Such was minzu tuanjie, according to
Guo Moruo, Communist China's "national poet" and the president of the Chinese Academy of Social Sciences. This "return" theme was a departure from the
"going out" theme in his 1923 play *Wang Zhaojun*.

Tian Han was initially critical of Mao's disastrous Great Leap policies. By
1959, Tian had just finished what many soon recognized as his best drama, *Guan
Hanqing*, concerning a playwright during the Mongol Yuan dynasty. Guan, living
under intolerable repression, rebelled by writing a play called *Dou E's Lament*, a
lament by a woman against the Mongol rule. Tian Han, a romantic loyal critic
of Mao, was perhaps expressing a passionate "anxiety of service" remonstrance,
critiquing Mao in the voice of a yin-person. According to Wagner, the politically
pugnacious "dialogue" between Tian Han and Guo Moruo led Tian to reply to
Guo's *Cai Wenji* within months in the form of a new historical drama, *Princess
Wencheng*: "His Tang princess is married off to a Tibetan (for the grand purpose
of cementing the eternal friendship between the Han and the Tibetans in 1959,
the year of Tibetan rebellion). In a pointed departure from Guo's plot, Tian has
the princess decide, from the very beginning, to stay in Lhasa and never look
back" (1990: 85–86). But it seems to me that Tian's *Princess Wencheng* was not
created simply for the purpose of battling against his personal rival—Guo. In
fact, Tian Han was cast into political limbo because of his outspoken criticism.
However, his political life was temporarily saved by Zhou Enlai and the Tibetan
uprising. According to Tian Han's biographer,

> On 10 March 1959, when rebellion erupted in Tibet, the question of safeguarding
> *minzu tuanjie* and unity of the motherland became a political "hot spot." Nine days
> later, before the rebellion was quelled, Tian Han was summoned to Zhongnanhai
> which housed China's top leaders, where premier Zhou Enlai gave him an assign-
> ment: write a drama "Princess Wencheng," using the story of *"heqin"* between Tang
> emperor Taizong and Tibet, to propagate the great significance of *minzu tuanjie*, and
> simultaneously prove that Tibet has been a part of Chinese territory from antiquity.
> Tian Han was a patriot with strong national consciousness; to write about such a
> theme, he would invest his emotion. (Dong 1996: 819–20)

Emotion Tian Han did indeed invest, and his "national consciousness" was also
expressed in minzu tuanjie. By June 4, Tian had already completed a first draft,

in which he wrote about class struggle between Tibetan slave-owners and slaves and the struggle between advanced Chinese civilization and ignorant and backward Tibetan culture. The sixth scene depicted Princess Wencheng rescuing a female serf. The serf fled her home because of debt and marriage and was employed by Wencheng. But before the princess was to meet her future husband, Srongtsan Gampo, the female serf was kidnapped by her master, a serf-owning "local nationalist." In her rescue mission, the princess encountered various obstacles from the barbarous local rulers and lost two of her most able assistants. In the end she failed, the girl's eyes were already gouged out as punishment for her flight. Infuriated by such barbarity, Princess Wencheng taught her new husband, Srongtsan Gampo, how to reform the old customs to benefit the masses. Srongtsan Gampo accepted her admonition and decided to learn from advanced Chinese culture. The play ends with a song trumpeting the triumph of Chinese civilization over Tibetan barbarity. But such an antagonistic tone, which was in tune with Guo Moruo's treatment of the Xiongnu in his play *Cai Wenji*, was not what Zhou Enlai was looking for. When the play was rehearsed on January 29, 1960, Zhou personally intervened to insist on minzu tuanjie, not class struggle. Tian Han rewrote it, downplaying class(-ethnic) struggle in favor of denunciation of certain "nationalists" who opposed minzu tuanjie. Tibetan nationalism was detected by the "wise king" Srongtsan Gampo, and finally the obstacles were removed, resulting in the great union—the wedding between Princess Wencheng and King Srongtsan Gampo.

Two things can be discerned here: Tian Han, a passionate Chinese nationalist with little patience for Tibetan "barbarism," wanted a decisive conquest of civilization over barbarity. For Zhou, an acute politician, wedding or great union was the ultimate end, and the immediate struggle was not class struggle but one geared to overcome all obstacles to great "union." But whatever the approach, both sought the legitimization of historical drama to strengthen Chinese claims to sovereignty over Tibet.

Throughout the writing process, Tian Han consulted one of the foremost historians, Jian Bozan, reportedly a sinicized Uyghur born in Hubei province. Jian entirely endorsed Zhou Enlai's plan, and indeed, after seeing a Shanghai-style drama, *Princess Wencheng*, he published an article about Wencheng, inviting her to "speak up" for Chinese sovereignty over Tibet in *Beijing Daily* on January 1, 1960 (Jian 1980a). Five months later, he wrote another piece in the national newspaper *Guangming Daily* (May 6, 1960), after viewing a performance of Tian Han's *Princess Wencheng* by the Youth Art Theater and a Kun-style drama of the same title, to "give the deserved historical place to Princess Wencheng" (Jian 1980b). In early February 1961, Jian Bozan published a piece on Wang Zhaojun, arguing that she was not a symbol of China's humiliation, nor should she shed tears for her emperor. Instead, "We should help Wang Zhaojun to wipe dry her tears and allow her to appear on stage as an active person to serve our time" (Jian 1980c: 489). She "knew" that her husband, Huhanye, was not an enemy of the Han dynasty but "the first Xiongnu shanyu who brought the Mongolian grassland into the Great Han Empire" (Jian 1980c: 488). A few days later, on February 11, Jian wrote to Guo Moruo:

> I recently wrote an article about Wang Zhaojun. I originally mentioned your modern drama *Wang Zhaojun* written in 1923, but fearing that it might get you into trouble, I deleted it. Even now people are interested in Wang Zhaojun's tears, but you helped her wipe away her tears more than thirty years ago. I think your *Wang Zhaojun* can still be put on. Why not? Of course, if you can write a new one, that would be even better. (1982: 34)

Jian's papers were a clarion call to reconsider the entire moral fabric of the Chinese people and to re-imagine the Chinese Nation. Inner Mongolian leaders responded by organizing a series of scholarly debates in *Inner Mongolia Daily* in 1961–1962. At the invitation of Ulanhu, the chairman of the Inner Mongolia Autonomous Region, a team of more than twenty of the most eminent Chinese historians and writers, including historians Jian Bozan, Fan Wenlan, and Lü Zhengyu and writers Lao She, Ye Shengtao, and Cao Yu, visited Inner Mongolia between July 23 and September 14, 1961. On September 12, they toured the Zhaojun Tomb (a.k.a. *Qing Zhong,* Green Tumulus) in the southern suburb of Hohhot, the capital city of Inner Mongolia. Almost all of them published poems or essays, denouncing the earlier "misrepresentation" of Wang Zhaojun, and they all attempted to restore the historical "truth" by removing the tragic hue from Zhaojun. She was not to be bemoaned but celebrated. Cao Yu, a renowned dramatist, known as China's Shakespeare, also was given a mission. As early as 1960, Zhou Enlai instructed Cao to write a play about Wang Zhaojun to encourage "Chinese women to marry national minorities" (Cao and Yu 1990: 415). His fellow travelers wrote poems to cheer him on. Lao She, for instance, in the preface to two poems about Wang Zhaojun, noted that his "friend Cao Yu is planning to write a play of *Wang Zhaojun,* I also, for the sake of celebrating *heqin* and neighborly peace, have written two short poems for him, hoping him to complete the play as soon as possible" (Lao She 1961, in Ban 1997: 55). Tian Han, fresh from his success with *Princess Wencheng,* also presented a poem to Cao Yu upon hearing Cao's plan (Cao and Yu 1990: 424). But for various reasons, Cao did not complete the play until 1978.

In October 1963 China's vice president, Dong Biwu, paid homage to the Wang Zhaojun Tomb and wrote a poem that was carved on a tablet, monumentalizing the *minzu tuanjie,* or marital union, between Han and Xiongnu and by extension the Mongols:

> Zhaojun has been alive for thousands of years
> Great is the vision of *heqin* between Hu[5] and Han.
> Agony and anxiety may poets express
> Futile is waving brush and dripping ink.

With a single stroke of the brush, almost two thousand years' history of humiliation was turned upside down; heqin was resurrected by the Chinese communists to achieve what Emperor Han Gaodi had failed to achieve. Kinship union, not bloody conquest, was to ensure Chinese sovereignty over ethnic minorities.

This sudden avalanche of "love" for Mongols apparently sent a message that also carried an opportunity to Mongol officials. In 1964, Chen Bingyu, the Mongol mayor of Hohhot, in response to the state's new interest in Wang Zhaojun, ordered the Green Tumulus completely renovated, making it a park to commemorate this ancient symbol of minzu tuanjie.

Ironically, soon, during the Cultural Revolution, lest such a minzu tuanjie discourse be seen as too soft on the minorities, heqin was denounced as a humiliation to the Chinese. Ulanhu and Chen Bingyu were then denounced for beautifying the Zhaojun Tomb. As a denunciation article wrote:

> Wang Zhaojun was a court woman at the time of Han Yuandi, she was a loyal instrument for the "*Heqin* Policy" of the ruling class of the Han dynasty. . . . Inner Mongolia's "reigning prince" Ulanhu and his loyal go-getter Chen Bingyu and his ilk . . . , however, lavished praise on Wang Zhaojun, going so far as to equate the capitulationist policy of "*heqin*" with our Party's nationality policy, representing *Zhaojun Going Beyond the Pass* as a so-called "symbol of minzu tuanjie," thus blotting out the class nature of the nationality question. (Jiansheju "Dongfanghong" Liandui 1967)

Behind the Marxist language of class were more assaults on ethnic minorities. A virulent Chinese onslaught on the Mongols was unleashed during the Cultural Revolution (Tumen and Zhu 1995).

WANG ZHAOJUN AND THE ENIGMA OF HER "LOVE" TODAY

One would have thought that after the brutal repression of minorities such as Mongols and Tibetans during the Cultural Revolution, the Chinese leadership would have shown some remorse and reexamined minority policies. This they did, but in a curious manner. They denounced the Gang of Four's "destruction of the correct Party policies towards nationalities" and vowed to restore the "correct" Party policies. Minzu tuanjie, a policy adopted in 1957 and rejected in essentials by the class struggle line of 1966 and the Cultural Revolution, was to be held aloft once again. Historians rushed to churn out another round of Zhaojun literature to "restore" minzu tuanjie, which was said to have been besmirched by the Gang of Four.

Cao Yu, recently rehabilitated, with a lofty sense of responsibility to China's national unity and to his unfulfilled promise to the recently deceased Zhou Enlai, returned to a play on Wang Zhaojun that he had initiated in 1961 but never

昭君怨，乌王爷也怨。千年 "青冢"
无人管。 我王爷为搞 民族分裂为 你重整
容。

3.2.   Ulanhu Worshiping at the Zhaojun Tomb
"Zhaojun lamented, so does Prince Ulanhu. For a thousand years, the 'Green Tumulus'
has been neglected. Now let me, the Prince, renovate it for the purpose of splitting
nationalities." (*Weidong Zhanbao*, October 3, 1967)

finished. The new Zhaojun literature and the discourse on minzu tuanjie were
presented as a Chinese goodwill gesture to the battered minorities. Cao Yu's five-
episode drama *Wang Zhaojun* was completed in 1978 to mark the thirtieth anniversary of the founding of the People's Republic of China. It was duly awarded
the highest national prize for literature.

In the preface to the drama, Cao candidly stated why he wrote it: "The
beloved Premier Zhou entrusted me with this duty when he was alive, to write a
historical drama about Wang Zhaojun. I grasped Premier Zhou's intention, that
is to use this theme to sing the praise of the unity and cultural exchanges
between various nationalities in our country" (1978: 37). The drama was thus
explicitly geared to serve the new state and Party ideology of minzu tuanjie.

How, then, was the new minzu tuanjie to be expressed artistically, especially
after the Chinese slaughter of Mongols? Cao never had to rethink the tragedy.
As he wrote, "Wang Zhaojun, there (in Inner Mongolia), is not a sobbing
woman (*funü*), but is a beautiful figure, a mythical person, a Han woman *loved*
by the Mongolian people" (quoted in Lin and Ma 1994: 187, emphasis added).
In other words, the drama was to forge the present day "unity" between Mongols
and Han, using a story that preceded the emergence of the Mongols as a people.
Cao masterfully restored historical "reality" by presenting the weakness of the
Xiongnu and the power of the Han. This "restored" historical background thus
set the stage for a Zhaojun who was no longer a reluctant victim, nor was she a
symbol of shame, but instead a witty woman who controlled her own fate and

who promoted friendship between the Xiongnu and the Han. No longer a lowly courtier, she was elevated to the position of "princess" (Cao 1978: 61). Far from being deterred by the prospect of living in a hostile land, she knew that Huhanye "knows well the custom of the Han dynasty, its language, and like other kings and dukes of many nationalities, looks up to Chang'an as a place of civilization" (Cao 1978: 51). Cao also used his mighty brush to remove the barbarity from the earlier representation of Huhanye's physiognomy. Now Huhanye has very manly features, yet "his eyes emit an attractive softness," befitting a legitimate petty ruler recognized by the central government. As if this was not enough, Cao also resorted to the age-old technique of genealogy, establishing the kinship link between the Xiongnu and Han, through the mouth of Huhanye himself, "Our Xiongnu and the Han are all the descendants of King Xia Yu; we are hands and feet; we are brothers. The Han and Xiongnu were originally one family, and this is our really basic cause for thousands of generations to come" (1978: 53). Such a blood relationship does not denote equality. Rather, Huhanye solemnly swears to the Emperor Yuan that he would be like "a good horse" that the Chinese emperor could rely on in life and death. "Such a horse isn't unruly in eating and moving, and [when you are] on its back, it does not bolt or run amok" (Cao 1978: 55).

With her wit, honesty, and sincerity, Zhaojun exposes the plot of the "Han chauvinist" Wang Long, the Han emperor's brother-in-law, and "local nationalist" Wendun, Huhanye's brother-in-law, to sabotage the marriage. Recovering from his grief over his dead wife, Huhanye withdraws the sword, a symbol of commanding power, from Wendun and gives it to Zhaojun to keep safe. Finally, the "traitor" Wendun is arrested. Huhanye is then advised by Zhaojun to send Wendun to Chang'an to be punished by the Han emperor, reasoning, "His Majesty will judge considerately and settle the matter satisfactorily" (Cao 1978: 109). Wang Long, the Han co-conspirator, receives no punishment.

In this new drama, Mao Yanshou, the corrupt court artist, disappears but perhaps reappears as Wendun. Recall that in Ma Zhiyuan's drama, the Xiongnu shanyu returns Mao to the Han emperor for decapitation. In Cao's drama, the shanyu turns in his own "local nationalist" brother-in-law to the Han court for punishment. The nature of the crime also shifts. Whereas in Ma's drama, the crime is letting Zhaojun marry the Xiongnu shanyu, in Cao's drama it is the prevention of or spoiling the marriage![6]

What is more extraordinary is the "love" Zhaojun shows to Huhanye, in addition to earlier representations in which she was presented as fulfilling a political mission of subduing and civilizing the "barbarians." Zhaojun's "love" for Huhanye is symbolized by a *hehuanbei* ("happy union quilt"), testimony to their sexual union. Zhaojun says to Huhanye, "Oh, Shanyu, this *hehuanbei* symbolizes the happiness of you and me, and may it also bring warmth to the hundreds and thousands of common people of the Han and Hu" (Cao 1978: 110). Charmed by this happy union quilt, Huhanye sets up an ancestral worship altar, and in a

grand ceremony, awards Zhaojun the title *Ninghu Yanzhi* ("Barbarian-Tranquiliz-
ing Consort"). But more miraculously than this conquering title, and perhaps
more happily, the hehuanbei suddenly turns into a big golden swan. Instead of
the sadly chirping sparrow flying south back home in the early representation,
under Cao Yu's facile pen, the quilt expands as the swan flies. The scenery is so
fantastic that Zhaojun exclaims, "It has changed to become as large as the sky,
without end!" Huhanye happily agrees, "It covers far and near, south and north
of the Great Wall, endlessly" (Cao 1978: 111).

That colonizing "love" has a contagious power. Later writers compete to
expand on that magical power. A grand song and dance drama, *Saishang Zhaojun*
("Zhaojun beyond the Great Wall"), was put on by the Hohhot Cultural Bureau
to celebrate the fortieth anniversary of the founding of the Inner Mongolia
Autonomous Region in 1987. In this drama, she shows her "love" (presumably
nonsexual) for the little prince, the son of Huhanye's deceased wife, who is said
to be opposed to the marriage between his father and Zhaojun. By sending gifts,
by worshiping at his mother's altar, Zhaojun finally wins his trust, and the little
prince finally calls her *qin ama* ("blood mom"). In real life, however, she eventually had to marry him, following the levirate tradition of the Xiongnu, a custom
the Chinese ridiculed for two thousand years. Levirate in socialist China is interpreted as a "backward" custom by ethnologists, and in the play it is conveniently
excised by the mighty pen, in favor of an "advanced" monogamy. Zhaojun practices monogamy in this play.

But mere sexual love is never enough; indeed, it is vulgar if divorced from
political mission. More work needed to be done to perfect Zhaojun and Huhanye's newly discovered sexuality and love. In August 1988, a ten-part TV play,
jointly made by Inner Mongolian TV and the Hubei[7] TV Drama Production
Center and originally dedicated to the commemoration of the fortieth anniversary of the founding of the Inner Mongolia Autonomous Region (too late for
1987), was shown simultaneously on fifteen provincial TV stations. As the literary adviser to the play, Lin Gan writes that it particularly emphasized two sets
of "sincerity": sincere reconciliation between the two supreme leaders, Huhanye
and Han Yuandi; and sincere "love" between Wang Zhaojun and Huhanye (Lin
and Ma 1994: 196).

That "love" and "smile" are said to be closer to "historical reality," a hard-
won victory. As Lin and Ma write in a self-congratulatory and triumphant mode
in their study of Wang Zhaojun: "After the propaganda and education of literary
and art workers and historians for several decades, people gradually freed themselves from the fixed mode of a sad and mournful Zhaojun, gradually accepted a
Zhaojun figure that is closer to historical reality: an envoy of nationality friendship. This is a gigantic, but also imperceptible, if gradual, change. The mega-
trend of nationality unity and friendship is after all irreversible" (1994: 199).

Of course, the northern frontier is no longer a hostile land where Zhaojun's

3.3. Huhanye and His Chinese Consort Wang Zhaojun Enjoying Minzu Tuanjie in Inner Mongolia (2000)

beautiful face was to be dusted by sand, or where she would be forced to gulp mutton and milk; it is now a land where what she is familiar with in her native land is abundant, and her husband is no longer an enemy, but someone who deeply "loves" her. Zhaojun finally "smiles," for the first time in history.

But irreversibility is also a Marxist trope, and the will of the people is beyond the manipulation of individuals. History is said to be created by the people, rather than by heroes. Lest this "imperceptible" mega-trend be doubted, an aura of authenticity is now given by "the people," in the form of folk stories. Lin Gan has documented many of those "folk stories." But "the people" are, of course, Chinese. I have tried in vain to find any "folk" literature on Zhaojun among the Mongols written in Mongolian, ancient or modern.

The new folklore has sprung up elsewhere in Zhaojun's home province, Hubei, too. Let us confine ourselves, however, to "folk stories" that are told by the Chinese, as I have found none by Mongols in Inner Mongolia. They are mostly about the Zhaojun tomb in suburban Hohhot. One story is related to Zhaojun powder (*Zhaojun fen*). It narrates the origin of the local lime mining industry: Women in the north were said to have no habit of applying powder to their faces; they only painted their walls with limewash, so that women's faces could radiate some brilliance through reflection. The lime came from a mountain called Yanzhi Shan ("Rouge Mountain"), but the mountain was burned to ashes, so there was no more lime. Ever since then, northern women "no longer had colors." After arriving in the north, Zhaojun wanted to make everyone beautiful, so she gave her own powder from the Han harem for them to use. But the local women did not have this custom and refused. Zhaojun then hid her powder in the mountains of Yanzhi, telling them there was lime there. Miraculously, Zhaojun's action revived the Yanzhi Mountains (Kuang 1990: 465).

This story is, of course, the product of a confused imagination, taking some information from a famous Xiongnu song: "Our Yanzhi Mountains are lost, making our women colorless." In fact, Han women during the Han dynasty knew nothing about rouge. Applying rouge was actually a Xiongnu tradition! Indeed, Cao Yu made this a spectacle in his drama, as Zhaojun's imitation of the Xiongnu women's fashion deeply offended her supervisor from the Han court! A "virtuous" woman was supposed to be "natural" looking, rendered immune from the social disease of conjugal infidelity.

Zhaojun is no longer a tragic figure, but she has more than a "civilizing mission." In a folk story recorded in Lin Gan's book *Zhaojun and the Zhaojun Tomb,* Zhaojun becomes a fairy sent down from heaven by the Jade Emperor to ease the conflict between the Han and Xiongnu. After marrying the Xiongnu shanyu, on their way to Xiongnuland in the cold windy and snowy winter, Zhaojun stops and plays her *pipa.* Suddenly, the wind stops, and a rainbow appears in the blue sky. The ice melts, and everything comes back to life. Lush grass begins to grow, and the Black River that once served as the border between Han and Xiongnu becomes crystal clear.

> Wherever Zhaojun goes, there is lush grass and sweet water, and both human beings and livestock flourish. . . . Zhaojun also has a beautiful brocade bag, from which she takes out some seeds. As soon as she drops them on the soil, there spring up crops beyond the Great Wall; she then takes out a pair of gold scissors, and cuts sheepskin into plows, carts, sheep and horses. As soon as they are put on the ground, there appear iron plows and wooden carts, and surrounding them are flocks of sheep, horses and camels. (Lin 1979: 70)

But the reality, unfortunately, is that Inner Mongolia has long suffered from rapid desertification, especially in the twentieth century, largely because of Chinese agricultural practices that transformed the grasslands and destroyed the fragile topsoil, exposing it to the fierce Siberian wind. A closer examination of the change of the Zhaojun image in the new folk stories reveals a systematic transformation, as Kuang summarizes succinctly:

> Today's bird of Zhaojun is no longer the autumn goose flying in the gloomy sky; she is a white dove soaring to great heights and hovering in the bracing spring breeze. What she is carrying is not Zhaojun's yearning for the emperor and her husband, but the welcome news of *"Huhan Heqin, Wanmin Tongqing"* (Xiongnu and Han are in *heqin,* Millions are joyful). . . . Today, Zhaojun rides a "golden pony" which is

frisking "in the beautiful grassland." . . . Today, the sound of Zhaojun's *pipa* is not only "like flying clouds and running water, like phoenix chirping; upon hearing, the sun stops its steps, and the wind hurries to send news." It now assumes a magical power: It "gushes out blue smoke, which extends from the east of the river to the west, and is transformed into a blue stone arch bridge, firmly straddling the Black River," and then "goes on to build a heavenly bridge for the Xiongnu and Han brotherly nationalities"! . . . Zhaojun still cries, but her tears are not "like a kite with broken string difficult to hold back," rather she cries for the drought inflicting the peaceful land beyond the great Wall, and she cries for the poverty and starvation of the herdsmen. She "is rather sad, she cudgels her brains, but is unable to find a way to resolve the pressing need," so she "sheds tears in agony under the moonlight." Zhaojun's tears are so useful! They "flow drop by drop into strings, and more and more," and "in a twinkling, they become a small stream like a jade belt," and on the soil "appear patches and patches of green grasses and fragrant wild flowers," and after that, the grassland restores to the beautiful scenery of "wind blowing the grass to bend, revealing cattle and sheep"! (1990: 479)

Interestingly, in contrast to the previous story, this one is highly sensitive to the drought condition.

The enigma of Wang Zhaojun does not just lie in her multiple representations; she can also be reincarnated in transsexual form as a man. In 1988 one of China's leading newspapers, *Guangming Daily*, praised Lin Gan, the Chinese scholar specializing in Xiongnu history who wrote extensively on Zhaojun, as a "contemporary Zhaojun" (*Dangdai Zhaojun*) (Lin, Wang, and Bailadugeqi 1995: 438–41). Through his historical and literary work, he himself ultimately has become a modern Zhaojun, a civilizer, whose pen portrays the "irreversible" mega-trend of minzu tuanjie through the representation of the hapless court woman Wang Zhaojun's marriage to the Xiongnu emperor. He was originally from south China, so he himself became a representative of those *zhibian* ("assist the frontier") immigrants who poured into Inner Mongolia in the 1950s and 1960s. He not only turned his tutelary goddess into a conqueror, but himself was duly reincarnated as the male side of the Janus-faced Wang Zhaojun. He edited a series called *Inner Mongolian Historical and Cultural Series*, which included a monograph on Wang Zhaojun penned by himself and a fellow Chinese historian, Ma Yi (Lin and Ma 1994). The purpose of the series, as explained in the preface by its patron, Wang Qun, a Chinese, then Party secretary of Inner Mongolia, is as follows:

Researching the history and culture of the Inner Mongolian region, understanding that the historical ethnic relations and ethnic changes in the Inner Mongolian region have important realistic and historical significance for strengthening the great unity between various nationalities, increasing the consciousness of the Chinese nation and patriotism of the people of various nationalities. (Quoted in Lin and Ma 1994: 1)

The fluidity of Zhaojun's reincarnations suggests that she can be anything and do anything for China. And that she is willing to go "wherever she is most needed." So it is not surprising that, recently, she does not even have to stay in Inner Mongolia. In the summer of 1993, a mummified young woman of the Pazyryk (a pastoral nomadic people of the sixth through the second centuries B.C.E.) was excavated by Russian archaeologists led by Natalya Polosmak, on the Pastures of Heaven in the Autonomous Republic of Altay in Russia, bordering China to the south, Mongolia to the east, and Kazakhstan to the West (Polosmak 1994). Called by archaeologists the Siberian Ice Maiden, she had been mummified and then frozen in freak climatic conditions around 2,400 years ago, along with six decorated horses and a symbolic meal for her last journey. Her body was covered with vivid blue tattoos of mythical animal figures. This was considered one of the most remarkable archaeological discoveries in recent decades, inspiring hopes that she will provide clues to the role and power of women in the nomadic peoples of ancient Siberia. Li Xiguang, a New China News Agency journalist, apparently has a different view. Li claims, in a book about his adventurous expeditions along the Silk Road, that the Ice Maiden is no one but Wang Zhaojun! Describing his conversation with Natalia Polosmak, Li wrote,

> Looking at the funeral procession, and the body of the "ice beauty" floating amidst the sea of flowers, Natalya *suddenly felt the pain of compunction* for destroying this sacred tomb, disturbing the several thousands of years' tranquillity of *this Chinese princess*. (1996: 332, emphasis added)

CONCLUSION: POLITICAL LOVE, NATURE, AND THE CHINESE NATION

This chapter is a conscious application of the genealogical approach to Chinese discourse of minzu tuanjie. It is not only a search for the discontinuities of history, but more important, as I hope to have succeeded in showing, an attempt to analyze "the tension between rupture and reinscription, between break and recuperation in discursive formations" (Stoler 1995: 61). The Chinese communist discourse of minzu tuanjie, as is clear from my discussion, builds on and transcends the ancient discourse and practice of heqin.

We need to recapitulate the main contours of this development. To some extent, we may conclude that Chinese nationalism has its moralistic origins dating back to antiquity; but what I have tried to highlight is the reverse of Chinese nationalistic concerns about "barbarians," from the original flirtation of a kinship alliance to the total rejection of "barbarians" and then finally to reestablishing the kinship alliance in a different form, transforming the "barbarians" into "national minorities," "one of us," blood relatives—*tongbao*. One of us . . . yet a lesser/subordinate one of us! In each phase of these fluctuations, the Chinese male anxiety about "barbarians" is expressed through female reproductive sexuality. Through heqin, it was hoped that "barbarians" could be made into conjugal relatives, so as to subjugate them through kinship moralizing; in other words, "barbarians" should show deference and obedience to the mother's father/ brother category. Neo-Confucianism ushered in an extreme gender inequality and lineage "fundamentalism," so much so that there existed no compatibility in marriage alliance between the Chinese and the "barbarians," for they were imagined to have either inhuman or demonic natures. Protecting women's chastity, controlling their sexuality, not only became a hallmark of Confucian morality, but also served to draw a strict boundary between Chinese and "barbarian." In other words, Chinese ethnicity and civility were invested in female sexuality. The Chinese communists have only flipped this representation (but not abandoned it) and used the motif of Wang Zhaojun and Princess Wencheng to simultaneously express national unity and Chinese sovereignty over the "barbarians." In this contradictory movement of morality and redefinition of group relations, we see a discursive bricolage whereby the older discourse of kinship and sexuality was first abandoned, then recovered, modified, and "encased" and "encrusted" in new forms (Stoler 1995: 61).

This chapter may also read like a Chinese saga of their women's *fanshen* from "on the bottom" to "on top." This ritualized national somersault in the sexual and kinship act is nonetheless invested with an aura of holiness, denoting not only the subjugation of minorities, but, more important, sovereignty over recalcitrant minorities. What is interesting, though, is that kinship, gender, sexuality, and love have been very much the site at which civilization and ethnicity have been demarcated in China. At each historical juncture, Inner Asians are "naturalized" as either compatible or incompatible in terms of copulation and reproduction to create worthwhile "Confucian" or "Chinese" subjects. If kinship and gender symbolize the incompatibility of the two peoples, hierarchically dichotomizing them into "civilized" and "barbarian," the latter being made beyond the pale of "humanity," they could also be used to prove the opposite. And this is done extensively by the communists. For communists who want to produce seamless socialist citizenry out of diverse ethnic groups, who may or may not accept the legitimacy of their rule, their device is invocation of the ancient kinship and gender discourse, repackaging these to naturalize the new hierarchical power relations between them. These gendered ethnic relations are set to nurture national "organic" unity or solidarity, as Emile Durkheim would say. This unity is said to come not only from biological union, but also from romantic love between them.

Benedict Anderson (1991), in his formulation of nation as an "imagined community," argues that the principal goal for consolidating the unity of a nation is to cultivate the "love for the nation." The "nature" of "political love"

> can be deciphered from the ways in which languages describe its object: either in the vocabulary of kinship (motherland, *Vaterland, patria*) or that of home (*heimat*

. . .). Both idioms denote something to which one is naturally tied. As we have seen earlier, in everything "natural" there is always something unchosen. In this way, nation-ness is assimilated to skin-color, gender, parentage and birth-era—all those things one can not help. And in these "natural ties" one senses what one might call the "beauty of *gemeinschaft*." (1991: 141, 143)

In this chapter, I have largely followed Sommer's (1990, 1991) path-breaking study of the foundational literature of romance in the nation-building process but have gone beyond the time-frame she set—the foundational period of nationalism. Instead, a genealogical approach enables me to trace the current discourse and practice of gendered national unity through longer history. This culture of "political love" instituted by the nation-building project is more about a means of achieving a National Unity than about its "effects." Despite the enormous resources, political and economic, that have been and continue to be invested in reproducing the nation—that is, fostering the minority's tie to the Chinese Nation "naturally"—it remains to be seen how successful it is. The problem stems precisely from the "nature" of such a unity. Although this may seem a "human" attempt to forge unity, or best of all, a nonthreatening one, as Chinese women may have "sacrificed" themselves on behalf of the patriarchal Chinese Nation to win over the patriarchal minorities, it actually "naturalizes" these identities of majority and minority and their "unity" "*by claiming for them an autonomy from human social agency*" (Yanagisako and Delaney 1995: 20, emphasis added). In other words, although this naturalizing power of biological union and love teleologically used for the production of National Unity has a remarkably disarming charm, behind the "human" surface, "all these identities and bonds are ascribed a *nonhuman* basis, whether in nature, biology or god. All legitimize hierarchies of difference in which power relations are embedded" (1995: 20, emphasis added). This one-way "love," however, does not say much about what minorities do or do not do, but more about the quaint morality of the majority Chinese. And I go further in arguing it also tells much more about the "nature" of building the Chinese Nation.

NOTES

1. Millward 1994 is a rare exception.

2. Women, then, were relatively free of the Confucian ethical constraint, enjoying a relatively high status, as widows could remarry. Widow remarriage was so natural that several emperors married divorced women or widows (Jiang Xiaowang 1995: 84). Women could thus play important roles, as in the case of princesses, such as becoming envoys, with a mission to make peace with hostile peoples.

3. Indeed, wars between the Han and Xiongnu were often conducted in a competition to win the support of wavering peoples. And their support was often secured, or intended to be secured, by marriage. In a crucial move, in order to obtain the support of the Wusun

in what is today's Xinjiang, the Xiongnu also married a princess to the king of Wusun, and this was different from tributary relations the Xiongnu initiated with the Han. Rather, I would argue, the Xiongnu adopted the Han kinship strategy. This is a subtle change, but a change of great significance.

4. Very few poems about Wang Zhaojun were written by women. This is a subject in its own right, but I cannot treat it in this chapter. The following poem is an example. The author, Xu Can (1622–1677), the daughter and wife of high officials, experienced exile along with her husband, but instead of lamenting the exile, she took pride in such a life:

> When a scholar fails to realize his ambition
> He can achieve renown by traveling to far-off places.
> Banchao, in arms, went to the far west;
> Wang Zhaojun dwelt in the northern kingdoms.
> With a sigh she got up from the dais,
> A hundred thoughts compact in her mind.
> How many years had she lived in the palace,
> And her exceptional beauty was only now recognized!
> Now, the Lord of Men, sighing in distress,
> Immediately ordered the portraitist's death.
> With jade pendants hanging across her carved saddle,
> With pearl studs sparkling on her horse's golden bit,
> She crossed a thousand, ten thousand, miles of yellow sand
> And abruptly reached the felt tents.
> Painstakingly she drew mournful sounds from her four-stringed lute,
> Sounds that inspire sorrow in a thousand generations—
> While those who in the Han palace had shone like clouds
> Have faded away like fireflies in the grass. (Saussy 1997: 303–4)

5. Generic name for Inner Asians.

6. Cao Yu's *Wang Zhaojun* drew criticism from many sides. It was criticized by Chinese intellectuals for being "literature written to order" (*zunming wenxue*), a term attributed to Lu Xun (Link 2000: 156–57). Link writes that Cao Yu's play *Wang Zhaojun* "was meant to show that China's minority nationalities are just as respectable as the Han people, so that marriage of a Han to a non-Han is actually quite normal and fine; but some young people in Beijing took the play to mean that the Party could no longer object to marriages between Chinese and Westerners" (2000: 293–94). The harshest criticism came from a prominent Mongol scholar, Munohoi (Mao Aohai) (1995a). In May 1981, he wrote an article entitled "Attempts to Analyze the Ideological Tendency in Some Nationality Historical Plays: Comments on Some Works by Comrades Guo Moruo, Cao Yu and Yu Boyuan." In the article, he launched a scathing criticism of Guo Moruo's *Cai Wenji* (1959), Cao Yu's *Wang Zhaojun* (1978), and Yu Boyuan's *Lady Shexiang* (1963) for insulting minority nationalities. All three plays demonstrated, he argues, blatant Chinese chauvinism: "The three nationality plays, under the guise of the key theme of praising nationality unity (*minzu tuanjie*) and state unity (*guojia tongyi*), have sung praise of, to various degrees, nationality inequality and nationality oppression in ancient times, and have made mistakes of various degrees in the ideological tendency towards the nationality question. Of them, the historical play *Wang Zhaojun*'s guiding thought is especially wrong for not fol-

lowing premier Zhou's demand, and has thus seriously hurt the dignity of minority nationalities" (1995a: 119). The article, written on the eve of the 1981 Mongolian student movement against the Center's No. 28 document (a document that endorsed plans to settle more Chinese immigrants in Inner Mongolia, etc.), was immensely popular among Mongol students. Munohoi himself, accused of being the black hand behind the movement, was imprisoned for seven days and then held under house arrest for ten months.

7. Wang Zhaojun was believed to be from today's Hubei province.

Part II

TENSIONS OF EMPIRE

4

⅄

From Inequality to Difference: Colonial Contradictions of Class and Ethnicity in "Socialist" China

PROBLEMS OF SUBALTERNITY
AND REPRESENTATION

I start with a problem, both theoretical and practical: Until 1947–1948 many landless Chinese immigrant tenants in Inner Mongolia worked for Mongols who possessed abundant land, thus forming a hierarchical ethnic-class relationship. Simultaneously, however, from the collapse of the Qing dynasty in 1911, successive groups of Chinese effectively controlled Inner Mongolia, the historical homeland of Mongol peoples. These were the warlords and the ruling Chinese Nationalist Party (GMD) government, from whose domination Mongols sought to escape.

In many respects, the situation of Inner Mongolia might appear to be an ideal case of "internal colonialism," in Hechter's (1975) terms. But it is not so simple. No matter how one interprets it, colonialism presupposes the clear-cut (ethnic) identity of the colonial self vis-à-vis a colonized other, the (political-economic) domination of an oppressed nationality by a ruling elite—and, above all, the confluence of these processes. The complexities of the Inner Mongolian issues are further underlined by the fact that the Mongols have long been a minority, even in their own ostensibly autonomous homeland—Inner Mongolia. This is the result of more than a century of ethnic Chinese settlement of the territory. But what happens when ethnic or national self-determination runs counter to the principle of class emancipation—specifically, a process in which landless

Chinese seek redress from landed Mongol elites? How do Mongol Communist Party leaders, who must negotiate between ethnic and class equality, resolve a situation that is beyond the clear-cut boundaries of "colonialism"? Finally, how does the increasing ethnic and cultural hybridity that results from Chinese in-migration and intermarriage, as well as changing Mongol lifestyles—influenced by political disruption, urbanization, education, and economic displacement—affect the "purity" of nationality principles that Mongol Communist Party elites claim to uphold throughout these struggles?

In 1947 Mongols, under the auspices of the Chinese Communist Party (CCP), established their own quasi-autonomous power by overthrowing Chinese war-lords and the GMD. Before they tasted the fruit of victory, however, Mongols faced the challenge of Chinese peasants, who demanded an equal share of land and property in the so-called democratic reform movement carried out in 1947–1948. Thus we have here the following paradox: The CCP helped "liberate" Mongols from the GMD and warlords, but at the same time it also enabled Chinese peasants to wrest land away from Mongol "landlords" in the name of revolutionary justice. In both cases, land was not only a focus in an emancipatory class struggle but also a symbol of identity in a postcolonial narrative of nationality self-determination and autonomy. The fact that the two processes overlapped poses a series of contradictory questions about the meaning of liberation from class and ethnic perspectives. The conflicting outcomes force us to inquire whether the regime of socialist egalitarianism is indeed "emancipatory" (and if so, for whom?) or just another form of "colonialism" (in which case, who are the colonizers and who the colonized?).

Central to understanding this class and ethnic violence are concepts such as "the people" and the "landlords." What caused the Mongols to lose ground and become a target for class-cum-ethnic struggle after the emancipation was precisely their failure to control these discursive concepts. This chapter thus discusses the changing boundaries of concepts, as communists responded to local situations in their attempt to apply to Inner Mongolia principles derived from experience in agrarian China, such as class struggle. I keep these boundaries alive in order to show the violence of these concepts. This approach eschews an easy moralistic representation of the subaltern other, often deployed in recent postcolonial critique. Instead, it attempts to problematize postcolonial neo-Marxist representation, drawing on materials from socialist Inner Mongolia of China.

Before turning to the case study, let us discuss briefly the binary opposition between the notion "subaltern" or its synonym, "the people," and national elites in recent postcolonial scholarship. The postcolonial historiographical project, represented by the South Asian Subaltern Studies school, is predicated on rescuing the voice of the subalterns, or "the people," and "speaking" on their behalf (Spivak 1988). However, there are many uncomfortable aspects of such a representation of the other. In criticizing the uneasy and shifting category of "the people" in socialist China, Gail Hershatter notes that subalterns speak in the language of the state: "this legacy of official subaltern-speak complicates enormously the search for subversive voices" (1993: 108). When "subalterns" did speak in the revolutionary narrative of "speaking bitterness," they demonstrated tremendous destructive power (Anagnost 1994, 1997). Recent studies show that the subaltern representation, as deployed by intellectuals, is often a self-empowering strategy; "it produces a way of talking in which notions of lack, subalternity, victimization, and so forth are drawn upon indiscriminately, often with the intention of spotlighting the speaker's own sense of alterity and political righteousness" (Chow 1993: 13).

Inasmuch as postcolonial critique borrows heavily from Marxist lexicons, there is now a need to study the terminology "postcolonially." "The people" in the subaltern analysis are the silent, the oppressed. But in the Marxist or Maoist lexicon, they become the loud-speaking majority, the masses, particularly a rural proletariat composed predominantly of landless and land-poor tenants and hired laborers who are mobilized to overturn the dominant minority landlord elite. The gallantry of the postcolonial critics intervening in this unequal relation on the side of the oppressed is laudatory, but how are we to grasp the power relations in a case in which "the people," as a majority, are also the dominant majority ethnic group in a multinational state, such as China? Many current world problems derive from ethnic conflicts, not infrequently in the form of majority violence (and, of course, many other forms of persecution) against the minority. It may be appropriate to suggest that ethnic minorities are not just failures in the "race for nation," but are in many instances colonized by modern nation-states that privilege the majority and sanction violence against minorities.

All this suggests the need to problematize the violent nature that is often concealed beneath classificatory concepts. In a recent volume, some historians and political scientists have examined the development and application of three paradigmatic concepts: nation/nationality, class, and civil society (Mudimbe 1997). According to Mudimbe, a paradigm dominated in a particular historical period, and the dominant paradigm "organized an intellectual configuration and a way of *thinking the political* by interpreting and reinterpreting the notion of social conflict, on the one hand, and of a community of interests, on the other" (1997: 3, original emphasis). The significance of this paradigmatic thinking is that intellectual representation of the other, the subaltern, ethnicity, class, or what not, should be premised on an awareness that class and ethnicity are ways of "thinking the political." There is also the implication of deploying such concepts, especially when the people they come to study also use them. Without this awareness, a blind use of these concepts, especially propelled by the postcolonial instinct of "resistance," could very well misread what happens on the ground. Bourdieu's warning is apt: "When the dominated quest for distinction leads the dominated to affirm what distinguishes them, . . . do we have to talk of resistance? . . . when, on the other hand, the dominated work at destroying what marks them, . . . is this submission?" (1990: 155).

MONGOLIAN CLASS NATIONALISM:
DOUBLE BOUNDARIES?

Inner Mongolia was a loose administrative unit created as a result of the Manchu conquest of the Mongols in the seventeenth century. It was one part of the "geo-body" of historical Mongolia, the other being Outer Mongolia. Inner Mongolia, by its very name, connotes internal and direct administration by the Qing dynasty. Nevertheless, Mongols in Inner Mongolia enjoyed a significant degree of autonomy and were political allies of the Manchus, an alliance consolidated through imperial marriages (cf. Rawski 1991; Zhang Jie 1997), thanks to the meritorious service of the Mongols in helping the Manchus to conquer China. As increasing numbers of Chinese migrated to Inner Mongolia to reclaim pasture for cultivation, in 1749 Emperor Qianlong ordered closure of the Mongolian border to Chinese immigrants in an effort to maintain Mongol purity and prowess. Nor would the Mongols be allowed to migrate to Chinese areas (Zhao 1994). However, the policy was not—perhaps could not have been—strictly enforced. Chinese peasants, especially famine refugees, continued to trickle in, encouraged by some Mongol nobles who employed them to cultivate land to increase the nobles' revenue. This started to transform the Mongolian land relations established by the Qing.

In the nineteenth century, banner nobles of various ranks owned *nutag*s, or pastures, and even ordinary Mongol subjects-cum-soldiers had their own smaller pastures for use, which were variously called *amiduralga-yin tariya* ("livelihood fields"), *erühe-yin tariya* ("family fields"), and so on (Wang 2000: 38). These lands, according to Qing law, could not be sold, but their use rights could be transferred. Regardless of their class status, it appeared that most Mongols leased their lands to Chinese peasants, thus becoming landlords (*tariya-yin ejen*) (Wang 2000: 61). And the ordinary Mongols constituted the majority of the landed class. Toward the end of the era of Manchu rule, the ethnic situation became increasingly complicated as a result of immigration and changing patterns of pastoralism and agriculture. Ironically, this Mongol practice of opening their land to Chinese peasants was challenged in 1902, when the crumbling Qing court decided to officially reclaim Mongol lands to pay for the Boxer Indemnity that resulted from the humiliating defeat in the hands of the Eight-Power Allied Forces in 1900. This policy abolished the earlier policy of immigration restraint, and a flood of Chinese peasants rushed into Inner Mongolia. By 1912, there were already 1.5 million Chinese—almost twice the population of Mongols, who numbered just over 800,000 (Song 1987: 50–62).

One fundamental change took place gradually: The Mongol princes-cum-landlords lost their rights to govern the Chinese tenants who settled on their land, as the Qing court and the subsequently established Republican Chinese government ruled that Chinese in Mongol banners would be administered by adjacent Chinese provinces and counties, rather than by the Mongol princes.

Eventually, administrations were set up within some banners to govern Chinese affairs, independent of the banner populations. Therefore, by the early twentieth century, numerous Chinese counties were set up in the territories of Mongol banners. As more Chinese flooded in, demand for land increased. Chinese land-dealers and earlier immigrants often rented their leased land to newcomers, usually at much higher prices. As a result, the beneficiaries of land transactions were usually not ordinary Mongols, not even the princes, but the original Chinese renters (Ba 1980). In other words, although the Chinese merchants and Chinese tenants had management rights, whereas Mongols, the proprietors, had the right to collect topsoil tax (known as Mongol tax, *mengzu*), the actual amount of taxes they collected was minimal because of the overwhelming power asymmetry. Profound social and economic changes took place, as more and more Mongols also started to settle down to cultivate land. Thus, apart from some banners to the north, most of eastern Inner Mongolia became overwhelmingly agricultural, and in the southern banners, ethnically mixed villages thrived. In western Inner Mongolia, lands along the fertile Tumed plain received the bulk of the Chinese immigrants. By 1949, while the Mongol population remained about the same as in 1912 because of wars and fertility decline due to spread of venereal diseases, the Chinese population increased to over five million (Song 1987: 54).

In other words, many of the complexities of communist-induced class/ethnicity struggles were already presaged by the long history of "ethnicity" leading up to socialism. Indeed, it was precisely this class/ethnic entanglement that triggered Mongol enthusiasm for national independence. In a sense, we do not need postcolonial theory to stress the significance of hybridity (Bhabha 1994a), when in fact hybridity, ethnic code-switching, and multiculturalism were all commonplace phenomena.

In this sense, we have a complex and hybrid social reality that renders difficult the definition of Inner Mongolia, specifically whether to view it as a colony or an internal colony. The declaration of independence of Outer Mongolia in 1911, and the subsequent establishment of the Mongolian People's Republic (MPR) with Soviet help in 1924, laid bare the logic that the other half of the historical Mongolia—Inner Mongolia—would have to be resolved in one way or another. However, Inner Mongolia was overrun by Chinese warlords; by 1928, the very name *Inner Mongolia* disappeared from the Chinese map. Between 1931 and 1945 the eastern part of the former Inner Mongolia came under Japanese sway, and the western part was controlled by Chinese Nationalist forces led by Fu Zuoyi. Under these circumstances, some Inner Mongolian nationalists saw their struggle as a national liberation movement; they projected Mongols as an oppressed small nation divided up, languishing under both Chinese and Japanese chauvinist and colonial rule. Mongol nationalists of various hues made numerous attempts, some pitting the Japanese against the Chinese, some vice versa, and some saw their only hope in linking up with the formally independent Mongolian People's Republic.

Chinese political forces at the time had, broadly speaking, two different attitudes toward Inner Mongolian nationalism split along ideological lines; the GMD, or the Chinese Nationalist Party, committed to Chinese nationalism and the unification of China, rejected all Mongolian demands for autonomy, let alone independence (cf. Jagchid 1999). The Chinese communists, locked in civil war with the GMD after 1927 and no less committed to Chinese nationalism and the unification of China, viewed sympathetically the Mongolian drive for autonomy, seeing Mongols as struggling against the same oppressive GMD regime that the communists sought to overthrow. Independence or freedom from oppression was viewed as just in communist ideology. At the end of the Long March, as the Red Army in Yan'an was squeezed between the GMD forces to the south, invading Japanese to the east, and threatening Muslims and Mongols to the north, ideological commitment and survival imperatives led Mao Zedong to make a declaration to the Inner Mongolian people in December 1935, on behalf of the central government of the Chinese Soviet People's Republic:

> We hold that it is only through a common struggle by ourselves and the nation of Inner Mongolia that we can rapidly defeat our common enemy—the Japanese imperialists and their running dog, Chiang Kaishek. At the same time, we are persuaded that only by fighting together with us can the Inner Mongolian nation preserve the glory of the epoch of Genghis Khan, avoid the extinction of their nation, embark on the path of national revival, and obtain independence and freedom like that enjoyed by the nations of Turkey, Poland, the Ukraine, and the Caucasus. (Schram, trans., 1999: 71)

Furthermore, Mao promised explicitly to return Inner Mongolia to the Mongols:

> We maintain that the six leagues, twenty-four sections, and forty-nine banners of Inner Mongolia, Chahar, the two sections of Tumute as well as the whole area of the three special banners in Ningxia, whether they have changed their status into *xian* or have been designated as grassland, should be returned to the Inner Mongolian people as part of their territory. The titles of the three administrative provinces of Re[he], Cha[har], and Sui[yuan] and their de facto administrative offices should be abolished. Under no circumstances should other nationalities be allowed to occupy the land of the Inner Mongolian nation or expropriate it under various excuses. (Schram, trans., 1999: 71)

Mao's statement was framed in terms of the "class nation" concept, viewing Mongols as a small, oppressed, colonized nation or people. As is well known, class, the central concern of Marxism and Leninism, was often appropriated to explain the hierarchy between different ethnic groups or racial groups. Imbued with this concern, the anticolonial liberation movement that gathered momentum from early in this century saw inequality between (ethnic) nations in class terms (cf. Duara, 1995).

In the Marxist-Leninist view endorsed by the CCP, class has its domestic and international forms. Domestically, a nation has its own dichotomous antagonistic classes, and internationally, a nation may also be viewed as a class. Actually, it was Li Dazhao, the co-founder of the CCP, who framed the most explicit notion of the Chinese nation as an oppressed proletariat as early as 1920, not slavishly following Marxist-Leninist categories (Meisner 1967: 188–94). However, class struggle for the CCP was a double-edged sword; it attacked foreign racial capitalists and imperialists, as well as militarists, bureaucrats, and land lords within the Chinese Nation, the intensity of each attack being determined by strategic machinations of the circumstances. Thus we may argue that the Chinese communist approach to non-Chinese nationalities before 1949 was deeply influenced by class-nation categories. The Mongols and other peoples were understood as oppressed and colonized nations, and they were promised self-determination as a way of achieving equality with the Chinese people. For the Chinese communists, Inner Mongolia was also a cultural-cum-national zone, somehow to be unified. Mao's 1935 declaration was perhaps the first Chinese communist political statement to define Inner Mongolia as a unified, homogenous, political, and national entity that cut across several provinces created under GMD rule. But there was a naïve conviction that Mongolian nationalist demands could be satisfied by simply dismantling the administrative structures—rooted, perhaps, in a lack of awareness of the social demographics. The overwhelming Chinese majority in Inner Mongolia was not addressed at all. This recognition of the Mongols' "subaltern" nation status was indeed the foundation for Mongol communists to work with Chinese communists to assure that they would deliver on their promises.

After the Soviet-Mongolian declaration of war against Japan in August 1945, Ulanhu, a Mongol communist, played a major leadership role in securing CCP victory in Inner Mongolia. He took the initiative to set up and lead an "Association of the Inner Mongolia Autonomous Movement" (*Nei Menggu zizhi yundong lianhehui*), a semi-party, semi-administrative entity cross-cutting the Chinese provinces with substantial Mongol populations, in an effort to provide a unified leadership to the Mongol autonomous movements.

Meanwhile, Mongols in eastern Inner Mongolia set up their own Eastern Mongolia Autonomous Government immediately after the Japanese surrender. Led by Mongol nationalists who viewed eastern Inner Mongolia as having been colonized by Japanese forces, and therefore cut off from both the MPR and the western part of Inner Mongolia that was subsumed under the Chinese provinces of Suiyuan, Gansu, and Ningxia, they aspired not only to unify Inner Mongolia, but also to join up with the MPR. The Eastern Mongolia Autonomous Government was led by a resurrected Inner Mongolia People's Revolutionary Party (IMPRP). Despite its nationalist tendency, the Eastern Mongolia Autonomous Government and its army were, however, also heavily controlled by the Chinese communists from the CCP Northeast Bureau in Manchuria (cf. Batubagan and Altanochir 1999).

There is no space to discuss the complicated process whereby the two groups came to work together for a unified Inner Mongolia or the strategic considerations the CCP took in supporting an "autonomous" Inner Mongolian government, rather than full-fledged independence. What I want to point out is that the founding of the "Inner Mongolia Autonomous Government," led by Ulanhu under the auspices of the CCP, in May 1947 raised a number of important questions—above all, to what extent was the "autonomous government" autonomous? Would it be led by the Mongols through their own party or would it be led by the Chinese Communist Party? The latter course at once posed issues of class and ethnicity, for the CCP was a purportedly Chinese proletarian class party that also claimed to represent the Chinese nation. But where was an Inner Mongolian proletariat to be found in a population of herders, peasants, and monks? Could the few Mongol members of the Chinese Communist Party represent the Mongol masses? These questions pervaded the debates and intrigues between two rival Mongolian factions that negotiated Inner Mongolian autonomy between 1946 and 1947.

Communism as an ideology was compelling to many who held what I call a "double class" view—that not only was there a class division within a nation, but that international relations could also be best grasped in class terms. The oppressor class within the oppressor nation was responsible for oppressing the smaller nationality, but the oppressor class of the smaller nationality would collaborate with the oppressor class of the bigger nationality. In such a case, ordinary Mongols were victims of both Mongol oppressors and Chinese oppressors, but the Mongol oppressor class was no match for the Chinese oppressor. Therefore, the smaller nation could initially be treated as undifferentiated and freed from the collective oppression of the bigger nation. Once that "autonomy" was achieved, the oppressor elements of the society would have to be eliminated. The correct interethnic or internationality relations, after the socialist victory, envisaged by Ulanhu, hinged on eliminating the oppressor classes of both Mongol and Chinese.

This vision led Ulanhu to conclude that the leading force of the Inner Mongolian revolution must be the Chinese Communist Party, which he joined in 1925, becoming by 1945 an alternative member of its Central Committee, the Party's highest-ranking minority official. Only through what he believed to be a nonethnic party, with its professed compassion for oppressed peoples, would it be possible to sort out the internationality conflicts or differences between Mongols and Chinese. Through this example, we can see the efficacy of communist ideology, as it had colonized the consciousness of some Mongol leaders such as Ulanhu, as Comaroff and Comaroff (1992) would say.

Ulanhu's insistence on this bifocal ideological boundary was challenged by the IMPRP leaders, but they proved no match for him and the CCP. The

IMPRP, as the leading party of this land, was an ethnic party that traced its origins to the 1920s, its membership open only to Mongols. The IMPRP leaders had two concerns: First, the social structure of Inner Mongols lacked a proletarian class. Therefore, IMPRP leaders concluded, there was no need for the CCP, whose real agenda concerned the industrial working class. Second, the IMPRP leaders viewed the CCP as a Chinese party. In fact, some even considered Ulanhu not a Mongol at all but rather a Chinese agent sent by the CCP to cheat Mongols, for Ulanhu was still known by his Chinese name, Yun Ze, at that time, and, like many assimilated Tumed Mongols, he could not speak Mongolian (see memoirs in Batubagan and Altanochir 1999).

The IMPRP leaders were thus crystal clear on the ethnic boundary: Mongol versus Chinese. But they remained ambiguous about the internal boundary— that is, the question of class divisions among Mongols. Class divisions among Chinese in Inner Mongolia were no concern to them either. Ulanhu insisted that class exploitation in the Inner Mongolian social structure warranted a radical revolutionary party such as the CCP to carry out democratic revolution to eliminate internal exploitation. Finally, Ulanhu won the debate, and in May 1947 an Inner Mongolia Autonomous Government (with jurisdiction limited to eastern Inner Mongolia) was founded, with Ulanhu as its chairman and military commander, as well as the general secretary of the Inner Mongolia Communist Party Work Committee.[1]

An interesting paradox can be discerned in Ulanhu's class-nation discourse. In order to justify his own power base—that is, the communist leadership—he *exaggerated* the Mongols' internal class conflict and emphasized their common interests with the CCP. We can say that Ulanhu's emphasis on class struggle helped to integrate Inner Mongolia into the new Communist Chinese state through a subaltern discourse of shared interests. But this simultaneously rendered "liberation" ironic and continued emphasis on ethnicity meaningless and, moreover, reactionary.[2]

Retrospectively, the triumph of Ulanhu's new class-nation discourse had two consequences: First, by de-emphasizing the Chinese colonialism that he had long fought against, he rendered Inner Mongolia an internal colony of China. To be sure, as Ulanhu saw it, the need for CCP rule was justified in terms of liberating Inner Mongolia from the colonial oppression of the GMD. But in so doing, he obscured the ethnic complexity of Inner Mongolia, thus fundamentally misrepresenting the nature of the Inner Mongolian polity, so that what resulted was not *minzu zhengquan* (nationality polity) but rather *minzu lianhe zhengquan* (joint nationality polity).[3] Although he should be credited for placing Mongols in positions of high authority, nonetheless, the Inner Mongolia Autonomous Government was no longer a vehicle for an autonomous Mongolian political system. In other words, Ulanhu clearly recognized and went about trying in his own way to address ethnic issues, by building a powerful Mongol component at all levels of officialdom, but his efforts were greatly handicapped by the political framing for which he was partially responsible, one that ruled out a genuine "autonomous" Mongolian political system. Under such a system, the equality that Mongols demanded from the Chinese now became a time bomb that could explode in their faces, for in the newly established Inner Mongolia Autonomous Region, Chinese had to be granted the same status as Mongols. Moreover, Chinese had to be given proper political representation, so that Mongols could not be charged with reverse colonialism, or even with what Arif Dirlik (1987) calls cultural hegemony.[4] Second, Ulanhu's emphasis on internal class antagonism, as opposed to the earlier stance that the Mongols collectively constituted a class-nation, thus warranting autonomy, left Inner Mongolia ill-prepared for the large scale violence in the subsequent "class struggle" land reform.

LAND REFORM IN 1947–1948: BLURRING BOUNDARIES

One of the distinctive features of Inner Mongolian ethnopolitics was the centrality of Ulanhu in all struggles. In a sense, the unusual developments in Inner Mongolia were personified in the diverse interests he attempted to negotiate or compromise in the creation of this new socialist Inner Mongolia. The complexity of the situation is magnified by Ulanhu's own sinicized "Mongolness," as he tried to represent the ethnic nation and his own socialist views as well. Here, I do not wish to privilege the voice of Ulanhu. His was only one among many, but, as the paramount leader of the Mongols after 1947, his opinion carried significant weight. Even there, his voice was never consistent, constantly shifting to define a position against the dominant yet often conflicting voices from the Party central leadership.

The Inner Mongolia Autonomous Government was far from "autonomous." A year before the founding of the autonomous government, eastern Inner Mongolia was already under the communist sway. In some areas, moderate land reform, in the form of settling accounts and rent reduction, began to develop under the CCP's Directive Concerning Land Reform, May 4, 1946 (cf. Selden 1979: 208–14). This immediately posed questions of ethnic relations, given the land tenure situation, including the question of whether the land reform movement should be carried out jointly by Mongols and Chinese or separately by nationality. Ulanhu, in his August 1, 1946, telegram to the CCP Central Committee about the Inner Mongolian land question, noted that Inner Mongolia had three regions: agricultural, mixed agricultural and pastoral, and pastoral. The agricultural region was concentrated in Jo'uda and Josotu leagues in eastern Inner Mongolia and the Tumed banners in Suiyuan province. He noted that the agricultural region was ethnically mixed, with Mongols in the minority:

> Large numbers of Chinese have already obtained land or land rights from Mongols for various reasons and by various means. Therefore, in the same region, the number

of Mongol landlords is far smaller than those of Chinese landlords. The Mongol landlords are simultaneously princes or nobles or bureaucrats, and the majority are Mongolian traitors and despots. Few Mongol peasants have no land, but their land is scarce or poor. The Mongol landlords do not rent their land to Mongols, but mostly to Chinese; Mongols, even though not landlords, rent their land to Chinese for cultivation. In the four banners of eastern Suiyuan, over 80% of the 7,000 Mongols rent their land to Chinese, and they don't cultivate themselves. (Ulanhu 1991: 1057)

Ulanhu further noted that each Mongol banner and monastery had "common land": "The sovereign rights (*zhuquan*) over these lands belong to the Mongols, but the lands are cultivated by Chinese; some lands are rented to Chinese through Chinese *er dizhu* (secondary landlords or land dealers)" (Ulanhu 1991: 1057). Therefore, he stressed that in the agricultural region, particular attention should be paid to ethnic relations and land rights questions.

Of particular interest is Ulanhu's insistence that all lands in Inner Mongolia belonged to the Mongols collectively. Therefore, the land of the Mongol landlords and despots could be redistributed to both Mongols and Chinese, but the latter must continue to "rent," not own, the land because the land belonged to the Mongols collectively. This was probably Ulanhu's initiative, an understanding premised on ethnicity. Chinese tenants, then, should "pay the lowest rent to the banner governments for the purpose of protecting Mongol land rights." As for the ordinary Mongols who rented land to Chinese, their land would not be redistributed or the rent be reduced. No land redistribution was advised for pastoral and mixed agricultural and pastoral regions. The Central Committee soon replied that it did not know the local situation and entrusted Ulanhu to use his own discretion. However, measures to provide protection to Mongols' interests were quickly swept away.

Soon after the founding of the Inner Mongolia Autonomous Government, the CCP and the GMD forces went into all-out civil war. The 1947–1948 engagement between the two forces in Manchuria was crucial to China's fate. The CCP designated the territory under the jurisdiction of the Inner Mongolia Autonomous Government as a "liberated region" (*jiefangqu*). It was during this period that the CCP's Land Reform Law (October 1947) was issued, calling for all-out land reform. The Inner Mongolia Autonomous Government, led by Ulanhu and the Inner Mongolian Communist Party Work Committee (subordinate to the Northeast Bureau of the CCP), fully implemented the 1947 Land Reform Law. Ulanhu, whether carried away by revolutionary enthusiasm or under pressure from the CCP, sought to thoroughly eradicate "feudalism" and distribute land in agricultural regions, directed by the slogan "land to the tiller." According to a retrospective account written more than forty years later by Liu Chun, Ulanhu's main Chinese assistant who led the land reform in Inner Mongolia, Ulanhu was also responsible for implementing a "leftist" policy in the pastoral region.

Ulanhu stated that "[t]he pastoral region will also exterminate feudalism."
Everyone in the leadership circle agreed with this suggestion (Liu 1993: 132–
33). Of course, that was precisely what the 1947 law demanded! We do not know
to what degree Liu may have wished, writing in the 1990s, to distance himself
from the leftist policy by attributing everything to Ulanhu. Whoever was responsible, we know that in the Mongol pastoral region, land reform took the form of
division of animals among poor herders, according to the slogans "livestock to
the herders" and "exterminate feudalism." In the pastoral region, livestock and
pastures of rich herders were distributed to individual herding households (but
with disastrous consequences, as the reduced size meant destruction of the reproductive capacity of the herd). Land in the agricultural region would be distributed equally to individual households, regardless of ethnic origin. "Mongol Tax"
(*mengzu*), paid by Chinese tenants to Mongol land proprietors, was abolished.
This was largely an ethnic-blind approach, whereby everybody would be treated
equally and fairly in terms of shares of land.

Land reform was, however, not just a matter of equalizing landholdings and
transforming social relationships involving class and ethnicity. It was also a
means of consolidating the revolutionary regime in the midst of civil war. In
Manchuria, land reform was an instrument for eliminating the social bases of
Japanese collaborators and GMD supporters, thus the class principle and the ethnic principle were fused in the movement. Land reform in Manchuria, from the
Chinese point of view, had a de-colonizing connotation; land belonging to local
bullies, traitors, and landlords, many of whom were associated with Japanese rule,
was redistributed to landless and land-poor peasants. Thus, land reform was welcomed not only by the Chinese rural poor, but also by agrarian ethnic minorities
such as the Koreans, many of whom had migrated to the area under Japanese
colonial rule (Olivier 1993: 55–57). The peasants who newly attained land
became staunch supporters of the CCP in its engagement with the GMD.

Since eastern Inner Mongolia had once been part Manchuguo, the de-colonizing agenda of the 1947–1948 land reform inevitably affected the Mongols. In
the Mongol area of Manchuguo, the Japanese had carried out a policy of "help
the Mongols and curb the Chinese" (*Fu Meng Yi Han*). The majority of nationalist leaders of the Eastern Mongolia Autonomous Government set up in 1946,
who were co-opted into the Inner Mongolia Autonomous Government, had
been former high civilian or military officials of the four Mongol provinces (later
to be called leagues in Inner Mongolia) of Japanese-controlled Manchuguo.
They included Buyanmandakh, leader of the new Inner Mongolian Congress
(*canyihui*), the former governor-general of four Mongolian Hingan provinces
under Manchuguo. Even Hafenga, the most popular, left-leaning leader of the
eastern Mongols, had once served in the Manchuguo embassy in Tokyo. These
people were Mongol nationalists who fought for Inner Mongolian independence
or autonomy, independent of Ulanhu's group. However, since land reform
sought to resolve the peasant problem by outright expropriation of land held by

landlords and "feudal" institutions, most of the top Mongol leaders, in the new class analysis, were vulnerable not only as traitors (having served the Japanese, despite later joining the resistance), but also as landlords and feudal elements who were the direct objects of struggle targeted by land reform. Struggle against former Mongol rulers who had served the Japanese (or the GMD) and expropriation of Mongol landlords' land became revolutionary priorities at the height of land reform. The violence was apparently so great that without "protection," the top Mongol officials could have perished (Ulanhu 1967 [1965]).

Violence during land reform in Inner Mongolia took two forms: interethnic and intra-Mongol. In the ethnically mixed agricultural region, land reform cadres used various means to spur people to violence. For example, a Party directive, published on December 21, 1947, for guiding the mass struggle to eliminate feudalism in a banner of the Hingan League explained,

[A]t the beginning of the movement, *we did not emphasize policies,* instead we used the method of igniting fires, used the simple slogans of redressing injustice and taking revenge to mobilize the masses, encouraging the masses to mobilize in the extreme hatred and demand for immediate practical interests. This is right. In the near future, we will continue to do this in newly opened up and half opened up areas. (Nei Menggu Gongchandang 1993: 30, emphasis added)

The same directive divided the population into several categories: despotic landlords and worst feudal force, ordinary landlords and not-so-bad nobles, despotic rich peasants, ordinary rich peasants, middle peasants, merchants, running dogs, rascals, bad cadres, GMD spies and other political criminals, and so on. It prescribed various measures to punish different categories of people and condoned killing the accused, if so demanded by "the masses." As this directive suggests, there were no specific ethnically based policies. Indeed, Party directives condemned the view that Mongols had no classes.

In ethnically mixed agricultural areas, violence was frequently ethnic in nature—specifically, Chinese tenants against struggling Mongol land owners. On July 30, 1948, in a report to a meeting of Inner Mongolian cadres, Ulanhu summed up the "left" deviations during the land reform:

[We] did not specify the struggle targets in the villages during the land reform according to the actual situation of Inner Mongolia, we did not designate classes according to the concrete situation of the Inner Mongolian economy. For instance, Mongol peasants are backward in agricultural work; it is not easy for them to rise to be rich peasants, so they should not have been struggled; Mongols have been forced to abandon pastoral economy and take up agriculture, and not knowing how to grow crops and for other reasons, they rented their family fields (*hukou di*), livelihood fields (*shengji di*). Those small landlords who retained lands should not have been struggled, either. As for the Mongol middle peasants, they were very few, so they should have received special attention and their interests should never have been violated, but in our struggle, we did not distinguish landlords from rich peasants, and in many areas we infringed upon the middle peasants. . . . therefore, before deviations were corrected, the scope of those struggled was very broad, averaging 20.8% of households and 25.6% of the population. (1987: 16–17)

In other words, as much as a quarter of the Mongols in agricultural areas were struggled against. Ulanhu further pointed out that excessive killings had taken place:

There was beating whenever struggle took place, and too many people were killed. This is a serious mistake; we should learn this lesson well. In Hingan, Non-Muren and Hulunbuir leagues, after mass work was launched, altogether 2,222 people (including some bandits and restoration army soldiers) were killed, the majority in equal land distribution campaign. In other areas the situation was worse. In Qiqihar village, 28 people were killed, constituting 1.2% of the population, and 248 people or 2.6% of the population were killed in Durbenshin of Jaraid banner. (1987: 17)

Nonetheless, although a more lenient policy was urged, land reform in agricultural areas of eastern Inner Mongolia was already a fait accompli. Land had been equally distributed to both Mongols and Chinese. Although the "Mongol minzu" still publicly owned (gongyou quan) the land, Mongols and Chinese had "ownership rights" (suoyou quan) to their individual pieces of land. Accordingly, Chinese were no longer required to pay any "Mongol Tax," but "they have equal obligations and citizen responsibility toward the Autonomous Government as Mongols" (Ulanhu 1987: 15).

It is interesting to note how land reform led Mongol peasants not only to struggle against Mongol landlords, but also to voluntarily give up lands to Chinese settlers. On July 22, 1948, at the same meeting that sought to correct left deviations, Song Zhending, a Chinese Party secretary serving in a Mongol banner reporting on the land reform in Hingan, noted the intense "class" consciousness of the Mongol peasants, which he disingenuously attributed it to their "simple mind":

1. They [the Mongol peasants] did not start immediately after the movement began, as they did not trust our policies. But after being mobilized, they were more radical than the Chinese. The Chinese were easy to mobilize, but it is difficult to build momentum among them. The Mongols were more difficult to mobilize, but once mobilized, they would not hesitate, and their action would spare no one's feelings. . . . 4. They [the Mongol peasants] tend to be emotional and retaliatory, this is also due to heavy oppression and their simplicity. (1993: 44–45)

Song reported that before the 1947 land reform, Inner Mongolian cadres were attentive to ethnic relations in ethnically mixed regions where Mongol landlords had many Chinese tenants. There was an explicit policy prohibiting division of

Mongol land and Chinese struggle against Mongol landlords. However, once land reform began in 1947, the earlier policy was reversed. The seizure and distribution of Mongol land were portrayed in Chinese documents as voluntary renunciation by Mongols who had gained higher communist consciousness:

> We [land reform cadres] originally decided that Mongols retained ownership rights even if their land was divided, and the Chinese should pay Mongol tax, one *sheng* (= litre of grain), two *shengs* or three *shengs* for one *shang* (= 15 *mu*) land according to the quality of land. This provoked discussion among Mongol peasants who wondered if Chinese here (in ethnically mixed regions) did not have ownership rights: what would happen to [us] Mongols if we [Mongol peasants] were not to be allocated land in predominantly Chinese counties? Since Mongol tenants elsewhere [in Chinese counties] were given land, here too the Chinese and Mongols should be treated equally. (Song 1993: 45–46)

The uncanny fact was that there were few such Mongol tenants in predominantly Chinese counties. Violence was not confined to agricultural regions. Land reform in the pastoral region did not involve distributing land to the Chinese, since few Chinese lived there, but intraethnic conflict in that area developed an international dimension. Since class labeling was introduced in accordance with the number of animals one possessed, rich Mongols, in order to avoid being labeled "herdlords" (hence feudal elements), both distributed animals to relatives and subordinates and slaughtered animals en masse. A herdlord risked not only confiscation of property but physical elimination. Poor Mongols, who had been allocated animals, were fearful that their share would put them into the category of herdlord and thus consumed as many animals as possible. Within a very short time, not only were some among the Mongol elite killed by the poor, but there was a catastrophic loss of animals.[5] Some herdlords put up stiff resistance, and others even rebelled, but they were put down by the Inner Mongolia Autonomous Government army. In February 1948, open rebellion broke out in Ulaanmod *nutag* in Hingan League, in which more than two hundred rebels killed land reform cadres and attempted to flee to the MPR with many followers and horses. The rebellion was brutally suppressed (Sun 1993). The violence in Inner Mongolia was so great that the MPR leadership expressed concern. The CCP central leadership also feared that continued ethnic violence might jeopardize the stability of Inner Mongolia (Liu 1993: 138).

The gravity of the Inner Mongolian land reform fiasco is evident from the belated self-criticism issued on June 23, 1949, from the Northeast Bureau of the Chinese Communist Party, which oversaw the land reform in Inner Mongolia. The document admitted the severe consequences for failure to distinguish Mongols from Chinese, mechanically applying Chinese practices to the Mongol areas in Chahar, Rehe, and northeastern provinces:

> Not a few Mongol cadres have been attacked and discriminated. In the agricultural area, in addition to usual leftist mistakes, most of the monasteries have been

destroyed, and even worshipping Buddha was prohibited. Even speaking Mongolian in the army was cursed as "asses braying." In the pure and semi-agricultural-semi-pastoral areas, the pastoral economy has suffered severe damages; most of the horses, cattle and sheep have been divided up, killed and eaten at will, leading to great casualties. Most of the monasteries have also been destroyed. All these have caused wide-spread resentment among the Mongol masses at all strata. (Dongbeiju 1991: 1249)

The self-criticism suggested that

In the future, *the central problem in the Mongolian area is to educate the cadres to under-stand nationality policy (minzu zhengce), to train new Mongolian cadres, to understand different policies that distinguish different regions* (agricultural, semi-agricultural-semi-pastoral, pure pastoral), and to understand that in the Mongolian area a more cautious and steady principle has to be adopted, and only a gradual democratic policy be implemented. (Dongbeiju 1991: 1249, emphasis added)

The necessity for such measures was not only to restore and develop pastoral and agricultural production. It is especially interesting to note the concern over the instability of the Mongolian army: "we should also be specially attentive to stabilizing the Mongolian army" (Dongbeiju 1991: 1249).

As part of the rectification seeking to redress problems associated with land reform, Ulanhu urgently assessed the Inner Mongolian situation. Before the meeting of high cadres of Inner Mongolia held in Harbin in July–August 1948, in light of the rebellion in Ulaanmod, Ulanhu had already called for a halt of reform in the pastoral region and pressed for a policy of "Three Nos and Two Benefits" (*san bu liang li*) for Inner Mongolia (Liu 1989, Baoyinbatu 1993). He proposed that in the pastoral region there should be no property distribution, no class labeling, and no class struggle. Herdlords (*muzhu*) and their herd workers (*mugong*) were regarded as symbiotic, with each benefiting the other (cf. Zhao 1998). According to Liu Chun, Ulanhu also proposed to add a phrase "help the poor herdsmen" (*fuzhu pingku mumin*)—that is, independent herders who were different from herd workers (Liu 1989: 109). This policy was made official in the Harbin conference.

This was not a rectification that endorsed the national Land Law and only blamed deviations, but an explicit statement that the law was not applicable among pastoral Mongols. Ulanhu thus introduced a new boundary. The Chinese method, drawing on the experience of agrarian China, was not to be applied in the pastoral areas (but it was implemented in agrarian regions) of Inner Mongolia because Chinese agrarian relations differed fundamentally from Mongolian pastoral ones. Therefore, apart from the princes and high lamas who were to be stripped of their privileges, the animal-rich Mongols, or so-called herdlords, were redefined as different from Chinese landlords. Herdsmen who worked for them were neither serfs nor slaves but salaried workers (*mugong*); in a word, these herd-lords were to be treated as national capitalists—that is, as progressive elements.[6]

Although no effort was made to stop land division in ethnically mixed agricultural regions, as land had already been equally divided up, measures were adopted to prevent Chinese peasants from further struggling against Mongol landlords. Mongol peasants, however, were allowed to participate in struggle sessions against Chinese landlords and bullies in agrarian areas (Hao 1997: 575).

It was indeed ironic that ideological unity meant ethnic division, for unrestrained class struggle eventually developed into national confrontation once again. It was also ironic that Mongols, once in a communist regime, came to be seen not as an oppressed small nation, an argument that initially won them a putative autonomy; instead, as the case in ethnically mixed agricultural areas showed, internal class relations were prioritized. Hence, many Mongols became targets of class struggle. I do not say that there was a deliberate policy on the part of Chinese communists to discriminate against the Mongols; rather, there was no policy that differentiated ethnicity.

THE "PEACEFUL" LAND REFORM: THE POLITICS OF DIFFERENCE

Demarcating Inner Mongolian territorial boundaries for the purpose of autonomy, winning the relative autonomy of Mongol herdsmen from the Chinese universalizing class struggle in land reform, and prevention of Chinese peasants from struggling against Mongol "landlords" all rested on the discourse of group difference, as well as on a revived subaltern identity. Taking advantage of conflict between class theory and practice with regard to ethnicity, Inner Mongolian communist officialdom succeeded in framing a strategy in which Mongols, especially pastoral Mongols, the symbolic center of Mongol identity, were recognized as a distinctive culture that warranted a boundary. This continued as a valid argument that Chinese leaders were prepared to accept, not only because their universalized land reform and class struggle had produced great "deviations," which Mao and other leaders came to deplore, but also because Inner Mongols, as a role model for soliciting support from other ethnic minorities in China and/or incorporation in a future "unified China," had to be treated leniently. Ulanhu's Three Nos policy achieved national status, becoming CCP policy in minority pastoral regions after the founding of the People's Republic of China.[7]

Should we then be optimistic about the limited but hard-won "nationality policy" in China? At stake is not only a theoretical issue, but direct responsibility for the subsequent majority backlash that cost Inner Mongolians their limited autonomy. I have already examined the process whereby the politics of difference had become a defining principle of Ulanhu's effort to draw boundaries to protect Inner Mongolian autonomy. This is not the end of the story, unfortunately. As long as the universalizing principle occupies the hegemonic position, the politics of difference will inevitably be criticized as the politics of privilege. In the West, conventional liberal democracy condemns minority rights as not only violating the principle of equality and citizenship but also undermining the stability of the nation-state. The rigid principle of conventional democracy and the movement for cultural recognition has produced an impasse. We need to examine further twists of this politics of difference in an escalating milieu of class struggle that came to define the essence of Maoism.

Land tenure was one critical dimension of the Chinese–Mongol relationship, as noted. As the Inner Mongolia Autonomous Region was established in the eastern part of Inner Mongolia, western Inner Mongolia, formerly colonized by Chinese warlords, continued to exist as a Chinese province—Suiyuan—until 1954. We can look at it a bit more closely, especially the Tumed region in Suiyuan.

Eastern Inner Mongolia had already gone through land reform before 1949, and the pastoral region in western Inner Mongolia followed the Three Nos policy until the 1960s. The Tumed region, as a part of the agricultural areas of Suiyuan province, underwent a "peaceful" land reform only in 1951, but that reform was resented by both Mongols and Chinese. The situation was complicated by Ulanhu, who had a personal stake there. He was not only a native of the Tumed, he was also born into a rich peasant family. The Tumed case was important as well because the banner is in the suburb of Hohhot, later to become the capital of a unified Inner Mongolia Autonomous Region, and political conflict there would produce reverberations in the capital and beyond.

Nationality policy was certainly a powerful weapon in the hands of Mongol officials once it was made a national policy. In 1951, even before Suiyuan province was returned to Inner Mongolia, Ulanhu, as China's leading minority official, managed to push and pass two documents specifically relating to land reform in purely agricultural Mongol banners in Suiyuan province.[8] Following the policy in the documents, Mongols were entitled to possess twice as much land as Chinese. Different criteria were also used to determine class status among Mongol peasants. Their class status would be determined exclusively by the volume of exploitation, rather than the amount of land owned. This was specified in articles 3 and 4 of the land law for Suiyuan Mongolian banners:

Article 3. Because the Mongols are in the midst of the transition from pastoralism to agriculture, because they still lack familiarity with agricultural production and productive skills, and because cultivation of their land depended previously on renting, so in classifying Mongols, land renters should be treated differently in accordance with their land holdings, exploitative income, and standard of living.

Article 4. Because the Mongols rent out land, in consideration of their special situation of being unable to collect land rent or to collect only low rent, classification should be based on their actual exploitative income.[9]

Ann Anagnost, in recasting "speaking bitterness narratives" in China, evokes Arif Dirlik's analysis of Mao's conceptualization of class located within hierarchies of power, "especially in terms of relations of exploitation," rather than "in their relationship to the means of production" (1997: 30). It appears in Inner Mongolia that the Chinese emphasized the means of production and that Mongols were land owners; Mongols, on the other hand, insisted that they were land owners in name, since Suiyuan was controlled by Chinese warlords, and seven counties were set up on the Mongolian banner territory. In fact, many Mongols were reduced to begging from their Chinese peasant-tenants.

In accordance with this reasoning, the Mongols' class status was consequently set one rung lower than that of Chinese with similar class statuses. Moreover, even if they rented out their land or employed hired hands, if their living standard was no higher than that of a Chinese middle peasant, they should be treated as "small renters" (*xiao tudi chuzu zhe*), not as "small landlords" (*xiao dizhu*). Consequently, their land would not be confiscated. Landless or poor Mongols would also be given twice as much land as Chinese in order to make up for their low-level farming skills. The measure effectively preempted an earlier yardstick, under which 20 percent of Mongols would have been classified as landlords and many more as rich peasants (Su and Zhang 1989: 117). Instead, of a total of 4,461 Mongol households (18,383 individuals) in six counties in western Suiyuan, the Tumed banner and four counties in eastern Suiyuan, and the Urad Front banner, which were subjected to land reform in Suiyuan province, 240 households (5.4 percent of the total) and 1,344 individuals (7.3 percent of the total) were classified as landlords, while 94.6 percent of households and 92.7 percent of the individuals were classified as tenants, poor peasants, middle peasants, and small renters. The percentage of landlord and rich peasant households and individuals appears to be substantially lower than the average of 8 percent of households and 10 percent of individuals for China, the cap set during the 1947–1948 land reform (Chinggeletu 1992: 26).

As can be seen, the achievement of Mongol dominance in Inner Mongolia resulted from a politics of difference based on a critique of Chinese discrimination, as well as on a reassertion of their subaltern status. This process conforms to Charles Taylor's cogent argument:

> The politics of difference grows organically out of the politics of universal dignity. . . . Where the politics of universal dignity fought for forms of non-discrimination that were quite "blind" to the ways in which citizens differ, the politics of difference often redefines non-discrimination as requiring that we make these distinctions the basis of differential treatment. (1994: 40)

Such "reverse discrimination measures," Taylor continues, have "been justified on the grounds that historical discrimination has created a pattern within which the unfavored struggle at a disadvantage. Reverse discrimination is defended as a temporary measure that will eventually level the playing field and allow the old 'blind' rules to come back into force in a way that doesn't disadvantage anyone" (1994: 40).

This new approach achieved several purposes. It made land available to Chinese tenants, hired laborers, and the land poor generally. Moreover, separate criteria of class designation avoided a situation of branding huge numbers of Mongols as landlords, so making the reality congruent with the earlier communist class-nationality principle, whereby ethnic minorities are viewed as oppressed and exploited by the majority. The rationale for granting more land to the Tumed Mongols was to elevate their "economic" status so that they could be equal to the Chinese in other arenas. This was what Mongols "gained" in the land reform in Suiyuan in 1951. However, neither Mongols nor Chinese were satisfied with the outcome. Mongols were unhappy because they lost most of the land that was historically theirs, and most saw their living standard fall. The Chinese were unhappy because they thought it unfair not only that they received smaller portions and usually poorer land, but also that the Mongols' class status was improved in an ideological sense—that is, lowered. Neither group saw the outcomes as embodying social justice.

Before the peasants began to enjoy their newly obtained private land, the individual landholdings were deemed unhelpful to the large-scale economic development that the emerging socialist China embarked on. Peasants were encouraged to form Elementary Agricultural Producers' Cooperatives (*chuji she*), in the ethnically mixed Tumed region. This meant that some Mongols could not form single-ethnic cooperatives and were required to form "nationality united cooperatives" (*minzu lianhe she*). In 1955, in what was then the Tumed banner (now Tumed East banner), 131 cooperatives were organized, of which only 1 was a pure Mongol cooperative, and 6 were Mongol-Chinese united cooperatives. By April 1956, 91.3 percent of Tumed banner peasant households had joined elementary or advanced cooperatives, of which 7 were pure Mongol and 293 mixed (Tumote 1987: 207). In these united cooperatives, each member was paid a dividend, according to his or her labor and individual contribution of assets (*gufen*), such as land, agricultural tools, and animals. In this way, by virtue of contributing double pieces of land, most Mongols received greater dividends than Chinese, at least those whose labor input was rated equal or nearly so. This practice angered the Chinese members, who were not only in the majority, but were also the main and the most skilled labor force in the agricultural cooperatives. They complained that Mongols exploited their blood and sweat money (*xue han qian*). Consequently, Chinese in the Tumed banner clamored to oust Mongols from the cooperatives. After 1956, with the introduction of the Advanced Agricultural Producers Cooperatives (*gaoji she*), income was no longer determined by both labor and assets invested in the cooperatives but exclusively on the basis of labor. Mongols were quickly impoverished, due largely to their lack of labor power, because not only did they have smaller families than the

Chinese, but many male adults were lost in the war. For instance, of thirty-seven Mongol households in Yunfeng cooperative of Bichechi township, twenty-two households saw their income reduced in the shift to advanced cooperatives (collectives) (Tumote 1987: 238). The drop in income was easily measured, because in November 1953, the state set three fixed targets for cooperative members and private peasants—that is, fixed production, fixed purchase, and fixed marketing, a kind of responsibility system. Many Mongols could not meet those targets, so their income dropped. Feeling deprived, many Mongols sought to quit the cooperatives and attempted to reclaim the land they had invested.

The response of the Mongol-dominated Tumed banner party committee was a program of land compensation (*tudi baochou*) to make up for the drop in income in Mongolian-Chinese joint cooperatives "so as to prevent those Mongol cooperative members from reduction of income from now on, and may even increase their income." Issued on April 1, 1957, the program specified that in joint cooperatives where Mongols were in the minority, according to their actual income drop, they could be given extra land that yielded no more than 30 percent of the income set in accordance with the state's three fixed targets (Tumote 1987: 238–39). But the program was never fully implemented. In 1959, as the anti-rightist movement swept in, not only were Mongols forced to "voluntarily" give up their land compensation, their grievances were also criticized as manifestations of "local nationalism" (Tumote 1987: 239–40). Then, in 1962, in the heyday of liberalization after the catastrophe of the Great Leap Forward and the virtual collapse of many communes, as pressure mounted from Tumed Mongols for land compensation, the banner party committee proposed reintroducing private plots, long eliminated in the collectivization drive, to substitute for the land compensation. Giving peasants private plots was a policy made by the state in 1959, in light of decreasing production of pigs as a result of communization. Inner Mongolia did not implement it until 1961. Apparently, the Tumed case was so special that in February 1963 the Inner Mongolia party committee and government headed by Ulanhu adopted a special measure to double the standard private plot allowance (5 percent) to the Tumed Mongols, so that they could grow sideline products to make up for their poverty (Tumote 1987: 955).

THE WRATH OF THE CHINESE "PEOPLE"

The geopolitical position of the Mongols and the hostility between China and the Soviet Union that erupted from the early 1960s onward further weakened the possibility for a discourse of "difference" in China. Class struggle again became the main approach to national integration; state unity and minzu tuanjie were the criteria to judge a minority's loyalty to the Chinese state. After reinitiating the class struggle through his battle cry "Never forget class struggle" in September 1962, in August 1963 Mao commented on the American Black civil rights movement, saying that "nationality struggle is, in the final analysis, a question of class struggle." This was quickly reformulated in Chinese propaganda as "The nature of the nationality question is class struggle." This reformulation, ostensibly equating the nationality question with class struggle, in fact replaced the nationality question with class struggle (Munohoi, 1995b). In other words, we witness the virtual abandonment by the Chinese communists of the nationality principle.[10] Chinese chauvinism was no longer deemed the problem that caused minority resentment, the logic being that in a socialist country where everyone was proclaimed equal, everyone must be equal. That some continued to raise the nationality issue was nothing more than backward thinking and, more ominously, a manifestation of backward class consciousness. The nationality question, if there was any, then must be treated as a class struggle problem. With the Chinese positioning themselves as proletarian, the problem focused on the minority and its continued backward (read feudal) class consciousness and practices.

This line of thinking was encouraged in the years 1963 and onward by the North China Bureau under the leadership of Li Xuefeng,[11] to "make up for the missed lesson of democracy" (*minzhu buke*) in ethnically mixed areas such as Tumed. Generally speaking, "making up for the missed lesson of democracy" was a euphemism for criticizing Ulanhu's 1948 Three Nos policy, which had been carried out in the purely pastoral regions well into the early 1960s, and the 1951 Tumed banner land reform—that is, it implied a class-struggle approach toward Mongols, both in the pastoral region and in ethnically mixed regions.

Difference, or nationality policy, was denounced as a mask to shield the class domination among the Mongols in the pastoral region and between the Mongols and Chinese in Tumed and other ethnically mixed areas. But tragically, the Chinese "subaltern" or "proletarian" outrage against so-called class domination or privilege turned out to be an assault targeting ordinary Mongols. Mao's class struggle line emboldened the Chinese opposition in Inner Mongolia to differentiate Chinese and Mongols; not only did some Chinese leaders of mixed-nationality communes refuse to give private plots to Mongols, they even called doing so a privilege (*teshu*), contrary to the socialist way of life. The land compensation and private land allowance to Mongols in the Tumed region, which was earlier justified as bringing about equality to the Mongols, became a target in the early phase of the Four Cleanups Movement (*cu xiantiao siqing*), which began in the winter of 1963–1964. In this so-called second land reform (*erci tugai*), which was characterized as "Red Storm" (*hongse fengbao*) in Inner Mongolia, the Chinese leadership demanded redesignation of the class designations made in 1950 and 1951. They made an issue of the fact that the Tumed Mongols had extra private plots. Was this not class privilege? they asked indignantly. Thus, 111 Mongol households were consequently reclassified to higher (that is, blacker) class labels as rich peasants and landlords. As landlords, they were subjected to struggle, and their land and other properties were confiscated (Tumote

1987: 224). While it was true that some Chinese also "enjoyed" an elevation of their class ranking, Mongols were not entirely helpless, especially while Ulanhu was still in power. In villages where Mongols were in the majority, they usually had the upper hand in counterattacks. There were also intra-Chinese struggles, as there were intra-Mongol ones.

Nonetheless, the Four Cleanups Movement in the Tumed banner was largely ethnic in nature, focusing on the fact that the Tumed Mongols had some extra land in the form of larger private plots. This was in part in reaction to the perceived power of their Tumed political patrons in the party and government of Inner Mongolia. The ultimate target of the Chinese attack was Ulanhu and other high-ranking Tumed Mongolian officials in the Inner Mongolian government and Party. Ulanhu's wife's relatives suffered particularly badly: of the 44 households in her natal village Xiaoyingzi brigade, 11 were reclassified as landlords or rich peasants, all of them her close relatives, as an anti-Ulanhu Cultural Revolution report subsequently revealed.[12] The Chinese felt that they were losers precisely because Mongol (communist) leaders of Inner Mongolia had suppressed the Chinese and supported Mongols.

Chinese indignity against the Mongols in the Tumed rested on egalitarian foundations, specifically rejecting the idea that Tumed Mongols should enjoy privileges. Typical questions from the Chinese were, for example, "You are a person, so am I, then why do you have a larger private plot than me?" (Li 1966: 129). "After liberation in the whole country, nationality oppression has been abolished and nationality equality realized, so why do we still need to draft a nationality policy?" Some (perhaps high-ranking cadres) denied there was any difference between Tumed Mongols and Chinese: "What difference is there between the Mongols and the Chinese in this place? Our labor is identical, all of us farm; our lives are identical, all eat *yumian* flour; our clothes are identical, all wear short coats; and we all speak the same language. I don't see any difference. Why then are there so many allowances (*zhaogu*) [for Mongols]?" (Li 1966: 84–85). Frustration among the Chinese sometimes led to verbal abuse, characterizing Mongols as parasites: "The Chinese feed the Mongols, and the good people feed the bad people" (Ulanhu 1967a: 55). A local Chinese leader said that he was for the Party, but "serving the people is contradictory to carrying out the nationality policy" (Li 1966: 157).

Throughout this struggle, to the annoyance of Ulanhu and his supporters, some eastern Mongolian officials rejected Ulanhu's viewpoint. They were also convinced that the Tumed Mongol demand for double plots was a privilege or an exercise of inequality, not just because they thought it unfair to the Chinese, but also because the eastern Mongolian peasants did not enjoy the same privilege. They joined with the Chinese, insisting that class was the central issue and that the Tumed Mongol privilege constituted a serious problem that should naturally be targeted in the Four Cleanups Movement. Ulanhu was furious: "Chinese chauvinism exists not only among Chinese cadres, but also among Mongol cadres. If minority nationality cadres commit the mistake of [Chinese] chauvinism, then the harm is greater!" (quoted in Li 1966: 97).

The accusations spiraled out of control. According to Li Gui, a Chinese Party secretary of Hohhot and Ulanhu's ardent supporter, some people in the Four Cleanups Team that was sent to Baishihu Brigade in suburban Hohhot, in order to dig out the "roots," even resorted to a house-to-house investigation, asking who had kinship relations with the people in charge in leading organs such as the Inner Mongolia Party Committee and what gifts local people sent them. Some openly clamored, making challenges and questioning, "What flag is the Inner Mongolia Party Committee carrying with regard to the nationality question? What flag is Ulanhu carrying?" (Li 1966: 363). They challenged the very principles of the Autonomous Region on egalitarian grounds. More ominously, by association, these criticisms spiraled to the higher plane of principle—that is,

4.1. Ulanhu Promoting Class Reconciliation
"The sky is blue, and the grassland is vast; the wind blows down the grass, revealing the cattle and sheep. Sheep are everywhere. There is no more wolf on the grassland." (*Jinggangshan: Tongda Wulanfu Zhuanhao*, October 8, 1967)

4.2. Down with Ulanhu's Class Capitulationist Policy
"No Division of Land, No Class Struggle, No Class Designation." (*Jinggangshan: Tongda Wulanfu Zhuanhao*, October 8, 1967)

suggesting that the Mongols, by enjoying a differential policy, were engaged in separatism. This was a charge that was particularly explosive in the tense international atmosphere of Chinese–Soviet polemics in the mid-1960s.

Instead of Mongol separatism, it was the Chinese who started to exclude Mongols from some new "revolutionary" organizations. In the Inner Mongolian class struggle surfacing in the context of the Socialist Education Movement of 1963–1965, class virtue, not birth or ethnicity, became the basis for an emerging new social and political structure. As in the rest of China, in the rural Tumed region, the "poor and lower middle peasant association" (set up on December 12–17, 1964) acquired political significance, with membership signifying one's standing in the entire social milieu. Membership was based on the virtue of low class status (as assigned in land reform). However, unlike in Chinese regions of China, virtue in Inner Mongolia was deeply embedded in ethnicity. Those deemed less virtuous—that is, now including many Mongols, for whom former land ownership now led to their reclassification as rich peasants or landlords—were excluded. The class virtue approach thus had an exclusionary function. In other words, subaltern politics began to show its menacing efficacy. Class was dichotomous, as Mao conveniently divided the classes into two antagonist camps. To be labeled a class enemy meant becoming "objects of the dictatorship of the proletariat," or "deprived of civil rights and, in some cases, of their freedom, constantly under suspicion and almost permanently subjected to ideological reeducation" (Billeter 1985: 152). This may be best illustrated by Ulanhu's resentment against the discrimination by the "poor and lower middle peasant association" against what he called "the Mongolian laboring people":

> Those holding a chauvinist viewpoint never conscientiously consider the demands of the Mongolian laboring people or patiently listen to their opinions. They regard the just demand of the Mongolian laboring masses, due to the improper treatment of some of their economic problems, as "carrying out capitalism"; [they] regard the Mongols' demanding separate brigades caused by economic conflict as "nationality separatism"; and they treat some ordinary disputes internal to Mongolian and Chinese peoples as enemy–us questions. They don't allow Mongols who withdrew from the brigade and who lodged complaints (*gaozhuang*) to Mongol leaders to join the "poor and lower middle peasant association"; they are not allowed to join the army or to become cadres, and in some cases, they have even been incarcerated. They have made the Mongolian poor and lower middle peasants unable to raise their heads, making them feel they have no future. This will inevitably cause conflict among nationalities, create tension in nationality relations, thereby diverting the main contradiction of class struggle. (Quoted in Li 1966: 120)

Ulanhu did not complain about the abstract principle of class struggle but objected to extending class struggle to ethnic relations, a direction that threatened Mongol interests and his political survival. It appeared that the only strategy left for him was to declare that the problem in Inner Mongolia was not one of class struggle but one of nationality relations. The nationality problem needed a nationality policy, he reasoned. By positing the Mongols as "poor and lower middle peasants," he was still working within the hegemonic discourse. Indeed, he was treading a very thin line over an abyss. He waged a double strategy, simultaneously creating a boundary for the purpose of ethnic equality and inclusion in the revolutionary process, but as a lower—hence more virtuous—partner. Ulanhu was thus a typical hybrid, both in and out, struggling to maintain breathing space.

But rhetoric was no longer sufficient. Ulanhu's ideological and ethnic positions became suspect. There were already accusations from some Chinese officials that he had personal territorial ambitions, thus challenging the very annexation of Suiyuan into Inner Mongolia in 1954, which had caused so much trouble for local Chinese immigrants. It seems that without this annexation, the Chinese in Suiyuan province would have had a free hand to carry out the class struggle to the detriment of Mongols. They denied that there was any nationality question in the Tumed region. Ulanhu retorted, "some are even Communist Party members, especially some CCP members holding power; they wantonly propagate that there is no nationality question, but if there is no nationality question, why do [we] want an autonomous region?" (Ulanhu 1967b: 70).

Angered by the Chinese challenge to Inner Mongolian autonomy, Ulanhu counterattacked in 1965 by reprinting and widely disseminating Mao's 1935 declaration on Inner Mongolia. He argued that the reason that there was an Inner Mongolia Autonomous Region today was because of Mao's declaration to the Inner Mongolian nation: "They should dig another root (apart from Ulanhu), the root is Chairman Mao's declaration published in 1935; we have built the autonomous region based exactly on this declaration" (Ulanhu 1967a: 55). This was tantamount to saying that if Chinese critics wanted to find a backstage master, they had best go directly to Mao. Ulanhu here used an interesting strategy: he occupied the strategic high ground, taking a historicist line, claiming that Inner Mongolia was not just a Mongol nationalist creation or fought for by Mongols alone, but promised and delivered by Mao himself. The retort served to justify the origins and continued validity of the autonomous institution. This, however, led to the Chinese backlash during the Cultural Revolution, one that would cost many thousands of Mongol lives in a genocidal witch-hunt of the alleged conspiracy of the so-called New Inner Mongolia People's Revolutionary Party fighting for Inner Mongolian independence (Tumen and Zhu 1995; Woody 1993). Ulanhu's alleged crimes were especially ominous; not only was he accused of being the chief of the conspiratorial party, he was also accused of forming a "Ulanhu Anti-Party Treason Clique." The campaigns led to the truncating of the Inner Mongolia Autonomous Region in 1969, dividing up most of its territory among several Chinese provinces, only to be restored once again in 1979.

TOWARD A CONCLUSION: PROVINCIALIZING UNIVERSALISM

In this chapter I have tried to demonstrate the trajectory of Chinese nationality policy toward Mongols in terms of class and ethnicity. To be sure, China's "nationality policy" is richer in content than I have been able to present here. However, this chapter is also meant to challenge both the Chinese communist *a priorist* claim that communism could deliver the liberation of the ethnic minorities and its critique, which tends to view Chinese "nationality policy" exclusively as a matter of bad faith or duplicity. I argue that nationality policy was more a minority demand, with Ulanhu as the representative figure in Inner Mongolia and beyond, than a majority blessing conferred from on high. Moreover, the very demand for nationality policy suggested the failure of communism in dealing with ethnicity. This failure came from both the internal dilemma of communist theories of ethnicity and the social reality that did not always match—at times, diverged far from—the theoretical recipe offered by communism. Mao's class struggle, for all its egalitarianism and "emanicipationism," reproduced a power hierarchy. In Inner Mongolia, the result was the reclassification of Mongolian class status with the effect of relocating many in the ranks of the enemy, thus subject to Chinese and class dictatorship and threatening the lives and livelihood of Mongols, individually and collectively. Without documenting the nature of domination and its resistance, silences, complicity, and displacements—above all, the hybridity of social reality—we risk naturalizing the communist discourse of nationality policy. To say the least, as I have shown, China's nationality policy emerged out of the debris of conflict between class and ethnicity and was predicated on the imbrication of class struggle and ethnic equity.

What we have seen here is that Ulanhu was long writhing within the confines of a kind of universalism—that is, the class struggle—which threatened to put many Mongols into the enemy camp. His political career had been marked by a conflict between the notion of class and ethnicity, two irreconcilable concepts that dominate ethnopolitics in many countries. Put differently, this is a conflict between difference and universalism. Universalism, or the difference-blind principle, is usually cloaked in neutrality, equality, dignity, and individualism. Its critics, on the contrary, frequently point out its hypocrisy as imposing "one hegemonic culture" and see it as "highly discriminatory" (Taylor 1994: 43). The violent provincialism of universalism has recently been criticized (Chakrabarty 1992). Since the Chinese communists could not resolve the unsavory binary dichotomy of class struggle and ethnic entitlement without destroying one or the other, in the end they chose the latter!

To dispute whether Inner Mongolia in a socialist China is an autonomous region or an internal colony is a moot point; we need to expand our basic definition of colony, grounded not only in ethnographic details, but also taking up issues beyond representation. To understand this, we grapple with how certain Western ideas, such as class and ethnicity, were introduced and how they left behind an ambiguous and politically explosive situation. In this sense, the seemingly bizarre complexity of Inner Mongolia defies any easy postcolonial representation.

The confusion over the class and ethnicity question may be better understood by applying Nancy Fraser's (1995) analytical distinction between class politics and identity politics or socialist/social-democratic politics and multiculturalist politics. She proposes to distinguish two analytically distinct understandings of injustice. One is socioeconomic injustice; another is cultural or symbolic. Justice requires both redistribution and recognition. "Recognition claims often take the form of calling attention to, if not performatively creating, the putative specificity of some group, and then of affirming the value of that specificity. Thus they tend to promote group differentiation. Redistribution claims, in contrast, often call for abolishing economic arrangements that underpin group specificity. Thus they tend to promote group de-differentiation. The upshot is that the politics of recognition and the politics of redistribution appear to have mutually contradictory aims" (1995: 74). These two opposing remedies might work in the ideal cases of class and homosexuality. However, Fraser identifies what she calls "bivalent" collectivities, such as gender and race, that have both economic and cultural faces. The remedies, both distribution and recognition, however, "are not easily pursued simultaneously. Whereas the logic of redistribution is to put gender out of business as such, the logic of recognition is to valorize gender specificity" (1995: 80). The imbrication of culture and economy, however, creates political dilemmas.

We may say that Mongol class-nation or class nationality poses something of a more acute problem than Fraser's bivalent dilemma. Fraser's theory is static, even rigid, as it presupposes only one possibility—that is, a discriminated cultural minority has to be one that also suffers from economic injustice. But the Mongols, as a minority (both in Inner Mongolia and in China as a whole), were attacked for inflicting economic injustice upon the majority Chinese. In this, the prescribed remedy envisaged by the majority Chinese was not redistribution, upgrading their economic status for eventual "equality," but "physical" class struggle to put the Mongols out of business as a group altogether. Given this choice of "elimination" through "redistribution" as "justice" and "elimination" through "violence" to redress injustice, Ulanhu naturally busied himself with either keeping the Mongols from class categorization altogether or lowering the class status or "proletarianizing" the Mongols, trying to shield them behind a "nationality policy."

In recent years, revisionist neoliberal scholars have begun painfully to abandon universalism and now believe that "equality" can only be achieved on the basis of "difference." Even practicing peacemakers in Israel, such as Daphna Golan, have confessed their confusion over universalism and particularism: "On the one hand, my work in the human rights movement is based on universal norms of justice and an ideology which stresses that each person, regardless of nationality, deserves basic dignity and rights superseding nationalism; . . . but . . . I have come to the conclusion that the only viable political solution is to draw a clear border between an Israel and a Palestinian state" (Golan 1997: 76).

However, merely "exposing the parochialism of universality," argues Frederick Cooper, "leaves a fundamental issue on the table." He writes, "an anti-universalist argument allows no possibility for dialogue about moral issues across cultural borders" (1997: 427). So we are still left with an impasse. What is the way out?

This chapter does not pretend to have proffered an answer; it shows only that issues of universalism/multiculturalism apply within socialist states as well, a terrain toward which people have previously looked mainly in terms of hegemony/resistance. The underlying oppression by the Chinese colonial rule of Inner Mongolia is not simple. Colonialism exists in different forms in different societies. Inner Mongolia is a story of a majority/minority ethnic colonial situation, too. I have, however, tried to show that "colonialism" is part of the sociopolitical system (socialism) and must be viewed in terms of its mutually conflicting concepts, which are nevertheless the tools to *think the political*. It does not lie in superficial racial or ethnic conflicts per se.

NOTES

1. The current name, Inner Mongolian committee of the CCP, was adopted in 1954. The IMPRP was disbanded in 1947, and most of its members joined the CCP or the Communist Youth League.

2. John Fitzgerald, in his discussion of nation-building in Republican China, suggests that class struggle often serves an important function of national integration. "Class struggle was conceived as a nation-building enterprise on a *centrist* model of the state" (1996: 162, emphasis original).

3. Of the 121 members of the Congress (*canyihui*) set up in 1947, 96 were Mongols, 24 Chinese, and 1 Hui (Hao 1991: 19).

4. Dirlik goes beyond simply debunking unequal relations between nations. He argues that a liberated nation very often develops its own cultural hegemony, whereby its internal inequality is legitimized. Dirlik thus suggests an approach that smacks of Mao's continuing revolution: to analyze the unequal relations within a society to make it an ideal one (Dirlik 1987). It appeared that reality was more messy than any class theory could handle. What characterizes Inner Mongolia is its hybridity, in the form of ideological and ethnic entanglement atop a multiplicity of social classes.

5. According to statistics from Jo'uda League, in 1946 the League had 1.43 million head of livestock. The number dropped to 0.93 million head by 1948, a loss of one-third (Hao 1997: 583).

6. In China landlords were regarded as feudal and had to be overthrown, whereas capitalists would receive better treatment in light of their contributions to developing the productive forces.

7. His points were embodied in a document issued by the Nationality Affairs Commission and approved by the Beijing government on June 15, 1953. "Nei Menggu ji Suiyuan, Qinghai, Xinjiang deng Di Muqu Muye Shengchan de Jiben Zongjie" (Basic Summary of Production in the Pastoral Areas of Inner Mongolia and Suiyuan, Qinghai, Xinjiang and Elsewhere) (in Ulanhu 1990).

8. One was "Suiyuan Sheng Mengqi Tudi Gaige Shishi Banfa" (Measures for Carrying Out Land Reform in the Mongolian Banners of Suiyuan Province), another "Guanyu Mengmin Huafen Jieji Chengfen Buchun Banfa" (Additional Measures on Designating Class Identities of the Mongols), in Nei Menggu Dangwei Zhengce Yanjiushi and Nei Menggu Zizhiqu Nongye Weiyuanhui, eds. (1987).

9. Nei Menggu Dangwei Zhengce Yanjiushi and Nei Menggu Zizhiqu Nongye Weiyuanhui, eds. "Suiyuan Sheng Mengqi Tudi Gaige Shishi Banfa" (1987).

10. This is rather similar to the liberal white retreat from race in the United States after the civil rights movement in the 1960s (Steinberg 1995).

11. The North China Bureau was one of the six regional bureaus of the Party, whose power increased in the aftermath of the disasters associated with the Great Leap Forward. One of the concerns of the North China Bureau was to find ways to feed the hungry by increasing agricultural output. One approach favored by the Bureau was to reclaim

pastureland, which was deemed wasteland. As the second secretary of the Bureau, Ulanhu resisted the Bureau's penetration into Inner Mongolia. A concerted effort was then made by the North China Bureau leadership to undermine Ulanhu's authority in Inner Mongolia by cultivating loyalty from discontented Chinese leaders and even some Mongol leaders.

12. "Wulanfu Wangchao' de Suoying—Guanyu 'Dangdai Wangye' Wulanfu zai Xiaoyingzi Dadui Dagao Zibenzhuyi he Fengjian Zhuyi Fubi de Diaocha Baogao (The Epitome of the "Ulanhu Kingdom"—An Investigative Report on the Capitalist and Feudal Restoration Carried Out in Xiaoyingzi Brigade by the Reigning Prince Ulanhu). *Wen'ge Ziliao* 27 (1967).

5

ᠵ

Rewriting "Inner Mongolian" History after the Revolution: Ethnicity, Nation, and the Struggle for Recognition

In chapter 4 I discussed the irony of Mongols caught in the contradictions of class and ethnicity. After huge losses during the land reform, Mongol communists pushed for a clearer conceptual, if not physical, boundary to provide protection from the very ideology and practices that ostensibly brought them "liberation." Here we inquire: How could the Mongol "revolution" against "Chinese" colonizers be accommodated within a communist China in which minorities, including Mongols, would continue to narrate a "glorious" revolutionary history? Insofar as the People's Republic of China was built on a series of "revolutions," Inner Mongolia was also unmistakably a product of revolution. Contrary to the conventional Marxist line, I contend that a revolutionary history in a nation is in fact a national history, as most socialist historiographies have testified (cf. Verdery 1991). In this sense, Mongolian revolutionary history, which legitimates a socialist reading of Mongolian nationality and creates institutions of Mongol autonomy in the Inner Mongolia Autonomous Region, must confront the fact that Mongols constitute only about 10 percent of the entire population of Inner Mongolia in the twentieth century. The overwhelming majority is Chinese, while the rest of the population, altogether comprising approximately 1 percent, consists of smaller minorities, including the Daur, Orochon, Ewenki, Manchu, and Hui.

This chapter explores one important dimension of interethnic dynamics, the competition over the revolutionary history of the Mongols in China in relation to the Chinese revolution and the formation of the nation-state. I see Mongolian revolutionary history, the quintessential material of "resistance" in essentialist narrative, not so much as an embodiment of "Mongol" revolution against China, as an implosion that not only affects factional refigurations within Mongol ranks, but also repeatedly redefines ethnic relations, notably those between Chinese and Mongols and between Mongols and Daurs. It examines how, in the process of writing Mongolian revolutionary history, Mongols repeatedly encountered problems of ethnicity such as the fact that one of the early Mongolian leaders, Merse, would later be identified as belonging to a newly created Daur nationality. It looks at Daur treatments of this figure in their history and at the recent "pluralization" of the Mongolian revolutionary historiographical discourse. We are thus treading on treacherous ground of what may be called a "postcolonial" or, more precisely, "postrevolutionary" ethnopolitics, including realms of history and memory. Postrevolution is not simply a matter of intellectual positionality or critique of colonial oppression or exploitation but requires an understanding of how the revolutionary victory reigns in legitimating power domination, managing ethnic relations, and consolidating national unity and how "contribution" or "disservice" to the revolutionary victory figures in the new postrevolutionary meritocracy.

Fred Halliday observes that

> "Revolution" as a term in political discourse and social science has a double character: like "nation," "society," "class," "war" and "community" it denotes both a reality, something that analysis can identify and study, and an aspiration, a concept with a normative dimension that protagonists advocate and opponents contest. At the same time just as the real character of revolution—the forms it takes, the forces it mobilizes, the outcomes it has—have [sic] changed, so too has its meaning, for political theorists and political actors, and above all for the social movements that mobilize in support of this idea. (1999: 4)

Revolution thus has multiple and shifting meanings, but its significance must be understood in the content of continuity and disjuncture of nation formation in international context. It teleologically represents a radical rupture of time in the development of a nation, symbolizing for its proponents the fulfillment of the national consciousness. This is as much so for the French and American revolutions as for communist revolutions. Whatever their transcendental premises or challenges to national sovereignty, "in practice, revolutionary regimes are the more determined defenders of the authority of states within" (Halliday 1999: 12). Étienne Balibar points out in his seminal essay "The Nation Form" (1991) that revolution plays an important role in marking the birth of modern nations. For a nation, there is only one single founding revolutionary event that marks the national identity. But if the founding moment is one, the origin myths are plural and subject to contradictory interpretations. As a result, "the myth of origins and national continuity . . . is therefore an effective ideological form, in which the imaginary singularity of national formations is constructed daily" (Balibar 1991: 87).

The Inner Mongolian communist-cum-nationalist revolution, which may be dated from the 1920s and which "succeeded" in 1947 with the founding of the Inner Mongolia Autonomous Government (later called Region), was the founding moment of a reborn "socialist" Mongol nationality within China. Yet this observation masks the fact that there was never a singular chain of revolutionary events or activities. The project of Inner Mongolian independence or autonomy was conducted by different groups and individuals with various ideological convictions and different projections of the future for Mongols. In a way, what later became known as the Inner Mongolian Revolution achieved parallel significance for Mongols with the original myth of the thirteenth century, when Chinggis Khan and his Mongol Empire put the Mongols on the world map. This new "revolutionary" myth of origin of a nationality invariably becomes a project of the historical imagination, especially in the case of a colonized nationality (but nonetheless, one masqueraded as emancipated) such as the Mongols, that requires reducing plural origins to a singular destiny. And this singularization invariably ends up in a monopoly of the revolutionary historiography by the single group in power. It is this monopoly, often violent, that sets in motion contention or competition between various groups, resulting in inclusion and exclusion in a multiethnic and multigroup setting like Inner Mongolia. In narrating this revolutionary history, Ulanhu, the communist Mongol leader who stood at the forefront of Chinese Communist Party efforts to establish the Inner Mongolia Autonomous Region, became the symbol of the essence of this nationality, ostensibly representing the will and aspiration of the "Mongolian people." Excluded from this "Mongolian people" are not only Mongols outside of China, but also those "bad" categories of Mongols, such as secular and ecclesiastical feudal lords, as well as all who stood on the wrong side of the ideological barricades. This historiographical representation of Mongolian nationality is problematic at best, as it is based on the premise of excluding the "bad" Mongols and allying with the "good" Chinese.

A central problem lies in avoiding teleology, particularly in writing the early stages of the revolutionary movement. I resist giving too much defining power to the Chinese communists early on, in contrast to the work of many scholars writing the histories of Chinese minorities (cf. Harrell 1995c). The general picture we get from their writing is that the minorities were the building materials for the construction of China—minorities specifically representing the lower stages, such as primitive communist, slavery, or feudal. Alternatively, minority history has been manipulated by Chinese authors to prove that minorities were "historically" part of China. And this perspective often induces a counterhistory, usually initiated by Western or Westernized intellectuals on behalf of the subalterns.

Ranajit Guha, a leading member of the Subaltern Studies Group working on Indian colonial history, holds that "the question of power in colonial South Asia or anywhere else in a land under foreign occupation can be phrased succinctly as 'Who writes the history of the subjugated people?' " (1997: xiii). The mission of his research is described thus: "Our attempt to inform this study of colonialism by the pathos of a purloined past is therefore not so much a matter of professional convenience as a strategy to situate the writing of a conquered people's history by conquerors at the very heart of the question of one nation's oppression by another" (1997: xiv). Such a perspective, locating the history of Mongols in China within the perspective of the Chinese revolution, requires that we untangle the complex issues of nationality and revolution.

One important dimension of this intervention is the carving out of "memory" as a domain of popular resistance against "official" or "colonial" History. This dichotomy is seen most clearly in Dipesh Chakrabarty's formulation: "Subaltern histories are . . . constructed within a particular kind of historicized memory, one that remembers History itself as a violation, an imperious code that accompanied the civilizing process that the European Enlightenment inaugurated in the eighteenth century as a world-historical task" (1996: 61). In the socialist context, memory as resistance to history may become even antiregime movements consciously undertaken by the actors themselves, as indicated by the articles in Rubie Watson's (1994a) edited volume entitled *Memory, History, and Opposition under State Socialism* (cf. Hein and Selden 2000). This chapter is not about the history/memory issue, though it lurks in the background. Instead of positing a dichotomy, I suggest that historiography constitutes an important site, the control of which is no less important for defining the legitimacy of history and its participants, as well as practitioners, in the national order of things (see chapters 6 and 7 for discussions of memory and ethnopolitics).

Inner Mongolian revolutionary historiography, inasmuch as it is the history of the "conquered" Mongols in China (in the sense that the Mongols were incorporated into the People's Republic of China) is more complicated than Guha's gallant but simplistic rhetoric conveys. The history was not written by the Chinese, or the "conquerors" per se, but was authorized and directed by Ulanhu, who was both the highest official of the Chinese communist state in Inner Mongolia and the representative leader of the Mongolian nationality. A profound ambiguity exists not only in the relationship between Mongols and Chinese, but also in that between Mongols and other ethnic groups—not to speak of intra-Mongol rivalry, a situation that defies any rigid dichotomy of colonizer and colonized. That the Mongols fought for their own liberation, by various means and through the activities of various groups, leading to the formation of the Inner Mongolia Autonomous Government in May 1947, two and a half years before the founding of the People's Republic of China, constitutes a complex situation, providing some room for a communist Mongolian self-representation. We must then explore the tortuous processes of fulfilling both the universalist (Chinese) national interest and the particularist Mongolian interest.

Inner Mongolian postrevolutionary historiography is not, therefore, a matter of an oppositional discourse of history versus memory but is intricately related to "nationality questions," to delineating ethnic boundaries, to demarcating territorial autonomy, and to representational ethnopolitics. It also involves analysis of a revolutionary politics that includes a significant Mongol dimension. Ann Stoler, in explicating the main message of Foucault's 1976 lectures on state racism, concludes that "if any single theme informs [Foucault's 1976] seminar, it is not a quest for political theory, but an appreciation of historiography as a political force, of history writing as a political act, of historical narrative as a tool of the state and as a subversive weapon against it" (Stoler 1995: 62). I suggest that in order to understand the production of Mongolian revolutionary historiographical knowledge, we must ground it in the concrete power relations among ethnic groups and between Inner Mongolia and the Chinese national state.

THE ORTHODOX INNER MONGOLIAN REVOLUTIONARY HISTORY

No official history of the Mongols in the twentieth-century communist revolution was forthcoming until 1962, almost fifteen years after the victory of the Inner Mongolian revolution. During this period, the Inner Mongolia Autonomous Region expanded from the eastern part of Inner Mongolia and took over several provinces on what was historically Mongolian territory, specifically Suiyuan in 1954, and parts of Gansu and Ningxia in 1956. The project of writing the *Inner Mongolian Revolutionary History* was initiated in June 1958, commissioned by Ulanhu, the paramount leader of the Inner Mongolia Autonomous Region. Although largely representing Ulanhu's vision of a Mongolian revolution leading to the creation of the Autonomous Region, it was by no means an easy process, as it had to simultaneously represent the interests of two dominant groups in Inner Mongolia: the Mongols and the Chinese, the latter being granted a certain primacy as representative both of the CCP and the Chinese state. The first draft was completed in 1962, when it circulated internally to solicit reviews from high-level cadres and revolutionaries. The final version was scheduled for official publication in 1967 to mark the twentieth anniversary of the Inner Mongolia Autonomous Region. However, with Inner Mongolia in turmoil from 1966 onward, much of the leadership, including Ulanhu, under attack; and the Mongol population subjected to terror, torture, and killing in the military-directed campaigns to purge a "New Inner Mongolian People's Revolutionary Party" of 1968–1969, it was not published until 1978, as part of the post-CR rehabilitation, and even then was not made available for public distribution. As the preface of the book indicated, the content was unchanged in order to refute charges against it during the Cultural Revolution. The book was denounced for allegedly "glorifying Ulanhu by erecting a monument and writing a biography for him" (Nei Menggu Geming Shi Bianji Weiyuanhui 1978). So I rely on it as a pre–Cultural Revolution text on Inner Mongolia's revolutionary history. What did it say, then?

The book contained several important points: The Inner Mongolian revolution centered on the CCP and was carried out under its guidance. The credit for implementing CCP policy for rejuvenating the Mongolian nationality was, however, given to Ulanhu. He was lauded not only for bringing about the unification of eastern and western Inner Mongolia, but also for spearheading Inner Mongolia's autonomy within China, rather than its independence. In other words, fighting for inclusion in China was as important as unifying two fragmented parts of Inner Mongolia, and fighting against internal Mongol nationalists and feudal elements was no less important than fighting against external colonizers, both the Japanese and the Chinese Nationalist Party (GMD). Both were necessary to achieve Inner Mongolia's incorporation within Communist China, with Mongols achieving equal status with other nationalities. This historiography was exemplary from an official Chinese perspective in achieving the twin goals of strengthening national unity and defending state unity.

Presenting Mongol agency in achieving this new vision was apparently deemed of equal importance as the ideological leadership and material assistance of the CCP. In this narrative, Ulanhu's revolutionary genealogy was traced to two important inspirations: (1) His teacher, Li Dazhao, one of the founders of the CCP, who was said to be particularly sympathetic to the Mongols; (2) Two "proletarian" uprisings led by Gadameiren (1931–1932) and Sine Lama (1926–1928), which took place in eastern and western Inner Mongolia, respectively, whose nature was interpreted as being both anti-internal feudal oppression and anti-external colonization. Both fought to recover and protect Mongol pastureland, which had been sold by Mongol nobles to Chinese colonizers. But both uprisings failed, allegedly due to their lack of long-term political goals or, most important in this historical verdict, correct ideological guidance—that is, from the CCP. The noble yet doomed subaltern resistance of the Mongols was contrasted to the movement led by a more sophisticated Ulanhu, who performed the miracle of unifying Inner Mongolia, saving the Mongols, and making possible their "equality," in the form of "Inner Mongolia Autonomous Region," in a "free" new Communist China.

This Mongol communist historiographic resolution of the ethnic conflict tortuously differentiates "bad" Chinese from "good" Chinese: the former colonized the Mongols, whereas the latter "liberated" them. To show how the Chinese communists came to the aid of the Mongols against the Japanese, a chapter was devoted to Chinese communist guerrilla forces (including a few Mongols) fighting the Japanese in the Daqingshan base of Inner Mongolia, ostensibly on behalf of (and with) the Mongols.

This cursory examination of postrevolutionary Inner Mongolian historiography shows indeed little of the primordial Mongol nation fighting for its own self-determination. Rather, equality and ethnic friendship within China became a substitute for self-determination, which was the original goal of the Mongolian revolution. There is something conspicuously missing, however. Eastern Mongols, who were unified into Inner Mongolia in 1947, were marginalized or largely excluded from this historiography. Likewise, other ethnic groups living in Inner Mongolia are also conspicuously absent. This is surprising, given the fact that western Inner Mongolia (i.e., former Suiyuan province) was only incorporated in 1954, whereas in 1947 Ulanhu set up the Inner Mongolia Autonomous Government on the basis of an already existing Eastern Mongolia Autonomous Government.

What is particularly interesting for our purposes is the treatment of Bayantai (Bai Yunti) and Merse (a.k.a. Guo Daofu), the chairman and secretary-general of the Inner Mongolian People's Revolutionary Party, a party founded in 1925 and which Ulanhu also joined in his youth. These sophisticated early Mongolian revolutionaries, rather than being presented as pioneers of the Mongolian revolution, like Sine Lama and Gadameiren, were denounced as traitors to the Mongolian nation and revolution. Instead, enormous space and praise were devoted to a youthful Ulanhu and his cohort absorbing Marxist-Leninist ideas. Ulanhu was elevated to the position of founding father of the new Inner Mongolia, a leader who embodied a new vision of Mongol internal unity and national unity with China, both presented as being in the best interest of Mongols.

In the mid-1980s, challenges emerged to this representation of history, not only from the eastern Mongolian communist veterans, but also, more important, from the Daur nationality, which now reclaims Merse's ethnic identity as Daur. The latter case is particularly intriguing because the controversy over the ethnic identity of one of the most important leaders of the Inner Mongolian revolution had implications not only for the revolutionary genealogy set by Ulanhu, but also for the very ethnic nature of the Inner Mongolian revolution, posing questions as to whether it is a "Mongolian" revolution or something else. In a way, this poses greater challenges to a Mongol historiography than the inclusion of the Chinese communists at the center of Mongolian revolutionary historiography. The immediate question is why this should be a problem in Merse's case. Can he not be treated as an "internationalist," as the Chinese are? After all, isn't it true that even in the Soviet Union, Stalin's Georgian ethnic background was no impediment to his becoming the leader of the Soviet Communist Party? Rather than looking at the issue from the Marxist canonical perspective, a closer examination of nationality formation in China and the concurrent history writing reveals that the issues of ethnic boundary have tremendous repercussions on the historiographical representation of individual revolutionaries and the movement. The immediate problem for the Mongols is that they have lost one of their preeminent revolutionary leaders as a result of nationality politics that rendered the Daur, once viewed as Mongol, as a separate nationality.

MERSE AS TRAITOR TO THE MONGOLS?

So, who was Merse? He was born in today's Hulunbuir League of eastern Inner Mongolia, into a Daur noble family in 1894. Showing early interest in politics, in 1918 he and his cohort set up what is known as the Hulunbuir Youth Party (also known as Mongolian Youth League or Mongolian Youth Party), perhaps the first political party in Inner Mongolia. In 1923, while working for the Chinese Foreign Ministry, he toured "Outer" Mongolia and the Soviet Union and wrote a book entitled *New Mongolia*, praising the revolution. For that, he was accused of being a "red element" and was sacked from his job as Russian translator. In 1924 he toured south China, including Nanjing and Canton, where he met Sun Zhongshan, the father of the modern Chinese nationalist revolution. Inspired by Sun's Three People's Principles, he published two books in the same year: *The Mongolian Question* (also known as *The Revival of the Yellow Peril*) and *The Mongolian Movement for National Self-Determination*. The latter book provided the theoretical ground for the emerging Inner Mongolian political activism. Merse played an instrumental role in the founding of the Inner Mongolian People's Revolutionary Party (IMPRP) in October 1925, a coalition party supported by the Comintern, the Mongolian People's Revolutionary Party, the Chinese Nationalist Party (GMD), and the Chinese Communist Party (CCP).[1] He was responsible for drafting its programs, its declarations, and even its official anthem.

The leadership of the IMPRP came mostly from eastern Inner Mongolia, including several "Daur Mongols." Bayantai, a Mongol, who became the chairman of the party, was pro-GMD, while Merse, the secretary-general, had extensive links with the Mongolian People's Republic (founded in 1924) and the Soviet Union. Merse was a radical communist revolutionary, eager to organize uprisings to overthrow Mongolian feudal rule and drive out all Chinese warlords from Inner Mongolia. In 1926 this led to deep disagreement with Bayantai, who insisted on relying on a pro-Soviet Chinese warlord, Feng Yuxiang.

When the GMD and CCP split in 1927, so did the IMPRP, both ideologically and organizationally. A new left-wing Inner Mongolia Youth Party was founded on the debris of the old Party, and Merse took up the leading position in it. As the GMD unified China and set up provincial administrations in Inner Mongolia in 1928, Merse and his fellow Daur comrade Fumintai led an uprising in Hailar to launch a Hulunbuir Autonomous Region, declaring:

> At the moment, deeply aware of the lack of condition necessary for setting up an independent state, we therefore announce autonomy externally and people's rule

internally. The goal of our movement is for the Mongolian People to rule Mongolia, we don't want the corrupt princely system, nor do we want the exploitation by the aristocratic class. We want modern democracy. (Nagudanfu 1985: 100)

However, lacking support from the MPR and the Soviet Union, the uprising failed and was brutally suppressed by the Chinese army. In order to offset further Chinese onslaught, Merse accepted the peace conditions offered by the Chinese general Zhang Xueliang and agreed to participate in the Hulunbuir administration. In exchange he was allowed to set up a Northeastern Mongolian Banner Normal School in Mukden (Shenyang), which became the cradle of Inner Mongolian modern education and nationalism. Merse, however, was soon removed from the school for propagating communism. When the Japanese invaded Manchuria in 1931, Merse refused to serve the Japanese and sought refuge at the Soviet consulate in Manzhouli in 1932 but disappeared thereafter.[2] Nonetheless, his idealism was carried on by his students. His best Mongol student, Hafenga, and his comrades revived the defunct Inner Mongolian People's Revolutionary Party immediately after the Japanese surrender in 1945 and set up an Eastern Mongolia Autonomous Government in 1946, after the MPR rebuffed their drive to unite with the MPR. It is this government and the territory under its jurisdiction that provided the base for Ulanhu's political activity, allowing him to establish an Inner Mongolia Autonomous Government in May 1947. Ulanhu, although he joined the IMPRP in his youth, was simultaneously a Chinese Communist Party member from 1925 onward, a situation analogous to that of Mao Zedong with dual membership in the GMD and the CCP in the years 1924–1927. Ulanhu's political base was in western Inner Mongolia in areas under Chinese communist control.

What, then, is Merse's place in Inner Mongolian revolutionary history? Although nothing official was written about the Inner Mongolian Revolution until 1962, for Inner Mongolia, the founding of the Inner Mongolia Autonomous Government in May 1947 was the defining moment for the new Mongol nationality. The moment needed to be theoretically packaged to flesh out its significance and difference from previous attempts. Ulanhu, as chairman of the Inner Mongolia Autonomous Government, made a speech to the Inner Mongolian cadres on July 23, 1947, in probably the first comprehensive analysis of the nature of Inner Mongolian society, the nature of the Inner Mongolian revolution, and the relationship between the Inner Mongolian revolution and the CCP. In this report, he paid tribute to the Duguilong movement led by Sine Lama in Ordos and an uprising led by Gadameiren in eastern Inner Mongolia as great anti-imperialist, antifeudal movements, turning an unprecedented and glorious page in the history of the Inner Mongolian people. In contrast, he accused Bayantai of being a murderer, a traitor to the Mongol nationality, whose "body is Mongolian, but whose thought is that of a Mongolian traitor." After denouncing other Mongols for their alleged treason or failure to persist, he mentioned Merse: "In 1929–1930, the great Chinese revolution failed, and the uprising led by Merse in Hulunbuir, (if we) judge its nature, was counterrevolutionary, (because) he was used by Dambadorji (an MPR leader), and also because of the Japanese [connection]; so, as a result, after the failure, he went to become a school principal for Zhang Xueliang" (Ulanhu 1967[1947]: 28). This set the tone for the later official history written in 1962. There, Merse and Bayantai were lumped together as representatives of the feudal upper class, who surrendered to the GMD, the enemy of both the Mongolian people and the Chinese Communist Party (Nei Menggu Geming Shi Bianji Weiyuanhui 1978: 50).

We need to understand the complex character of Ulanhu's revolutionary historiography. To his credit, it was not simply unprincipled slavish obedience to the CCP, but an adroit discourse that appropriated the CCP for the benefit of Inner Mongolia, and perhaps vice versa. Ulanhu's revolutionary historiography derived from his sense of nationalism, as well as from his understanding of Mongolian society as a hierarchical one riddled with class conflicts. He thus staunchly opposed the Chinese Nationalist Party, the GMD, for its rejection of the rights and identities of non-Chinese peoples, seeing the future of China in the assimilation of minorities on the basis of equality. The CCP, by virtue of its position as an opposition party in opposition to (but sometimes in united front with) the GMD, and its voicing of Marxist-Leninist principles of national self-determination, made many rosy promises to the Mongols, including the right to establishing an independent state (see chapter 4).

The CCP's promises, as well as its social programs, were important for people like Ulanhu, who was attracted to communism in his youth. The ideological conflicts between the CCP and the GMD, and the Inner Mongolian connection to the two parties, had acquired symbolic significance for distinguishing who was really fighting for the Mongol cause: Mongol CCP or Mongol GMD. Bayantai's support for the GMD, therefore, did much to taint the reputation of the Inner Mongolian People's Revolutionary Party (IMPRP) despite Ulanhu's own youthful participation in the party. The reputation of the IMPRP was further damaged because of the translation of the Party's name in Chinese—that is, Nei Menggu Guomindang (Inner Mongolian GMD)—thus giving the impression that it was an underling of the Chinese GMD.

But Ulanhu proved to be a nuanced politician. He was clearly aware of the split of the IMPRP in 1927 between Bayantai and Merse. Rather than attributing it, however, to the disagreement between pro-Mongolia/Soviet leaders like Merse and pro-China leaders like Bayantai, he presented it as a split between Chinese GMD and CCP supporters. In 1965 Ulanhu presented his vision of the contours of the Mongolian revolution, in lectures to Chinese journalists from Beijing who had been invited to prepare for reporting on the twentieth anniversary of the founding of the Inner Mongolia Autonomous Region, scheduled for May 1967. He lumped together Merse and Bayantai as traitors to the Mongol nation: "After that batch of princes and aristocrats of the Inner Mongolian GMD, including Jin Yunchang, betrayed, a batch of party members followed them to Nanjing and became officials, and made profits." In contrast, here clearly alluding to himself and his co rades, "those trained in the Mongolian-Tibetan school, especially the group of Communist Party members and Mongolian cadres trained in the revolutionary process, went to villages to work among the masses" (Ulanhu 1967 [1965]: 13). This version, of course, also aligns Ulanhu with Mao in going to the countryside after the GMD-CCP split in 1927–1928.

The importance of the name change was clearly spelled out by Ulanhu: "In Inner Mongolia, after the second congress of the GMD (in 1927), the Inner Mongolian *Guomindang* (GMD) was turned into Inner Mongolian *Renmin Gemingdang* (people's revolutionary party)" (Ulanhu 1967 [1965]: 13). This is Ulanhu's revolutionary historiography, through hairsplitting linguistic manipulation, both denouncing the pre-1927 IMPRP and appropriating the post-1927 IMPRP to boost his own credentials. The success of this manipulation, of course, hinged on using Chinese, rather than Mongolian.

After Ulanhu's death in 1988, there has been a slow movement to rewrite the Inner Mongolian revolutionary history. In the 1997 edition of the *Inner Mongolia Revolutionary History* (Hao 1997), Merse was still located in the "rightist" camp of the IMPRP, but the book fell short of branding him a traitor. This ambivalence shows something more than merely a question of historiographical accuracy. Indeed, there has been a lessening of charges against him as time has gone by. To some extent, the IMPRP came to be personified by the treasonous Bayantai. This official Mongolian low-key treatment of Merse and the excessive bashing of Bayantai, the quintessential Mongol traitor, betray a profound uncertainty or anxiety over Merse's ethnic identity as a Daur. Moreover, writing an Inner Mongolian revolutionary history as a distinctly "Chinese" experience brought in tension between a revolution that transcended national boundary and a domesticating desire of a nation-state. In fact, even in the 1962 version, Merse was denounced not for his pan-Mongolist activities, but for his alleged treason in surrendering to the GMD. One may argue that the side-lining of Merse must also be related to his more "subversive" status than Bayantai, for he offered an alternative model of revolution for the Mongols to the dichotomy of the CCP and the Chinese GMD—that is, his link with the Soviet Union and the Mongolian People's Republic proved to be too embarrassing to discuss. To recognize the pan-Mongolian characteristics of the IMPRP and criticize its leaders for pan-Mongolist activities would no doubt delegitimate the IMPRP. In Ulanhu's Inner Mongolian revolutionary historiography, the IMPRP was legitimate, but its legitimacy lay in its Chinese domestic characteristics. The battle line was along working either with the Chinese Communist Party or with the Chinese Nationalist Party—the former "our friend," the latter "our enemy."

As we have observed, the Inner Mongolian revolutionary historiography, for all its communist overtones, was crystal clear concerning ethnic boundaries—that is, whether one betrayed or defended Mongol interests. For all his treason-ous crimes, Bayantai was recognized as a Mongol. Indeed, this ethnic identity particularly aggravated his crime. Similarly, I submit, Merse, by being recognized as of a separate nationality—the Daur—had to be distanced, not only from this intra-Mongol controversy, but indeed his very involvement proved embarrassing to a historiography that was defined as a Mongolian revolution. In this light, he could not be fully incorporated into a "Mongolian" revolutionary history with-out transforming the very ethnic parameters of that revolution and its history.

This poses an interesting question: how to represent a non-Mongol in a "Mon-golian" revolution, and conversely, how a non-Mongol people—in this case, the Daur—should represent its ethnic members who fought for "others'" interests. And yet, this question is still too simple to capture the complexity of the issue. The Daurs called themselves "Daur-Mongols" between 1911 and 1956, and in this sense, Merse was fighting for the cause common to Daur and Mongol. The separation of the Daurs from the Mongols in the 1950s had, then, dramatic repercussions on their historiographical representation and by extension their political standing in Inner Mongolia. Before discussing the Daur representation of Merse in their modern history, we must study the historical circumstances wherein Merse and his fellow Daurs projected themselves as Mongols.

GENEALOGICAL IMAGINATION AND THE POLITICS OF HYPHENATION

The Daurs, an important but numerically small group, are today scattered in eastern Inner Mongolia and the neighboring Chinese province of Heilongjiang. There are also some in Xinjiang.[3] Once tributaries of the Horchin Mongols, they were conquered by the Manchus and organized in the imperial Manchu eight banner system, separate from the Mongols. During the Qing dynasty they were closely identified with the Manchus, so closely that they were called "new Man-chu." However, they were not confused with the Manchus. All the banners were separately labeled "Solon," "Daur," "Barga," and so on (see Lattimore 1969). As the boundary between the Qing and Russia was drawn in the treaty of Nerchinsk in 1689 and the treaty of Kiakhta in 1727, some Daurs, along with other groups such as Ewenki, Orochon, and Barga (Mongols), were sent to Hulunbuir, where the Daurs played a dominant role in defending the Qing border. Toward the end of the Qing empire, the prominent place enjoyed by the Daurs began to crum-ble—as did the positions of all other northern peoples, including the Mongols—when the Manchus began to identify with Chinese interests. The Daurs' alienation from the Manchus was accompanied by their increasing identification with the Mongols, especially the Daurs in Hailar city of Hulunbuir.

Early in the twentieth century, the Russian Far Eastern Railway turned Hulunbuir into a hot spot for international contention. As the ruling group in Hulun-buir, the Daurs felt political pressure more acutely than local Mongols. The independence movement in Outer Mongolia found immediate echo in Inner Mongolia, and in 1912 Hulunbuir under Daur rule declared itself a sovereign part of newly independent Mongolia under Jebtsundamba Hutagt.[4] This cultural and political identification with the Mongols was further facilitated by the new ethnic policy initiated by Republican China, envisioning China as a union of five officially recognized nationalities: Chinese, Manchu, Mongol, Tibetan, and Muslim. Under such circumstances, it became imperative that the Daurs firmly stand on the side of the Mongols and indeed provide leadership to the Mongols to resist Chinese colonization. A new hyphenated identity was born—Daur-Mongol—but one bereft of any official designation by any Chinese force.

Hyphenation was not, however, a common practice among the tribally divided Mongols. Among Mongols, one would not normally speak of Halh-Mongol or Barga-Mongol; it was unnecessary to hyphenate Halh with Mongol in order to emphasize their "Mongol" identity, for that Mongol identity was known and taken for granted. This is an important area for research: How did the Mongols identify themselves in the thirteenth century and subsequently, and what impact did the Qing policies toward Mongols have in determining who should or should not be considered Mongol in relation to the Qing governance? For the moment, I argue that at the turn of the twentieth century, the underlying Mongolness was no longer assumed but had to be reaffirmed, so hyphenation began to emerge among groups in order to emphasize their Mongolness to others.

The first public mention of "Daur-Mongol" I can find appeared in Merse's book *The Mongolian Question*, written in 1924. As mentioned earlier, the book was a survey of Mongolia on behalf of the Chinese Foreign Ministry, but because of Merse's pro-Mongolian stance conveyed in this book, he was sacked. There Merse wrote that the Mongol Nation consisted of five main groups:

> The Halh living in Outer and Inner Mongolia, who were the descendants of wise and heroic Chinggis Khan and his meritorious generals, the Ööled-Mongol living in Qinghai and north of the Tianshan mountains; the Daur-Mongols numbering one hundred thousand living in Heilongjiang province's Hulunbuir and Butaha; the Buryat-Mongols numbering five hundred thousand who live in the Baikal state and Ilkusk province of Russia; and the Kalmyk-Mongols numbering two hundred thousand who live in the Volga river region of Russia. (Guo 1924: 17)

He then commented on the cultural unity of the groups by emphasizing their common Mongol language, common belief in Buddhism, and common pastoral economy. Presumably, these were thought to be part of the common fund of cultural property of the Mongols that makes up the distinctive traditions passed down through the generations. Unfortunately, he did not elaborate, but whatever he thought specifically, the inclusion of the Daurs as a major Mongol group enabled Merse to speak authoritatively on behalf of all Mongols to the Chinese authorities about the "Mongolian Question." He spoke as a legitimate member of the Mongol nation. It is interesting to note that while he called Mongols in Outer and Inner Mongolia Halh without differentiating tribal differences or hyphenating it with "Mongol," he hyphenated all other groups with "Mongol." It is obvious that for Merse, Halh was coterminous with Mongol and was accorded the central place, whereas other groups had to be specifically identified as Mongol.

The centrality of Outer Mongolia can be seen most clearly from the Buryat nationalism at the beginning of the twentieth century. And indeed, much of Daur-Mongolian nationalism was inspired by the Buryats, with whom Daurs had extensive contacts. Although a Mongol-speaking people, Buryats had their own genealogical tradition that was not linked with "Mongol" genealogy, as defined by Chinggisid. Indeed, the Baikal region that the Buryat inhabit had never been under Mongol or Qing jurisdiction; instead, Russia had ruled the area since the seventeenth century. But Buryat nationalism in nineteenth century Tsarist Russia emphasized their Mongolness and their identification with Mongols elsewhere. This nationalist activism, cultivated largely through education, was soon suppressed by the Tsarist Russian government, and while some Buryat intellectuals were banished to Outer Mongolia around 1910 (Dugarova-Montgomery and Montgomery 1999), most went of their own accord, and some of the more influential of them did so after the Soviets' takeover (e.g., Elbegdorji Rinchino). The experience enabled numerous Buryat intellectuals to play prominent roles in spearheading Mongolian nationalist and communist revolutions in Outer Mongolia (subsequently, in the Mongolian People's Republic).

By no means accidentally, the Buryat Mongolian intellectuals in Russia who were heavily involved in the Mongolian nationalist movement were active in demonstrating their cultural achievement. Ts. Zamcarano, a Buryat, was a pan-Mongolist and was the first person to advise the independent Mongolian government to use the symbol of Chinggis Khan to rally the Mongols (Bulag 1998). In Mongolia he published the first newspaper in the country—*Sine Toli* ("New Mirror"). He was the founder of the Institute of Books and Texts (*Sudur Bicigun Huriyeleng*), which was the predecessor of the Mongolian Academy of Sciences, and initiated and directed almost all the first scientific research in the young republic. Typical of a cultural nationalist, Zamcarano was particularly concerned with both historiography and folklore. He himself published a comprehensive survey of folklore of all groups in the Mongolian People's Republic (1934) and a comprehensive study of the Mongol chronicles (1955). During his trip to Inner Mongolia in 1910, he obtained a copy of the *Secret History of the Mongols* in Chinese transliteration, known as *Yuanchao Mishi*. It was a thirteenth-century text of the family of Chinggis Khan, a narrative tracing the rise of the Mongol Empire. The text mentioned numerous tribal or clan groups. During the Ming dynasty, the book was used by the Ming to train experts in Mongol affairs and thus was transliterated into Chinese, with Chinese annotations. The original Mongolian version was lost, however. In 1916 Zamcarano placed an advertisement in the *Capital News* (*Niislel Hureenii Sonin Bichig*), soliciting books about Chinggis Khan.

According to Ardyajab (1991), a prominent Daur scholar specializing in the study of the *Secret History of the Mongols*, his grandfather Tsend Gung (1875–1932) responded to Zamcarano's call and transliterated the *Yuanchao Mishi* into Mongolian. Tsend Gung, once the leader of the Left Wing office of the Fudutong government of Hulunbuir in the last years of the Qing, went to join the cause of Mongolian independence, led by the lama Jebtsundamba Hutagt. He was ennobled as *bodlogot baatar gung* ("resourceful hero duke")[5] in 1913 for his heroism in the Mongolian expedition sent to liberate Inner Mongolia. And in 1915, he served as deputy foreign minister for Jebtsundamba's Mongolian government (Handsuren 1997: 7–8). Completing the transliteration in 1917, he spelled out his intention in the preface of his transliteration "In order for modern Mongolian children to read ancient Mongolian and know the heroic and majestic deeds of Mongols famous among many countries of the world, I, not fearing my own lack of knowledge and using spare time after work, have endeavored over a year to complete the transliteration" (in Ardyajab 1991, also Handsuren 1997: 4). The work was not published for eighty years, until 1997 in Ulaanbaatar, when it was brought out by Tsend Gung's daughter Handsuren. This was the first attempt to transliterate the *Secret History of the Mongols* into Mongolian in its entirety. Zamtsarano highly appreciated the value of the transliteration, and he took it to the Soviet Union for publication, but before he could do so, he was killed in Stalin's great purge. The manuscript was, however, deposited in the Leningrad branch library of the Oriental Research Institute of the Soviet Academy of Sciences. Although not published until 1997, the manuscript has been used by various scholars working on the *Secret History of the Mongols*, and Ts. Damdinsuren, the literary doyen of the MPR, popularized the *Secret History of the Mongols* in contemporary literary language, based on Tsend Gung's transliteration. Zamcarano, a Buryat Mongol, and Tsend Gung, a Daur Mongol, thus played instrumental roles in helping Mongolia and Mongols at large to reclaim their foundational cultural heritage, thereby also proving staunchly the Mongolness of both the Buryat and the Daur.

Tsend was not the only "Mongol" who transliterated the *Secret History of the Mongols* into Mongolian. Merse, in his busy and dangerous revolutionary career in the late 1920s—possibly after the Inner Mongolian People's Revolutionary Party split in 1927–1928—was also involved in transliterating the *Secret History of the Mongols*, demonstrating his sophisticated mastery of both classical Mongolian and classical Chinese. Zamcarano specifically mentioned Merse[6] in his discussion of the transcription of the *Secret History of the Mongols*:

> We quoted above texts from the Altan tobci and the Yuan-ch'ao pi-shih in the transcription by A. M. Pozdneev, who lays a claim to a scientifically accurate transcrip-

tion of the Chinese characters. An example is provided by the transcription of the same text by the Mongol scholar Merse, a Dagur, who knew his Dagur mother tongue, who knew spoken and written Mongol, and who worked on a Mongol-Chinese dictionary which was published during the Ming period. He distinguished h before vowels, when this aspirate occurred, and he gave the possible variant reading in so far as the Mongol alphabet admitted of such a possibility. (1955: 62)

The job was not an easy one because it required a sophisticated command of classical Chinese. Moreover, the text contained ancient Mongolian vocabulary lost to contemporary Mongols but largely preserved in the Daur language. This linguistic affinity with ancient Mongolian testified, Tsend and Merse must surely have thought, that the Daurs were Mongols. In any nationalist project, the essence of which lies in the national heritage, such a substantial claim was a powerful boost. Perhaps one reason why the *Secret History of the Mongols* became so fascinating to these Daurs and Buryats was precisely because it represented an imagination of the organic "unity" of all the Mongols. Since then, the Daurs have proved to be best endowed with the skills and interest to translate and study the *Secret History of the Mongols*, the foundational Mongolian text that informed the origin and rise of the Mongol nation.[7]

Buryat nationalism, although temporarily suppressed in late nineteenth century and early days of the twentieth century, gained momentum as a result of the Buryats' pan-Mongolian outlook when Outer Mongolia declared independence in 1911. The Bolsheviks' takeover of the Buryat lands did nothing to stop this tendency, and in 1923 a Buryat-Mongolian Autonomous Soviet Socialist Republic was founded in the Soviet Union. Note this unprecedented official hyphenation. It is perhaps not far-fetched to speculate that the Daur hyphenation with the Mongols as Daur-Mongol had the Buryat-Mongol exemplar for emulation. In any case, it had roots in the pan-Mongolian movement, looking toward an independent Mongolia as the Mecca for all Mongols. Small wonder that Merse made repeated visits to Mongolia and wrote several small books about what he saw there. Like the Buryats, who had been outside of Mongolian cultural and political hegemony, yet played such an important role in the pan-Mongolian revolution, Daur intellectuals like Tsend, Merse, and Fumingtai were modernists and nationalists—above all, pan-Mongolists. Like the Buryats, they were involved in reclaiming the cultural heritage of the Mongols, and like the Buryats, they "educated" the so-called proper Mongols. Whereas the Buryat intellectuals like Zamcarano set up the first modern school and the first research institution in Mongolia, Merse and fellow Daurs opened the first Mongolian school in Hulunbuir in 1916, and in 1929, after his failed uprising, Merse took up the task of setting up the most prestigious Northeastern Mongolian Banner Normal School. To be Mongol, they had to fundamentally redefine the genealogical parameters of the Mongols.

Not all Daur intellectuals were attracted to the revolution in Mongolia. Some attained high positions in Beijing. Guo Kexing, a distant relative of Merse, was a prominent scholar who worked in various capacities in the Ministry of Transportation in Beijing and as a professor at the Transportation University. He was also a senior editor of several publication series and journals of the Chinese Army. In 1926, while editing comprehensive data on China's transportation and military affairs, Guo published the eight-volume *Heishui Guoshi Jiacheng*, of which three volumes survive (Ao Dong 1989). This was an ambitious project to unravel the entanglement of tribal groups and banner systems in Heilongjiang, as well as his own clan history. Merse was one of its peer reviewers. Guo Kexing, however, had a completely sinocentric view of the origins of the Daur. *Dahuer* (Daur), he wrote, was originally descended from *huaxia*, that is, the Chinese. But as they moved to the northern steppe, they adopted a pastoral economy and became "barbarian" (*yong yi bian xia*). He lamented the lack of written tradition that contributed to the obliteration of the true history of the *Dahuer*:

> When people talk about nationalities in Heilongjiang province, they usually refer to the Solon, Manchu and Mongol. And the Daur people also shook the world as the crack force of the Solon, and when the Manchus and Mongols moved in and ruled China, they [the Daur] were also proud of being Solon, Manchu or Mongol, forgetting who they were. Pity! Forgetting ancestors would be ridiculed by people. (Guo 1987: 127)

The book no doubt catered to the then prevalent Chinese nationalism, seeking to establish that all five nationalities recognized at that time were branches of the Chinese, thereby establishing a racial-genealogical Chinese Nation, a vision later canonized in 1943 in Jiang Jieshi's *China's Destiny* (Chiang 1947).

While Guo Kexing extolled the unity of the Chinese Nation, others felt that the Chinese, with their claim of Five Nationality Harmony, were precisely the source of oppression, control, and assimilation. The Daurs at the time closely identified with Mongols, and indeed, Merse even personally told Lattimore, who worked in Manchuria and Inner Mongolia in 1929–1933, that "the Daghors are 'descendants' of Habto Hasar, a brother of Chinggis Khan" (Lattimore 1969: 183), thereby aligning the Daurs with the other eastern Mongols who claim a similar ancestry.

In 1933 a book appeared, entitled *Textual Research on the Daur-Mongol* (Altangata 1980). Built on Merse's classification of the Mongol groups, the book tried to prove the existence and validity of such a Daur-Mongol group. Through evidential scholarship, the author, Altangata, a Daur, a follower of Merse, traced the genealogy of the Daurs to the ancient Tartars, a Mongol tribe known in the *Secret History of the Mongols*. Based on linguistic analysis, Altangata argued that the name Daur was a modern corruption of Tartar. It is interesting to note that the book was sponsored by Ba Jingbao (a.k.a. Fu Liting), a Daur notable in the Butaha region, who became the governor of the Hingan East Province under

Manchuguo. Degulai, another prominent Daur politician, who wrote the preface, was to become an important official working for the Mongolian border government of the Mongolian prince Demchugdonrob, and he later became a leader of the Mongol community in Taiwan after fleeing the mainland in 1949. Published in January 1933, the book was widely distributed by the Eastern Butaha Eight Banner office, thus lending official weight to the idea of Daur-Mongol identity in Manchuguo. The Daurs' Mongol identity was officially affirmed in Japanese controlled Manchuguo.

Daur-Mongol identity resided, then, in both a linguistic and a genealogical imagination. Curiously, there was little effort on the part of the Mongols to claim that the Daurs were their lost brothers, and indeed, as of today I have yet to find a single piece written by Mongols insisting that the Daurs were Mongols. The Daurs had to confront an entrenched Mongol identity, which was the project of Mongolian historiography since medieval time and which kept lists of tribes constituting the "Mongols." There had been little ambiguity during the Manchu empire concerning who were Mongols and who were not and where the boundary was of each of the hundred-odd Mongolian banners. In none of the Mongol chronicles were the Daurs mentioned as Mongols. In fact, by organizing the Daurs in the Manchu eight banner system, rather than the Mongol eight banners, the Qing rendered them non-Mongol, indeed "New Manchu." For the Daurs to enter the traditional Mongol "national" genealogy, established first by the founding of the Mongol state in 1206 and enshrined in the *Secret History of the Mongols* (which contains detailed genealogical information of different clans and tribes and their overlords), it would require broadening the genealogical boundary of the Mongols, which was in fact shrinking or hardening as a result of Qing administrative classification of banners. And precisely because Mongol is a genealogical and racial category, the Daurs could only categorically prove their Mongolness through genealogy. *Textual Research on the Daur-Mongol* was, in my view, also a response to implicit Mongol rejection of the Daur claim to Mongol identity. Degulai, who prefaced the book, placed its significance in consolidating the "unity" of the Mongols. This internal Mongol "unity" was placed in opposition to the Chinese discourse of unity of the five nationalities. He expressed regret that after Chinggis Khan's conquest of Eurasia, Mongol tribes had been dispersed across the vast territory of Europe and Asia, some being assimilated, some being conquered, so that some no longer recognized that they were Mongol, thus affecting the unity of the Mongols.

> Take the Daur-Mongol in the Onon drainage region for example. At the beginning of the Yuan dynasty, they either fought each other or expanded their influence moving inside the territory of the Manchu. Later, as the Manchu ruled China, they conquered the Daur tribe, who were defeated, reorganized, and subjected to their control for hundreds of years. Also because they were placed near their subgroup Honku, i.e., Solon, to engage in pastoral economy, those not well versed in history

and geography sometimes mistook the Daur for a group of the Tungus people. (Altangata 1980: 1)

Degulai complained that this was caused by both the colonization of Chinese historiography and the physical dispersion of Mongols, which caused the loss of their racial identity, making them unable to unite with each other against external enemies. "This is only because there is no traditional history (written) by the Mongol themselves. Our history has been written by others, who can then manipulate our national consciousness." He lauded the publication of the book as both correcting existing incorrect views and "also contributing greatly to the unity of our Mongols" (Altangata 1980: 1).

The ambivalence of the Mongols to the Daur claim of Mongol identity was evidenced in the new nickname given by Mongols to the Daurs—"September 18 Mongol,"[8] implying that they became Mongols only after the Japanese conquest of Manchuria on September 18, 1931. The Daurs were in a precarious betwixt-and-between position. When the Japanese scholar Ikeshiri (1982) published a book in 1943 entitled *Daur Nationality*, many Daurs were enraged, accusing the Japanese of attempting to split the Mongolian nationality (Tegusi, interview 1996).

Nevertheless, their identity as Mongols and their cultural sophistication put them in an advantageous position in Manchuguo. The Manchuguo emperor Pu Yi's wife Wan Rong was a Daur. The highest Mongolian commander within Manchuguo was a Daur, Guo Wenling. Together with Lingsheng, another Daur notable from Hulunbuir, Guo was instrumental in persuading Pu Yi to become the emperor of Manchuguo in 1932 (Zhang 1990: 239). In 1942, as the commander of the No. 9 Military Control Zone (*junguan qu*), Guo Wenling also played a key role in building the Chinggis Khan temple (completed on September 30, 1943), the central symbol of Mongol nationalism in eastern Inner Mongolia (Zhang 1990: 247). Although numerically small, their power was so extensive that of the four Mongol provinces within Manchuguo, the Daurs initially controlled two: Hingan North Province and Hingan East Province.

On the other hand, the Daurs' fiercely independent character was a constant challenge to Japanese expansionism. Their insistence on their autonomy from Japan was treated by the Japanese as indicative of strong Mongol nationalism. In 1936 Lingsheng, the Daur governor of Hingan North Province, and three other Daur leaders, were executed by the Japanese for allegedly colluding with the Mongolian People's Republic, thereby becoming the most prominent "Mongol" resistance martyrs to Japanese imperialism and exposing the fragility of the Mongol fantasy of Japanese help to the Mongols in their struggle against China. A purge of Daurs from the Manchuguo leadership followed (Erhenbayar 1985). Thereafter, sixty-eight disillusioned Daur youths and intellectuals moved out of Manchuguo to work for Prince Demchugdonrob's Mongolian Borderland government (Guo 1989).

In short, the hyphenated appellation Daur-Mongol made the Daurs either ardent Mongol nationalists or ambivalently aware of their "out of place" status. Their initial political sophistication was soon reduced, as their high-profile leaders were either executed or punished by the Soviet Union, the MPR, or the Japanese. Many Daur pan-Mongolist revolutionaries, including Merse and Fumingtai, perished in Stalin's Great Purge in 1937–1938 (Odongowa 1996: 168). Other high-profile Daurs involved in Manchuguo met with tragedy after the war. Guo Wenling was punished by the communists as a war criminal. Many Daur-Mongols working for Prince Demchugdonrob's government were permanently removed from Inner Mongolian politics. Some fled to Taiwan. As a result, after the collapse of Manchuguo, it was Merse's Mongol students, and not the Daurs, who would play a major role in the postwar politics of Inner Mongolia.

The postwar political configuration is too complex to be treated here in detail; suffice it to say that the Daurs felt an increasing marginalization in the new Inner Mongolian politics. They played little role in setting up either the Eastern Mongolia Autonomous Government or the Inner Mongolia Autonomous Government.[9] We may be tempted to say that it is the cumulative result of this marginalization that led to their secession from Mongol nationality and ultimate reclassification as Daur nationality. But what triggered their change of ethnic identity appears to be related to the Chinese communist initiative to identify nationalities and realign ethnic relations in order to "solve nationality problems."

Not all Daurs lived in Inner Mongolia. Some lived in Heilongjiang province and others were in Xinjiang. These Daurs were not under the purview of Mongolian nationalist discourse or administration. After 1946 when the CCP controlled Manchuria, it began to practice a new ethnic policy that promised more equity and encouraged ethnic autonomy. As a result, the Daurs in Heilongjiang province set up an autonomous Daur township in August 1952, naming it the "Longjiang County Daur Nationality Autonomous Region." They were encouraged to send a delegation to Beijing, representing their own "Daur nationality." New China's nationality policy also compelled other Daurs to seek a more authentic representation. In March 1954 the Daurs in Xinjiang, who were sent by the Qing to garrison as part of the Solon garrison force, insisted on restoring their ethnic identity as Daur, as opposed to Solon. In the same year, the Chinese government established a "Gurban Siheri Dahuer Nationality Autonomous Region" in Xinjiang. The Daurs in Inner Mongolia proved to be a difficult case because of their extensive entanglement with the Mongols. As early as 1952–1953, anthropologists, historians, and linguists from Beijing[10] arrived in Inner Mongolia to identify the Daurs. Although there was no consensus among the Daurs, they were identified as a separate nationality soon afterward. The Daur nationality did not, however, become an official category until 1964, as a result of the second national census (Huang 1995: 150).

DE-HYPHENATING THE DAUR-MONGOL: MERSE, TRAITOR
TO THE DAUR NATIONALITY?

How, then, did the Daurs narrate their new nationality? Or how was it narrated on their behalf? Prior to the People's Republic, there was little written about "Daur" history per se, either by the Daurs or by outsiders who were easily accessible to the Daurs. And indeed, the most important text produced by the Daurs was written to prove their "Mongol" identity. Now that the Daurs were classified as a separate nationality, a history had to be written for them; the new nationality had to be narrated. At this juncture it is particularly interesting to examine what the new Daur history has to say about their past, and especially about Merse, their most prominent intellectual-politician.

The first significant book was published in 1985, *A Social and Historical Investigation of the Daur Nationality*. However, it was actually prepared by the Institute of Nationalities of the Chinese Academy of Social Sciences in the early 1960s, though not published until the 1980s, when it appeared with revisions. The text was originally prepared to serve as raw material for the writing of three series: The National Minority Brief History, The National Minority Brief Information, and The Outline of Nationalities in the Autonomous Regions. A "preliminary version" of the *Combined Volume of the Daur Nationality Brief History and Brief Information* was issued in 1963 to solicit comments. All of these projects were torpedoed by the Cultural Revolution, and their publication was postponed until the mid-1980s, when they could be published with post–Cultural Revolution perspectives.

The book, like the preliminary version of *Combined Volume of the Daur Nationality Brief History and Brief Information*, which synthesized materials collected in the 1950s and 1960s, made no mention of the fact that the Daurs had only recently been recognized as a separate nationality. Instead, it traced the nationality as it appeared in the historical record from the mid-seventeenth century, giving the impression of a natural, uninterrupted flow of historical time, uncontaminated in its national essence. The authors, mostly Daur and Mongol, did a remarkable job of identifying the location, population, and organization of the "Daur" since the mid-seventeenth century. Similar to the revolutionary historiography of the Mongols, what was deemed important to demonstrate their revolutionary credentials were two uprising stories-cum-legends narrating Daur resistance to Chinese colonization during the Republican period. These were deemed important for demonstrating class-nationality consciousness, as prerequisites for their "autonomy." One uprising was organized by Shaolang and Daifu in Qiqihar of Heilongjiang province. According to this story, class cleavages among the Daurs deepened as Chinese penetrated their region. Chinese merchants also added to the impoverishment of many Daurs, forcing them to rebel. The direct cause of the rebellion was apparently the arrest of Shaolang and his cousin Daifu, who were accused of stealing and selling a landlord's (presumably, a Chinese landlord's) horse in 1913. Breaking out of prison along with other prisoners, they carried out a heroic action of robbing rich landlords to aid the poor. But in 1916, as their numbers grew to sixty, the team split up because of internal feuds, and they were finally crushed by the Chinese

The second story tells of an uprising in Morindawa in 1931, on the eve of the Japanese invasion of Manchuria, during which the Daurs rebelled against the Chinese immigration that disturbed the local livelihood. The Morindawa uprising was said to "defend the homeland and national interest." The rebels consisted of young students and hunters and was led by an adult hunter, Ying Dengbao. Attracting over two hundred people, the rebel army attacked Chinese government forces and local Chinese bandits. The army was never defeated by the Chinese, but it accepted Japanese reorganization in 1932. "Then, the one year long Morindawa uprising finally failed" (Nei Menggu Zizhiqu Bianjizu 1985: 19).

Merse disappeared from this version of Daur revolutionary history. Indeed, apart from these two uprisings led by lower-class Daurs, there was no other "revolutionary" involvement by the Daurs. This primitivization of the Daur modern revolutionary history stemmed not just from the Marxist demand for agency of "the people," but more important, it was premised on a new "national" or "ethnic" essence. Heroes had to fight specifically for nationality, including class-nationality. In this sense, an ethnic history, especially a communist-induced one, is a tortuous process of ethnic exclusivity, one that conceals the great efforts by communists to extend the united front to various nationalities. It cleanses not only ambiguities, but also what is teleologically considered damaging to the newfound essence and morality of the nationality. To reclaim the history of Merse and his comrades would delegitimize the raison d'être of the claim for a separate Daur nationality status, because Merse and his comrades fought for the Mongols (Daur as part of Mongol) and as Mongols. Deletion of sophisticated Daur revolutionary heroes was also facilitated by the denunciation of Merse in the official Inner Mongolian revolutionary history. However, renouncing this history altogether inadvertently demonstrates that the Daurs were an unimportant and backward people who fully deserved and required the warm concern of the Party and the state. And curiously, in this new historical underrepresentation, the Daurs transformed themselves from the leading group spearheading the Inner Mongolian revolution to ineffective rebels, seeking justice. And their "liberation" was delivered not by themselves (for they were supposedly weak and backward) but by the Chinese Communist Party.

The absence of modern Daur revolutionaries in Daur history was directly related to ambiguities in the Daur-Mongol identity. In the most important document that set out the reasons for identifying the Daur as a non-Mongol nationality, written by Fu Lehuan, it was also necessary to confront some Daurs in Hailar who insisted on their Mongol identity (1955: 27). Fu Lehuan suggested that those who identified with Mongols were a small number of ruling aristocrats, opportunists who, in their own interest, identified themselves as "New Manchu" during the Qing. Although he showed some sympathy for the structural dilemma of the Daurs, who were "banner soldiers" who had no place to go after the Qing and therefore had to rely on the Mongols, Fu condemned the ulterior motives of a small number of Daurs: "Here we should distinguish another small group of people, who sought to ally with the Mongols to wage a 'Mongolian National Revival' movement, and advocated 'pan-Mongolism,' such as Guo Daofu (Merse)" (1955: 28). His pan-Mongolian nationalism was denounced as no more than selfish interest.

> Guo Daofu, in the 8th and 9th years of the Republican period, identified himself as a "Mongolian" representative, collected donations by "praying" for Mongols. . . . He was obsessed with the idea of becoming the "premier" of "Great Mongolia." Once he disguised himself as a revolutionary and together with Fumingtai organized the "Mongolian Youth Party," and launched an "uprising.". . . After its failure, he became an advisor to Zhang Xueliang and set up the "Mongolian Banner Normal School" in Shenyang, continuing to propagate bourgeois nationalism, claiming that Daurs were Mongols. (Fu 1955: 28–29)

This Mongol nationalism was conveniently linked to the Japanese attempt to "rejuvenate Mongolian Nationality"; hence it was dubbed anti-Soviet, anticommunist, and anti-Chinese, but pro-Japanese. It is interesting to note that those who continued to insist on their Mongol identity were considered no more than conspiring with the Japanese:

> Some reactionary Daur upper elements, in order to satisfy their own political ambitions, inherited Guo Daofu's mantle; they too identified themselves as "Mongol." Taking advantage of this opportunity, they mobilized and obtained "high posts" in the "Hingan East Province" and "Hingan North Province" set up by the Japanese and the puppet regimes. (Fu 1955: 29)

Since this Mongol identity was no more than a conspiracy of the Japanese and the politically ambitious Daur, "this conspiracy was struck a counterblow by the great masses of the Daur people" (Fu 1955: 29), who insisted on their authentic Daur identity.

It is clear that to justify the Daur as a separate nationality, the Daur-Mongol identity had to be ruthlessly suppressed. In doing so, virtually all Daur intellectuals and politicians had to be denounced as pan-Mongolist and/or pro-Japanese, two of the biggest enemies of China. Their revolution and their struggles were deemed incompatible with the new Daur nationality, whose identity has been cherished by the "people." Revolution was a people's revolution, whereas a revolution of nonpeople could only be "counterrevolutionary" and must necessarily be denounced and cleansed from history. For a Daur to be Mongol is to be pro-

Japan! Insofar as Merse and other Daur intellectuals advocated Mongol identity for the Daur, they were the enemies of the Daur people.

But immediately after the triumphal declaration that "[a]fter Liberation, the reactionary political activities of Guo Daofu and a small number of Daur elite elements in the Japanese and Puppet government period had long been convicted by the great masses of the Daur people," Fu Lehuan noted that "Guo Daofu–style education still has some lingering influence. Meanwhile, such anti-science and history-betraying books about the Daur genesis as *Textual Research on the Daur-Mongol* are still wide spread among the Daur people under historical conditions of a shortage of historical readings. To that small number of people who judge the nationality identity question solely from blood lineage, the book still retains influence" (Fu 1955: 29).

MAPPING THE DAUR NATIONALITY IN INNER MONGOLIA

The consequences for changing ethnic identity are great. A socialist ethnic identity would have to be justified by meeting all of Stalin's criteria, including that a nationality must have a common language, common territory, common economy, and common psychological makeup or culture. But these criteria are as much a precondition for determining a nationality as they are targets to meet and blueprints to fulfill. The historiographical delineation is only the first step.

Broadly speaking, there were two kinds of ethnonationalism during the Republican era that forced the relatively weak Chinese Communist Party to grant autonomous status. The first is territorial nationalism associated with the Mongols and Tibetans. Of the two, Mongols were more intimately related to the international movement and involved in the communist movement and Japanese colonialism. This kind of ethnonationalism engaged the Chinese political movements, including both nationalist and communist, from the collapse of the Qing. The other kind is less a territorial nationalism and more an ethnic demand for recognition, such as that associated with the Hui (Muslims), Zhuang, and numerous other groups whose populations are more widely scattered throughout China. Some anthropologists and historians have suggested that these latter nationalities were later "invented" by the socialist Chinese state (cf. Gladney 1991, Kaup 2000). The Daurs are an exceptional case; they stood between the two patterns because of their strong identification with the Mongols and their leadership role in the framing of Mongol ethnonationalism. And yet, as discussed earlier, not all the Daurs came under this Mongol identification, and it was those who were outside the Mongolian cultural and political purview who first reacted to the Chinese state's new ethnic policy of recognition of new nationalities. The result was to place the Daurs under tremendous pressures to dissociate themselves from the Mongols and create an autonomous identity, which in turn required a sweeping reconstruction or invention of their history and culture.

Mapping Daur autonomy is no easy process, given the people's dispersed residential pattern. This situation is perhaps not so dissimilar to the problem of mapping the galactic, nonterritorial Southeast Asian polities into a Siam geobody, delineating rigid territorial boundaries (Thongchai 1994, 1996). It was yet more complicated because granting of autonomous banners to the "small" ethnic minorities in Inner Mongolia was carried out at a time when the Inner Mongolia Autonomous Region was extending its jurisdiction over the former Suiyuan province (created in 1928), as a matter of reclaiming what was historically Inner Mongolian territory. This was indeed a Pyrrhic victory, whose result was to increase the ratio between Chinese and Mongols from 4 to 1 to 7 to 1. But for Mongols, what determined this geographical unification drive was their memory of historical injustice done to them through the influx of Chinese settlers in the first half of the twentieth century and the political weight they carried as an important nationality with "compatriots" in the independent Mongolian People's Republic.

This territorial expansion was a curious compromise between the Chinese policy of regional autonomy (which prescribes autonomy for minorities that constitute the majority in a particular territory associated with them) and the Mongol demand for an "independent autonomy" (modeled after the post-1915 and pre-1946 MPR status as an autonomy that recognized China as its suzerain state). Ulanhu called Inner Mongolian Autonomy—Unified Autonomy (*tongyi zizhi*), demanding the creation of an expanded Inner Mongolia Autonomous Region that would bring all Mongols in historical Inner Mongolia under a unified territorial institution. This symbolism of unity of eastern and western Inner Mongolia carried greater weight than other practical considerations, such as how a small minority (one-seventh of the total population in Inner Mongolia) could exercise the titular (*zhuti*) autonomous rights over a territory in which the Chinese were the overwhelming majority. It proved to be a costly enterprise. Not only had Chinese leaders in Suiyuan province to be given equal official positions in the Inner Mongolia Autonomous Region, their "revolutionary history" also had to be accommodated.

But politics can be contagious. It is the Inner Mongolia concept of "unified autonomy," rather than the regional autonomous banner granted to "small" nationalities, that inspired many Daurs. Curiously, until 1958 the Daurs had no separate administration within Inner Mongolia. The Hulunbuir autonomous government, based on the Hingan North Province set up by the Daurs immediately after the anti-Japanese war, was abolished in 1946 and taken over by the Inner Mongolia Autonomous Government, and the Non-Muren League, which was built on the basis of the Hingan East Province, was soon abolished. There remained no political niche for the Daurs. Moreover, the Daurs were now scattered in two provinces: Heilongjiang and Inner Mongolia, if we do not count the small number of Daurs in distant Xinjiang. In 1957, during the short-lived Hundred Flowers Movement, some Daur leaders called for a Daur autonomous prefecture, to cover Hulunbuir, Morindawa of Inner Mongolia, and Qiqihar in Heilongjiang, restoring the former political sphere of the Daurs. The Daurs, finding a new mission in such an enterprise, enthusiastically set out to explore it. Unfortunately, such a territorial vision clashed directly with the Mongol vision, for it threatened to remove a large chunk of what Mongols claimed as their territory. Ulanhu expressed his opposition to the proposal in May 1957 at the Propaganda Conference of the Inner Mongolian Party Committee. I quote his remark at length, as it was remarkably frank, allowing us to understand how the Mongol officials thought at that time:

> With regard to the question of Daur nationality autonomy, the Inner Mongolian Party Committee is very cautious. First, there is a need to identify whether the Daur are a separate nationality. . . . According to research, 60% of the Daur vocabulary is the same as Mongolian. In the past, I also heard Guo Daofu [Merse] say that the Daurs are the authentic Mongols. Mongols used to believe in shamanism, and the Daur now still believe in this religion. But after we looked at the Soviet situation, we felt that it was possible for the emergence of some [new] nationalities after the revolution. After liberation we adopted an attitude of doing research first, not rushing to decide. Besides, there is disagreement within the Daur nationality. Later we sent people down to listen to people's opinions. They were very happy to become a separate nationality; it was then decided to recognize the Daur as a nationality.

He then discussed the difficulty of putting all the residentially dispersed Daurs into a single territorial unit and the justification for rejecting an autonomous prefecture for the Daurs:

> Then, we set out to study the question of Daur autonomous institutions. The Inner Mongolian Party Committee discussed the question in February and March last year. The crux of the matter is to establish appropriate levels of autonomous institution, whether autonomous prefecture or autonomous county. To solve this question, one criterion should be the size of the nationality's concentrated residential area, then consider the size of the population. Historically, the upper area of the Non River is the hunting area of the Daur. Now they live interspersed throughout Inner Mongolia and Heilongjiang. The concentrated residential areas are some natural villages. The [Daur] population in Inner Mongolia is over 20,000, in Heilongjiang over 20,000, and altogether about 50,000 in the whole country. To establish an autonomous prefecture, it would be necessary to consider merging part of Inner Mongolia with a part of Heilongjiang. But conditions do not exist for establishing an autonomous area. . . . Since the Daur nationality have no large compact residential community, we suggested that the Central Government set up an autonomous banner (county), and this suggestion was approved as early as May last year (1956). We proposed setting up a Daur autonomous banner on the basis of the Morindawa banner, where 24,000 Daur people reside. But some comrades of the Daur national-

ity were not content, and they demanded nationality unified autonomy, they demanded an autonomous prefecture, this is without any realistic justification. But because opinions differed, the decision was postponed. Now the Inner Mongolia Party Committee is waiting for the central government to convene a meeting to discuss the matter. (Ulanhu 1967 [1957]: 19)

Although the Daurs had proposed setting up a Daur prefecture under the jurisdiction of Inner Mongolia, the prospect of turning part of the historical Mongol territory into a non-Mongol territory, albeit within Inner Mongolia, frightened Mongol leaders, and they rejected this proposal. The proposal also met with strong opposition from Heilongjiang province. After the Center approved the Inner Mongolian proposal to set up an autonomous banner instead of a prefecture for the Daurs, some Daur cadres continued to persist in their demand. This episode indicates that the structure of the CCP did allow for certain types of local initiatives, but some balance of forces or hierarchical relations limited the opportunities and could result in heavy penalties for those who contested official policy. Unfortunately for the Daurs, their campaign coincided with the hostile political atmosphere of the anti-rightist movement. In February 1958 the Party Center condemned "unprincipled" demand for expansion of territory under minority autonomy and elevation of autonomous administrative status as a manifestation of "local nationalism" (see Wang 1958). But while Inner Mongolia was unable to undertake any further expansion—that is, to include many Mongols remaining in Heilongjiang, Liaoning, and Jilin provinces—the consequences for the Daurs were far greater. Not only did the Daur campaign collapse, but most of the leaders involved in the prefecture-building campaign were sacked or punished.[11] After this ruthless purge, a smaller Morindawa Daur Nationality Autonomous Banner was set up within Inner Mongolia on August 15, 1958, when "the people danced and sang songs, joyfully celebrating this significant and glorious day of the people of the Daur Nationality" (Wang Duo 1992: 416).

In this struggle for territorial rights as prescribed for defining a "nationality" (which has to have a "common territory"), the Daurs lost legitimation by losing most of their leaders. Their failure, I argue, stems not only from their small number, but more important, from their primary interest in fulfilling the territorial conditions for a separate nationality. Since the latter necessarily required dissociation from the Mongols, territorially, culturally, and politically, the Daurs inevitably clashed head on with Mongol interests.

In the ethnic quota system implemented in Inner Mongolia to assure strong Mongolian "representation" in leadership positions as a means of exercising their ethnic rights, Mongols remained vigilant concerning the Daurs, many of whom were highly educated and better qualified than Mongols, being trilingual in Mongolian, Chinese, and Daur. Their taking up leadership positions would mean diminishing the Mongol percentage. In the 1950s Mongols called the Daurs "Mongolian Jews" by virtue of their intellectual achievements and their familiarity with Mongol (and Chinese) culture. Although this constituted a rec-ognition of their superior talent, Daurs who experienced that painful historical era remember it with disdain and bitterness. Young Daurs, less versed in history and experience, feel immense pride in this stereotype.

The Daurs, then, had to stay where they were supposed to be—that is, they were supposed to be content as a "small" ethnic minority. This status was consol-idated after the Cultural Revolution, and they now have only one "Daur" repre-sentative in the People's Congress and a leader in charge of nationality affairs in the Political Consultative Conference. As socialist subjects like workers or women, a nationality should have its prescribed "place," no more no less.[12] Such was the fate of the de-hyphenated Daur nationality in socialist China.

DEBATING THE DAUR ETHNOGENESIS
AND THE REINSTITUTION OF MERSE

Historians and anthropologists have noted a profound change in China's policy toward minorities since the Cultural Revolution. This was partly due to the demise of the class approach, as central to the Chinese regime's understanding of social relations, and the emergence of stress on the moral authority of the state and nation. Historians noted a reversal of the dominant historiographical paradigm (Dirlik 1996), in which many whom the CCP identified as traitors have been reappropriated as national heroes (Guo and He 1999). It is interesting to note that treason toward China, as understood by the CCP, turned out to be a simultaneously Han-centric and class-ridden concept. Zeng Guofan, a Chinese commander from Hunan province, who crushed a powerful Chinese peasant uprising in late Qing, had long been condemned by Chinese communists as a traitor to the Chinese Nation not only for his suppression of the revolutionary "masses," but for supporting the alien Manchu dynasty. In the 1990s craze for new heroes, Zeng has been redefined as a Chinese national hero and his suppres-sion of Chinese rebels deemed a noble deed, not for supporting the Manchu per se, but for defending the "country," "state," or "people" of China—a pan-Chi-nese Nation—a neutral moral entity beyond the parochial Han-centrism pro-moted by Chinese communists (Guo and He 1999).

The new post–Cultural Revolution emphasis on cultural diversity within the Chinese nation, rather than pressing for the withering away of ethnic identities, also led to ethnic revival among China's national minorities, which began to celebrate their cultural accomplishments. The key to understanding this ethnic revival is the notion of culture. It implies a transition of nationality, from its political, territorial, economic, and linguistic overtones—a bounded political entity—to "ethnic groups" with colorful "cultures" within the Chinese Nation. Emily Chao (1996) argued, in her study of the Naxi nationality in the post-Mao era, that the state project of re-imagining the nation engendered the re-presentation of the Naxi as a learned, civilized, and advanced minority through sanitizing and secularizing religion. The colorful "cultural diversity," noted others (cf. Schein 2000), has been packaged for domestic and international consumption. In this respect, it is pertinent to examine how the Daurs' rewriting of their history constituted a challenge to Mongolian historiographical representation.

Victor Shnirelman (1996: 6) argues in his study of the competition for the past that in the authoritarian Soviet Union the field of ethnogenesis was one of the few spheres that ethnic intellectuals could legitimately engage in. Historical origins were manipulated to fit the desire of the Soviet's and each nationality's place in history, present and future. Because of the contrived ethnogenesis of the Soviet era, after the collapse of the Soviet Union, attempts to rewrite history and ethnogenesis in Russia and the new states have led to acrimonious disputes between ethnic groups over their ancestry. The same is true in Inner Mongolia. After the Cultural Revolution, in the atmosphere of ethnic revival, there emerged a debate over Daur ethnogenesis so important that it has become a subdiscipline within Daur studies. Two broadly opposing ideas can be discerned: one claims that the Daurs descended from the Mongols, and another traces their origins from a pre-Mongol people—the Khitan. This debate, which is almost entirely among the Daurs, with occasional input by seemingly disinterested Chinese scholars, has been largely avoided by Mongol scholars.

Some (see especially Ounan Wuzhuer 1995; Wulisi Wurong 1987) have argued that the Daurs were forced to proclaim a Mongol identity since the Chinese government did not recognize a separate Daur identity in the 1920s. In this view, early Daur intellectuals were opportunists who "lied" about their ethnic identity in order to be able to pursue careers outside of their community. However, this "lie" was said to be "ridiculed" by their compatriots, who often made fun of their newly acquired Mongol identity. For this reason, according to supporters of a separate Daur identity, those Daur-Mongol intellectuals never identified themselves as Mongol when they went home. It is clear in this view that "the people" recognized the absurdity of the hyphenated claim, both by their silence and by the occasional joke that became the site of resisting the "Daur-Mongol" identity.

Their main focus of attack was Altangata's book, which made the case for the Mongol identity of the Daur. After several decades, the ghost of the book lingers on: For those who emphasize a separate nationality, the book is an irritant, as it suggested voluntary identification with the Mongols. Although it is easy to debunk the book's claim because of its obvious "ridiculous" mistakes, such as that the word *Daur* is the corrupt pronunciation of Tartar, its central argument cannot so easily be dismissed. In the view of critics, to accept the genealogical link with the Mongols as proposed by Altangata would seriously undermine the integrity of the Daurs, implying not only inauthenticity, but also subordinating the Daurs as "followers" of the Mongols, as the word *Daur* would imply in the *Secret History of the Mongols*. *Daur* was then explained not through Mongolian but through Chinese. Proponents of this view (Ayong 1982; Meng 1995) hold that the name *Daur* is a corruption of *Dahe*, a clan of the Khitan. This is so because the Qianlong emperor, in his compilation of frontier people's genealogy, thought that the Daurs were the descendants of the Dahe. Qianlong's designation in this view becomes the earliest indication of Daur ethnogenesis. The symbolic importance of this claim is great, as it implies that the Daurs are descendants of the Khitan, a more culturally and economically civilized people than the Mongols by virtue of their being closer to the Chinese. Although Mongols also claim to have relations with the Khitan, and indeed, the Khitans are said to be proto-Mongol, the point of direct relations with the Khitan is to prove that the Daurs existed prior to the emergence of the Mongols as a nation. This genealogical seniority is psychologically important, for it proves that the Daurs, far from being "followers" of the Mongols, are the "grandfathers" of the Mongols, as a Daur researcher confided to me in 1996. It should be recognized that this view, that the Daurs are a separate people from the Mongols, is also an official, government-sponsored view of the Daurs. Not incidentally, the view is upheld by those politically "in power."

However, this argument, which remains politically dominant and correct among both Daur and Chinese scholars and officials (although this does not necessarily mean that a majority of Daurs hold this view), continues to be challenged by others (see Ayong 1998; Badaranga 1998) who insist that their predecessors' choice of Mongol identity was not entirely political opportunism. Rather, there are linguistic and cultural bases for such identification. The Mongols and the Daurs are linguistically close, sharing over 60 percent common vocabulary, and culturally, they are both pastoralists, although Daur agriculture is more advanced. Badaranga states, "In accordance with the above mentioned common characteristics in language, their geographic and environmental locale, as well as customs and traditions from time immemorial, and religious beliefs, that the Daur once self-identified as Daur-Mongol is not something casual or without basis" (1998: 465). Some senior Daurs whom I interviewed in 1996 argue that the denial of their Mongol identity and denial of that part of the revolutionary history from 1911 to the 1940s deprived the Daurs of their rich history. However, suspicion of the motives of Daur leaders for identifying as Mongols unnecessarily generated conflicts and mutual suspicion among the two peoples. The reality, they argue, was that the Daurs and Mongols had common interests, both were colonized by Chinese, and it is this common fate, common experience, neighborly friendship, and common culture that led to Daur identification with the Mongols. They claim further that Daurs provided crucial leadership and visions for the Inner Mongolian revolutionary movement against feudalism and imperialism. Menghe wrote passionately,

> In the past, under specific historical conditions, it is not something strange or incomprehensible that the Daur used as their own ethnonym the name of the Mon-

gols who are intimately related to themselves. We are also proud of the emergence of such people as Guo Daofu. However, some people went so far as to say that the Daur's calling themselves Mongols was to use force and influence the Mongols in order to get on the political platform. We beg to disagree with such views. (1996: 46)

He argued that this was tantamount to blaming the victims, as the responsibility lay not with the motivation of the Daur intellectuals but with the discriminatory nationality policies of the reactionary oppressors of Republican China. One must caution not to read this pro-Mongol ethnogenesis debate too far; no one is openly claiming that the Daurs should change or abandon their identity as Daurs.

The debate over Daur ethnogenesis is a fierce one, with both sides trying to prove their points "scientifically," but it is never far from the Daur-Mongol hyphenation established by Daur revolutionaries. Therefore, both sides continue to study the motivations of early revolutionaries, especially Merse. Was he really convinced that the Daurs were Mongols and that it would be in the best interest of the Daurs to completely Mongolize themselves, or did he show some interest in the Daurs specifically?

Scholarly research reveals that Merse was not exclusively a Mongol fighter; he also took the interest of the Daurs to heart. While some have revealed his linguistic excellence in translating the *Secret History of the Mongols*, others note that he also devised perhaps the first Latin script for Daur, and that he actively taught the Daurs to read their own "language." Unfortunately, it is said, this experiment was cut short by the Japanese invasion and Merse's early demise. It has also been discovered that Merse in fact was one of the readers of a book written by the Daur scholar Guo Kexing, which proclaimed a Khitan origin for the Daur, thereby suggesting that Merse may also have been sympathetic to this view. This latter is a most egregious after-the-fact reading of history. Nonetheless, what emerges in this research is the agency of Merse in defining his ethnicity and his preoccupation with it. More important, Merse was not just interested in training Mongol students; he also encouraged Daurs to study in Mongolia and the Soviet Union. The cumulative effect of this study of Merse has been to show that for him "Mongol" became a generic term covering many different groups. There was an internal diversity within the Mongol Nation, which Merse acutely recognized. And retrospectively, for the Daurs, the Mongolian revolution was in the interest not just of Mongols, but also of other groups identified as Mongols, including the Daur.

This Daur reinstitution of Merse as a Daur with a Daur heart had to take account of the official *Inner Mongolian Revolutionary History*, which still brands him as a villain. Nonetheless, Daur historians began to present him as their hero for the first time in the mid-1980s. The first *Brief Daur History* (Dawuer Zu Jianshi Bianxiezu 1986), which was part of the state-recognized official history, made a fine distinction between Merse's position and that of Bayantai, the Mongol chairman of the Inner Mongolia People's Revolutionary Party and the chief villain in Inner Mongolian revolutionary history. It is stated that the split within the Inner Mongolia People's Revolutionary Party was caused by a conflict between Merse and Bayantai, thereby establishing Merse's "left" (positive) position. This claim was supported by the evidence that he did not betray the revolution to the Chinese Nationalists. Rather, he organized another uprising against Chinese colonization, whereas Bayantai implemented the Chinese colonization policy in Inner Mongolia. The uprising failed, not because of Merse's mistakes, but because of the betrayal of the Soviet Union and Mongolia, which did not send reinforcement troops as they had promised, for fear of getting involved in Chinese politics. It is Merse, it is argued, who, in order to prevent the Chinese massacre of the people, accepted a compromise offered by an enlightened "patriotic" Chinese general Zhang Xueliang. And he set up a school to train Mongolian, Daur, and other nationalities' students and spread revolutionary ideals among them, for which he was removed from the school. Unlike anybody else who accepted Japanese rule, Merse was known to have openly condemned the Japanese for invading China, proving that he was a heroic patriot.

Interestingly, in the effort to make him a politically correct person, Merse is said to have advocated no independence for the Mongols; rather, he is said to have fought for the equality of the various nationalities of Inner Mongolia. Merse is even commended for having been able to establish cordial relations with Sun Zhongshan and Zhang Xueliang, a sign of his ability to "unite with" the Chinese people. In 1997 Daur intellectuals held a jubilee meeting to commemorate Merse's one hundredth birthday. There was unanimous agreement and praise for Merse as one of the great revolutionaries of Inner Mongolia. His greatness, in the words of Manduertu, a famous Daur researcher at the Chinese Academy of Social Sciences in Beijing, lies in, among other things, "patriotic spirit" and advocacy of "minzu tuanjie" (1996: 40). This patriotism is better explained by three Daur elders who were once Merse's students:

> He, in alliance with determined people in Inner Mongolia and China's advanced intellectuals, under the direct guidance of the Comintern, founded the Inner Mongolia People's Revolutionary Party, demanding national autonomy and self-determination in accordance with Mr. Sun Zhongshan's Three People's Principles. He repeatedly emphasized in his books, "The present-day Mongolian Nation must not establish an independent country." He advocated democratic reform and people's rule for achieving the highest goal of national liberation within the autonomous rights. These measures and theories of his can now be universally recognized. (Enkebatu, Erhenbayaer, Se'ershentai 1996: 60)

The implications of such a claim are not only to establish Merse as the original theorist and practitioner of what would be achieved under the Chinese communists and Ulanhu, but to challenge negative representation of him in Inner Mongolian Revolutionary History and undermine Ulanhu's position as the father of Inner Mongolian autonomy. Yi Ming, one of Merse's daughters, a retired professor of history, challenged head on the long-held official verdict of Merse as a "nationality splittist":

> Mr. Guo Daofu's political thought was democratic revolutionary thought against imperialism and feudal aristocracy. As a revolutionary of the frontier minority nationality, he had been struggling unceasingly for properly resolving the questions of Inner Mongolia and Hulunbuir. He resolutely advocated regional autonomy and the democratic system in accordance with Mr. Sun Zhongshan's Three People's Principles, and he opposed nationality splitism, defending the integrity and unity of the Chinese Nation. It can be affirmed hence that Mr. Guo was not a nationality splitist; instead he was an outstanding statesman and educator, the pioneer of the early national democratic revolution in Inner Mongolia. (Yi 1996: 90)

Through this tortuous historiographical and ethnogenetical analysis, Merse has been both domesticated and elevated, simultaneously opposing Mongol nationalism, promoting Daur identity, and defending Chinese unity. A flurry of articles emerged recently that reminisced on the communist revolutionary activities of the Daurs fighting for the liberation of the Daur and China. Taken together, they represent a profound paradigm shift, a shift that is premised on the moral authority of the Chinese Nation, and a protest against the marginal status of the Daurs in Inner Mongolia.

PLURALIZING INNER MONGOLIAN REVOLUTIONARY HISTORY: BLEEDING FOR THE CHINESE NATION

The contours of the new Daur historiography and ethnogenesis unexpectedly reveal that the Inner Mongolian revolution is not even necessarily or exclusively a Mongolian revolution for the Mongols.

As recently as the 1997 edition of *Inner Mongolian Revolutionary History*, Merse was still considered a rightist, along with Bayantai. But he was acquitted of the charge of surrendering to the Chinese Nationalists. And he was credited with initiating the "Republic of China Mongolian Party Implementation Committee" (Zhonghua Minguo Mengdang Zhixing Hui) in January 1925, which was the embryo of the future Inner Mongolian Nationalist Party (Nei Menggu Guomindang)[13] (Hao 1997: 111). More important, the authors no longer placed Ulanhu at the center of the Inner Mongolian revolution; instead, a multitude of groups, including herders, intellectual youths, aristocrats, non-Mongol minorities, and Chinese, all united in common opposition to colonialism. We thus see pluralization of the foundational myth of the Inner Mongolian Revolution. This, according to the key author of the book, constitutes a radical departure from

5.1. Merse's Bust in Morindawa Daur Banner (photo courtesy of Ardyajab, 2000)

what he called the earlier "leftist" approach that concentrated on Ulanhu's monopoly of the Mongolian revolutionary discourse to a pluralistic approach recognizing the contribution of other peoples in this revolution. It implies more equity in the ethnic relations in the revolution. However, this postrevolutionary equity raises another important question. That is, what are the criteria of inclusion of people in Mongolian revolutionary historiography? I have suggested that this hinges on their fighting not for the interests of the Mongols alone, but for the interests of all Inner Mongolian people, a multiethnic regional entity, a legitimate component of the People's Republic of China.

This point is more clearly illustrated by the inclusion of many eastern Mongols who had been excluded from Inner Mongolian revolutionary history for their "un-Mongol" behavior, according to Ulanhu's revolutionary nationalist criteria. Here, interestingly, eastern Mongols, as far as revolutionaries are concerned, form an alliance between Daurs and Mongols, for indeed, there would be no "eastern Mongol" without the prominent participation of the Daurs, including some providing leadership.

In 1987, on the eve of celebrating the fortieth anniversary of the founding of the Inner Mongolia Autonomous Region, an article entitled "History's Choice," written by Lu Yan (a pseudonym of one Ulanhu's daughters), appeared in *Liao Wang*, an influential Chinese journal. It portrayed a heroic Ulanhu, who survived alone an ambush by bandits on his way to eastern Mongolia and managed to found the Inner Mongolia Autonomous Government, amid the saber-rattling demonstration of hostile eastern Mongols outside the conference hall.

> At the most crucial moment the conference started; hundreds of delegates poured into the conference hall. And yet just when the conference was in session, those upper elements brazenly deployed their army into the city, and paraded cavalry and artillery in front of the conference hall, and someone even attempted to plant a bomb in the conference hall. They had already prepared everything.
>
> It was at this conference that Yun Ze (Ulanhu) made a political report representing the CCP. Outside gun carriages were rumbling, and inside everybody was at daggers drawn. In the report, Yun Ze elaborated in detail and analyzed the struggle between two viewpoints and two roads that had existed since the time of the Great Revolution. He hit the nail on the head when he rebutted the fallacy held by some upper elements, pointing out that the real liberation of the Mongolian nationality was by no means "independence" and "autonomy" [advocated by] the minority of upper elements, rather it must be realized by the great masses of the people under the leadership of the Communist Party.
>
> The election started, but the will and determination of the people were not anticipated by the upper elements: Chinese Communist Party member Yun Ze was elected by an overwhelming majority as chairman of the Inner Mongolia People's Government. The Inner Mongolian people, after many years' bleeding and sacrifice, struggle and exploration, finally made their historical choice. (Lu 1987: 19)

The article immediately provoked protest and refutation from many of Ulanhu's one-time eastern Mongolian communist supporters. They were mostly in their sixties and seventies, and having become "retired senior cadres," they had nothing to fear. They began to write long reminiscences of the founding of the autonomous government, noting that they had become communists long before Ulanhu arrived. They claimed they were recruited by Chinese communists from the Northeast Bureau who had penetrated into Eastern Mongolia, advising them to fight against the Chinese Nationalists, as the Chinese Civil War began in Manchuria and eastern Inner Mongolia. To buttress their claim of their earlier revolutionary credentials, they called on the surviving Chinese advisers to prove their effectiveness in converting them from nationalists to communists.

In 1996 I interviewed Wang Haishan, a high-ranking Daur military commander, who commanded the first cavalry division of the Inner Mongolia Self-Defense Army in 1947. He was compelled to respond not as a Daur but as an eastern Mongolian revolutionary whose integrity was being challenged. He said that after he read the article, many of the survivors wrote a letter of protest to the journal. They also wrote letters to central leaders in Beijing, including Chen Yun, Peng Zhen, and Zhang Pinghua, who were once leaders of the Northeast China Bureau, directly in charge of eastern Inner Mongolia. Zhang Pinghua (a Chinese) was the military commissar of the Western Manchuria Military District. Wang had a special fondness for Zhang for having raised the slogan

"Descendants of Chinggis Khan, unite!" For this, he was persecuted during the Cultural Revolution. Wang said that he also wrote to Zhang Ce, then leader of the Hingan Province Party Committee, the main representative of the CCP in eastern Mongolia, who also reportedly disliked the article.

> We wrote many letters to the Inner Mongolian Party Committee, to Wang Qun (party secretary). Li Fuchun had died. He was in charge of Inner Mongolia, and he knew the truth, as we were introduced into the Party by him. It was approved by the Western Manchurian Branch Bureau. Our political commissar was Zhang Ce. Liu Chun was also present (when we joined the Party). I also wrote to Ulanhu. Wang Qun had a word with Buhe (Ulanhu's eldest son who was then, in 1987, Chairman of the Inner Mongolia Autonomous Region). What kind of cadre is he? Didn't he once play the *erhu* (two-stringed bowed instrument)? He said, "I didn't quite know. I only saw people in Lenin suits with guns coming and going." Is wearing a Lenin suit a crime? I was then commander in charge of city defense. I had over one hundred picket soldiers. I was in charge of the security of the conference. The uniforms of the pickets were different from those of the army, they were black, Lenin style. They were guarding the conference hall, carrying guns. Security outside and inside the city was the responsibility of the first division. The first regiment was inside the city, the third was outside, and the second was at the war front. It arrived just as the election started. How could she say gun carriages rumbling, and we were demonstrating our power? At whom were they shooting their guns? Ulanhu was holding the conference. If we demonstrated militarily, could he continue?
>
> I heard she recently wrote another article, along similar lines. We are prepared to write another response, to fight to the end. Did Ulanhu have an army? How many people were from the western part? Was it just one guard squad? When you arrived, I went to meet you in Baichengzi, and we lined up along two sides of the road and shouted: Long Live Chairman Ulanhu! What came of you? Buhe is your son, but how dare he say those words? Am I afraid of you? Even today, the contradiction between eastern and western Mongolia is like this. Personally, there is no problem. I get along with the Tumed Mongol brothers, they are very good. But why don't they recognize the revolutionary events of eastern Inner Mongolia?

Here, there is no division between Mongol or Daur but between eastern and western Inner Mongols, not in terms of tribal division but in terms of revolutionary credentials. The significance of this new demand for "recognition" of their revolutionary credentials must be understood in the treatment of eastern Mongols by Ulanhu. In much of Ulanhu's political career, he had tried hard to present a Mongolian communist front to the Chinese. Although staunch supporters of Ulanhu, who played an instrumental role in consolidating Ulanhu's position in the Inner Mongolia Autonomous Government, the eastern Mongolian (including Daur) communists had at least two liabilities: their pre-communist careers as soldiers in the Japanese-controlled Hingan army of Manchuguo and their onetime support for the unification of Inner Mongolia with the MPR. These "historical dark spots" brought them repeated career setbacks after the anti-rightist movement of 1957, when class background was increasingly emphasized, further increasing their vulnerability. They thus became victims of Ulanhu's overzealous monopoly of Inner Mongolian Revolution historiography. Many lost their jobs in 1965–1966, replaced by Ulanhu's Tumed Mongols, who had been trained in Yan'an. But this internal dynamic was temporarily brought to an end by their common victimization during the Cultural Revolution. The Daurs, despite their newly attained nationality identity, did not escape being persecuted for allegedly betraying China. In addition to being persecuted for being members of the New Inner Mongolian People's Revolutionary Party, many were punished for both Daur "nationalism," as they were accused of being underground "Justice Party" (Zhengyi Dang) members, and for pan-Mongolism, as they were denounced for organizing the "Unification Party" (Tongyi Dang), advocating the unification of Inner Mongolia with the Mongolian People's Republic.

The buzzwords *communists* and *nationalists* must not be understood in their de-contextualized dictionary definitions. They should instead be understood in the specific contexts of Chinese ideological practices and the experiences of people in Inner Mongolia. To be labeled a nationalist signifies different things for different nationalities; it means patriotism for Chinese but treason or secessionism for Mongols and other minorities! The former is a legitimate and glorious attribute, whereas the latter would incur punishment. Communism, whatever its reputation outside of China, still commands a certain aura of respect in Inner Mongolia and in various ethnic regions of China. Communism provides for a higher moral ground, enabling Mongols to criticize Chinese chauvinist and racist attitudes and practices. Therefore, emphasizing the communist credentials of the Mongols and shedding all "nationalist" associations were Ulanhu's strategies for maintaining Mongolian autonomy in the increasing hostile atmosphere in the early 1960s, when class struggle became the sole criterion to analyze social relations and even ethnic relations (see chapter 4).

The eastern Mongolian (and Daur) revolutionaries' struggle for recognition succeeded in the 1980s and 1990s. Their contribution to the Inner Mongolian revolution and to the founding of the Inner Mongolia Autonomous Region has been duly recognized. Whereas in the first edition of the *Revolutionary History of Inner Mongolia,* the Eastern Mongolia Autonomous Government was said to be hostile to the CCP and Ulanhu's effort to set up the Inner Mongolia Autonomous Government in 1947, the 1997 edition noted that at the people's congress that inaugurated the Eastern Mongolia Autonomous Government in January 1946, "Hu Bingquan delivered a speech at the congress as a representative of Yan'an, elaborating the CCP's nationality policy and united front policy. His speech was enthusiastically welcomed by the majority of the delegates" (Hao 1997: 461). This edition credited the CCP Northeast Bureau as the earliest inspiration for the eastern Mongol's acceptance of CCP leadership, which ran counter to the once-orthodox Ulanhu version that he alone "saved" Eastern Mongolia from its road to nationalism or unification with the MPR. It is this prior communist consciousness that paved the road for their agreement to unify with Ulanhu's western Mongolian autonomous movement in April 1946, which further led to the founding of the Inner Mongolia Autonomous Government a year later.

We have seen a curious phenomenon: Once Ulanhu's monopoly of Inner Mongolian revolutionary historiography is broken, and the Inner Mongolian revolution is defined to benefit all the peoples of Inner Mongolia, it becomes clear that Eastern Mongols, Western Mongols, and Daurs have all tried to project themselves as "communists" but not "nationalists." The dynamic of locally informed interplay of nationalism and class struggle determined that one must try at all cost to avoid being called a nationalist.

I have to this point performed perhaps some kind of postcolonial criticism of the Mongolian revolutionary historiography and have, I hope, identified some plural voices that have begun to challenge the Mongolian revolutionary historiography monopolized by Ulanhu.[14] But the trouble is that, while the postcolonial scholarship of the subaltern school, if I understand it correctly, repudiates the Nation and its capitalized History and celebrates differences in power, I find that in the Inner Mongolia case, the resistance to the Ulanhu's Mongolian revolutionary history, while having performed a noble service in pluralizing it, in fact strengthens the claims of Chinese National power.

Here I find Katherine Verdery's treatment of the socialist state and the production of history in Romania particularly illuminating. Her subtle analysis of the resistance or oppositional activities among historians reveals that this actually helped to strengthen Party rule. Since the Party presented itself as the guardian of the Romanian Nation, which is the central reference point for any legitimate Romanian history, and since existing socialism tends to concentrate resources in the hands of the political apparatus, "one of the chief mechanisms for this outcome was competition *within the intellectual 'space,'* rather than between scholars' and 'Party'" (1991: 240, original emphasis). If we apply this insight to the production of Mongolian revolutionary history, we note that Ulanhu's earlier struggle for a revolutionary historiography was not entirely one between him and the Party because he was an agent of the Party, too. Rather, he was trying to firmly establish Inner Mongolia as legitimate, convincing Mongol skeptics that being part of a socialist Chinese state was both a project against oppression by "bad" Chinese and also a destiny associated with "good" Chinese. This was a powerful discourse, which both suppresses internal opposition and seeks to expand the scope of Mongolian autonomy. Ulanhu's earlier Mongolian revolutionary historiography retained discursive power against Chinese oppression. In this, it exercised some, albeit limited, Mongolian agency.

Post-Mao China has, however, much in common with Ceausescu's Romania; the entire Chinese people, or the Chinese Nation, has become the central reference point. This means that, while recognizing the plurality of ethnic categories, "de jure" equality of all nationalities is preempted. This is in contrast to the earlier recognition that "Chinese Chauvinist" oppression of minorities constituted a problem. Thus, it would be foolish to celebrate such a pluralism, because this pluralism has become precisely the material for constructing the Chinese Nation, a new racialized category that encompasses the "entire Chinese people" against any enemies of the Chinese state, imagined or real.

This observation, also developed in chapters 2 and 3, can be further corroborated by Geremie Barmé's (1999a) colorful summation of avant-garde Chinese nationalism as "to screw foreigners is patriotic" (see also Zheng 1999). As a new oppositional category, the Chinese Nation requires internal unity and makes minzu tuanjie (national unity/amity between nationalities) the new, to quote Brackette Williams, "ideological specification of criteria for the evaluation of fair and foul competition and cooperation as features of nation building and the construction of civil society out of which these categorical distinctions are produced" (1989: 434–35). Reversing the earlier revolutionary discourse that enabled Mongol revolutionaries to retain a limited critical voice, the new Chinese nationalist ideology is premised on a "dialectic of sacrifice and betrayal." Contribution to or sacrifice for the nation is rewarded by inclusion in the moral national community, which guarantees equal citizenship and will be rewarded by a place in national history. This Williams describes as "bleeding for the nation" (1989: 436). Now, in Inner Mongolian postrevolutionary historiography, various Mongol groups, including the Daur, as well as the Chinese, compete for the status of having laid the foundation of the Inner Mongolia Autonomous Region and, by extension, for the establishment of the People's Republic of China.

In other words, in the postrevolutionary struggle for recognition, Mongolian and Daur revolutionaries have become complicit with the nationalist discourse of the Chinese Nation. The irony is, ultimately, that by relying on the moral authority of the Chinese Nation to widen the scope of the admittedly oppressive Mongolian revolutionary historiographical discourse, they have lost their own agency in "evaluating" the Chinese Nation and have allowed the Chinese Nation to judge whether and how much they have contributed to the Chinese Nation. And it is by this criterion that they are to be rewarded or penalized, either in the local power structure or the National History of China. It is this competition that simultaneously separates the Daurs from the Mongols, creating both as distinct and "equal" categories, and links the Daurs and the Mongols genealogically and even perhaps genetically to the Chinese Nation, to be possessed by China as China's Mongols or China's Daurs.

What, then, is the point of postrevolutionary historiography more than half a century after the revolution? Merse and Ulanhu have died. Many communist revolutionaries have passed away or will soon. Perhaps the quest for historical meaning, as Michel de Certeau writes, "aims at calming the dead who still haunt the present, and at offering them scriptural tombs" (1988: 2). Their scriptural tombs still haunt us today, for history "deals with death as an object of knowledge and, in doing so, causes the production of an exchange among the living souls" (de Certeau 1988: 47). But the greater tragedy, apart from their death, is that the exchange among the living souls is no longer predicated on an under-standing of revolution in terms of equality, democracy, friendship, or a more equitable world, but on whether the revolutionaries were fighting for "splitism" or Unity of the Chinese Nation.

NOTES

1. For a comprehensive study of the rise and fall of the Inner Mongolian People's Revolutionary Party, see Christopher Atwood (1994).

2. In 1989 the Soviet Union finally released information, recognizing him as a revolu-tionary. He was said to have been sentenced to ten years' forced labor. The Soviet docu-ment did not say what came of him after that or when he died (Aria, personal interview, 1996).

3. According to the first national census in 1953, there were 48,000 Daurs in China, 19,500 in Inner Mongolia, 22,700 in Heilongjiang, and 5,800 in Xinjiang. The 1990 cen-sus indicates that the total Daur population increased to 121,463, of which 71,484 were in Inner Mongolia, 42,319 in Heilongjiang, and 7,660 in Xinjiang (Sheng and Gao 1998: 54).

4. This political allegiance completed a shift from identification with the Manchus to the Mongols. And the Daurs at the time did not use their ethnonym Daur, for the wider political reality was that they represented the titular Mongol group Barga. Tsend, an able and knowledgeable Daur, who was to serve as a deputy foreign minister under the new Mongol emperor, was ennobled as a duke (Gung) of the Barga Mongols.

5. Bilid (1998) noted, however, that Tsend was a *ulus-tu tusalahci gung* ("state-assist-ing duke").

6. Merse and other Daurs in Ulaanbaatar assisted Nicolas Poppe in his study of the Daur language when he was visiting Ulaanbaatar in 1927. He was in fact advised by Zamcarano, who told him, "These people speak a very archaic Mongolian language, and I think it would be a very good idea if you investigated it" (1983: 43). In his publication entitled *Dagurskoe Narechie*, Poppe mentions that Merse invented a Latin-based Daur script in 1920 (1930: 6–7).

7. Urgunge Onon, a prominent Daur Mongol scholar resident in Britain, is an ardent Mongolist. He translated the *Secret History of the Mongols* into English, bringing out both a scholarly and a popular version (Onon 1990, 1993). In 1996 he reminisced on his understanding of Daur shamanism in *Shamans and Elders: Experience, Knowledge, and Power among the Daur Mongols*, co-authored with Caroline Humphrey (Humphrey with Onon 1996). This is a memory work, a particular and partial one (as memories always are). Also, it is one of the few books in English to mention Merse and other Daurs. Note the subtitle of the book, "Daur Mongols." The leading authorities of the *Secret History of the Mongols* in Inner Mongolia include Tsend Gung's son Eldentai and his grandson Ardyajab.

8. Wulisi Wurong (alias Wu Weirong), a Daur from Heilongjiang, who later played an instrumental role in having the Daur recognized as a separate nationality reminisced

acidly, "In the period of old China's tangled fighting between warlords, when the Daur people offered military grain and livestock to the ruling warlord government, officials would reprimand upon hearing the Daur speak their national language: don't speak your beastly language. In the era of Manchuguo ruled by the Japanese imperialists, under the cheating signboard of the five nationality harmony of the Han, Manchu, Mongol, Hui and Tibetan, the Daur people even lost their rights of survival. In the national situation investigation (population census) conducted in the first year of Datong of Manchuguo which required filling out the item of ethnic identity, officials objected (to the Daur's demand) saying: 'What Dahuli (Daur), there is no such nationality in Manchuguo,' thereby openly depriving the ethnic minority of their rights. As a last resort, the Daur could only report themselves as 'Meng Xi ren' (person of Mongol category) or 'Meng Qi ren' (person of Mongol banner), attaching themselves to the name of Mongolian nationality, trying to make a living by borrowing the name of an alien nationality. Under such circumstances, some individuals of the Mongolian nationality even insulted the Daur people [by saying they] were '9–18 Mongol,' meaning that they were surrendered Mongols after the September 18 Manchurian incident. However, the great masses of the Daur people, especially the Daur intellectuals had been thinking even in their dreams, for the sake of their national dignity, restoring the nationality name, and obtaining the real equality of nationalities, that one day the Daur nationality could emerge in the ranks of the great family of the Zhonghua Minzu as a *danyi* (single or unitary) nationality" (Wulisi Wurong 1993: 644).

9. There was a great deal of resentment against the Daur officials by virtue of their link with the Manchuguo regime, despite their simultaneously pro-Mongol sentiment. The crack in this pan-Mongolian identity could only be attributed to the Mongol sub-ethnic identity, marking of boundaries by each tribal group. There was a short period of autonomy for Hulunbuir before it was incorporated into the Inner Mongolia Autonomous Government. In a report by Zhang Pinghua to the North China Bureau, Barga Mongols in Hulunbuir were enthusiastic for incorporation with the then Mongolian Hingan province under the Mongol leadership, whereas two leading Daur officials opposed the unification, insisting on autonomy, to the chagrin of Barga Mongols, who claimed, "But they are not Barga, how can they represent the Barga Mongol?" It is clear that Hulunbuir was no longer considered a Daur-dominated area but was closely identified as a Barga Mongolian place. The Hingan East Province was temporarily renamed Non-Muren League before it was abolished. The abolishment provoked strong Daur resentment. According to Liu Chun's reminiscence, after the founding of the Inner Mongolia Autonomous Government in May 1947, "Some reactionary elements in Hulunbuir League and Nawen Muren (Non Muren) league organized a so-called Zhengyi Dang (Justice Party), attempting to organize a reactionary government in these two leagues. They carried out a counter-revolutionary uprising in Zhalantun (Jalan Ail), and the people's government suppressed this counter-revolutionary activity" (Liu 1989: 101). Wulisi Wurong wrote that in June 1947, the Fifth Division of the former Inner Mongolian Self-Defense Army arrested over forty Daurs in Zhalantun as illegal "Justice Party" elements. They were completely rehabilitated after 1979 (Wulisi Wurong 1987: 137).

10. The earliest Chinese investigation was conducted in the summer of 1950. Led by two famous Chinese anthropologists, Lin Yaohua and Cheng Yongling, a delegation consisting of teachers and students from departments of oriental languages, economics, and

history departments of Yenching University, Qinghua University, and Beijing University arrived in the then-called Huna League (i.e., combination of Hulunbuir and Non-Muren leagues) to study the ethnic minority situation. Approved by Ulanhu, the investigation did not aim specifically at the Daurs but surveyed all groups in Hulunbuir. The report submitted in 1951 (eventually published in 1997) treated the Daur as one of the Mongol groups (Yenjing Qinghua Beida 1951; Nian Shuqi Nei Menggu Gongzuo Diaochatuan 1997).

11. This resulted in the greatest cleavage between the Daurs and Mongols, which continues until today, with Daurs often accusing the Mongols of being *bugou yisi* (showing no sense of obligation to friends). The first sign of Mongol remorse came from Tegusi, a prominent Mongol politician, the former deputy chief of the Propaganda Department of the Inner Mongolian Party Committee:

> Circa the tenth anniversary of the founding of the Inner Mongolian Autonomous Region, some Daur cadres and masses, in accordance with the nationality regional autonomy policies, raised a demand to establish a Daur autonomous prefecture. Regarding such an important question, whether it should be raised, how to be raised, it certainly needed discussion, deliberations and consultations among the people, and it was discussed in a formal meeting within specific limits. After the anti-nationalist rightism struggle started, who would have thought it would become a serious incident, drawing in many Daur nationality cadres, who had been subjected to criticism and investigation for a long time, some even being punished as "nationalist rightist" (*minzu youpai*), and some subjected to disciplinary action? Looking at the question today, thirty years later, it is clear at a glance. Whether a minority nationality should implement autonomy, how to implement it, whether to build an autonomous prefecture or an autonomous banner, this should be considered from all angles, proceeding from actual conditions. If the demand raised wasn't realistic, they should be given patient explanation and persuasion. But raising a demand is equitable and legitimate, and it is permissible to review and discuss within certain limits. That autonomy should only be granted from above, and the practice of not even allowing them to discuss and review, is a violation of the democratic principle, nor is it in line with the nationality policy of the Party and the state. The improper handling of the question hurt many Daur comrades' feelings, and it is necessary to learn a lesson from this bitter experience. (1993: 57–58)

Wang Duo, the Chinese leader directly in charge of establishing Daur autonomy, continued to insist on the legitimacy of the punishment in his memoir, although acknowledging its excess:

> After this decision [building an autonomous banner instead of a prefecture] of the Center and Inner Mongolia was transmitted to the Daur cadres, some of the Daur cadres still held to their own view, and continued to engage in *chuanlian* (making contacts among themselves and lobbying) activities. Because of this, the Inner Mongolian Autonomous Region sternly dealt with some comrades. This had a considerable educational impact on the comrades who were persistent in their erroneous views at the time. Later the department concerned corrected the excessive disciplinary punishment meted out to some people. (1992: 414–15)

This view was strongly protested by some leading Daur cadres whom I interviewed in 1996.

12. Their political and cultural relations with Mongols are not, however, that easy to sever. Some Daurs are versed in Mongolian and others in Chinese but not in their own language, which has no official script. Those who write in Mongolian must, however, contribute to Mongol culture. Tong Fu, a very gifted Daur musician, contributed some of the most popular "Mongolian" songs. Many Daurs were implicated in the anti-new IMPRP witch-hunt during the Cultural Revolution by virtue of their earlier participation in the Inner Mongolian Revolution.

13. The Inner Mongolian Nationalist Party is also the Inner Mongolian People's Revolutionary Party. The book now uses two names interchangeably.

14. There is a Party-sponsored institute called "Ulanhu Research Institute," devoted to writing biographies and histories of Ulanhu and his fellow comrades. An Ulanhu Mausoleum built in 1992 perpetuates his cult. See chapter 7.

PART III

MODELS AND MORALITY

6

🦋

Models and Morality: The Parable of the "Little Heroic Sisters of the Grassland"

A story that is famous throughout China is set in Inner Mongolia. One day in the middle of the harsh winter of 1964, Longmei and Yurong, two Mongolian sisters aged eleven and nine, were entrusted by their father to look after one of the collective's flocks of sheep close to home while he went out to help his neighbors. The two girls, ignoring their father's words, drove their herd farther away to a better pasture. The weather in February on the grassland is subject to sudden change. A blizzard swept in before they could round up their flock and head home. The frightened sheep ran with the roaring wind. Fearing that the sheep would be lost in the blizzard, the two sisters followed them. The temperature dropped to 37 centigrade degrees below zero, but the two sisters continued to run after their sheep in the blizzard, taking care that the sheep not scatter. Yurong, the younger sister, lost one of her boots while running. The girls drove off eagles hovering above their prey and also protected the flock against a Mongol herdlord who attempted to steal the sheep. After running after the flock for one whole day and a night, covering thirty-five kilometers in the blizzard, they finally reached a railway station at the Bayanoboo Mine. Yurong was no longer able to walk, but Longmei stumbled toward the station. A train was rushing past and was about to run over Longmei when a Chinese railway signalman, Comrade Wang, rescued her. With the help of several other Chinese railway workers, under the leadership of Bayandüren, a Mongolian Party secretary of the Bayanoboo Mine, Yurong was also found and saved. Prompt medical care by the local hospital and the Inner Mongolian hospital enabled both sisters to survive: Longmei suffered frostbite, and one of Yurong's legs was crippled. Only two sheep died in the blizzard; the remaining 380 sheep survived.

Ulanhu, who was then the paramount leader of the Inner Mongolia Autonomous Region and China's leading ethnic minority official, immediately praised the sisters' heroic deeds. He graced the front page of the March 14, 1964, issue of the *Inner Mongolia Daily* with an inscription in his own calligraphy:

> *Longmei and Yurong, little sisters, are revolutionary successors from amongst the people of the grassland, growing up nurtured by Mao Zedong Thought. Youngsters of all nationalities in our Region will try hard to learn from their exemplary behavior and noble character.*

Ulanhu penned the inscription just one year after Mao had anointed the sainted People's Liberation Army martyr Lei Feng in the magazine *China Youth*[1] with a call to "Learn from Comrade Lei Feng." The *Inner Mongolia Daily* editorial noted, inter alia, that the Chinese participants in the drama of the two girls had demonstrated "class friendship and love, and minzu tuanjie" toward Mongols, and they were duly rewarded. The two sisters were also immediately accepted as Young Pioneers and henceforth lionized.

Very soon the story of the two little sisters was transmitted not only all across the Inner Mongolian grassland, but throughout China via films, plays, and picture books. It was even adapted as a lesson in national primary-school textbooks. The two sisters were depicted as happy children of a poor herdsman's family in the fertile grasslands of Inner Mongolia, nourished by the radiance of Mao Zedong Thought. The girls were among the best known in the Chinese communist pantheon of exemplars, including Lei Feng, Wang Jie, and others, and were said to have been particularly appealing to teenagers. Their signal difference was that they were Mongol, not Chinese, and had been ennobled when they were alive, whereas others were honored posthumously. They inspired two generations of young children—myself, a Mongol child in Inner Mongolia, among them. I not only was enraptured by the films and picture books, but kept their beautiful stage photos on my wall, both admiring their beauty and following their example, doing my best to become a good student of Chairman Mao. In learning from the two sisters, we were simultaneously taught to hate our Mongolian exploiter class enemies and to cherish the generous assistance of the brotherly Chinese.

I, and I believe many of my compatriots, never questioned the story at any time until 1993, when a torrent of newspaper articles appeared, reporting that the two little sisters had actually been saved not by Comrade Wang but by a Mongol man called Haschuluu. It was further pointed out that Haschuluu had been portrayed as the unnamed sheep rustler in the story. In the summer of 1996, I interviewed Haschuluu and obtained some documentation from him but was not able to interview the two sisters.

Examination of this political myth makes it possible not only to shed some new light on ethnic relations in Inner Mongolia, but also to look into the complex moral dimensions of ethnic representation in China. I treat the emergence of the two little exemplars as a strategy of resistance by the Inner Mongolian

6.1. Little Heroic Sisters of the Grassland (*Little Sisters of the Grassland*. Peking: Foreign Languages Press, 1973)

leadership against the Party Center in Beijing, through a Mongolian representa-tion of ethnic relations and socialist fervor. This kind of resistance came with a price, of course. It was achieved through disempowering a bad-class Mongol and showing deference to the Chinese by creating a myth of salvation at the hands of Chinese. But this was precisely the morality of socialist ethnic relations, one that was carefully constructed to maintain the status quo of the Mongols. How-ever, this morality of ethnic resistance, which otherwise would be sustainable, has been complicated by Haschuluu's recent revelations. Haschuluu, who had long been vilified as a sheep rustler and class enemy, not only long resisted, but also eventually challenged, this representation. We are then left with questions about how to deal with such socialist ethnic heroes in the postsocialist period.

Nowadays, it is almost impossible not to discuss domination and resistance when we treat power relations. And yet, there has been a general tendency toward what Lila Abu-Lughod (1990) calls "the romance of resistance." Such a romance of resistance is a reflection of the author's philosophical orientation, informed by a liberal emphasis on free human spirits, viewing all kinds of domi-nation or oppression as loathsome, rather than as a reflection of objective real-ity.[2] I follow Abu-Lughod in viewing resistance as a diagnostic of power, offering clues to power configurations in the society concerned, rather than for the sake of resistance: "Instead of taking these [sorts of resistance] as signs of human freedom," she argued, they should "tell us more about forms of power and how people are caught up in them" (1990: 42).

In studying ethnicity, social scientific studies exhibit a strong propensity to dichotomize the opposition between minority and majority-cum-state and to invariably view sympathetically the minorities, who are very often perceived to be the victims of majority-cum-state violence. This rests on viewing categories such as nation and ethnic group as "internally homogeneous and externally distinctive and bounded objects," as Eric Wolf puts it (1982: 6). Despite my conviction that the Mongols are in general subordinated and oppressed politically, economically, and culturally in China, a conviction that I hope is amply documented in this volume, I choose in this and other chapters to traverse the terra incognito of the internal tensions *among* the Mongols against the wider Chinese political background. This task is perhaps best accomplished by discovering the subjects, giving them voice, and letting them represent their own interests. In this way, the monolithic category of the subaltern naturally dissolves, opening a way for us to gaze into Mongolian society, both its internal dynamics and its relationship to the dominant Chinese society.

POLITICAL EXEMPLARS

The two little sisters were what Caroline Humphrey (1997) calls exemplars, one of the techniques used by a regime to project and instill official ideology. Ideology is abstract and cannot be effectively inculcated through mere slogan shouting or propaganda. What is abstract must be made concrete, human, and attainable through examples. Humphrey suggests that Mongol morality is largely based on exemplars.

Despite the wooden character of many socialist exemplars, we should avoid treating them teleologically, but rather should appreciate and analyze their role in socialist (and not only socialist) societies. The Confucian—or, for that matter, Mongolian—moral exemplar and the socialist exemplar all stress a need for self-cultivation and self-discipline, requiring a large degree of human agency on the part of the emulator and, from the elite point of view, enhancing social control through the active cooperation of the inculcated.[3] The socialist regime also sought social change through this process, in that the socialist exemplar is based on a socialist-defined morality, a world of its own with a new hierarchy of honor and shame, distinction and mediocrity. The highest prestige or esteem in a socialist society is supposed to lie with those who conform to the socialist ideal, however that may be defined. Anita Chan (1985), in her study of Chinese political socialization, describes how young people in China before the Cultural Revolution feverishly tried to outdo their peers in emulating heroes or exemplars. The key here is not "learning" but displaying what one has learned, captured by the Chinese phrase *biaoxian*. The psychological pressure upon youngsters was tremendous, generating a competitive political activism. Activists, according to Chan, when talking about activism or activist organization during the Cultural Revolution, "often turned to the word 'glorious' (*guangrong*), connoting both spiritual achievement and personal prestige" (1985: 7). While models have the capacity to project and personalize exemplary behavior, individuals and groups can also manipulate them in the pursuit of personal interests. Ironically, pursuit of socialist exemplar status frequently became a means to establish claims to personal glory, even while eschewing self-interest.

In a parallel fashion, Mao's class struggle engendered a self-interested subjectivity. Ann Anagnost suggests that Mao had launched a "class subject," especially in the "speaking bitterness" narrative promoted during land reform against alleged wrongs done by landlords. "Speaking bitterness" would be repeatedly resurrected in subsequent campaigns. Anagnost argues that "by giving 'voice' to the subaltern class subject, the Party engaged in a metaphysics of presence, one that authenticated its leadership as representing the constituencies its own discourse had constituted" (1994: 265). In other words, Mao's political conceptualization of class located actors within hierarchies of power, "especially in terms of relations of exploitation," rather than in their relationship to the means of production (Dirlik 1983: 196). In this way, the subaltern was transformed from victims into a force to transform society. This was in the interest as much of the subaltern as of the Party. The consequences of such a subaltern subjectivity were fully evident in the brutality during both the Land Reform and the Cultural Revolution (Huang 1995; see also chapter 4).

THE POLITICAL BACKGROUND OF THE "LITTLE HEROIC SISTERS" TALE

Inner Mongolia is one of the five so-called autonomous regions in China. It was established in May 1947, two-and-one-half years before the founding of the People's Republic of China. Stretching along the northern borderland, neighboring Mongolia and Russia, it is presently home to over three million Mongols—numerically insignificant Daur, Ewenki, Orochon, Hui, and Manchu minorities—and about twenty million Chinese. Its incorporation into the People's Republic of China, as opposed to independence or unification with the Mongolian People's Republic (MPR, now known as Mongolia), was facilitated by Ulanhu, a veteran communist, who worked with the CCP, applying Leninist lenses to comprehend the Inner Mongols as a small oppressed nationality that deserved autonomy within a Chinese state.

However, this kind of autonomy did not prevent ethnic violence during the land reform period when naked class struggle was launched, which effectively allowed Chinese settlers to expropriate Mongol land. A politics of difference was subsequently pursued by Ulanhu to provide a kind of buffer for pastoral Mongols, partially shielding them from the consequences of the class struggle approach until 1966, when the Socialist Education campaign, the predecessor of the Cultural Revolution, threatened to break through the ethnic boundary. In the early 1960s Mao's simulated class struggle approach became ubiquitous, and collectivization and communization became the dominant political discourse and organization. This now made the earlier policy differentiating Mongol and Chinese, and pastoral and agricultural conditions, not only obsolete but reactionary.

The new class struggle policy called for intra-Mongol class struggle to shape a socialist Mongolian nationality as a basis for class unity between Chinese and Mongols. Ironically, the emphasis on class obliterated the boundary between Chinese and minorities, the basis for providing "autonomy" to the latter. However, this class unity was never ethnic-blind. As the flag-bearing nationality of China, the Chinese projected themselves as the embodiment of modernity, the destiny, whereas the minorities were enjoined to learn from the "elder brother" Chinese. This new hegemony rendered any minority "autonomy" as rejection of socialist ideals and insistence on ethnic boundaries as regressive.[4] In this new ideology, the burden of new ideal socialist nationality relations was imposed on minorities, who must transform themselves so as to be worthy of the friendship and assistance of the advanced Chinese elder brothers. This new class struggle offensive was extremely effective in breaking down ethnic boundaries, opening doors for both the state and the Chinese penetration into minority area, which resulted in further integration.

Under such circumstances, the question confronting Mongols was not so much a pressure to overthrow class enemies as it was to maintain Mongol leadership without losing out ideologically to the Chinese. Furthermore, Mongol communists faced a greater challenge, as the deteriorating Sino-Soviet relationship and increasing tensions between China and the MRP made Mongol communists increasingly susceptible to charges of ideological and national treason. This extraordinary situation necessitated a politically astute response from Mongol communists, requiring expressions of loyalty to China and its version of socialism. And it was in this what I call performative loyalty, that Mongols, especially Ulanhu, demonstrated their creativity.

As early as 1960 and 1961, during the three-year Great Leap famine that left millions dead throughout China, Ulanhu arranged for Mongols to adopt three thousand Chinese orphans, ranging in age from several months to six years. When dozens of orphanages in Shanghai, Jiangsu, Anhui, and Zhejiang provinces appealed to Beijing for help in late 1959, China's premier Zhou Enlai approached Ulanhu, the Mongol leader of China's Inner Mongolia Autonomous Region, to see if he could provide some relief goods, as Inner Mongolia was among the few regions of China that had not been hard-hit by the famine. According to recent much-publicized reports in China (Hao and He 1997; Ma 1997), Ulanhu suggested instead that Mongol herders adopt and raise some of the orphans. Mongol herders, he reasoned, had been afflicted with severe venereal diseases in the past, leaving many women sterile. They were hungry for children. The Mongol adoption of the children neatly solved two problems, if only on a small scale: it helped alleviate the anxiety of childless Mongols, and it lightened the burden of Chinese struggling in the face of famine.

It turned out that helping the Chinese orphans was only part of Ulanhu's effort to "share the worry" of China (*wei guo fen you*), for he also arranged to donate 320,000 tons of grain free of charge and to sell 30,155 tons of grain to the state, thereby winning high praise for demonstrating "socialism, patriotism and collectivism" from the editorial of the *People's Daily* (January 1, 1962). As this case reveals, instead of the Chinese "elder brothers" helping the minorities, as Chinese propaganda invariably claimed, this was an instance of Mongols helping Chinese in the name of patriotism. This Mongol patriotism served Mongol interests, simultaneously raising the image/place of Mongols in the PRC—that is, in an important sense, reordering the rungs of ethnicity.

Over the next few years, Ulanhu's ideological offensive was manifested in several moral exemplars, including the two little sisters, all of whom were used not only to demonstrate Mongolian commitment to socialist revolution and to the Chinese state, but also to provide an effective Mongol form of ideological propaganda.

That the models were created from below—that is, by the Mongols themselves rather than by Mao or other Chinese leaders in Beijing—enables us to investigate the notion of Mongol agency rather than total subservience to what is handed down from the Center. Models are the building materials for ideological competition.[5] An exemplar is susceptible to manipulation to serve the ends of its creator. Thus, in our story of two little sisters, what started out as a simple event came to be endowed with at least four distinct ideological messages. The first is that the Mongols, even children—and above all, two girls—were devoting their lives to the socialist cause. Their actions embodied the spirit of love for collective property, and they risked their lives to protect it. The second is clearly the motif of internationality friendship in the form of Chinese people helping—and in this case, even saving—Mongols. Third, there is an inherent sexual overtone here: it is not just friendship, it is the elder brother (Chinese) helping or saving the younger sister (Mongol)! It is possible that this, as well as the new class motifs, made the story particularly attractive at the highest levels of the Party. The fourth is the threat to socialism in the form of resurgent class enemies to the Mongol proletarians, exemplified by a former herdlord, the unrepentant class enemy.

Let me analyze the story of the little sisters in light of this historical and theoretical context. What is extraordinary is that within the short space of a month—the incident occurred on February 9–10, 1964—by March 14, a model was being promoted, with the story published prominently in the leading newspaper of the Inner Mongolia Party and officially patronized by Ulanhu.[6] Two weeks later, on March 27, the Peking Opera Ensemble of the Inner Mongolian

Art Theater performed a Peking Opera called *Little Heroic Sisters of the Grassland*, and Ulanhu personally attended the first performance. It is significant that a Peking Opera ensemble and not, say, a Mongol dance troupe performed. Chinese artists were the first to seize the opportunity to associate themselves with the two heroic models and their rescuers, which pleasantly surprised Ulanhu. He mounted the stage to honor the playwright-director and actors after the show, noting, "This play has been rehearsed well. You've gone ahead of us. You've already presented the heroes on stage even before they're discharged from hospital. (In the play) the two heroes have gone back to the grassland." In April 1964, at his instruction, the opera premiered in Beijing and was highly praised by Premier Zhou Enlai, General Luo Ruiqing, and other central leaders (Wurijitu 1997: 585). The story of the young heroines had been mounted on the national stage. The timing of Ulanhu's eulogy of the girls and the opera performance suggests that both Mongols and Chinese were politically acute in identifying the ideological significance of the story, but perhaps each for different purposes. In promoting the two-sister story, Ulanhu not only astutely gauged the increasing importance of revolutionary Peking Opera,[7] but also showed the top leadership, and Mao in particular, that the Mongols were committed to the socialist cause.

Interestingly, during the same period, Ulanhu promoted another art form, one with a specific Mongol character, the Ulan Muchir, a mobile song and dance ensemble consisting of twelve to thirteen performers. This ensemble was to propagate Mao Zedong Thought and all the messages of China's socialist construction to the remote herding camps that were inaccessible by other means. This, too, became an exemplar; indeed, many song and dance ensembles throughout China were thereafter renamed Ulan Muchir. In 1965 Ulanhu anointed Ushenju (Wushenzhao), a pastoral commune in Ordos, "the Pastoral Dazhai"—that is, the pastoral equivalent of Mao's agrarian model village of Dazhai—and elevated Boroldai, a Mongol woman who cleared poisonous weeds and planted bushes in the desert, into a national model. Boroldai was a female Mongolian counterpart to the male Chinese national agricultural model Chen Yonggui, who was elevated to the heights in 1965. Gender is not the focus of this chapter, but it is a fact that several Mongol females, but no males, were projected as major icons in the 1960s, while the Chinese models were overwhelmingly male. We have already noted that gender and ethnic-nationality are intricately intertwined: minorities are often feminized by the majority nationality Chinese (cf. Gladney 1994; Schein 2000). But feminization of minorities may not be merely erotic fantasy concerning minorities on the part of the Chinese. Rather, I contend that it also should be understood as a political strategy by Mongols to simultaneously manifest loyalty to the national enterprise and to present themselves as posing no threat to the Chinese, as, for example, the image of a warrior such as Chinggis Khan would evoke.[8] (See chapter 3 for an in-depth historical analysis of gender and nationality in China.)

Briefly, Ulanhu's extraordinary model-building activity was not only directed toward winning the support of Mao, Zhou Enlai, Lin Biao, and Jiang Qing for his version of socialism in minority regions, but, in light of the wider political and ethnic context discussed earlier, it may be understood as a kind of resistance to Mao's notion that "nationality struggle, in the last analysis, is class struggle," highlighting instead a politics of alliance between Chinese and Mongol. This perspective brings out the subtlety of Ulanhu's leadership: opposed to the application of class struggle to ethnic relations, he adroitly used the hegemonic class struggle discourse to represent Mongols as an ideologically advanced nationality and one that constituted no threat to China's rulers.

REPRESENTING A MONGOLIAN CLASS

I have deliberately teased out certain ironies in Ulanhu's exemplar-building activity, revealing it as a kind of resistance-within-collaboration. The representation of nationality amity, however, demanded redrawing the internal ethnic boundary.

Ulanhu's selective representation of the socialist Mongol identity to the Center altered the nature of Mongol cultural content and social structure. The regime required a uniform ideological shape—in other words, an oppressed class (poor herders or farmers)—which in turn required an active Other. In the Inner Mongolian nationalist representation, there used to be an ethnic Other—that is, the Chinese colonizers. Indeed, Mao invoked Guomindang repression of the Mongols in his 1935 address to the Mongols. To continue to project the Chinese as the Other could not be sustained once Mongols became an ethnic minority within socialist China. Mongols could ill afford to paint a picture of vicious Chinese merchants or warlords rapaciously exploiting the Mongols, as that might have become the basis for their ethno-nationalist ideology antagonistic to the Chinese, who wielded power at the national level. The Other now had to come from among the Mongols themselves. The Chinese had to become, as the ideological representation in minority areas, elder brother figures, selflessly sacrificing their comfort to help Mongols. We can see this as Mongol pandering to the Chinese. And, of course, it is. But we can also see it as a political strategy to encourage the Chinese to define themselves in this way, to make the ideological norm for the Chinese the provision of help for minority peoples, specifically the Mongols. As Ann Stoler argues, "Colonial cultures were never direct translations of European society planted in the colonies, but unique cultural configurations, homespun creations in which European food, dress, housing, and morality were given new political meanings in the particular social order of colonial rule" (1989: 136–67). One of the homespun representations of the Chinese in Inner Mongolia was that they were essentialized into a beneficent symbolic monolith.

It is important, however, to situate representation of the Mongol "Other" in a specific political and historical context. The herdlord (*muzhu*), the equivalent of the Chinese landlord (*dizhu*), was different from the feudal secular and ecclesiastical aristocrats who had already been overthrown. Mongolian nationalism in this century had targeted two groups: externally, the Chinese merchants, warlords, and settlers who were held responsible for the misery of the Mongols; and internally, the aristocrats and lamas. Aristocrats had put their own interests before those of their fellow Mongols by selling Mongol land to the Chinese, which provoked many rebellions throughout the first half of the twentieth century, and the lamas were blamed for reducing Mongol prowess because of their preaching of nonviolence and their withdrawal from the reproductive pool of the Mongols. These two categories of people were unacceptable to the Mongol nationalists, who were convinced that colonial liberation lay in secularism and class equality. An autonomous Inner Mongolia was proclaimed in May 1947 as a result of a hybrid nationalist-communist revolution that recognized Chinese sovereignty. But history did not stop there. Despite the demise of aristocrats and lamas and victory of the "Inner Mongolian people," in the context of China's land reform, it became necessary to delineate class hierarchy among the Mongols. The classificatory language of the 1947–1948 land reform in the pastoral areas used a term, *bayan*, which was translated as *muzhu*—that is, herdlord—to refer to a category of rich Mongols. But in Inner Mongolia class carried less significance than in Chinese regions, until the Socialist Education Movement in the early 1960s. This was thanks to Ulanhu's policy, learning from the land reform disaster in 1947–1948, defining policy in the pastoral region in terms of "Three Nos [no division of property, no class struggle, no class designation] and mutual benefit between the herdlord and herd workers" (see chapter 4).

The Four Cleanups launched a re-examination of the Mongol class structure and Ulanhu's Three Nos. Under the direction of the North China Bureau, led by Li Xuefeng, reading back into the history of the region prior to the land reform of 1948, the herdlord–herder relationship was henceforth to be classified as antagonistic (rather than "mutually beneficial"). But such a reclassification threatened not only the former herdlords, or those so classified, but also Ulanhu, who hitherto had shielded the pastoral Mongols from class struggle. In this politically charged context, in 1965 Ulanhu all but conceded under pressure that it was necessary to conduct class struggle against all exploiting classes, including those in the ranks of pastoral Mongols. In the face of sharp political challenge, Ulanhu sought to advance a new theory, defining Mongols as essentially a proletariat, which would, in pursuit of its class interests, ally with the Chinese proletariat. He now advanced a theory of three bases (political, economic, and cultural) that would shape a harmonious relationship between the Mongols and Chinese and that, in a time of looming international conflict, would guarantee a safe borderland and unified Chinese state in the face of threats from the Soviet Union and its MPR ally. It is not surprising that the only option available for Mongols was to celebrate the Chinese–Mongol alliance and friendship, leaving the Other to be found among the Mongols, as in the little sisters story. Behind this ethnic amity was, of course, the bigger Other, the hostile and "revisionist" Soviet Union and its ally, the MPR.

This analysis takes us to the question of how the story of the two sisters was forged. The original March 14 story posited no Mongol enemy. The enemy was nature, the blizzard, and eagles hovering above, preparing to pounce upon the lambs. The opera mounted by the Baotou Opera House soon afterward "invented" a Mongol herdlord who attempted to steal the sheep and pilfer collective property, taking advantage of the two little sisters. In the play the alert class-conscious members of the proletariat caught and punished him. And, of course, as in the original story, the opera highlighted Chinese heroism in saving Mongols. This representation, inasmuch as it was created in Inner Mongolia, was based on self-deprecation. It meant dividing the Mongol populace along class lines and embedding the Mongols in a subordinate position to Chinese in a dialectics of power and subordination. The opera version had profound implications for former herdlords long bereft of all property and power in the new phase of class struggle.

WHO SAVED THE TWO SISTERS?

In 1993 many Chinese newspapers reported a dramatic story told by Haschuluu, claiming that he was the true savior of the two sisters. Chinese and Mongol authorities, in publishing the story, tacitly approved the claim. His version of the story runs as follows in brief:

> On the 9th of February, Haschuluu went to see off an old classmate at the Bayanoboo railway station. He took his eleven-year-old son with him. The next day, they started off for home, as he worried about his own two daughters who had been looking after livestock. Not far from the railway, to the west, they saw several hundred sheep squeezing into a gully. He and his son assumed that their own animals had been blown there by the blizzard, because west of the railway there were no sheep other than those belonging to their brigade. They discovered one dead goat and a white dead lamb. Haschuluu decided to deliver them to the railway station for temporary storage, as they were the commune's property, asking his son to keep the flock together. Haschuluu took the dead goat to the railway station, but a young Chinese worker named Wang Fucheng was reluctant to let him keep it there, and only agreed when Haschuluu promised to take it away by 6 P.M. Heading northwest again, Haschuluu discovered his son with a girl. She was Longmei, the daughter of their fellow brigade member Tianxi. She was already frozen, and only managed to say that her sister was still in the mountains. Haschuluu quickly led her to the switchroom, and his son followed. As they neared the station, Wang raised his signal torch and ordered them to stop, as a passenger train was approaching. When the train was still two hundred meters away, Haschuluu pulled the girl by the arm and crossed the railway lines. He asked Wang to go find help, but Wang was reluctant to do so. Soon, however, four or five Chinese workers arrived. Alarmed by Longmei's

swollen face, they started to rub snow on her face and feet. Asking them to find the missing girl, Yurong, Haschuluu raced off to the post-and-telecommunication office and placed a call to the Sinebulag commune. He then rushed to the Bayanoboo Mine Headquarters, and asked if they could lend a truck to help transport two frozen girls to the hospital. Wu Long, the director of the Mine, responded quickly and organized a rescue team. The two girls were saved.

The new version of the story did not question the two sisters' heroism. It differed from the earlier version, however, in two important dimensions—that Haschuluu and his son had discovered and saved Longmei and that some other Chinese workers, not Wang, had rescued Yurong. The mine Party secretary, Bayandüren, was absent in this account, but the mine director provided a truck and organized the rescue team. This new story was not entirely subversive and did not throw into disarray the carefully constructed myth that a Chinese worker had saved the two Mongol girls as a demonstration of "class friendship and love, and minzu tuanjie." Actually, it tells a slightly different story: that is, cooperation between Mongol and Chinese led to the rescue. Haschuluu was adamant that most of the Chinese involved had acted honorably to save the girls. This stance may well have been warranted, but it was also politically astute, because Chinese political culture in the 1990s certainly did not allow for any general questioning of Mongol–Chinese ethnic amity and friendship.

There were other hidden dimensions to the story. Readers may have noted that the two Mongolian girls had Chinese names, Longmei and Yurong. The sisters are from a family of Harchin Mongols, who had settled in the region in 1960. The Harchin are a highly sinicized Mongol group whose homeland straddles the Mongolian and Manchurian borderland.[9] In the territorial configuration after 1947, the greater part of Harchin territory fell outside of Inner Mongolia in Liaoning province. In 1957, at the time of the Hundred Flowers movement, some Harchin openly complained that they suffered from discrimination at the hands of the Chinese and requested to settle in Inner Mongolia. Ulanhu once remarked that it would be all right for other Mongols also to immigrate to Inner Mongolia if Chinese immigration could not be stopped. The subsequent Great Leap Forward movement essentially lifted the lid on immigration, and several million Chinese, as well as smaller numbers of Mongols, rushed into Inner Mongolia over the next several years. At the time, Inner Mongolia was better off than most parts of China, which in the aftermath of the Great Leap Forward was afflicted with a horrendous famine, claiming millions of lives. The two sisters' family was among that tide that swept into Inner Mongolia during the Leap. They settled in a pastoral brigade in the fertile grassland near Baotou. As the Harchin had long been highly sinicized, many had adopted Chinese names. The two sisters' father was called Tianxi. However, despite their Chinese names, the two girls could not speak Chinese well as of 1965, since the people of the new homeland where they had lived for over four years were almost entirely Mongol-speaking.[10]

Haschuluu was a Horchin (not Harchin) Mongol from the eastern part of Inner Mongolia. Born in 1918, he had served as a platoon leader in the Japanese-controlled Mongolian Hingan Army for three years in the early 1940s. After the founding of the Inner Mongolia Autonomous Government in May 1947, he became a military researcher at the General Staff office of the Inner Mongolian Liberation Army. He was a gifted intellectual. In July 1949 he was employed as editor for the journal *Changchun Public Security,* produced by the Changchun City Public Security Bureau. In 1952 he returned to Inner Mongolia and worked as an assistant editor at the Mongolian Editorial Department of the Inner Mongolian Publishing House in Hohhot. But personal and ideological differences with his immediate Mongolian superiors at the publishing house in the aftermath of the Great Leap Forward resulted in the expulsion of Haschuluu from his work unit in 1958. Unable to settle the dispute in Inner Mongolia, he lodged a complaint against his superiors to the Party Center in Beijing, only to be arrested and incarcerated in 1960. He was sentenced to two years' "labor under surveillance" (*laodong guanzhi*) for the errors of (1) making complaints to the Party Center; (2) quarreling with police and disturbing social order; (3) eating pork when living in a Muslim neighborhood; (4) and repeatedly quarreling with his wife. In July 1962, as a result of widespread economic hardship, a population dispersion program was carried out in order to alleviate urban food shortage. Just one month before finishing his service, Haschuluu was hastily sent to the countryside and was promised that, if he agreed to go, all charges against him would be dropped as soon as the sentence expired. Otherwise, he would have to serve two more years. He and his whole family were exiled to where the two sisters lived: Narangerel Brigade of Sinebulag Commune in Darhan Mumingan Banner, near Baotou city. He was still laboring under surveillance when the events of February 1964 unfolded.

When I interviewed him in 1996, Haschuluu, a gaunt old man at the age of seventy-eight, was still angry when he recalled his life story. Indeed, nothing was more important to him than this event. Although his career had already been ruined earlier, he could handle it as many did. But punishing him for saving the two sisters, who became heroes while he languished as a criminal, deeply contravened his sense of basic human morality.

TRUTH AND POWER

The story is not only a matter of truth or lies. It is also about morality. Indeed, what is truth? Michel Foucault (1980) holds that "truth" is linked to power/knowledge. Knowledge linked to power not only assumes the authority to determine "the truth," but also the power to monopolize truth.[11] In Maoist categories, especially those of the Cultural Revolution, "truth" was constructed in the class struggle, while in Ulanhu's Inner Mongolia, it had an additional dimension—

ethnic relations. In light of Foucault, we should pay attention to how the combination of discourse and power produced a certain conception of crime and the
criminal, as well as of heroism, conceptions that had profound effects not only
for criminals and judicial officials, but for the entire population for whom the
two sisters modeled the interaction between class struggle and nationality bonds.

Haschuluu's account permits a glimpse into some of the ways in which this
regime of truth functioned. Haschuluu shows how Wang had trumped up the
story of the rescue to his personal advantage. According to Haschuluu, in 1964
Wang, in his interview with the journalists who came to report on the two little
sisters, reaped proletarian virtues for himself while discrediting Haschuluu. As
Haschuluu reconstructed, Wang fabricated the following story:

> Haschuluu crossed the railway lines and immediately seeing the dying Longmei, he
> sneered and walked past her. Suddenly, he saw two dead frozen sheep not far from
> Longmei. Thinking that no one could see him, and that the girl would soon die, he
> thought why don't I get my hands on them? So, pulling the sheep's leg, he threw it
> over his shoulder, and was stealthily attempting to slip away when a railway worker
> passed by. After all, it was the working class, the bowstring of "never forget class
> struggle," that was drawn tight. He [Wang] stopped Haschuluu, asking in a stern
> voice: "Where are you taking this sheep?"
>
> "Oh, oh, nowhere, who says—Ah, ah, I want to—," Haschuluu hemmed and
> hawed. "No, where did you get it? Let's go back and have a look!" The railway
> worker escorted Haschuluu to the herd, and then he saw Longmei, who was dying
> of frost. He angrily ordered Haschuluu not to move and he carried Longmei to the
> railway station. Comrade workers eventually rescued Longmei.

Haschuluu said that this version of the story was transmitted in propaganda documents called "Xiang Yingxiong Xiao Jiemei Xuexi" (Learn from the Little
Heroic Sisters) (no. 1 and no. 2), published in 1964, almost immediately after
the incident, by the Bayanoboo Mine people's committee. This propaganda
transformed the tale of the two sisters, who no longer fought only against the
blizzards, but also against the class enemy. The story was enthusiastically adapted
by the Baotou Opera House, as mentioned earlier. The truth was reconstructed
by those who had access to the media, and the truth was constructed around a
class enemy—the Other—who by "definition" was fit for precisely such a robe.

This should not be construed as suggesting that the higher authorities lacked
information about who had saved the girls. According to a later official investigation, Wang Zaitian, a Mongol Party secretary in charge of law and order in Inner
Mongolia, and the deputy banner governor of Darhan Mumingan banner, also a
Mongol, deliberately suppressed the truth. Wang Zaitian and the deputy governor had tried to strike a deal with Haschuluu. In consideration of Haschuluu
being "an element under surveillance," they would not be able to commend him
publicly, but he would be deemed to have "expiated his crime by his good deeds."

This he accepted, believing it was the only hope for a return to normal life. How dared he not trust the Party?

The Mongol authorities then installed a Chinese as the savior of the Mongol girls, fully aware of the fabrication, and the Mongol savior was exorcised lest he ruin the tale's message. Ultimately, for the sake of the message, he would in fact be presented as the Other in propaganda. Thus, not only would Haschuluu not be discharged as promised, he would accumulate further negative political labels. The difference between fiction and reality began to blur. To provide the tale with more meaning, he was accused of being a sheep rustler, counterrevolutionary, and herdlord. By suggesting that he stole the girls' sheep, taking advantage of their frozen status, he was virtually accused of committing the offense of attempted murder. This concocted story took on its own momentum. In 1966, as soon as the Cultural Revolution started, the Party secretary of the Sinebulag Commune, a Mongol, forced Haschuluu to endure a "struggle session" for three days and nights. Moreover, Longmei, then thirteen years old, was brought into the struggle, a form of class struggle education. The two sisters would soon publicly repeat the story of Haschuluu's perfidy everywhere.

Subsequently, in the mounting international tension between China and the Soviet Union and its ally the Mongolian People's Republic, many Mongols during the Cultural Revolution, Haschuluu among them, were labeled as "agents of the revisionist Mongolia," "historical counterrevolutionaries," "active counterrevolutionaries," and "New Inner Mongolian People's Revolutionary Party (IMPRP) members," the latter referring to an alleged vast Inner Mongolian conspiratorial plot to secede from China. This gave rise to a witch-hunt and pogrom of the "New IMPRP" members that cost over sixteen thousand Mongol lives and several hundred thousand injuries, by official reckoning. Haschuluu was borrowed for "struggle" everywhere in Darhan Mumingan banner. He was finally released from his sentence in July 1967, but as the witch-hunt against the "New IMPRP" escalated, he and his family were expatriated to his hometown Jirim League, in eastern Inner Mongolia in September 1968. In Darhan Mumingan banner and his hometown, Khuree banner, he served more than three years in prison, on and off. He was finally politically rehabilitated in February 1975. This may have been related to an ongoing effort to partially rehabilitate the victims of the "New IMPRP" witch-hunt, which Mao had admitted in 1969 had "gone too far" (*kuodahuale*). Tragically, the two sisters have never publicly acknowledged that Haschuluu was their savior, although Yurong, the younger sister, did so in private.

That Longmei has been unwilling to recognize Haschuluu as having helped her is not entirely surprising. Longmei was eleven years old at the time. Unlike many other models who suffered greatly during the Cultural Revolution because of their link with overthrown Party officials, Longmei and Yurong did not suffer, despite their link with Ulanhu. Indeed, Mao's wife Jiang Qing used Longmei to criticize Ya Hanzhang, a famous Chinese scholar, who was noted for his support of Ulanhu and Ulanhu's nationality policy. Longmei, by being utilized by the rebels in Inner Mongolia and by Chinese leaders at the national level during the Cultural Revolution, had her importance as a national hero heightened.[12] Longmei's own subsequent political career rested on clinging to the official version of the story. In a 1990 interview, she remarked that the person she admired most was still Lei Feng, the model revolutionary whom Ulanhu doubtless had in mind in creating the myth of the two sisters of the grasslands (Du 1990).

STRUGGLE OVER THE TRUTH: THE "POST-SOCIALIST" REGIME OF HARMONY

The Maoist regime of truth produced legions of victims and victimizers, as the hegemonic culture of class struggle was built on a widening gap between representational and objective reality. After the Cultural Revolution, these contrasting realities became a battleground between Maoists and their opponents. The public transcript (to use James Scott's term) that ultimately won the battle usurped Mao's own dictum: *shishi qiushi* ("seek truth from facts"). It was, of course, never central to Mao's thought, though he did apparently use it a couple of times. It was Deng who made it his cardinal principle after the Cultural Revolution. Philip Huang offers an interesting analysis of the Chinese expression:

> The Chinese expression in fact conveys a good deal more than the narrow empiricism suggested by that translation [Seek truth from facts]. *Shishi* suggests immediately the connotation of "real facts" as opposed to phony facts. And *qiushi* conveys not so much the connotation of the amoral "truth" that the discursive context of English lends the term as a more moral "what is right and true," as opposed to "what is wrong and untrue" (as in *mingbian shifei*, or "distinguish clearly between right and wrong"). The fact that this expression has become the reigning slogan of the post–Cultural Revolution era demonstrates the depth of the reaction against the rupture between representational and perceived reality in the Cultural Revolution. *Shishi qiushi*, or "seek what is right and true from real facts," is a call to realign representational reality with objective reality. (1995: 135)

The effect of this battle cry was tremendous. Vera Schwarcz (1994: 46) writes that "[o]nce the boundaries of truth telling had been expanded officially from above . . . a flood of memory, pain, and remorse rushed up from below." It launched a reverse "speaking bitterness" narrative, affirming the subjectivity of the victimization of the Cultural Revolution and the injustice to which many had been subjected. While Mao successfully mobilized the subaltern consciousness and subjectivity, Deng's initial strategic use of "Seek truth from facts" ultimately proved threatening to his own limited reform, as it created a "subjective capacity for 'moral memory'—an act of recollection that refuses to identify the past only with what is collectively useful in the present moment" (Schwarcz 1994: 47). What was immediately emphasized by the Deng regime was social harmony, as victims and victimizers were urged to put their former sufferings behind them, even to forget what had happened, and promote economic reform. "The Truth" still refuses to be dissociated from knowledge/power. Indeed, as F. G. Bailey argues, truth may be seen as harmony and is conditioned by the "social need" for harmony. A truth that does not support what is perceived as social harmony is immoral and must be suppressed: "Society requires for its survival the practice of deceit" (Bailey 1991: 27).

The new/old Chinese culture of harmony that has been counterposed to the Maoist culture of disharmony need not be celebrated. We should not assume that this will naturally give rise to a utopia in which conflict and contradiction are eliminated. Rather, we need to deconstruct the ways in which the rhetoric of harmony "masks the realities of the social coercion that maintains some semblance of peaceful co-existence despite on-going antagonisms" (Colson 1995: 70). The enforced need in Inner Mongolia, unlike the Chinese regions of China, is for ethnic amity. Although in post-Mao China people have abandoned socialist models, and the nouveaux riches have become the new models,[13] abandoning the socialist models in Inner Mongolia would have different political implications, as it might affect ethnic relations. The new regime of harmony in Inner Mongolia subscribes to a "don't or else" policy: "Don't say or do anything detrimental to minzu tuanjie."

Although Haschuluu was acquitted of criminal charges in 1975, the injustice done to him in the fabrication of the story of the two sisters still stood. In July 1978 Haschuluu and his son submitted to the Inner Mongolian Party committee a 119-page complaint entitled, "How we discovered and rescued the heroic little sisters of the grassland, Longmei and Yurong—Thoroughly exposed the serious crime of Wang Fucheng, Bayandüren and Baoxiao in cheating various newspapers and journals of the whole country and their journalists and in cheating the Party Center and Chairman Mao, as well as people of various nationalities." They demanded the restoration of their reputations with regard to the innuendo in the two little sisters story, but to no avail. Undaunted, Haschuluu wrote letters to the *People's Daily*, and the latter finally brought the case to the attention to the CCP secretary-general Hu Yaobang. In April 1979 Hu urged that the case be settled. Only then did the Inner Mongolia CCP propaganda department (*xuanchuan bu*) investigate the affair. It is worth noting that the propaganda department, not the judiciary, was in charge of this affair. Although Haschuluu was then able to return to his work unit, the Inner Mongolia Publishing House, a long silence ensued. Finally, in 1984, at the prodding of the organization department (*zuzhi bu*) of the Party Center, the Inner Mongolia Youth League Committee, where Longmei worked, and the Inner Mongolia Publishing House, Haschuluu's work unit, investigated and confirmed Haschuluu's testimony. On January 8, 1985, the year's first circular from the organization department of the

Inner Mongolia CCP called on the propaganda department to take appropriate measures to remedy the damage to Haschuluu's reputation. The propaganda department was urged to give him a monetary reward and public praise. But following the standard formula of Deng Xiaoping's dictum of *yi cu bu yi xi* ("better crude than meticulous") with regard to the Cultural Revolution, the instruction following the circular emphatically pointed out that the comrades at the Hohhot Railway Bureau should do "ideological work" on Wang to free his mind of misgivings. In other words, Wang was not to be discredited; he had simply made a mistake, he was still a good comrade. In Deng's version of a pan-Chinese "communitas," to use Victor Turner's (1969) term, rehabilitation was to soothe animosity and bring amity among contenders, rather than equity.

But had harmony been restored? We have already noted the reluctance of Inner Mongolian officialdom to rehabilitate Haschuluu. It took four to five years to settle the matter and then only after the intervention of the Party Center and its secretary-general. Even after the reconciliation decision, nothing substantial was forthcoming. There was a media blackout.[14] The reason for this silence was that an unnamed leader in the Party Center (*zhongyang shouzhang*) had ordered, "The influence of the original propaganda about the heroic little sisters from the grassland was very great, now it is not necessary to carry out a correction propaganda." So there was to be no negative propaganda that might vilify Mongolian heroines, either. But who was this influential central leader who was so interested in protecting the two little sisters? Haschuluu was reticent to name that *zhongyang shouzhang*.

It is not entirely impossible, however, to speculate about the identity of the leader. The only high official at the Party Center with a personal stake in the story of the two sisters was Ulanhu. He was then China's vice president. For want of better terminology, we may suggest that the relationship between Ulanhu and the two sisters was one of patron-client, by virtue of the fact that Ulanhu had created and propagated the model in 1964. Their relationship was temporarily severed by the two sisters during the Cultural Revolution, when Ulanhu was overthrown and they denounced him. But this did not reduce Ulanhu's grandfatherly affection for them. When Ulanhu visited Inner Mongolia for the last time in August 1987 to commemorate the fortieth anniversary of the founding of the Inner Mongolia Autonomous Region, Longmei and Yurong were among the local dignitaries who had an audience with the aging leader, who died the following year.[15] It is therefore not surprising that Ulanhu would have sought to block Haschuluu's rehabilitation. Moreover, Inner Mongolian officialdom between 1979 and 1992 was dominated by Ulanhu's son Buhe and other family members.[16] It is ironic that the official version harped on the very class struggle line that Ulanhu had long striven to overcome.

TOWARD A CONCLUSION

Socialist China is not only a polity that disciplines its citizens into socialist subjects, but also can be understood as a system of cultural significance. Socialism as an ideology is abstract, and the abstract must be concretized and made manifest for the masses less attuned to subtlety. Like modern nations, socialist subjects require not only novels, flags, museums, and other monuments (Anderson 1991), but also constant guidance. The state presents models for socialist subjects to look up to and to guide them in remolding themselves (cf. Friedman, Pickowicz, and Selden 1991). As such, models are not individual human beings, but embodiments of an ideal, a crystallization of collective wisdom. During its heyday of socialist revolution, China produced numerous novels, plays, operas, comic books, and movies, to represent the Past, Present, and Future in melodramatic forms. According to Peter Brooks (1994), melodramas are the best form to represent revolutionary morals, for in melodramas, the humble people rise against the evil and the evil is always punished in the end. Daniel Gerould (1994) also argues that melodramas of revolutions in France and the USSR often adopt the Manichean view of the world, voice the need for heroes and villains, and preach simplistic moral lessons. It is interesting that our two little heroic sisters were both modelized and melodramatized. They were turned into paragons of people upholding communist enthusiasm for production, "ideal" ethnic relationship—minzu tuanjie (*as beneficiaries of Chinese salvation*), and even waging intra-Mongol class struggle (*as victims of Mongol class enemies*). As paragons, they have been taken out of history to lead a reified existence. In such melodramas, truth is necessarily constructed.

However, pointing out the fabrications in the "Little Sisters" story is both easy and difficult. It is easy for an outsider. But it is also difficult, first because several of the protagonists are human beings who are still living in such roles and have great stakes in maintaining the status quo. There is no sign that they themselves have spoken about it reflexively. It is no guarantee about the absolute truth of Haschuluu's story. It would be wise to beware of replacing one myth of selflessness and class struggle with another myth of selflessness and nationality harmony. Second, dismantling such a political dinosaur would have great implication for the morality of the socialist Mongolian minzu. Although the myth of Chinese "saving" the Mongols has been proved to be contrived, the "little sisters" were not abandoned as Mongols, and in fact, they now are listed among the thirty communist Mongolian military and political celebrities in contemporary China. Of course, in the newly restored "truthful" story, the "Little Heroic Sisters" have reconciled with their Mongolian savior, Haschuluu (Bayar 1998: 159–64). Third, it is in the interest of socialist China to continue to uphold such a model—a newly sanitized version, of course—however contrived the entire thing may be, simply for the sake of the regime living with glorious past memories. In a scheme to further monumentalize the socialist ideal, perhaps to inculcate some altruistic ideal into millions of children and youths brought up eating McDonald's and watching Hollywood blockbusters, the All China Young Pioneers are planning to erect a Memorial to Heroic Chinese Children and build an Exhibition Hall for the Chinese Children. They plan to display the little sisters' heroic deeds along with those of juvenile martyrs such as Xiao Erhei and Liu Hulan (Bayar 1998: 160).

It is perhaps unfair for me to go further into what Doris Sommer would call a "pretty lie" (1991: 90), not least because the protagonists and their melodrama continue to have significance for the socialist Mongolian minzu and socialist China, which is struggling to maintain a regime of harmony and economic prosperity in the era of globalization. At a minimum, however, we can challenge here the inherent romanticization of resistance of minorities against the majority in recent postcolonial critical scholarship, by identifying several kinds of socialist subjects. Subjects are understood in Foucauldian terms, viz. they are produced within a discourse. These subjects may produce some forms of "resistance," but they speak or act within the limits of—or indeed they must be subjected to—the episteme, the regime of truth, or the regime of harmony. Phrased in this way, we may find the "subjects" writhing within the discursive regime defined by the state, being at once resisters and accomplices, or sometimes one and sometimes the other.

What may also be inferred from this study is the moral constraint the regime of truth places on the maintenance of the ethnic boundary in Inner Mongolia. This is not to suggest that there is no longer an ethnic boundary. Rather, I suggest that the boundary is maintained by the moral discourse that takes its reference from the regime of truth. This study tries to show the overlapping structures of ethnicity and state and insist that to understand ethnicity in socialist China, we stand to gain much insight into the "failure" of ethnic resistance by analyzing relational complicity. Complicity in this sense does not imply conscious collaboration with the powerful but the curious fact that action and the discourse of "resistance" very often operate within the framework of the existing order of domination.

NOTES

1. Lei Feng was by no means the first model used by Mao, nor was such a model inherently socialist. Mao took his inspiration from the exemplary models for children that had been commonplace in teaching Confucian morality and were developed in the revolutionary base areas in Jiangxi in the late 1920s and early 1930s and in the wartime resistance bases in the years 1937–45. But the most direct lineage for the Chinese socialist exemplars appears to emanate from Mao's hero emulation movement in the Yan'an years of the 1940s, which was also inspired by the Soviet models of the Stakhanovite movement. See Patricia Stranahan (1983); Friedman, Pickowicz, and Selden (1991); and Selden (1971).

2. Sherry Ortner (1995) has criticized the current state of "resistance" ethnography and found three forms of what she called "ethnographic refusal": sanitizing politics, thinning of culture, and dissolving actors. Paul Willis (1997) recently criticized two kinds of weakness in anthropology: empiricism and humanism. The problem with humanism is

that "since you've traveled so far to the field, and you have a bounded notion of the field despite protestations to the contrary, you see the agents involved in that field as in charge of their own destiny in some way or another. It might look traditional, irrational, old fashioned, religious or whatever, but our job is to show the real truth, to show ultimately, another people's culture is human and rational, with Centered human beings in some way controlling their own forms" (1997: 184).

3. To be designated a labor hero or model is thus to convey a title of prestige, and prestige, as William Goode (1978) argues, is one of the factors that enables social control. The other three control factors are force and threat of force, wealth, and friendship-love-affection. I would point out that the title can become a source of mockery or challenge in periods when regime legitimation falters, as this study shows.

4. This was testified to by increasing denunciation and punishment of "nationality rightists" (*minzu youpai*) or "local nationalists," starting in 1958. Whereas "great Chinese chauvinism" had been earlier denounced as oppressive of and discriminatory to minority nationalities, and minority "nationalism" was encouraged to combat "great Chinese chauvinism," a great reversal occurred beginning in 1963. Great Chinese chauvinism, in fact, came to be equated with socialist class position, with "elder brotherly" help, imbued with ideological progressiveness.

5. Mary Sheridan (1968) identified the proliferation of military and civilian heroes in the power struggle between army generals and civilian leaders. In discussing the Chinese model of moral exemplar, Lucian Pye distinguishes a hierarchy in terms of the goal of self-improvement: "The goal of self-improvement was moral perfection according to established standards, and hence it sought excellence in terms of conformity to cultural norms, not in terms of the uniqueness of the individual. There was a hierarchy of moral achievement in which only the elite could strive for self-development while the mass of the people were ruled by example" (1996: 19–20).

6. Ulanhu's enthusiasm for the two girls was matched only by that of local officials. The first detailed report in the *Inner Mongolia Daily* would indicate that the Mongol leader Bayandüren, party-secretary of Bayanoboo Mine, was instrumental in promoting this story in the first place. Most of the officials involved, as well as the saviors of the girls and later helpers, were explicitly identified as "Communist Party members." These leaders seemed to be extremely conscious of the political capital they could gain from being identified as helping the two heroines. Their enthusiasm for the girls went beyond the bounds of "concern" by fatherly cadres for the safety of the people under their jurisdiction. The potential rewards unleashed a tremendous enthusiasm not only from Mongols but also Chinese, vying to demonstrate their ideological virtue. What started as a demonstration of the embodiment of Communist morality of altruism became the vehicle for an acute struggle for self-interest. All of the people involved were duly praised or rewarded.

7. We should bear in mind the national context of the socialist education campaign and Lin Biao/Jiang Qing efforts to reform the Peking Opera at precisely this time. See Lowell Dittmer (1981). But it is extraordinary that Ulanhu, a Mongol, played a role in harnessing the Peking Opera to spread Maoism among the people in and out of Inner Mongolia. After the birth of the *Little Heroic Sisters of the Grassland*, Ulanhu remarked that the modern Peking Opera should emphasize the themes of minority nationalities. In a CCP Politburo meeting, Ulanhu proposed organizing a festival of Peking Opera on contemporary themes. That proposal was apparently accepted by Jiang Qing and others

active in the movement to revolutionize Peking Opera, as in early July 1964, an All China Festival of Peking Opera Modern Play Demonstration was held in Beijing.

In 1964 Ulanhu's contribution to the new Peking Opera in socialist education was recognized by one of China's veteran artists, Xia Yan, who said: "It was Comrade Ulanhu who first mobilized the Modern Peking Opera Festival (*xiandai jingxi huiyan*). Comrade Ulanhu especially was concerned with modern Peking Opera. It is an especially important question of how to infuse the national form into the performative art of Peking Opera. The modern opera festival was very important" (quoted in Baoyindalai 1990: 154).

8. Amy Mountcastle suggests that in recent years the exiled Tibetans have similarly sought to cast their struggle for independence in feminine terms. But in this instance, it is a case of capturing the attention of the world and particularly Americans. As feminine, the exiled Tibetans hope to present an image of a "gentler race," as victims of Chinese aggression. Mountcastle argues, "if the Tibetan nationalist enterprise is portrayed in 'softer,' feminized, universally meaningful terms, then the Chinese are portrayed as masculinized aggressors whose interests are nationalistic, self-serving . . . " (1997: 138).

9. Their princes were the first in Inner Mongolia to promote modernization and nationalism, taking their inspiration from Japan's Meiji Restoration. Harchin intellectuals subsequently led the Inner Mongolian People's Revolutionary Party, a nationalist-democratic party under the leadership of the Comintern and the Mongolian People's Revolutionary Party. However, the political position of the Harchin in Inner Mongolia was eclipsed during the Chinese civil war of the late 1940s as they supported the losing side— the Chinese Nationalist Party.

10. Nevertheless, characteristic of Mongolian tribal politics, the Harchin newcomers faced discrimination as outsiders. Longmei reportedly said in the March 14, 1964, report, for example, that if she and her sister did not look after the flock, her brigade neighbors would comment negatively about their family. Moreover, *contra* the formal story that the father was a poor herder, his class background was actually higher. Haschuluu told me that the father was actually of aristocratic origin. Why had not such a bad class background barred them from becoming socialist models? Haschuluu's explanation was that their father had been able to conceal his class background and that Mongol officials decided to ignore their class background in their eagerness to discover a powerful model.

11. Foucault argues, "Truth isn't outside power. Truth is a thing of this world; it is produced only by virtue of multiple forms of constraint. And it induces regular effects of power. Each society has its regime of truth, its 'general politics' of truth; that is, the types of discourse which it accepts and makes function as true, the mechanisms and instances which enable one to distinguish true and false statements, the means by which each is sanctioned, the status of those who are charged with saying what counts as true" (1980: 131).

12. Longmei joined the PLA when she was seventeen. Initially, she worked as a nurse in a military hospital and then went to study medicine at the Baotou Medical College and the Inner Mongolian Medical College. She later worked as a Communist Youth League leader in Inner Mongolia. She is currently a deputy chair of the People's Congress in the Donghe District of Baotou Municipality.

Yurong, the younger sister, was permanently crippled as a result of frostbite. She is now a deputy chair of the Inner Mongolian Association for the Disabled. Haschuluu did not bear many grudges against Yurong, the younger sister. Even during the Cultural Revolution, after saying that Haschuluu stole their sheep in her speeches at schools, Yurong would come and tell him that she would never forget his kindness for saving her life. Unlike her sister, Yurong has always been close to Haschuluu's family and looked after his ailing wife. On March 15, 1993 Yurong attended her funeral.

13. We should not, however, draw a premature conclusion concerning the demise of the Lei Feng model in China. Even today, there seems to be what is called "Lei Feng Spirit," which shows a tremendous power of adaptability, combining ancient Chinese virtues with modern Communist ideology. According to Lockwood, "the mantle of Lei has descended on a Ms. Du Chunyan. After being laid off by a state-owned enterprise on the verge of bankruptcy—a common story, as China grapples with the task of reforming tens of thousands of loss-making businesses—Ms. Du opened her own shop. Since then, she has been training other laid-off workers, in what the newspaper describes as an attempt to repay her debt to society. . . . With millions facing unemployment as China allows its loss-making state-run businesses to go bankrupt, a great deal of Lei Feng Spirit is going to be needed" (1998).

14. Haschuluu claimed that numerous journalists from the *People's Political Consultative Daily, Guangming Daily, Inner Mongolia Daily,* and *Inner Mongolia Pictorial* came and interviewed him and his son. But nothing appeared in the press.

15. Indeed, Ulanhu was said to be eager to see his models, and they talked for over ten minutes at the railway station before his departure for Beijing. Longmei and Yurong wrote a memorial article, expressing how Ulanhu satisfied their demand to write the school name and youth palace at their own constituency in 1986 and 1987 (Longmei and Yurong 1990).

16. Ulanhu died in December 1988. While it was impossible to criticize his model so long as he was in power, in 1990 some Inner Mongolian newspapers published hints of revelation, pointing out that Haschuluu was the true discoverer of the girls. But the full explosion of the story only came in late August 1993, one year after the removal of Ulanhu's son from his position as the chairman in Inner Mongolia.

7

§

The Cult of Ulanhu:
History, Memory, and the
Making of an Ethnic Hero

U lanhu (1906–1988) has figured prominently in my discussion of many areas of Inner Mongolian ethnopolitics. Ulanhu, or "the red son of Communism," as his name would be translated, was the founder of the Inner Mongolia Autonomous Region and was its supreme leader from its origins in 1947 until he was ousted in the early days of the Cultural Revolution. Long the nation's top official minority cadre, in the 1980s he served as China's vice president, the highest position any minority cadre has ever held. We are thus left with an intriguing question: How has Ulanhu been evaluated by Mongols and Chinese in his lifetime and after his death? In this chapter I make no attempt to use public opinion surveys or other quantitative measures to take the pulse of Mongol and Chinese views, an impossibility in the current political atmosphere in China. Rather, I focus on a phenomenon emerging in Inner Mongolia in recent years— that is, an attempt by both Mongols and Chinese to set up a posthumous cult of Ulanhu. By cult, I do not refer to political-cum-religious venerational worship, as was the case of "Mao Craze" or Mao Cult in the 1980s and 1990s (Barmé 1996). There is no Ulanhu badge being used as a protective charm, nor is there Ulanhu cuisine to reenergize the body and soul. What is at issue, and thus the focus of this study, is the different *meanings* of Ulanhu as a great minority leader to the Chinese state and to the Mongols, who are a minority both in their own Autonomous Region and in China.

Here I treat Ulanhu as someone betwixt and between two worlds, Mongol and Chinese. He was a hybrid in multiple terms; he was a Mongol but could not speak Mongolian. He was a representative of the Mongols; indeed, he was said to represent the entire minority nationality population of China, attaining the status of a *minzu lingxiu* ("minority nationality leader"), and simultaneously a party-state leader as the "pre-eminent nationality work leader" (*zhuoyue de minzu gongzuo lingdao ren*), as the Party's official evaluation states. Ulanhu then offers an interesting opportunity to examine ethnic relations within the frameworks of Chinese socialist ethnopolitics and of regional and global politics. I will examine the Chinese state's and Mongols' changing evaluation of him. Here an anthropological and qualitative approach, combining documentary analysis and personal interviews, yields particularly interesting results.

CONSTRUCTING AN ULANHU CULT

When Ulanhu died in Beijing on December 8, 1988, he was deputy chairman of the National People's Congress. The Party's official evaluation was that he was a "reliable Communist soldier, distinguished Party and state leader, outstanding proletarian revolutionary, pre-eminent nationality work leader." When Ulanhu died, however, there did not seem to be any breast-beating mourning either in China for a while or in Inner Mongolia. Indeed, life went on, and nobody paid too much attention to the news of his death. His funeral was quietly held in the auditorium of the PLA general logistics headquarters in Beijing. Apparently, no organized mourning ceremony was held in Inner Mongolia. Only about four to five hundred people attended the funeral in Beijing. In addition to official mourners, including ranking Party, government, and military leaders, most of those in attendance were Tumed Mongols, especially Ulanhu's family members. Some arrived from Inner Mongolia uninvited. According to informants who attended the funeral, the mourners were quickly led around the corpse and ushered out after performing the usual three-bow ritual, leaving no time for people to express their grief. Buhe, Ulanhu's eldest son, then chairman of the Inner Mongolia Autonomous Region, was said to have requested that a proper funeral be held in Inner Mongolia, but Deng Xiaoping reportedly vetoed this. He further requested that a small mausoleum be built in Inner Mongolia. Deng again did not give permission. Finally, Buhe was pressured to agree to cremating Ulanhu's body, his ashes to be kept at Babaoshan Cemetery in Beijing, where the ashes of heroes of the revolution are usually kept. It is rumored that Buhe was also confined to Beijing for a period following the funeral.

Ulanhu's low-profile funeral may be contrasted with the mourning following the deaths of two prominent leaders in early 1989: the death of the Tibetan Buddhist leader, the Panchen Lama, in January and that of the disgraced Chinese leader Hu Yaobang in April. I consider first the Panchen Lama. Upon the Panchen's death in January 1989, a memorial service was held in the Great Hall of the People, and Buddhists all over China, most notably in Tibet, organized memorial services to commemorate him. The People's Government of the Tibet Autonomous Region and the Democratic Management Committee of the Tashilhunpo Monastery were made responsible for building a stupa and a memorial in his honor. Both were to be erected in the Tashilhunpo Monastery itself, so that, according to the official account, "future generations may honor the memory of the man who accrued so much patriotic and Buddhist merit" (van Grasdorff 1999: 188).

Why the difference? It was explained to me by a Chinese politician that the reason is that Ulanhu was a communist, while the Panchen Lama was a Buddhist. Ulanhu was China's vice president from 1983 to 1988 and at his death was a vice chairman of the National People's Congress. Ulanhu's funeral was said to be in line with the CCP policy to hold simple funerals for communist leaders. This explanation undoubtedly underestimated the high stakes in the maneuvering between China and the international Tibet lobby being played out around the Panchen Lama. Chinese authorities invariably compared the Panchen Lama's patriotism to the Dalai Lama's apostasy and betrayal of his Chinese motherland. In this light, the difference may not be simply a separation of state from church, but may lie rather in the political symbolism carried by the dead Panchen in relation to the Chinese state and the Tibetans.

An insight can also be gained from consideration of the death and funeral of Hu Yaobang a few months later. Born in 1915 and joining the CCP when he was eighteen, Hu Yaobang made his political career by working in the Chinese Communist Youth League. For fourteen years, between 1952 and 1966, he was the first secretary of the Youth League. After the Cultural Revolution, thanks to his close relationship with Deng Xiaoping, Hu was appointed secretary-general of the CCP Central Committee in 1980. But he finally fell in 1987 when he angered Deng over his stand on the question of bourgeois liberalization (Yang 1988). He suddenly died in April 1989, in the middle of student protest in Tiananmen Square. The refusal of the Party to the student petition for an explanation of the background to Hu's resignation as secretary-general of the Party in 1987 and denial of student participation in the official memorial service held inside the Great Hall of the People prompted students to turn Hu into a cult hero. On April 22, challenging the official memorial service, students staged their own ceremony, thus managing to "convert an official ceremony into a counterhegemonic performance" (Perry 1994: 77).

It does not, therefore, seem correct that Ulanhu's low-profile memorial service can be adequately explained by the Chinese Communist Party policy with regard to its deceased leaders or their official rank upon their deaths. "Fancy funerals" for leaders were banned only after October 1991, and then only briefly. According to Reuters on October 11, 1991, which reported the declaration of the Central Committee of the Chinese Party, "when senior officials of the Party and state die, their funerals must follow the principle of simplicity." The declaration further stipulated that dead leaders would be cremated and their ashes buried, no tombs were to be built, and no ashes could be scattered (Watson 1994b: 82–83). Why was the Party's lofty principle applied to Ulanhu retroactively?

The Chinese state's apparent apathy toward his memorial service and the ban on the funeral being held in Inner Mongolia came as a great surprise, and even a shock, to many Mongols, giving rise to speculation that Ulanhu might have made mistakes and fallen out of favor with Deng Xiaoping. People cracked bitter jokes, saying that the scale of Ulanhu's funeral was smaller than that of Li Sheng a few years earlier; he was a friend of Ulanhu's and a veteran Tumed Mongolian revolutionary who held a minor post as the director of the Hohhot Nationality Affairs Committee. Li had become hugely popular among Mongol students in the 1981 Mongolian students' movement, supporting their demands. His cortege was said to have paraded from Hohhot to Lama Dong some fifty kilometers away, a place associated with his revolutionary activities during the anti-Japanese war. Some explained to me that the Chinese leadership was worried that those who suffered from the anti-new Inner Mongolian People's Revolutionary Party movement and anti-Ulanhu movement during the Cultural Revolution might gather at his funeral and cause a disturbance. It is difficult to ascertain precisely the Chinese government calculus at the time; the official handling of the funeral and the general response of the Mongols may be indicative of the diminution of Ulanhu's political value for the Chinese party-state. Certainly in 1988–1989, Ulanhu did not have the stature to Mongols that the Panchen Lama had to Tibetans or Hu Yaobang to Chinese.

What is certain is that a turn occurred in the official policy toward Ulanhu three years later. In June 1992 the Propaganda Department of the CCP officially permitted a modest mausoleum to be built in Hohhot, the capital of Inner Mongolia. The decree of the center, which is carefully displayed in the mausoleum, reads:

> June 12, 1992: Central Propaganda Department: [We] in principle agree that a small scale (*xiao xing*) mausoleum can be built for Comrade Ulanhu. [We] suggest that the scale should be set in accordance with the principle of frugality and modesty. The cost should be born by the autonomous region. Office of the Chinese Communist Party Central Committee.

This appeared to be an after-the-fact approval. In May, one month before the approval, construction had already begun in western Hohhot inside a Botanical Garden, under the Inner Mongolia Party Committee and Government. The construction was completed hurriedly, but rather than the modest structure that the Propaganda Department had stipulated, a great structure emerged, fashioned after the model of the Chinggis Khan Temple in Ulaanhot and the Chinggis Khan Mausoleum in Ordos, only bigger. Officially opened on December 23, 1992, the mausoleum is 2,100 square meters. By comparison the Chinggis Khan Temple covers 822 square meters and the Chinggis Khan Mausoleum 1,500 square meters. In the absence of the body or ashes, one huge standing statue was erected in front of the mausoleum, much like a returning Ulanhu walking on the grassland of his homeland. Inside the main hall is a sitting statue, surrounded with wreathes presented by individuals and organizations when special memorial services are held. These are strikingly similar to the statues of Chinggis Khan in Ordos, except that Chinggis Khan is armored. As in the Chinggis Khan Mausoleum, there are very few actual "relics." Instead, their respective careers and accomplishments are chronicled through photographs and paintings. Outside the hall, there is a tablet inscribing the names of every prefecture government and party committee in Inner Mongolia as donors.

The new mausoleum has been designated as a "base for patriotic education." On women's day (March 8), children's day (June 1), and army day (August 1), the government orchestrates pledge-taking rituals, initiation rituals, thus turning Ulanhu's mausoleum into not only a public display of the patriotic deeds of Ulanhu, but the political ritual platform of Inner Mongolia. The official purpose of the mausoleum is captured in the following words, written by one of Ulanhu's daughters:

> Under the new situation of reform and opening, organizing Comrade Ulanhu's Mausoleum exhibition has important historical and practical significance; it has provided us a necessary platform and lively education materials for conducting education in revolutionary tradition and patriotic education. It will always educate later

7.1. Statue of Ulanhu in Front of His Mausoleum (2000)

7.2.   Statue of Chinggis Khan in Front of His Mausoleum (2000)

generations to learn from the glorious spirit of the older generation of proletarian revolutionaries, and complete their unfinished causes. (Qiqige 1993: 48)

ETHNOPOLITICS AND POSITIONAL SUBJECTIVITIES

What we have seen is an interesting return of Ulanhu to Inner Mongolia, from which he had been removed for twenty-two years after 1966. In 1966 he was declared a counterrevolutionary, a traitor to China, a campaign that resulted in the catastrophic purges not only of Ulanhu but of virtually the entire Mongol leadership of Inner Mongolia, and a situation that resulted in numerous casualties of ordinary Mongols. And yet after his death, he apparently made a comeback as the ultimate embodiment of the state, as a representative of the state, a Mongol hero, a symbol of Chinese patriotism, a defender of the Chinese nation, all of which were meritorious at a time when internal and external forces were said to be trying to split China apart. I argue that the timing of Ulanhu's return, from a low-profile treatment in 1988 to pomp and grandeur in 1992, was closely related to efforts by Beijing to assure stability and control in the autonomous region. This was also the result of pressures from certain Mongols to restore his honor and to use him to strengthen the position of Mongols in Chinese politics and society.

It is useful to briefly examine the ethnopolitical situation in Inner Mongolia in the 1980s and early 1990s. In the course of the 1980s, many of Ulanhu's children and relatives regained power and held high government positions in Inner Mongolia—indeed, forming an important factional political force in the region. Buhe, Ulanhu's eldest son, was the chairman of the Inner Mongolia Autonomous Region for ten years, between 1982 and 1992, when he succeeded to his father's position as the deputy chairman of the National People's Congress in Beijing. He was never the Party secretary; in fact, the position has always been held by a Chinese since Ulanhu's removal in 1966–1967. It is important to note that no one, least of all a Mongol, ever replicated Ulanhu's many-sided power—for example, Party, government, and army chief in Inner Mongolia, simultaneously holding many important Party and state positions in Beijing. In the popular perception, Buhe's domination in Inner Mongolia did not derive from his personal capability; rather, it hinged on his being the son of Ulanhu. This is not entirely unique to Inner Mongolia, but common to China, where many senior communist leaders' offspring have assumed leadership positions, the prime example being Li Peng, the adopted son of the later premier Zhou Enlai.

Ulanhu's family domination in Inner Mongolia was derided in numerous stories. One story tells that when someone went to the Inner Mongolian government building and shouted, "Lao [senior] Yun!" almost half of the office windows were opened. Realizing his mistake, the person shouted, "Xiao [junior] Yun!"; the other half of the windows then opened. Yun was Ulanhu's Chinese surname, a name shared by many Tumed Mongol group, to which Ulanhu belonged. A similar story is that there were so many Yuns seeking to attend Ulanhu's funeral in Beijing that it became difficult to buy train tickets.

Ulanhu's family domination in Inner Mongolia was not just about tribalism, but was also about official corruption. China's market reforms opened venues for those with political connections to reap vast personal profits. This official corruption led to the protest and demand for more transparent polity in Tiananmen Square in 1989. Anticorruption movements called for popular justice. There was outcry against the collaboration between Buhe's wife and Li Peng's son to line their pockets by speculating in cashmere, a newly booming commodity of Inner Mongolia. Chinese and "democratic" criticism of Ulanhu as a "Mongolian King" and his dynastic rule of Inner Mongolia was published in an overseas dissident publication, *Zhonggong Taizidang* (*CPC Princes*) (Ho and Gao 1992). This was rather reminiscent of the charges against Ulanhu during the Cultural Revolution that he had become a "reigning prince" (*dangdai wangye*) and was building an "independent kingdom" (*duli wangguo*).

Here we note two important issues that are not always reconcilable: the intra-Mongol struggle and the internationality struggle in Inner Mongolia. Assuming an oppositional rhetoric against "tribal" politics in a multiethnic situation could be an effective way to cut across the ethnic barrier. For the criticism of "corrupt" Tumed Mongols had the effect of criticizing not only the "corrupt" officials but the "Mongols." Characteristic of modern politics, whether communist (democratic centralization) or liberal democratic (electoral legitimation), in Inner Mongolia "the people," of course, are overwhelmingly Chinese. There is no easy solution to this situation, especially in Inner Mongolia, where the Mongols are an absolute minority in their own "autonomous region."

Perhaps in response to "popular" resentment of the Tumed Mongols, who no longer had Ulanhu's support, toward the end of 1991 Buhe's younger brother Uje, mayor of Inner Mongolia's largest city, Baotou, who was poised to succeed Buhe as chairman of Inner Mongolia, was removed from Inner Mongolia and made a vice-governor of Shanxi province. Buhe, after retiring from his post as chairman of the Inner Mongolia Autonomous Region in 1992, was kicked upstairs to become a vice-chairman of the People's Congress, a post his father, Ulanhu, had held until his death. That is, he was removed from his power base in Inner Mongolia. Since his departure, most of the Tumed Mongol elite, especially those bearing the same surname, "Yun," in the upper echelons of political power have been removed from office, making way for eastern Mongols and Chinese. At the same time, in a curious way, to curb eastern Mongolian domination, the Party institutionalized tribalism by alternating the chairmanship between Tumed Mongols and eastern Mongols and leaving out many other significant Mongol groups.

To these internal dynamics of ethnopolitics were added exogenous events, specifically, democratic movements in the Mongolia People's Republic (MPR) and various Asian nations and the collapse of the Soviet Union. Inner Mongolia, because of the close ethnic link with Mongolia, was clearly affected, although Inner Mongolia did not experience violence or the emergence of a separatist movement on a scale comparable to that in, for example, Xinjiang. Nevertheless, Wang Qun, the Party secretary of Inner Mongolia, wrote an alarmist report in the *People's Daily*, on May 14, 1990: "Since last spring and summer, there have been two incidents in the Inner Mongolia region in which a small number of people started up trouble. At first a small number of people exploited ethnic issues to stir things up in a vain attempt to destroy nationality solidarity and the unity of the motherland" (quoted in *Crackdown in Inner Mongolia* 1991:7). The state subsequently cracked down on two Mongol organizations in Yekejuu and Bayannuur Leagues. The main charges against these organizations included organizing family meetings and lectures in which they discussed Mongolian cultural renewal and national modernization. The groups distributed anti-Soviet nationalist pamphlets written by the famous MPR democrat-nationalist leader Baabar and established contacts beyond Inner Mongolia (see *Crackdown in Inner Mongolia* 1991). These mild cultural and civil society–type movements met with heavy-handed responses from a paranoid Party. Not only were they declared illegal, but leading Mongol participants were incarcerated for years. An anti-Mongol nationalist campaign was carried out in Inner Mongolia. According to an appeal and a statement issued by an overseas Mongolian human rights organization, Inner Mongolian League for the Defense of Human Rights,

> Wang Qun, the present secretary of the Communist Party in the Inner Mongolian Autonomous Region, is using high-handed methods to intimidate and threaten Mongolian intellectuals and cadres. Many Mongolians fear this incident may evolve into a campaign of political persecution. It has not only effectively silenced the Mongolian intellectuals but also caused great unease among certain high-level Mongolian officials. This is because their memory of the massacre known as "unearthing the new Inner Mongolian People's Revolutionary Party" in which tens of thousands of people were killed 22 years ago is still fresh. (*Crackdown in Inner Mongolia* 1991: 15)

What is of interest for this chapter, though, is whether and how Mongol officials resisted in this time of crisis. To his credit, Buhe was sympathetic to the intellectuals and was reluctant to suppress Mongol demands for greater nationality rights. Buhe was known to have had much friction with the Party secretary Wang Qun. Wang, an "imperial envoy" eager to bring Inner Mongolia into closer integration with China, implemented the Center's policies, often with excessive passion. Buhe, however, insisted, as his father had during his long rule, that Inner Mongolia had its own peculiarities and sought to adapt central policies to the local situation in many areas. Many Mongols evaluated Buhe positively for his handling of this matter. Nevertheless, Buhe and other Mongol officials were eventually forced to toe the official line, insisting on defending national unity (minzu tuanjie). How do we reconcile these two stances taken by Mongol officials?

Here it is useful to invoke James Scott's theory of the arts of resistance (1990). He distinguishes two modes of political discourse: public transcript and hidden transcript. The term *transcript* refers to a kind of political discourse that may take such forms as speeches, gestures, and practices. For Scott, public transcript is a protective mask worn by the subordinates in interaction with the powerful, in the manner of showing deference or consent. The hidden transcript is always an offstage performance, which conveys the true feelings of the subordinate after removing the mask of disguise. It is important to note that public transcript, as a kind of hegemony, may serve the subordinate as much as the powerful. He convincingly argues that subordinated groups, in their protest, usually do not have an alternative ideology, but embrace the bulk of the dominant ideology: "most protests and challenges—even quite violent ones—are made in the realistic expectation that the central features of the form of domination will remain intact" (1990: 92). In the struggle, strategic actions usually emphasize loyalty to the institution or person. "Any dominant ideology with hegemonic pretensions must," Scott argues, "by definition, provide subordinate groups with political weapons that can be of use in the public transcript" (1990: 101).

Concerning this "use value of hegemony," Mongol intellectuals and officials, I suggest, have learned how to use official ideology for their own purposes. "Minzu tuanjie" (nationality unity/amity between nationalities) is a hegemonic slogan designed by the party-state to force nationalities into line. The hegemony of this term lies in its absolutist assumptions: the objective of the state is national unity, and only socialism can bring about national unity. This "national unity," however, ultimately privileges the interests of the Chinese. The official injunction is that no one should say or do anything detrimental to minzu tuanjie (*bu shuo/zuo bu li yu minzu tuanjie de hua/shi*). This injunction seeks to effectively foreclose any legitimate way to express politicized ethnic grievance, lest it undermine "national unity." "Preserve state unity and consolidate national unity" is a slogan raised at every sign of ethnic unrest. Mongol officials and intellectuals would be paraded on TV and radio to declare where they stood on nationalism. Invariably, all would express their resolute opposition to any attempt to undermine minzu tuanjie, thereby creating the impression that "nationalism" was more harmful to the Mongols than to the Chinese state. However, while minzu tuanjie is an ultimate state weapon, the praxis can be more complex.

As our case shows, indeed, the battleground is the keyword *minzu tuanjie*. The importance of keywords in politics is underscored by Daniel Rodgers (1987). Political struggle for him is over the control of these metaphors of legitimation. In his fascinating study of the concept of *fengjian* or feudalism in Chinese history, Duara (1995: 146–75) shows that the indigenous term initially provided impetus for the federalist movement across Chinese provinces. Empowering local people and governments was seen as a way to preserve the Chinese nation in the light of the ever-weakening central state in the final decades of Manchu rule. However, the federalist movement lost its ideological legitimacy when *fengjian* was later invested with negative meanings, identified as feudalism, as the Other of the master narrative of History.

The fortune of the term *fengjian* highlighted an important principle defining the relationship between state and society in the face of external threat. Local autonomy, ethnic or nonethnic, is often seen as undermining state unity and sovereignty. Whereas *zi zhi* ("self-rule" or "autonomy") or even self-determination were positive keywords that indeed were used in the names of many national minority organizations, such as the Inner Mongolia "Autonomous" Region, in the early 1960s, the escalating Sino-Soviet rift required absolute loyalty of the frontier Mongols to the beleaguered Chinese state. Ulanhu's insistence on local autonomy—that is, the protection of Mongol rights in the autonomous region—then became the very basis for charges of his alleged crime of splitting China, and he himself was purged. In July 1981, in a seminal article published in the *People's Daily* to defend minority nationality autonomy, which he championed, Ulanhu argued, "Once nationality regional autonomy is conscientiously implemented, the minority nationality peoples would then be deeply convinced that they are not only the masters of their own homeland, but also of the motherland;

their spirit of loving the motherland, loving their own nationalities would be greatly elevated" (1999: 371).

This line of argument over what constitutes the condition for nationality autonomy and national unity clearly reveals competing visions and positions. Mongols are desperate to make sure that their demands for limited autonomous rights are not understood by the Chinese as weakening state integrity. Losing this precarious legitimacy in a neurotic China, hypersensitive to the "nationality question," would invariably invite the state's ruthless suppression. Minzu tuanjie, by virtue of its ambiguous meanings, referring either to "national unity" or to "amity between nationalities," has been embraced by both Chinese and Mongols for different purposes. Whereas "national unity" tends to obscure Mongols as a political and cultural unit, minzu tuanjie, understood as "amity between nationalities," recognizes and highlights difference and equality between nationalities. The universalistic and particularistic dimensions of minzu tuanjie could, therefore, be pitted against each other. An assimilationist policy could be criticized for not cementing minzu tuanjie but destroying it. For their part, the Chinese would hold that ethnic differences and demand for equality and autonomy, which are seen by minorities as conditions for minzu tuanjie, would lead to minzu fenlie (national splitism). The following incident illustrates an interesting process whereby positioned subjectivities are expressed in manipulating the meaning of minzu tuanjie.

In the early 1990s, as democracy and nationalist movements spread across Mongolia, the Chinese government became nervous, fearing that Inner Mongols would also join a pan-Mongolian movement, spurring independence and democracy in Inner Mongolia. Wang Qun, the Party secretary of Inner Mongolia, made repeated speeches, harping on minzu tuanjie and the dangers of splitism, to the dismay of many Mongol officials and intellectuals. As some Mongols confided to me, this was a typical ploy of frontier colonial officials bidding to consolidate their power. To take another example, Han Maohua, a deputy Party secretary, made reports in 1993 at the Inner Mongolian Party School that Mongols were latecomers, settling in the territory of Inner Mongolia only eight hundred years ago, whereas historical and archaeological evidence showed that the Chinese had lived in Inner Mongolia since time immemorial. This was an attempt, Mongols asserted, to deny them their rights of autonomy. Wang's and Han's speeches and their underlying goal incurred a barrage of criticism from Mongols. Some high-ranking Mongolian leaders asserted that it was Wang and Han, not the Mongols, who wanted to drive the Mongols away from Inner Mongolia, splitting China. Mongol leaders also accused them of violating the Chinese Constitution and the Law of Nationality Regional Autonomy, which defined Mongols as the titular nationality of the Inner Mongolia Autonomous Region. They swiftly reported the case to Beijing, leading to an investigation. They demanded that the Chinese officials not distribute Han's speech to the public, especially to Mongol students. Had Mongols not exercised caution, had they reacted angrily in public, this could have provided local Chinese officials with ammunition to prove to the Chinese central government that Inner Mongolia was indeed in trouble, and it was necessary to crack down on alleged Mongol "splitists" in order to defend the "motherland." In this struggle, Wang Qun was criticized by the Party Center, but he was not punished; instead, he added the post of chairman of the Inner Mongolian People's Congress, the highest self-ruling organ of the autonomous region, one usually reserved for the Mongols. Han Maohua was subsequently removed from Inner Mongolia but appointed Party secretary of Ningxia Hui Autonomous Region, clearly a promotion for his meritorious service. Although Mongols were not entirely happy with this outcome, it nevertheless constituted a small victory in removing Han from the Autonomous Region and blocking the circulation of his poisonous thesis. Whether this was a victory worth winning may be disputed, but it must be understood within the specific context of Inner Mongolia in which Mongols are on the defensive against the state's desire for more direct control and in which frontier Chinese cadres' special role is to serve as guarantors of Chinese national security. Victory, from the Mongol point of view, is not secession—a victory that would virtually guarantee war—but is maintenance of the precarious status quo.

It is in such a geopolitical context that the meaning of Ulanhu's political career assumes great importance. In 1989, in the aftermath of the Tiananmen Square incident and the unrest in Tibet, a massive campaign by the Inner Mongolian government, headed by Buhe, was carried out in Beijing and Hohhot to propagandize Ulanhu, portraying him as a staunch communist, a patriot who successfully solved China's ethnic problems in Inner Mongolia. They did not hesitate to point out that while Tibet was troubled with ethnic riots and calls for independence, Inner Mongolia, thanks to the fruit of Ulanhu's effort, was stable and prosperous, having unshakable trust in the Party's leadership. A huge exhibition of Ulanhu's life was mounted in Beijing in 1991. Under Buhe's direction, a Ulanhu Revolutionary History Materials Compiling Office was set up in 1989 and an Ulanhu Research Association in 1990, with its own journal, *Ulanhu Research*. Housed in the Inner Mongolia Archives, the association was charged specifically with studying Ulanhu's patriotic thought and revolutionary contributions. In the next few years, a biography, a memoir, a pictorial, and a six-part teledrama were produced, displaying Ulanhu's outstanding contribution to "solving" the Inner Mongolian question.

This effort catered to the needs of the beleaguered Chinese state, which was desperately seeking legitimacy, especially in the ethnic field. In a way, we could argue that ethnic unrest in the late 1980s and 1990s lent urgency to the Chinese government, requiring that it justify the incorporation of Tibet, Xinjiang, and Inner Mongolia into China not as Chinese "liberation," but as the willing act of patriotic minority communists like Ulanhu. These internal and external political atmospheres compelled both Mongol and Chinese Party leaders to take Ulanhu on board. In this new cult of Ulanhu, the discourse of power relations in Inner Mongolia could then be referred back to Ulanhu and the institutions Ulanhu helped set up, providing resources that could be used by both Mongols and Chinese. Now that Ulanhu was presented as a symbol of Mongol revolution and patriotism, Mongols and Chinese—indeed, the entire Inner Mongolian officialdom—rushed to become patrons of the mausoleum. Suddenly, Ulanhu became a great man, no longer an ambiguous figure. No one could then afford to dissociate from him. Ulanhu is dead! Long live Ulanhu! The dead Ulanhu became part of the state's magic, the "attraction and repulsion" of which being, as Michael Taussig so eloquently writes, "tied to the Nation, to more than a whiff of a certain sexuality reminiscent of the Law of the Father, and lest we forget, to the specter of death, human death in that soul-stirring insufficiency of Being" (1997: 3).

Then, who was Ulanhu? What did he actually mean to the Chinese state and the Mongol people? Before sketching his life history and contemporary remembrances of his "contributions" in the following two sections, I want to briefly discuss the subjectivity and positionality of social analysts.

Renato Rosaldo (1993: 166) defines the analyst as a "positioned subject." This perspective emphasizes reflexivity on the part of the anthropological analyst vis-à-vis the "culture" one studies. In an ethnopolitical situation, we deal with more than one culture and more than one group. The cultures and groups are relational and at times oppositional. This requires us to recognize that in an ethnic conflict situation, the views expressed by opposing group members are also "positioned." It is important to take seriously the sometimes clashing views of the "positioned subjects" on the ground and treat them also as kinds of social analysts.

This kind of relational and positional subjectivity is marvelously captured by Andrew Shryock in his study of the binary rhetoric in writing and maintaining genealogies or histories among Bedouin tribal sheiks under conditions of segmentary social and political relations. Truth is locally and relationally understood and therefore changeable (Shryock 1997). Likewise, Michael Herzfeld proposes what he calls "reflexive comparativism," the goal of which is not to treat history-making of the sort Shryock describes "as though it belonged to exactly the same mode as western historiography." The advantage of reflexive comparativism is that "instead of making 'our own' mode the immovable touchstone for the evaluation of all others, we treat it as an interesting cultural object in its own right" (Herzfeld 2001: 65). Following this reflexive comparativist approach, I do not try to find an objective truth in what Ulanhu actually did or did not do; the truth is always relational, and this is perhaps especially so in a socialist state, as I noted in chapter 6 with regard to the two heroic little sisters. Rather, in examining the ritually constructed cult of Ulanhu, we can make sense of relationally positioned subjectivities maintained by Mongols and Chinese, especially the Chinese state.

THE MEANING OF ULANHU TO CHINA

In this section, I examine Ulanhu's communist career path to gauge what he meant to the Chinese Communist Party state. Ulanhu's life history showed that from the very start of his revolutionary career, he constantly crossed the ethnic line. To China, his greatest value seems to be his "loyalty," rather than fighting for Mongolian interests.

Born into a sinicized Tumed Mongolian peasant family in 1906, in the suburb of today's Hohhot, the capital city of Inner Mongolia, Ulanhu received his education in Beijing's Mongolian Tibetan school, where he became a Chinese Communist Party member in 1925. His revolutionary mentor, Li Dazhao, one of the legendary founding fathers of the Chinese Communist Party, known for his alternating positions on nationalism and internationalism (Meisner 1967), was sympathetic to Mongols. Ulanhu never forgot to narrate this revolutionary genealogy (Ulanhu 1989). Trained in Moscow from 1925 to 1929, Ulanhu made many friends who later proved to be extremely useful for his career: Wang Ruofei, Zhou Enlai, Wu Xiuquan, and so on (Hao 1997). Unlike other Mongol communists who attempted to revive the defunct Inner Mongolian People's Revolutionary Party, which Ulanhu also joined in 1925, Ulanhu and his Tumed Mongol cohort returned to Inner Mongolia in 1929, set up a cell of the Chinese Communist Party, and established international communication lines between the CCP and the Comintern. Ulanhu's early communist activities in Inner Mongolia made two lasting impressions on fellow Chinese communists. Wang Ruofei, a high-ranking Chinese communist, came to work in the base established by Ulanhu in Suiyuan province. Under Wang's leadership, Ulanhu tried to instigate Mongolian rebellion against the ruling GMD. After Wang was captured by the enemy in 1931, Ulanhu played an important role in the rescue operation. In 1936 Ulanhu instigated the desertion of troops from the Mongolian nationalist leader Prince Demchugdonrob's army, consisting mainly of Tumed Mongols. Although most of the troops were later annihilated by the GMD army, the uprising was symbolically important for the Chinese, as it was a first shot fired at the Japanese and their Mongolian collaborators. Following the second CCP-GMD coalition against the Japanese invasion, Ulanhu joined the Mongolian army under GMD control, and he managed to recruit many CCP members. The symbolic and political capital he earned was enormous. His was the only communist and Mongolian resistance movement leaning toward the Chinese Communist Party.

In 1941 when his communist activity was considered intolerable to the GMD, which threatened to kill him, Ulanhu was summoned to Yan'an, where he became the most trusted "minority" communist within the ranks of the CCP, thanks in part to his friendship with many of the CCP's top leaders who had been his acquaintances or classmates in Moscow in 1925–1929. He then directly participated in the Party's formulation and practice of policy toward minorities.

Serving first as a dean of studies of Yan'an's College of Nationalities and surviving the 1942 rectification movement in Yan'an, Ulanhu emerged as an alternate member of the CCP Central Committee in the Party's Seventh Congress in 1945. As the Second World War drew to an end, Ulanhu became the CCP's point man to solve Inner Mongolian questions.

Ulanhu demonstrated his remarkable skill at solving the Inner Mongolian "question" for the CCP when he was dispatched by General Nie Rongzhen to dismantle the Provisional Government of the Republic of Inner Mongolia, a pro-independence Inner Mongolian government set up in 1945 by Prince Demchug-dongrob's officials after the Soviet-Mongolian invasion and occupation of much of the central and eastern parts of Inner Mongolia. Without firing a shot, he managed to become the "chairman" of the government and later dismantle it and recruit its members into his own Inner Mongolian Association of Movements for Autonomy, a semigovernmental organization set up in 1946. Then, moving to eastern Mongolia, he replaced the more militarily savvy Eastern Mongolia Autonomous Government with his own association, which paved the way for founding the Inner Mongolia Autonomous Government in May 1947 (Hao 1997; Nei Menggu Zizhiqu Dang'an'guan 1989). This latter government was a strategic gift to the Chinese Communist Party in its race for control of Manchuria in 1947–1948. A CCP-controlled Inner Mongolia guaranteed not only a strong base for the CCP operation, but also Mongolian support for the CCP. The Inner Mongolia Autonomous Government was also significant for the CCP, as it was the Party's first major success in resolving territorial and nationality issues. Ulanhu, as the man who delivered all this to the CCP, was, of course, richly rewarded for his meritorious service, as he was accorded the full control of Inner Mongolia and allowed to restore the historical Mongolian territories under the jurisdiction of the Inner Mongolia Autonomous Region.

This brief biographical note shows that Ulanhu's rapid rise within the CCP hierarchy was directly related to his remarkable success in "solving" the Inner Mongolian "question." One does not have to doubt his skill, but the efficacy of his skill must be understood within larger power relations. There was no other option for Inner Mongols but to cooperate with the Chinese Communist Party. After all, the CCP also promised to dismantle the Chinese provinces and return them to Mongols. Instead of positing a mysterious magnetic gravity of China to minorities, as Chinese communists-cum-nationalists maintain, we should perhaps think of Ulanhu and other Mongols' decision to work within China as strategic maneuvers. In all Chinese representations, the CCP's military power, with its million-strong army contending for supremacy with the GMD in Manchuria, is downplayed. Rather, the inclusion of Inner Mongolia into China is represented as a struggle and as a "desire" by Ulanhu and other Mongols who supposedly knew that Mongols' future interest lay only in China.

The idyllic Chinese representation of Ulanhu's struggle for China nevertheless allows us to understand the "effect" of Ulanhu on the nature of the Inner

Mongolian revolution. I argue that by "solving the Mongolian question" for China, Ulanhu transformed the Inner Mongolian issue from one of Chinese and Japanese colonization to one posing a threat to Chinese national sovereignty. This is not to deny that as a Mongol himself, who started his revolutionary career out of a desire to improve the livelihood of his impoverished Tumed Mongols, Ulanhu was a kind of nationalist, and communism, a doctrine that preached colonial liberation, was enormously attractive to him. He was, however, oblivious to the tendency that the CCP, although initially endorsing internationalism—the altruistic passion for the liberation of all humanity—became increasingly nationalistic because of the Japanese invasion. National salvation, rather than social equality, became its priority. As a member of the Chinese Communist Party, Ulanhu constantly had to choose between his Party loyalty and loyalty to the Mongols. In the face of eastern Mongolian criticism in 1947, he insisted that the Inner Mongolian question was organically linked with the Chinese revolution, and only after the Chinese revolution succeeded could the Inner Mongolian question be solved. This vision led him to organize unconditional Mongolian support for the CCP to ensure its victory over the GMD (Ulanhu 1999). However, the CCP struggle against the GMD was simultaneously a nation-building effort. Once the CCP won the war and founded the People's Republic (in 1949), to insist on independence or self-determination became a reactionary activity, as it was interpreted as splitting from the progressive forces. Ulanhu thus, in effect, became a person who was instrumental in delivering Inner Mongolia into the CCP and later PRC jurisdiction. And this double role—that is, leading the Mongols to fight for equality or "autonomy" and solving the "Mongolian question" on behalf of the CCP—made him both a "nationality leader" and a Chinese communist cadre.

Given his career experience and his special status as a Mongol communist with extensive links to the MPR and the Soviet Union, he became a member of the Central People's Government and a member of the National Committee of the People's Consultative Conference in late September 1949, a position that clearly indicated that he was a founding member of the People's Republic of China. His diplomatic skill was recognized; he was elected the "executive chairman" of the presidium of the conference of the Sino-Soviet Friendship Association on October 5, 1949. He subsequently added the posts of the standing committee member of the Political Consultative Conference and deputy commissioner of the Nationality Affairs Commission. His position as a state leader vis-à-vis minorities was confirmed on September 1, 1950, when he was appointed by the State Council as the deputy director of the PRC's first National Day Reception Committee, in charge of entertaining ethnic minority representatives. In September 1954 Ulanhu was elected vice premier of the State Council, National Defense Committee member, and commissioner of the Nationality Affairs Commission. On September 27, 1955, he was awarded the military title general (*shangjiang*), second in rank only to marshals. His standing within the

Party hierarchy was further elevated in September 1956, when he was elected an alternate member of the Politburo, the only officially recognized minority member in the highest power organ of the CCP. These impressive positions were held concurrent with all the top positions in the Party, government, and army of Inner Mongolia until the beginning of the Cultural Revolution.

The positions he achieved had to be managed carefully. His continued importance to Chinese national politics hinged on his ability to keep Inner Mongolia fully integrated into China. This had advantages and disadvantages, for diminished "difference" on the part of the Mongols would also reduce his political weight. Thus the imperatives of ethnopolitics led Ulanhu, throughout the 1950s and early 1960s, to engage in two sets of powerful discourses: first, whether or not Inner Mongolia should be a part of China. In this, Ulanhu was unequivocal in his determination to safeguard the territorial integrity of China. As a Moscow-educated communist who went through the Yan'an rectification training, Ulanhu was well versed in the Party's two-line (*luxian*) struggle theory—that is, the struggle between capitalism and socialism. In Inner Mongolia, in addition to the two-line struggle, Ulanhu constantly rehearsed a two-road (*daolu*) struggle—in other words, to be part of China or to be independent. Unfortunately, in order to establish his unequivocal patriotic credentials, he set up an Other, the long-defunct Inner Mongolian People's Revolutionary Party (IMPRP). He tirelessly narrated the struggle between his Yan'an road and eastern Mongols' IMPRP road, alluding to the tension between the two in the months before founding the Inner Mongolia Autonomous Government in 1947. The IMPRP road, in his view, was for independence, associated with the GMD and the Japanese militarism; it was thus anti-Mongol and unnationalist! The Yan'an road, on the other hand, while predicated on the progressive and good Chinese, was better for the national development of the Mongols. To some extent, this discourse made Mongols geographically split, as it put many eastern Mongols into a potentially disloyal camp and the western Mongols, represented by his Tumed Mongols, as the vanguard of the Mongolian future. Indeed, this prospect required continued narration of the danger of independence and justified the repeated condemnation of Mongolian regional nationalism (see Ulanhu 1999 and chapter 5).

Ulanhu's second set of discourses was, however, an attempt to cultivate Mongol support to offset overt Chinese infringement on Mongol rights. If the first set of discourses derived from Ulanhu's political identity as a Chinese "patriot," the second one was from his ethnic identity as a Mongol. Ulanhu's career was geared largely for the liberation of Inner Mongols from the oppression of the Chinese. In the Leninist definition, this would mean liberating the oppressed small nation from an oppressor nation. The creation of the Inner Mongolia Autonomous Region was therefore his version of the liberation of Mongols. Unification of Inner Mongolia, defusing the ethnic tension between Mongol herdsmen and Chinese peasants by making pastoralism a legal part of the Chinese national economy, indigenizing Inner Mongolian administration, and so on, were among numerous measures he adopted. These measures were to make Mongols the principal nationality of the autonomous region and to make their status congruent with the administrative power. In this effort, Ulanhu effectively defined the Chinese as helpers of the Mongols. His criticism of Chinese chauvinism was particularly harsh. There were two tools in his hands: first, he would quote Mao's words in denouncing Chinese chauvinism and celebrate Mao's promise for ethnic equality. He tried to define and legalize the autonomous institution. Many of China's minority autonomy legislations in the 1950s, however inadequate from today's vantage point, were the result of his effort. In this manner, we can then see an interesting development in Inner Mongolian ethnopolitics. To uphold the autonomy was very much like upholding a mini-nation-state sovereignty. Border, administrations, language, education, and so on, were all important things that needed to be protected for Mongols. The diminishing status of the autonomy, the interference of the state and Party without mediating through Ulanhu, would be resisted and sometimes denounced as showing Chinese chauvinism. In this situation, Ulanhu would bypass all the channels and talk directly to Mao Zedong and Zhou Enlai. This created an interesting impression in Inner Mongolia: Mao and Zhou were kind to Inner Mongolia, but there were a lot of bad local Chinese (Hao 1997).

Briefly, Inner Mongolia in the 1950s and early 1960s was full of contradictions; the population of Inner Mongolia was broadly divided into four camps: pro-China Mongols; pro-MPR Mongols; anti-minority Chinese at the lower-level; and pro-minority Chinese at the center, such as Mao and Zhou. By balancing these, Ulanhu reaped enormous political capital. There was a kind of personality cult in the 1950s, largely encouraged by Mao himself, who saw the role of such minority leaders as crucial in ruling the minority region. According to Jiang Ping (1995), who was once the commissioner of the State Nationalities Affairs Commission, he saw Ulanhu's portraits in the guest house of Sunit banner along the Sino-Mongolian border in 1965. Apparently, this was allowed by Mao, as Jiang writes, "Chairman Mao remarked many times before his death: In Inner Mongolia, you should hang Ulanhu's portrait, and shout Long Live Ulanhu. We need batches of most prestigious mass leaders who had intimate relationship with the masses. This was absolutely indispensable in the revolutionary war, so is it in present period of socialist construction" (1995: 169).

This seemingly happy apotheosis of Ulanhu defies representational politics in a liberal democracy, in which a leader shows allegiance to his constituency. That he was simultaneously a representative of the Party to the Mongols and that of the Mongols to the Party denies much moral integrity that can be accorded to any one representative. Gleason gives a vivid description of the characteristics of local officials in Soviet Central Asia:

> Of necessity, local officials serve powerful central patrons. At the same time, however, the resourceful and clever local official may simultaneously seek to promote

the interests of his native homeland and ethnic brethren. As the representative of the center, the native local official might exploit the fusion of political and economic decision making, endemic scarcity and personalistic control over allocative decisions in seeking to mobilize resources to satisfy the wishes of his central patrons. At the same time, as a representative of the locality, he may use these self-same instruments to advance the interests of his ethnic counterparts. Whose man is the local official in the Soviet periphery? The clever local official may be able to answer in the classic retort of the native colonial official: "I am everybody's man." (1991: 614)

But such dual allegiance is fraught with dangers. One cannot please everybody. It may be argued that it was this dual allegiance that ultimately brought down Ulanhu during the Cultural Revolution. On the one hand, he could impose his will as a heavyweight state leader in Inner Mongolia and bargain for more state resources to his own constituent region of Inner Mongolia by virtue of his position in the central government and his direct access to Mao Zedong, Zhou Enlai, and Zhu De. He also managed to make the experiences of Inner Mongolia exemplary to other minority areas of China. Indeed, in 1958 Zhou Enlai praised the Inner Mongolia Autonomous Region as a model region. On the other hand, although extremely effective in cutting red ribbons, this power could also be resented by both his subordinates in Inner Mongolia and his superiors in Beijing. This was especially so when he blocked or modified the Party's policies or directives by insisting on the "difference" of the Inner Mongolian situation. For instance, class struggle was successfully avoided in the pastoral region. And land reclamation was resisted. His position as the alternate member of the Politburo and the second secretary of the CCP North China Bureau (appointed in November 1960) became a point of dispute between him and Li Xuefeng, the first secretary of the CCP North China Bureau. Insisting on his being an alternate member of the Politburo, he defied Li Xuefeng, his superior in the North China Bureau, and effectively blocked North China Bureau intervention into Inner Mongolian affairs, either directly or by making himself the Bureau's representative in Inner Mongolia, much to Li's chagrin.

This seems nothing unusual, for politics means conflicts. But what is at issue here is that the entire fate of Inner Mongolia hinged on one charismatic politician. However, this kind of "personality" politics showed its weakness in times of crisis or when his use value expired or his power became a liability rather than an asset. His defense of Inner Mongolian autonomy, in the form of printing and circulating Mao's 1935 Declaration to the Inner Mongolian people in 1966; his defense of the Tumed Mongols from being struggled against in the Four Cleanups Movement; his promotion of Tumed Mongols in an effort to maintain "revolutionary" authenticity and "Mongol" control of Inner Mongolia; and his insistence on the nationality policy, rather than on the application of universalist class struggle in the multiethnic Inner Mongolia, all backfired (see chapter 4).

These issues became the primary reasons for the denunciation of Ulanhu in the North China Bureau's marathon conference at the historic Qianmen Hotel in Beijing in May–July 1966, which launched the Cultural Revolution (1966–1976). In a combined effort by his subordinates in Inner Mongolia and his humiliated superior in the North China Bureau, Ulanhu was accused of creating an independent kingdom, advocating Inner Mongolian independence, and conspiring with the Soviet Union and the Mongolian People's Republic. At one point in the meeting, Ulanhu was charged with planning a coup on the occasion of celebrating the twentieth anniversary of the founding of the Inner Mongolia Autonomous Region in 1967, when he would massacre the Chinese, and for which purposes he had already had a mass grave dug in the suburb of Hohhot (Hao 1997: 261). In the fifty-plus days' denunciation meeting, the North China Bureau officially charged Ulanhu with five crimes that were formally approved by the Party Center on November 2, 1966:

> Ulanhu's mistake is the mistake of opposing the Party, socialism and Mao Zedong Thought; it is the mistake of destroying state unity, carrying out nationality separatism and revisionism with an aim for an independent kingdom; in nature he is the biggest power-holder taking the capitalist road in the Party organization of Inner Mongolia. Exposure and criticism of Ulanhu's mistakes is tantamount to having dug out a time bomb buried inside the Party. (Tumen and Zhu 1995: 23)

Between August 16 and November 2, 1966, the Party Center stripped Ulanhu of positions as first secretary of the Inner Mongolia Party Committee, second secretary of the North China Bureau, commander and commissar of the Inner Mongolian Military Zone, and president of Inner Mongolia University. But he was allowed to retain the position as chairman of Inner Mongolia, in name only, until mid-1967.

The denunciation of Ulanhu was initially a Party-orchestrated activity. He was not punished by the rebels unleashed by Mao to destroy the bureaucratic obstacles to his revolutionary vision. To some extent, Ulanhu was rather analogous to Liu Shaoqi, who was now presented as embodying the very antithesis of Mao and the Party's revolutionary program. Lowell Dittmer argues that in the criticisms of Liu Shaoqi, Liu became at different times and for different reasons "1. a *symbol* for all 'capitalist-roaders' that was used as a rallying call for rebellion against an entire category of elites, 2. a *scapegoat* for other capitalist-roaders, a villain against whom both friend and erstwhile foe could unite in common vilification" (1998: 248–49). However, he argued, the two functions Liu served alternated, so that "the Red Guards were inclined to use Liu as a 'symbol' for attacks on diverse local targets, whereas the official press tried to use him as a 'scapegoat' to *deflect* attacks from these same targets" (1998: 250, original emphasis). What's peculiar about Ulanhu's situation is that while Liu Shaoqi was tortured to death, Ulanhu survived and did not seem to suffer much physi-

7.3. Ulanhu Accused of Biting Off Lands from Neighboring Provinces (*Jinggangshan: Tongda Wulanfu Zhuanhao*, October 8, 1967)

cally. After the Qianmen Hotel conference, Ulanhu was kept in Beijing and later transferred to Hunan province under military protection.

Mao and Zhou's decision not to allow Ulanhu to be sent to Inner Mongolia for struggle may have been based on a genuine belief that Ulanhu would be killed by the angry factions, but contrary to Mao and Zhou's much-touted love for "nationality cadres," their refusal to clarify their own evaluation of him, either as a "revolutionary" cadre or as an enemy, made the case worse and created further problems for Ulanhu. In fact, it was Zhou Enlai who chaired the Qianmen Hotel conference that overthrew Ulanhu.

The ambiguity of Ulanhu's position is evident in the fact that he was denounced by the Party Central and the North China Bureau, but he was not allowed to be physically struggled by the factions in Inner Mongolia. Moreover, he continued to appear on the Tiananmen Rostrum, together with Mao and Zhou, until 1967. In fact, he continued to keep his positions as chairman of the Inner Mongolia Autonomous Region, alternate member of the Politburo, and vice-premier of the State Council until 1967. It was fear of Ulanhu's return and retaliation that drove some of his Chinese subordinates and the North China Bureau leaders to wage an all-out propaganda war against Ulanhu throughout Inner Mongolia, gathering concrete evidences to prove his alleged nationalist secessionism and other crimes, so that the Party Center could do away with him once and for all. Although he was openly denounced by the Party, declared the

7.4.   Ulanhu Dragging the Inner Mongolia Autonomous Region Out of China
**"I am over 60 years old, and I have been fighting Chinese chauvinism for more than 40
years. I can still. . . ."** (*Jinggangshan: Tongda Wulanfu Zhuanhao,* October 8, 1967)

ultimate enemy of all the people of Inner Mongolia, and stripped of all his posts
in May 1967 when Inner Mongolia was put under the military control of the
Beijing Military District, the Center's refusal to surrender him to be subject to
the revolutionary justice in Inner Mongolia continued to confound both rebels
and loyalists. Ulanhu had to be demonized by all sides, a symbol conveniently
used by different factions to attack each other for serving Ulanhu at one point
or another. This anti-Ulanhu orgy persisted well into the early 1970s. Ulanhu
was the central figure in what was later called three unjust cases that engulfed
the entire Inner Mongolia: the "Ulanhu anti-party treason clique," the "February counter current in Inner Mongolia," and the "New Inner Mongolia People's
Revolutionary Party." In a report to the Secretariat of the Central Committee
of the CPC on July 16, 1981, Zhou Hui, the Party secretary of Inner Mongolia,
admitted that "[t]hroughout the region, 790,000 people were directly incarcerated, struggled against, or kept incommunicado under investigation mainly as a
result of these three cases. Of these, 22,900 people had died and 120,000 were
crippled" (*Crackdown in Inner Mongolia* 1991: 29).

Given such a heavy-handed denunciation of Ulanhu and Mao's all-too-brief verdict in May 1969—suggesting no more than that the punishment of the Mongols had gone too far but was not wrong—Ulanhu's rehabilitation was far from easy. After Lin Biao's death in September 1971, Mao approved a list prepared by Zhou Enlai of old cadres to be "liberated," and it included Ulanhu's name. It is interesting to note how Zhou Enlai then ostensibly defended Ulanhu. According to Hao Yufeng (1997), the official biographer of Ulanhu, in late 1971 in a meeting preparing for the Party's Tenth Congress, Jiang Qing, Wang Hongwen, and others of the group that would eventually be branded the Gang of Four insisted that Ulanhu was guilty of promoting secessionism and revisionism, and the great revolutionary masses of Inner Mongolia would never accept his liberation.

Zhou Enlai defended Ulanhu thus: "Ulanhu is a Mongolian cadre since the early days of our Party; he has made many important contributions to the Chinese revolution!" He then specifically pointed out that Ulanhu's outstanding contributions included abolition of the Provisional Government of the Republic of Inner Mongolia, which aimed to split China and destroy national unity. He praised Ulanhu's heroism in this incident as *dandao fuhui*—that is, he went to the enemy camp all by himself, disregarding personal safety. His efforts to organize the Inner Mongolia movement for autonomy and the founding of the Inner Mongolia Autonomous Government were all part of his remarkable contributions. His mistakes were secondary, and he confessed his mistakes to Mao and was determined to correct them. Finally, Zhou Enlai remarked, "In a great country like ours, which has 56 nationalities, it is abnormal that we don't have a nationality leader coming out to work" (Hao 1997: 281–82). Zhou Enlai was clearly embarrassed that all minority leaders had been overthrown and punished.

Here one should note that Ulanhu was liberated largely because of his "Mongolian" identity and his status as a "nationality leader." Moreover, he was praised for his role in destroying Mongolian independence and bringing Inner Mongolia into China. His pro-Mongol work after 1947 was, however, labeled "mistakes," for which he apologized. He was then given high positions within the Party and government organizations in Beijing. For instance, he was elected first deputy chairman of the Political Consultative Conference in February 1978, second to Deng Xiaoping, who was the chairman. Deng apparently also appreciated Ulanhu's status, as he said to Ulanhu after their elections,

> You are the nationality leader of our party, and in the work of nationality you have accumulated rich and concrete experiences. Comrades Mao Zedong and Zhou Enlai highly respected you for this point when they were alive. Look, our country was left in a terrible state by Lin Biao and the "Gang of Four"; I hope you can help the Party Central to clear up the mess left by the Gang of Four. (Hao 1997: 289)

Ulanhu was subsequently appointed the chairman of the United Front Department of the Party Central to "clear up the mess" for the Party Central.

During this period, he was a full member of the Politburo and was vice-chairman of the PRC, and at his death in 1988 he was a vice chairman of the National People's Congress. However, in spite of his high positions in the Party, he was permanently severed from Inner Mongolia. More important, he was supposed to represent the Party in his capacity as a "minority" leader but was deprived of his constituency. The Party's official appraisal of Ulanhu upon his death noted that comrade Ulanhu was a "reliable Communist soldier, distinguished Party and state leader, outstanding proletarian revolutionary, and pre-eminent nationality work leader."

ULANHU IN MONGOL EYES

Taken at face value, the Ulanhu cult may manifest a common desire by both Mongols and Chinese, by appealing to Ulanhu's communist spirit, to further ethnic unity and common prosperity. Behind the seeming solidarity with regard to the Ulanhu cult, we can nevertheless see that Ulanhu represents different values to Mongols and Chinese. It would be preposterous to suggest that from a Mongolian point of view, however sinicized some Mongols were, they would only emphasize and celebrate their own subordination.

The inspiration of Ulanhu to Mongol leaders is that he placed Mongol interests on an equal footing with the interests of the Chinese state, making the case that the protection of Mongol interests and of harmony among nationalities held the key in Inner Mongolia (and not only in Inner Mongolia) to the enhancement of China's national interests, including security interests. Although Ulanhu's Inner Mongolia was short of independence—and, indeed, power was monopolized by him, his mainly Tumed associates, and his family members—Ulanhu nevertheless did several things beneficial to all Mongols during his lengthy rule of Inner Mongolia. Inner Mongolia under his leadership offers a good contrast to today's Inner Mongolia, one so sharp that many Mongols recall his era (1947–1966) as a lost paradise. By this technique of contrast, Ulanhu and his era have come to represent to many not only tolerable ethnic relations, but, above all, the glory of Mongol control of Inner Mongolia. This constitutes the core of his value and his cult to the Mongols.

Several features stand out to characterize his leadership. These are qualities especially stressed not only by ethnic Mongolian leaders, but also by ordinary Mongols and, to some extent, even by local Chinese, who see little benefit in the conflict between the center and the region. Further on, I will summarize certain attributes of Ulanhu stressed by some Mongol officials, especially by Zhao Zhenbei, a Mongol leader, who made his name by expelling illegal Chinese immigrants in the early 1980s while governor of Silingol League. Their comments were published in two 1990 volumes commemorating Ulanhu. On the one hand, the authors are speaking to Mongols. But at the same time, their words must be more or less acceptable to the Chinese authorities, who also vet the manuscript and read the book.

Zhao describes Ulanhu as a great son of the Mongolian minzu. His contribution lay in his "creative" application of Marxism to the reality of Inner Mongolia, a claim precisely analogous to that made for Mao with respect to the sinification of Marxism. And this retains great significance for guiding nationality work in Inner Mongolia. What, then, is this creative work of Ulanhu's? Zhao claims that Ulanhu developed a complete series of "thought" regarding nationality work, especially in the pastoral region. Ulanhu single-handedly demonstrated that the pastoral economy is not something backward, as agriculturist Chinese would have it, but is a legitimate part of the national economy. Thus, he fundamentally transformed the perception of the Chinese leadership toward the pastoral economy. Ulanhu maintained that pastoralism was the key to the economy of Inner Mongolia. Consistent with this policy, Ulanhu resolutely opposed reclamation of pastureland for crop growing, activities initiated by both local Chinese and the Chinese leadership of the North China Bureau and the Ministry of Agricultural Reclamation (*nong keng bu*). Ulanhu insisted that the pastoral Mongols had a different class structure from that of farmers, thereby resisting the blind imposition of Mao's agrarian-based class categories in Inner Mongolia. Instead, he devised a new policy appropriate to Inner Mongolia: no redistribution of land, no struggle, no class classification (the "Three Nos"), and moreover, he held that the herdlord and herder relationship should be mutually beneficial (see chapter 4 for a detailed discussion). At the height of the communization craze, Ulanhu, according to Zhao, opposed any such reorganization in the pastoral area. What he did, paying lip service to the center, was merely change the names of the Mongol *sumu* (township) to communes but staunchly resisted the leveling practices associated with the communes elsewhere. What made Ulanhu great was his independent and creative thought, an ability to hold to the truth in defiance of erroneous policies from the Center. In contrast to the general disaster wrought to all other provinces and regions by Mao's revolutionary zeal, culminating in the Great Leap famine, during Ulanhu's twenty-year leadership in Inner Mongolia, the Mongolian population increased from 800,000 to 1.3 million, and livestock numbers grew from 8.41 million in 1947 to 41.7 million in 1965, a prosperity unparalleled in any part of China (Zhao Zengbei 1990). These bold statements are not unreasonable; of course, Zhao ignores Ulanhu's shortcomings. While Zhao attributed this achievement to Ulanhu's creative thought and independent leadership style, a Chinese commentator, who praised the same achievements made by Ulanhu, resolutely insisted that "[t]his is the result of Comrade Ulanhu leading various nationalities of Inner Mongolia to stride forward along the correct direction of Marxism-Leninism and Mao Zedong thought; this is the inevitable result of the Party's nationality regional autonomy policy. It is bound to be futile for anybody to deny it" (Zhao Yuting

1990: 140). While noting certain common elements, what is most striking is the fundamental difference in approach between the two.

Mongols who recalled Ulanhu almost invariably stressed his creativity and independent spirit. For Buyandalai, a vice director of the Cultural Department of Inner Mongolia, Ulanhu laid the foundations for a new Inner Mongolian culture. Recalling Ulanhu's initiative in organizing the Inner Mongolian Cultural Ensemble (*Ulan Muchir*) in the late 1950s and early 1960s, which became a model for propagating the Mao Zedong Thought adopted throughout China, he pointed out that it was Ulanhu who insisted that Mongols had a rich culture that others should also learn from. Ulanhu's greatest contribution was showing that Inner Mongolian culture should be Marxist in content but national in form. And this was said to be in stark contrast to the later and still ongoing deliberate suppression by Chinese authorities of the Mongolian form of Inner Mongolian art and culture. Buyandalai concluded his recollection with praise:

> Ulanhu has gone and left us, but *long live his radiant nationality culture and art thought, and the nationality cultural enterprise to which he devoted his entire heart.* The purpose of remembering him is to inherit his legacy, and to develop more numerous, newer and better culture and art to console his soul up in heaven. (1990: 170, emphasis added)

Particularly surprising are the claims of Ulanhu's contribution to the Mongolian language. The Mongol language, one of the symbols of Mongol political equality, from the founding of the People's Republic, was challenged in the state's new discourse. Chinese (Mandarin) was privileged, becoming the direct medium not only for the transmission of Mao's doctrine, but in virtually all government activities, from administration to education to the military, even in the Inner Mongolia Autonomous Region. This association of political correctness and linguistic chauvinism posed a stark choice to Mongols: to remain politically and scientifically "backward" (thereby inevitably subjecting themselves to the Chinese civilizing mission) or to "catch up," in the first instance by incorporating key loan words from Chinese but ultimately losing the Mongol language in favor of Chinese. While a few Chinese-leaning Mongol linguists advocated taking in not only borrowed words from Chinese but even sounds and grammatical components, most Mongol officials resisted this by forming a committee to borrow words from the Cyrillic Mongolian used in the Mongolian People's Republic. They rejected the idea that only Chinese was an appropriate source of loan words.

The state-imposed language loss was exacerbated by the social environment Mongol elites found themselves in. Following the 1947 founding of the Inner Mongolia Autonomous Government, in 1952 the seat of government moved to Hohhot, originally a monastic town, divided between Manchu (army), Chinese (merchants), and Mongol (monks and pilgrims) quarters, that quickly became overwhelmingly Chinese with the migration of tens of thousand of workers and officials from north China (cf. Jankowiak 1993, for the contemporary "Chinese" characteristics of this city). Very soon, the children of Mongol cadres and intellectuals lost their language because of the combination of peer pressure from Chinese children (the overwhelming majority) and classroom instruction in Chinese, rather than Mongol (cf. Bao 1994). The rapid loss of language stirred strong resentment among Mongol officials and intellectuals, who voiced their criticism in the Hundred Flowers Movement in 1957. If, in old China, Mongols had lost their language because of the oppression of Great Han chauvinists, they asked, what could account for the loss of the Mongol language in the New China, in which ethnic oppression was supposed to have been eliminated and all nationalities were equal? It was agreed that Mongol language use had to be strengthened. However, one month later, this officially sanctioned criticism was targeted as a veiled attack on the Party and the Chinese Nation. Language became an issue precisely because it was one of the defining principles of Mongol nationality (Tegusi 1993: 56). Coupled with this was the fact that Mongolian was defined as the first language of the Inner Mongolia Autonomous Region, and it was decreed as early as 1947 that official documents must be prepared in Mongolian and Chinese. The difficulty in maintaining the dual-language policy after 1949 was resented by Mongols, not only because it inconvenienced many Mongol cadres and intellectuals, but also because the Mongol language was a powerful symbol of their status and identity. To be deprived of that status had profound political implications: it was a sign of the assimilation of the Mongols, one that could warrant the rescinding of Mongolian autonomy, the very basis of their status, authority, and position. Ethnic autonomy was, after all, based on difference.

Mongol linguistic resistance was poignantly demonstrated in 1957 by Ulanhu, the leader of Inner Mongolia, who deliberately spoke Mongolian on the tenth anniversary of the founding of the Inner Mongolia Autonomous Region. Many Mongols were moved to tears and could not forget it even after his death in 1988. Mongols interpreted his Mongol speech as defiance against the increasing Maoist and Han chauvinist onslaught on Mongol culture. It was sensational because Ulanhu could not speak Mongolian, as he belonged to the Tumed Mongol group, which had lost the Mongolian language a century ago. He read his speech from a text written in Cyrillic that was translated from his original Chinese (he spoke Russian fluently).

Thus, for Shenamjil (1990), a veteran linguist, Ulanhu was the founder of new China's Mongolian language work. He credits Ulanhu with inscribing an article (Article 53) in the Common Program ratified by the Chinese People's Political Consultative Congress (which served as a Constitution) between 1949 and 1954: "All national minorities have the freedom of developing their dialects and languages, preserving or reforming their customs, habits and religious beliefs" (in Hinton 1980: 55). Ulanhu, as a non-Mongol speaker himself, insisted that every Mongol and Chinese cadre should be bilingual in Mongolian and Chinese. And indeed, Ulanhu made it compulsory for Chinese cadres to learn Mongolian, stating that it would be used as a yardstick to measure whether they were here in Inner Mongolia to serve the Chinese or Mongols. Shenamjil particularly mentioned that in 1957 Ulanhu addressed the Mongolian People's Republic delegation in Mongolian, which made a great impression on many (1990: 285). A famous Mongol writer, T. Damrin, recalled that in 1987, at a celebration held in Beijing, Ulanhu "greeted [Inner Mongolian artists] in Mongolian, everybody was greatly moved, full of tears in their eyes" (1990: 274).

These few illustrations suggest that admiration of Ulanhu on the part of some influential Mongols may be genuine. But that genuine admiration goes hand in hand with the tactical use of Ulanhu to make the points that they wish to make regarding the present regime. Through celebration of Ulanhu and glorification of his achievements, these Mongols express their strong resentment toward the present situation. Mongol tears at Ulanhu speaking Mongolian contrast with the erosion of Mongolian language in Inner Mongolia in the 1980s and early 1990s. Many of the Mongolian language schools set up after the Cultural Revolution had collapsed, for the Chinese-dominated market economy made any Mongol education unsustainable, indeed useless. Nor is admiration for Ulanhu limited to the Mongol elite who once worked for Ulanhu. It extends to ordinary Mongols, Tumed and non-Tumed. They express their utmost contempt for some Mongol leaders, who are known to forbid their children to speak Mongolian when Chinese guests visit them. Critics say, "Look at Ulanhu; he was a real man. He not only tried to speak Mongolian himself but also tried to make the Chinese learn it!" Here, obviously, the issue is not that Ulanhu himself had indeed managed to learn Mongolian—in fact, his Mongolian was no more than signing his name in Mongolian script and uttering some simple everyday sentences—neither is it how many Chinese had learned Mongolian, but it is Ulanhu's "intent" or "effort."

When Mongols looked back at the Ulanhu era, they found at least two things: First, Mongols as a whole in Inner Mongolia were relatively better off economically than people in most of the country. This was true not only through the 1950s but also during the Great Leap Forward famine of the early 1960s. Politically, they also enjoyed more rights than they do today.

The Mongols quoted previously portray Ulanhu as a Mongol hero. The heroism of his deeds is based on comparisons of then and now. It is also based on a comparison with Mao. Although I suggest that this is a strategy chosen by Mongols largely as a means to engage in power discourse, nevertheless, their genuine feeling for Ulanhu cannot be dismissed. I would like to show that new criteria to evaluate a leader may be emerging in Inner Mongolia.

What Mongols see of themselves in assessing the twentieth century is that they are weak and overwhelmed by the Chinese, and that they are themselves hopelessly divided, unable to either become a united people or defend their interests in the face of the combination of a powerful Chinese state and large-scale Chinese migration to Inner Mongolia. Their decline in this century is a sharp contrast to their history of glory and valor. Their constant yearning for Chinggis Khan is, in this sense, a yearning for the recovery of Mongol prowess. Making things worse, the Mongol "feudal" lords early in this century, in the eyes of Mongols, indulged their selfish interests at the expense of the people. Not only did they collaborate with Chinese warlords, they also suppressed Mongols. These social vices seen in Mongol traditional lords indicate that Mongols would like to have a leader who could protect their interests against Chinese colonization and stand equal with the Chinese. The quality they would like to see in a Mongol leader is, first of all, strength and power, and that power should be directed outward, rather than inward.

Mongols love to point out that Ulanhu concurrently held the top Party, government, and army posts in the Autonomous Region, as well as being vice-premier (elected in both 1954 and 1965) and an alternate Politburo member, the only minority Politburo member. All of these were underscored to display his importance to Inner Mongols, both as the supreme leader of the autonomous region and as a major figure at the national level. This is impressive, not only in Inner Mongolia, but also in all other minority regions, where no one held all these positions simultaneously. This achievement is contrasted strongly with today's situation, in which the army, Party, and National People's Congress are all controlled by Chinese. And even when a Mongol is chairman, he lacks the authority in that position that Ulanhu had built because of the primacy of the Party secretary, always a Chinese. Ulanhu's monopoly of power, although at times contested in the sphere of intra-Mongol relations, has become one of his greatest merits, and it is now immensely admired by virtually all Mongols.

A number of miraculous signs linking Ulanhu with Mao are also widely remarked. Ulanhu is favorably compared to Mao Zedong: (1) both lived to the age of 82; (2) both Mao and Ulanhu shared one character in their names: *ze* (Ulanhu's Chinese name is Yun Ze), which means "pool" or "pond," and by extension "beneficence"; and (3) they physically resemble one another; Ulanhu was even taller than Mao. These signs underscore Ulanhu's quality as a great man, comparable to Mao.

How should we understand this? Hevia, in a fascinating study of different notions of koutou ritual, rejects defining it as "rituals of abject servitude." Following Catherine Bell's study of ritual as a "strategic mode of practice" that "produces nuanced relations of power, relationships characterized by acceptance and resistance, negotiated appropriation, and redemptive reinterpretation of the hegemonic order" (1992: 196), Hevia sees koutou as "empowering the lesser in a dependent relationship with a superior" (1994: 193). In his view, the koutou is a negotiation process involving power relations. Not everyone is permitted to koutou; "the subject must be encompassable," that is, the subject must also be powerful in the sense of having attributes and capacities desirable for incorporation into the imperial rulership. Indeed, we know that in history, tributary relations with the Chinese often demonstrate the strength of the nomadic kings, and what was negotiated worked to the material advantage of the latter. The importance of such ritual also lies in confirming the support of emperor/empire for the rule of a local ruler. This historical precedent may have contributed to a notion that a strong leader within the ritual realm will be able to obtain greater benefits for his people. Seen in this light, Ulanhu's joining the Chinese symbolic world creates expectations that the communists would deliver more—that is, restoration of the fragmented Inner Mongolia—and indeed assure some kind of autonomy, something Mongols could not achieve without help. Similarly, Mongols would concur that the ascendance of Ulanhu to the power center of the Chinese state did not mean that he was just a puppet but that he was strong and a force to be reckoned with by the Chinese government. Mongols may also see his high position in government as a demonstration of collective Mongol power in the configuration of the Chinese ethnic hierarchy, wherein greater autonomy and benefit could be wrestled out for the Mongols.

How this kind of dual allegiance and power relations was supposed to have worked is illustrated in the case of Ulanhu. The dismantling of the Inner Mongolian autonomy that Ulanhu had created, and his own demise, as well as the suffering of the Mongols during the Cultural Revolution, tended to bridge the gap between Ulanhu and the Mongols through shared suffering. Ulanhu also did his best to restore the fractured territorial autonomy of Inner Mongolia in the 1970s. According to a Mongol who was directly involved in restoring lost Inner Mongolian territories, Ulanhu played the role of a strong man after he was released from "protective custody" (*jian hu*) and allowed to resume work in 1973. Hua Guofeng, Mao's successor, was said to be less knowledgeable in minority affairs, and other leaders responsible for minority work were not yet reinstated, so he allowed Ulanhu a free hand in this realm. In his capacity as the minister for the United Front, and in close cooperation with other Mongol leaders, in 1979 Ulanhu then ordered the restoration of the territorial boundaries of Inner Mongolia Autonomous Region. This was no small job. There was opposition from three sides: the central ministers, the five provinces and autonomous regions, and Mongol leaders within those provinces. The latter were against the unification because they already held some positions of power. Unification would mean a reshuffle that could threaten their positions. This narrative highlighted one man using his skills to maneuver within the Chinese leadership, contrasting Ulanhu with selfish Mongol officials who preferred to remain within Chinese provinces. The narrative thus transformed Ulanhu from a traitor to an ethnic hero. Mongols acknowledge today that without Ulanhu, there might never have reemerged a unified Inner Mongolia; indeed, there would be no "Inner Mongolia Autonomous Region" at all. A Mongol dissident who would not concur with Ulanhu's other merits nevertheless acknowledged Ulanhu's outstanding performance in defending the Autonomous Region. He felt obliged to attend Ulanhu's funeral in Beijing uninvited and wrote an elegiac sentence, "In memory of twice unifying Inner Mongolia!"

The strength or ability (*chadaltai*) of Ulanhu is also favorably assessed along with his second quality, Mongol heart (*Mongol setgel*). The notion of Mongol heart is eclectic. It allows a person to fail in doing something; what matters above all is loyalty to one's nation. This is perhaps the ultimate test for Ulanhu. "Mongol heart" always distinguishes "one of us" from "one of them," or "for them" from "for us." As long as that "for us" is made clear and proved, even a complete failure may be turned into a martyr. Alternatively, a man of great accomplishments may be disowned (see chapter 5, for the Daur reevaluation of Merse).

Indeed, Ulanhu's "heart" is also the battleground of the posthumous evaluation of Ulanhu by the Chinese state and Mongols. In a memorial article published in the *People's Daily* on Ulanhu's ninetieth jubilee on December 23, 1996, Qiao Shi, then chairman of the National People's Congress, emphasized Ulanhu's solid Party spirit: "Comrade Ulanhu was loyal to the causes of the Party and the people; under all circumstances and in whatever posts he held, he had been resolutely following and implementing the Party line and its various principles and policies, always placing the fundamental interests of the Chinese Nation and collective interests of the State before everything else" (Qiao 1996). He was praised for fighting hard against any Mongol attempts to betray China. Ulanhu's greatness, in this official evaluation, lay in his *Chinese* heart.

There is no denying that deep in their hearts, Mongols deeply resent Ulanhu's so-called great patriotism—that is, his loyalty to the Chinese Nation. But this was a fait accompli, one that could not be disputed by any Mongol official in the People's Republic. Rather, Mongols try to find every sign that shows Ulanhu's Mongol heart after 1947. The accumulation of stories, from his trying to speak Mongolian to his concrete efforts to promote Mongol rights and his purges by the Chinese, almost vindicated earlier suspicions that he might be a Chinese agent. Mongols, especially eastern Mongols, were deeply suspicious of Ulanhu's ethnic identity in the 1940s. As he was called Yun Ze and assumed the title chairman of the Inner Mongolian Autonomous Movement Association, he was rumored to be a Chinese agent disguised as a "reincarnation" of Prince Yondonwangchug, the first head of the Mongolian Local Autonomous Political Affairs' Council, a political movement initiated by the famous prince Demchugdonrob. Prince Yondonwangchug, who died in 1939, was also known as Prince Yun in Chinese abbreviation (Jagchid 1999). An image of Ulanhu has been built through gossip and anecdotes, a classical arena where hidden transcripts are staged. These social constructions, which may involve a highly selective reading of his activities as viewed by many Mongols, portray him above all as a man who always placed Mongol interest before all else.

Some Mongol intellectuals, who were long suspicious of Ulanhu, now suggest that he might just have had a Mongol heart, but regrettably he was convinced that communism would deliver liberation to Mongols, and he made the fatal mistake of allying with the Chinese Communist Party. When he realized the problem, he was already on the pirate boat. He could not get off, but had to carry on. Many Mongols now understand, in light of increasing evidence, that there was no choice for Inner Mongols but to accept incorporation into China, particularly since the Soviet Union and the Mongolian People's Republic steadfastly refused to render any assistance to Inner Mongols in their desire for independence.

Other Mongols would say that no matter how masterful he was in nationality affairs, Ulanhu was extremely ignorant of the Chinese mentality, although he thought he understood them from his life experience. These remarks are from some eastern Mongolian intellectuals, who have every reason to say something critical. But no doubt they see Ulanhu not so much a deliberate traitor as a victim of his own internationalist enthusiasm. The blame is therefore directed toward those Chinese who cheated Ulanhu, who was sincere, typical of a Mongol.

There are numerous stories of Ulanhu's awakening—that is, becoming more ethnically conscious. I mentioned that it is a great comfort for some Mongols that Ulanhu, who once was ignorant of Mongolian language, managed to read a text in Mongolian in 1957. An eastern Mongolian cadre told me a story to convince me that Ulanhu was indeed knowledgeable in Mongolian. In the 1950s, after the new Chinese currency was printed, he spotted a mistake in the translation of "bank." The Mongol translation *mongon ger* was a literal translation of the Chinese *yinhang*, which means "silver/money house." Ulanhu immediately spotted and suggested that it be retranslated as *bank*, a well-established international loan word in Mongolian. Not only this, he managed to persuade the Center to retrieve the printed currency and issue new correct notes.

One important story concerns how Ulanhu insulted Wang Zhen. Wang, a ranking military man and minister of the Agricultural Reclamation Ministry, turned a large part of Mongol pastureland in Hulunbuir into agricultural fields in the early 1960s. It is said that Ulanhu got extremely angry when Mongols complained to him about the loss of their pastureland. He then went to Hulunbuir and ordered Mongol herders to let in horses to eat up all the crops, thus spoiling the scheme. This is certainly an exaggeration. But it was remarkable that Ulanhu managed to persuade Wang Zhen to restrain his activity in Inner Mongolia, while in Xinjiang his military production and construction corps, *bingtuan*, became a major colonization force (cf. Seymour 2000).

Another story tells of a famous Mongol singer in Beijing who experienced discrimination at the hands of the Chinese director of the Central Nationalities Song and Dance Ensemble. One day she went to see Ulanhu to ask if he could do something to help her. A few days later, at a meeting of the Nationality Affairs Commission, Ulanhu said to the minister in his typical Tumed Chinese dialect:

"Hey, I heard that X is a bastard, bullying our poor Y, can you do something about it?" As the story goes, before long the director was sacked.

These two stories among Mongols indicate that a strong Mongol heart, protecting Mongols, and defying the Chinese are the basic criteria for approving of a Mongol leader. His action is justified and given high approval from Mongols, and that is exactly what is expected of a strong man who has a Mongol heart.

Another important series of stories, known by almost all Mongols, illustrates a sense of despair shown by Ulanhu. According to this story, Ulanhu did not want to be transferred to Beijing. The motif in this genre is that of a caged tiger, crippled, yet always thinking of going back to Inner Mongolia. Some Mongols would say that he was disappointed at how Inner Mongolia had developed and worried at its prospects. Deng Xiaoping in this story is an uncompromising hardliner. On the fortieth anniversary of the founding of the Inner Mongolia Autonomous Region, Ulanhu managed to return to visit Inner Mongolia, but only after a tough negotiation with Deng. Deng eventually allowed him to go, but with these preconditions: First, he must praise what he has seen, and second, he must not incite any trouble. Perhaps the most moving part may be that of Ulanhu going to pay homage to Chinggis Khan. His pilgrimage was not on the agenda. Ulanhu had again to ask Deng's permission, and he was granted two hours there. Before Chinggis Khan's shrine, Ulanhu was said to have bitterly wailed. So do many Mongols nowadays. He stayed more than four hours before finally being pushed by his security guards onto the helicopter, never again to return to Inner Mongolia. It is said that after wailing in grief, the old man of eighty-one stood up and murmured, "Still, minzu tuanjie is good."

These stories portray Ulanhu as a kindly old Mongol, kidnapped by the Center. Mongols and Ulanhu wailing together in front of Chinggis Khan's shrine somewhat ties their fate together through Chinggis Khan, the ultimate symbol of the Mongol people. That Ulanhu worshiped Chinggis Khan is not entirely new. As early as 1939 he had been involved in removing the Chinggis Khan shrine from Ordos to a relatively safe area in Gansu, when Japanese forces attempted to seize it. In 1946 he raised the slogan "Descendants of Chinggis Khan, Unite!" as a war cry to inspire Mongols to fight for the autonomy of Inner Mongolia. In 1954 he officially arranged to bring back the shrine from exile and ordered that a three-domed mausoleum be built to house the shrine in 1956. On that occasion, he personally officiated at the Chinggis ceremony, as he did in 1962. According to charges levied during the Cultural Revolution, Ulanhu tried to become Chinggis Khan the second. Like many other Mongol patriots, perhaps Ulanhu always identified himself with Chinggis Khan. His cry before Chinggis Khan is a symbolic gesture, indicating that he thought he had failed, but it is also a message that he tried his best, following in Chinggis Khan's steps. We do not know what he thought, but his cry before Chinggis is interpreted by Mongols as repentance before the supreme Mongol ancestor.

Humphrey (1997) distinguishes two types of morality, Asian and European.

She suggests that unlike rule-based European morality, Asian, and particularly Mongolian, morality is constructed in the discourse of exemplars. In such a society there is no absolute wrong or right. The exemplar morality allows for individual difference and social hierarchy. In Mongolia, everybody, at some point in life, should have a teacher. The teacher is someone who advanced and improved himself or herself in relation to some moral principle, such as "bravery," "purity of thought," or "compassion." In our case, Ulanhu might be regarded as a political exemplar by the Chinese in order that people learn and conform to the political message. Mongol perceptions of exemplars can be multidimensional. Humphrey notes that exemplars have little or no control over what teachings their disciples derive from them. It is the disciple's task to make certain points exemplary in his own moral construction. This insight might help us to understand how Mongols make sense of Ulanhu. For Mongols, Ulanhu embodies numerous messages, contrary to the simple model of patriotism that the Center wishes Mongols to learn from him. To say the least, Ulanhu is seen as a quintessential exemplar *not* to trust the promises of the CCP. Mongols try hard to figure out the meaning of his "teaching" of "minzu tuanjie"; they believe that, being a great and clever man, Ulanhu must have a hidden message in his words. The hidden message, if it is hidden at all, was expounded by a Mongol scholar in an article that recently won a prize. He argued that Ulanhu had advocated not only internationality unity, but also intranationality unity. His exposition is worth quoting at length:

> Our country's elder generation proletarian revolutionary, outstanding leader of minority nationalities, and the founder of the Inner Mongolian Autonomous Region, Comrade Ulanhu, in his remaining years, even on his deathbed, was always deeply concerned about this problem. In 1987 on the occasion of the 40th anniversary of founding the Inner Mongolian Autonomous Region, he reiterated this point in his own article on this special topic: "unity includes the unity of all nationalities in the whole country, the unity between various nationalities in Inner Mongolia, and the unity within a nationality. Only when this unity is strengthened, when the state unity is consolidated, only when there is a strong unified great motherland, and when the region that has achieved nationality regional autonomy has internally united would various causes better develop. . . . The formation and development of the Mongol nationality is also the result of the unity between various tribes." He, in his 1988 conversation with Comrade Wenjin, in his sincere words and earnest wishes, looked forward to better unity between various nationalities in Inner Mongolia, and among Mongols. This is the greatest expectation from our revered Comrade Ulanhu before he departed from the world forever. When this testament of his was publicized by vice chairman Wenjin in 1988 after the formation of the new administration of the Inner Mongolia Autonomous Region, in a form of journalistic question-answer on TV and radio, it was praised and endorsed by cadres and masses of all nationalities of the region. (Orchilon 1993: 124)

7.5. Ulanhu as a State Leader to the Mongols (2000)

"TOTALITARIAN NOSTALGIA"
FOR STRONGMAN ULANHU

As we have seen, the Mongol cult of Ulanhu emerged as a result of "contrast" between past and present. The past is necessarily multilayered, forming the legendary or mystical Golden Age, the dark medieval times, informing the rise and fall of a people. The past represented by Ulanhu was not necessarily a Golden Age, but it embodied certain hopes after a hellish dark age. And this recent past of hope, with its limited promise, established a link with the ultimate Golden Age of Chinggis Khan. Historical contrast is an institution in all modern nationalist historical consciousness, punctuated by linear time. It gained particular salience as a mechanism for political legitimacy in Communist China: By constantly contrasting the present with the past, one yearns for a brighter future. But this future-looking contrast can also be reversed in the form of nostalgia—looking back to the past with fond memory, a yearning that targets the present as the dark age, and looking in horror at the uncertain future. The past serves as something known, certain, and stable. Barmé writes that "nostalgia develops usually in the face of present fears, disquiet about the state of affairs, and uncertainty about the future. Confronted with social anomie and disjuncture, nostalgia provides a sense of continuity" (1999b: 319). He points out that the new cult of Mao Zedong of the late 1980s and early 1990s was caught in a dialectic of irony and nostalgia. The irony is that despite Mao's purge and terror, Mao, like Stalin, "was the embodiment of both history and the national spirit, so to deny him would be to negate not merely one's own history but also vital facts of the national character" (1999b: 320). The nostalgia for Mao at a time of economic uncertainty and social anomie under Deng Xiaoping's rule invested in him a mystical image of being a "representative of an age of certainty and confidence, of cultural and political unity, and, above all, of economic equality and incorruptibility." Thus the Mao cult is both what he calls "totalitarian nostalgia" and a kind of resistance. And precisely here, Barmé points out, lies its irony and limited value: it offers a simple model of what it was in the past, "but it did not offer new or viable political solutions to China's problems" (1999a: 321).

To a certain extent, the cult of Ulanhu may be understood as a "totalitarian nostalgia." It is also based on the institution of contrast. But unlike the Mao cult, the yearning for Ulanhu is an aspiration for a viable solution to China's ethnic problems (i.e., from a Mongol perspective, the Chinese constitute a problem to the Mongols, not vice versa) that Ulanhu had so long fought for, albeit with limited success. And that is to foreground the role of the state and its constitution in the ethnic relations sphere. Here is the crucial site of struggle: Whereas the Center and the Chinese appropriate him only to obtain Mongol loyalty in a crude manner, Mongols reclaim his Mongol identity not only to point out the Center's hypocrisy, but also to suggest a new kind of politics. Mongol officials are now successfully appropriating Ulanhu and his complete set of ideas in order to resist further incursion into rights that are seen as rightfully theirs. Significantly for the Mongols, Ulanhu is not only the engineer of that objectifying machinery, but also part of the machinery—that is, the state. If he is really recognized as a state leader, as having once been China's vice president, if the law he engineered is recognized as legitimate and binding, there is no reason (many Mongols say) why he should not be granted the greatest respect by Mongolian officialdom. Mongols are most emphatic that Ulanhu is "patriotic" for China, thus firmly establishing the base that Chinese cannot fault.

Ulanhu has become an institution upon which people can rely and bargain with the state. What is interesting is that Mongols, especially students, often raise Chinggis Khan's portrait and demand rights once exercised by Ulanhu in Inner Mongolia! In terms of generations of leaders, with the ever greater decline of the Mongols' ethnic rights in Inner Mongolia, people do miss Ulanhu: If he were alive, they say, Inner Mongolia would be different. Only he could stand up to Chinese discrimination and abuse. Here, Mongols have started to appropriate him as an ethnic hero, along with Chinggis Khan. This cult transforms Ulanhu from an ambiguous figure into what James M. Burns (1978) calls a "heroic leader."

This heroic leadership does not necessarily mean that Ulanhu actually possessed heroic qualities that delivered tangible benefits to the Mongols. Heroism does not necessarily pivot on success. Moreover, heroic leadership is "not simply a quality or entity possessed by someone: it is a *type of relationship* between leader and led" (Burns 1978: 244, emphasis original). Whatever quality or attribute is possessed by the heroic leader, worship of him or her is an outcome of an expectation, a projection of one's fears, aggressions, and aspirations onto some social objects that allow a symbolic solution to conflicts. "Heroic leadership provides the *symbolic* solution of internal and external conflict" (Burns 1978: 244, emphasis original).

Both Chinggis Khan and Ulanhu, however, have also been appropriated by the Chinese state as its national heroes. The addition of Chinggis Khan and Ulanhu to the Chinese national pantheons is a complex process, with resistance and complicity from the Mongols, reflecting the complex relationship between Mongols as an ethnic minority that wishes its culture and heroes to be properly represented by the state and the state's desire to integrate minorities, including Mongols, into a national state. In the latter case, Chinggis Khan can also be de-Mongolized, making him into a racialized pan-Chinese hero, whose highest function may be to display Chinese racial and military superiority to White Others. Likewise, Ulanhu may also be de-Mongolized and made a Chinese "nationality work leader," as a paragon of loyal minorities, representing a Janus-faced circle: to conquer the state to be ruled by the state.

Whatever mixed and entangled feelings Mongols have about this Chinese appropriation, from a Mongol perspective one senses a difference between Chinggis Khan and Ulanhu. Chinggis Khan is an ultimate identity-giver to the Mongols, and his worship is religious-cum-nationalistic, whereas Mongols' respect for Ulanhu, as this book shows, is not a celebration of their identity, but a weapon for dealing with the Chinese state and their current dilemma, or a *symbolic* solution of their problems. He thus provides a point of reference against which every Mongol leader must be compared. One may raise this question: Would a new Mongol leader be able to stand firm and be reckoned with by the Chinese central government? But perhaps such questions are impossible to answer, as Ulanhu's status was contingent on his earlier communist career and intimate links with the Soviet Union and Mongolia. With these factors gone, it is doubtful that any Mongol could achieve comparable significance within the Chinese polity. What is certain is that Ulanhu does remain a symbolic aspiration.

In summer 2000, during my latest trip to Inner Mongolia, I went to visit the Ulanhu Mausoleum—indeed, not just once. In contrast to earlier times, the gigantic mausoleum was virtually deserted. There were very few people in the botanical garden, still less in the mausoleum. Protected by fee-collecting guards at the entrance to both the botanical garden and the mausoleum, Ulanhu enjoys a secluded serenity, unperturbed by either the bustle of the streets or the dust blown up by the faintest wind. As I gazed at the gigantic statue, my mind was filled with a famous passage uttered by Pavel Korchagin, the hero in the Soviet writer Nikolai Ostrovsky's novel *How Steel Was Tempered,* a novel that inspired millions of idealistic people in China from the 1950s to the 1980s:

> Man's dearest possession is life. It is given to him but once, and he must live it so as to feel no torturing regrets for wasted years, never know the burning shame of a mean and petty past; so live that, dying, he might say: all my life, all my strength,

were given to the finest cause in all the world—the fight for the Liberation of Mankind. (1959, part 2: 114)

Later, when I mentioned this to a senior Mongol, he said with a deep sigh: "But he died with regret and shame. His cancer was caused by his increasing anxiety in his later years."

Bibliography

Abu-Lughod, Lila. 1990. "The Romance of Resistance: Tracing Transformations of Power through Bedouin Women." *American Ethnologist* 17(1): 41–55.

Altangata. 1980. *Dawuer Menggu Kao.* Huhehaote: Nei Menggu Zizhiqu Shehui Kexueyuan Minzu Yanjiushi.

Anagnost, Ann. 1994. "Who Is Speaking Here? Discursive Boundaries and Representation in Post-Mao China." Pp. 257–79, in *Boundaries in China*, ed. John Hay. London: Reaktion.

———. 1997. *National Past-Times: Narrative, Representation, and Power in Modern China.* Durham, N.C., and London: Duke University Press.

Anderson, Benedict. 1991. *Imagined Communities: Reflections on the Origin and Spread of Nationalism.* London: Verso.

Ao Dong. 1989. "Boxue Duocai de Xuezhe Guo Kexing." *Dawuer Ren.* (September 30).

Ardyajav. 1991. "Guanyu Chengde Gong Huanyuan bing Fanyi de "Yuanchao Mishi." *Dawuer Ren* (July 10).

Atwood, Christopher P. 1994. *Revolutionary Nationalist Mobilization in Inner Mongolia, 1925–1929.* Unpublished Ph.D. dissertation. Bloomington: Indiana University.

Ayong. 1998. "Guanyu Dawuer de Zuyuan Wenti." Pp. 381–86, in *Dawuer Ziliao Ji*, vol. 2. Beijing: Minzu Chubanshe.

Ayong Batu. 1982. "Qidan Houyi de Dawuer Zu Shehui." *Dawuer Zu Yanjiu* 1: 26–40.

Ba Jingyuan. 1980. "Baotou Mengmin de 'Chuzudi' yu Mengzu de Laili jiqi Yanbian." *Baotou Shiliao Huiyao* 3: 130–38.

Badaranga. 1998. "Dui Dawuer Zucheng ji Zuyuan Wenti de Kanfa." Pp. 463–67, in *Dawuer Ziliao Ji*, vol. 2 Beijing: Minzu Chubanshe.

Bailey, Frederick G. 1991. *The Prevalence of Deceit.* Ithaca: Cornell University Press.

Balibar, Étienne. 1991. "The Nation Form: History and Ideology." Pp. 86–106, in *Race, Nation, Class: Ambiguous Identities*, by Étienne Balibar and Immanuel Wallerstein. London: Verso.

Balzer, Marjorie M. 1999. *The Tenacity of Ethnicity: A Siberian Saga in Global Perspective.* Princeton, N.J.: Princeton University Press.

Ban Lan, ed. 1997. *Huhehaote Shici.* Huhehaote: Nei Menggu Renmin Chubanshe.

Bao, Wurlig. 1994. *When Is a Mongol? The Process of Learning in Inner Mongolia.* Unpublished Ph.D. dissertation. Seattle: University of Washington.

Baoyinbatu. 1993. "Wei Shenme Wulanmaodu Muqu Meiyou Shixing Pingfen Shengxu—Huiyi Jiergele Qizhang de Yiduan Hua." *Xingan Dangshi Wenji* 2: 152–53.

Barlow, Tani. 1994. "Politics and Protocol of Funü: (Un)Making National Woman." Pp. 339–59, in *Engendering China: Women, Culture and the State,* ed. Chris Gilmartin et al. Cambridge, Mass.: Harvard University Press.

Barmé, Geremie R. 1996. *Shades of Mao: The Posthumous Cult of the Great Leader.* Armonk, N.Y., and London: M. E. Sharpe.

———. 1999a. "To Screw Foreigners Is Patriotic." Pp. 255–80, in his *In the Red: On Contemporary Chinese Culture.* New York: Columbia University Press.

———. 1999b. "Totalitarian Nostalgia." Pp. 316–44, in his *In the Red: On Contemporary Chinese Culture.* New York: Columbia University Press.

Batubagan and Altanochir, eds. 1999. *Wei Minzu Jiefang er Fendou de Yidai Qingnian.* Shenyang: Liaoning Minzu Chubanshe.

Bayar. 1998. *Menggu Xieyi.* Beijing: Minzu Chubanshe.

Bell, Catherine. 1992. *Ritual Theory, Ritual Practice.* Oxford: Oxford University Press.

Besio, Kimberly. 1997. "Gender, Loyalty, and the Reproduction of the Wang Zhaojun Legend: Some Social Ramifications of Drama in the Late Ming." *Journal of the Economic and Social History of the Orient* 40(2) (May): 251–82.

Bhabha, Homi K. 1994a. *The Location of Culture.* London and New York: Routledge.

———. 1994b. "DissemiNation: Time, Narrative, and the Margins of the Modern Nation." Pp. 139–71, in his *The Location of Culture.* London and New York: Routledge.

Bilid, Bilig. 1998. "Cengde Gung-un 'Ger-un Uye-yin Bicimel'-un Tuhai." *Ovur Monggol-un Neiyigem-un Sinjilehu Uhagan* 3: 35–39.

Billeter, Jean-Francois. 1985. "The System of 'Class Status.' " Pp. 127–69, in *The Scope of State Power in China,* ed. S. R. Schram. London: School of Oriental and African Studies, University of London.

Birch, Cyril, ed. 1965. *Anthology of Chinese Literature.* New York: Grove.

Bourdieu, Pierre. 1990. "The Uses of the 'People.' " Pp. 150–55, in his *In Other Words: Essays towards a Reflexive Sociology.* Stanford, Calif.: Stanford University Press.

Brennan, Timothy. 1990. "The National Longing for Form." Pp. 44–70, in *Nation and Narration,* ed. Homi K. Bhabha. London and New York: Routledge.

Brooks, Peter. 1994. "Melodrama, Body, Revolution." Pp. 11–24, in *Melodrama: Stage, Picture, Screen,* ed. Jacky Bratton, Jim Cook, and Christine Gledhill. London: British Film Institute.

Brubaker, Rogers. 1996. *Nationalism Reframed: Nationhood and the National Question in the New Europe.* Cambridge: Cambridge University Press.

Bulag, Uradyn E. 1998. *Nationalism and Hybridity in Mongolia.* Oxford: Clarendon.

Burchell, Graham, Colin Gordon, and Peter Miller, eds. 1991. *The Foucault Effect: Studies in Governmentality, with Two Lectures by and an Interview with Michel Foucault.* London: Harvester Wheatsheaf.

Burns, James MacGregor. 1978. *Leadership.* New York: Harper & Row.

Buyandalai. 1990. "Wulanfu Tongzhi dui Nei Menggu Wenhua Shiye de Gongxian." Pp. 146–70, in *Wulanfu Jinian Wenji,* vol. 2, compiled by Wulanfu Geming Shiliao Bianyanshi. Huhehaote: Nei Menggu Renmin Chubanshe.

Cairenjia. 1983. "Huiyi Ma Bufang Shiqi de Mengzang Wenhua Jiaoyu." *Qinghai Wenshi Ziliao* 11: 120–28.

Cao Shujun, and Yu Jianmeng. 1990. *Cao Yu.* Beijing: Zhongguo Qingnian Chubanshe.

Cao Yu. 1978. "Wang Zhaojun." *Renmin Wenxue* 11: 37–111.

———. 1979. "Zhaojun Ziyou Qianqiuzai—Wo Weishenma Xie 'Wang Zhaojun.'" *Minzu Tuanjie* 2.

Chakrabarty, Dipesh. 1992. "Postcoloniality and the Artifice of History: Who Speaks for 'Indian' Pasts?" *Representations* 37: 1–26.

———. 1996. "Marx after Marxism: History, Subalternity, Difference." Pp. 55–70, in *Marxism beyond Marx,* ed. Saree Makdisi, Cesare Casarino, and Rebecca E. Karl. New York: Routledge.

Chan, Anita. 1985. *Children of Mao: Personality Development and Political Activism in the Red Guard Generation.* London: Macmillan; Seattle: University of Washington Press.

Chao, Emily. 1996. "Hegemony, Agency, and Re-Presenting the Past: The Invention of Dongba Culture among the Naxi of Southwest China." Pp. 208–39, in *Negotiating Ethnicities in China and Taiwan,* ed. Melissa J. Brown. Berkeley, Calif.: Institute of East Asian Studies, University of California, Berkeley.

Chatterjee, Partha. 1993. *The Nation and Its Fragments: Colonial and Postcolonial Histories.* Princeton, N.J.: Princeton University Press.

Chen Bangyan. 1981. " 'Jihai' Yanyuan he 1940 Nian de Jihai Qingkuang." *Qinghai Wenshi Ziliao Xuanji* 8: 63–68.

Chen Binyuan. 1986. *Ma Bufang Jiazu Tongzhi Qinghai Sishi Nian.* Xining: Qinghai Renmin Chubanshe.

Chen Guangguo, and Xu Xiaoguang. 1992. "Lun Qinghaichao dui Menggu Lifa de Zhengce Yiju yu Jiben Yuanze." *Qinghai Minzu Xueyuan Xuebao* 4: 60–65.

Chia Ning. 1993. "The Lifanyuan and the Inner Asian Rituals in the Early Qing (1644–1795)." *Late Imperial China* 14(1): 60–92.

Chiang Kai-shek. 1947. *China's Destiny & Chinese Economic Theory,* with notes and commentary by Philip Jaffe. New York: Roy.

Chinggeletu. 1992. "Suiyuan Sheng de Tudi Gaige Yundong." *Nei Menggu Dangshi Tongxun* 1.

Chow, Rey. 1993. *Writing Diaspora: Tactics of Intervention in Contemporary Cultural Studies.* Bloomington and Indianapolis: Indiana University Press.

Chun, Allen. 1996. "The Lineage-Village Complex in Southeastern China: A Long Footnote in the Anthropology of Kinship." *Current Anthropology* 37(3): 429–50.

Cohen, Myron. 1993. "Cultural and Political Inventions in Modern China: The Case of the Chinese 'Peasants.'" *Daedalus* 122(2): 151–70.

Cohn, Bernard S. 1983. "Representing Authority in Victorian India." Pp. 165–209, in *The Invention of Tradition,* ed. E. Hobsbawm and T. Ranger. Cambridge: Cambridge University Press.

Colson, Elizabeth. 1995. "The Contentiousness of Disputes." Pp. 65–82, in *Understanding Disputes: The Politics of Argument,* ed. Pat Caplan. Oxford: Berg.

———. 1996. "Ethnicity, Nationalism, and the Politics of Difference in an Age of Revolution." Pp. 162–83, in *The Politics of Difference: Ethnic Premises in a World of Power,* ed. Edwin N. Wilmsen and Patrick McAllister. Chicago: University of Chicago Press.

Comaroff, John, and Jean Comaroff. 1992. "The Colonization of Consciousness." Pp. 235–63, in their *Ethnography and the Historical Imagination.* Boulder, Colo.: Westview.

Cooper, Frederick. 1997. "The Dialectics of Decolonization: Nationalism and Labor

Movements in Postwar French Africa." Pp. 406–35, in *Tensions of Empire: Colonial Cultures in a Bourgeois World*, ed. Frederick Cooper and Ann Laura Stoler. Berkeley, Los Angeles, and London: University of California Press.

Couture, Jocelyne, Kai Nielsen, and Michel Seymour, eds. 1998. *Rethinking Nationalism*. Calgary, Alberta: University of Calgary Press.

Crackdown in Inner Mongolia. 1991. An Asia Watch Report. United States: Human Rights Watch.

Crossley, Pamela, K. 1990. "Thinking about Ethnicity in Early Modern China." *Late Imperial China* 11(1): 1–34.

———. 1999. *A Translucent Mirror: History and Identity in Qing Imperial Ideology*. Berkeley: University of California Press.

Dalby, Michael T. 1979. "Court Politics in Late T'ang Times." Pp. 561–681, in *The Cambridge History of China*, vol. 3, *Sui and T'ang China, 589–906, part 1*, ed. Denis Twitchett. Cambridge: Cambridge University Press.

Damrin, T. 1990. "Jingdu, Nanwang de Juhui." Pp. 273–78, in *Wulanfu Jinian Wenji*, vol. 2, compiled by Wulanfu Geming Shiliao Bianyanshi. Huhehaote: Nei Menggu Renmin Chubanshe.

Da Qing Gaozang Chun Huengd Shilu. 1964. Taibei: Hualian Chubanshe.

Dawuer Zu Jianshi Bianxiezu. 1986. *Dawuer Zu Jianshi*. Huhehaote: Nei Menggu Renmin Chubanshe.

de Certeau, M. 1988. *The Writing of History*. New York: Columbia University Press.

Deleuze, Gilles, and Félix Guattari (trans. and foreword by Brian Massumi). 1987. *A Thousand Plateaus: Capitalism and Schizophrenia*. Minneapolis and London: University of Minnesota Press.

Di Cosmo, Nicola. 1998. "Qing Colonial Administration in Inner Asia." *The International History Review* 20(2): 287–309.

Dirlik, Arif. 1983. "The Predicament of Marxist Revolutionary Consciousness: Mao Zedong, Antonio Gramsci, and the Reformulation of Marxist Revolutionary Theory." *Modern China* 9(2): 182–211.

———. 1987. "Culturalism as Hegemonic Ideology and Liberating Practice." *Cultural Critique* 6 (Spring): 13–50.

———. 1996. "Reversals, Ironies, Hegemonies: Notes on the Contemporary Historiography of Modern China." *Modern China* 22(3): 243–84.

Dittmer, Lowell. 1981. "Radical Ideology and Chinese Political Culture: An Analysis of the Revolutionary Yangbanxi." Pp. 126–51, in *Moral Behavior in Chinese Society*, ed. Richard W. Wilson, Sydney L. Greenblatt, and Amy Auerbacher Wilson. New York: Praeger.

———. 1998. *Liu Shaoqi and the Chinese Cultural Revolution* (revised edition). Armonk, N.Y.: M. E. Sharpe.

Dong Hanhe. 1995. *Xilujun Chenfulu*. Lanzhou: Gansu Renmin Chubanshe.

Dong Jian. 1996. *Tian Han Zhuan*. Beijing: Beijing Shiyue Wenyi Chubanshe.

Dongbeiju. 1991. "Dongbeiju Guanyu Menggu Diqu Tugai Yundong de Jiantao, 1949, 6, 23." P. 1249, in *Minzu Wenti Wenxian Huibian*. Beijing: Zhonggong Zhongyang Dangxiao Chubanshe.

Donnan, Hastings, and Thomas M. Wilson. 1999. *Borders: Frontiers of Identity, Nation and State*. Oxford and New York: Berg.

Dorji. 1984. "Huiyi Wo zai Qinghai Xuanju Menggu Zu Guoda Daibiao Shi de Yi Duan Jingli." *Qinghai Wenshi Ziliao* 12: 88–95.

Dreyer, June Teufel. 1976. *China's Forty Millions*. Cambridge, Mass.: Harvard University Press.

Du Yongtao. 1990. "Longmei: Bing bu zong shi Chenxing." *Zhongwai Funü Wenzhai* (August).

Duara, Prasenjit. 1988. "Superscribing Symbol: The Myth of Guandi, Chinese God of War." *Journal of Asian Studies* 47(4): 778–95.

———. 1995. *Rescuing History from the Nation: Questioning Narratives of Modern China*. Chicago and London: University of Chicago Press.

———. 1996. "De-Constructing the Chinese Nation." Pp. 31–55, in *Chinese Nationalism*, ed. Jonathan Unger. Armonk, N.Y.: M. E. Sharpe.

———. 1998. "The Regime of Authenticity: Timelessness, Gender, and National History in Modern China." *History and Theory* 37(3): 287–308.

Dugarova-Montgomery, Yeshen-Khorlo, and Robert Montgomery. 1999. "The Buriat Alphabet of Agvan Dorzhiev." Pp. 79–98, in *Mongolia in the Twentieth Century: Landlocked Cosmopolitan*, ed. Stephen Kotkin and Bruce A. Elleman. Armonk, N.Y.: M. E. Sharpe.

Dutton, Michael. 1988. "Policing the Chinese Household: A Comparison of Modern and Ancient Forms." *Economy and Society* 17(2): 195–224.

Ebrey, Patricia. 1993. *The Inner Quarters*. Berkeley and Los Angeles: University of California Press.

Edwards, Louise P. 1994. *Men and Women in Qing China: Gender in the Red Chamber Dream*. Leiden and New York: E. J. Brill.

Elliott, Mark C. 2001. *The Manchu Way: The Eight Banners and Ethnic Identity in Late Imperial China*. Stanford, Calif.: Stanford University Press.

Enkebatu, Erhenbayaer, Se'ershentai. 1996. "Women Yongyuan Huainian Ta—Jinian Guo Daofu Xiansheng Dancheng 100 Zhounian." *Dawuer Zu Yanjiu* 5: 50–60.

Eoyang, Eugene. 1982. "The Wang Chao-chün Legend: Configurations of the Classic." *Chinese Literature: Essays, Articles and Reviews* 4: 3–22.

Erhenbayar. 1985. "Wei Man Shiqi de Lingsheng Shijian." *Hulun Bei'er Wenshi Ziliao* 3: 38–54.

Farquhar, David. 1978. "Emperor as Bodhisattva in the Governance of the Qing Empire." *Harvard Journal of Asiatic Studies* 38: 5–34.

Fei Xiaotong. 1989. "Zhonghua Minzu de Duoyuan Yiti Geju." Pp. 1–36, in *Zhonghua Minzu de Duoyuan Yiti Geju*, ed. Fei Xiaotong et al. Beijing: Zhongyang Minzu Xueyuan Chubanshe.

Fitzgerald, John. 1996. *Awakening China: Politics, Culture, and Class in the Nationalist Revolution*. Stanford, Calif.: Stanford University Press.

Fong, Grace S. 1994. "Engendering the Lyric: Her Image and Voice in Song." Pp. 107–44, in *Voices of the Song Lyric in China*, ed. Pauline Yu. Berkeley, Los Angeles, and Oxford: University of California Press.

Foucault, Michel. 1980. *Power/Knowledge*. Brighton: Harvester.

Fraser, Nancy. 1995. "From Redistribution to Recognition? Dilemmas of Justice in a 'Post-Socialist' Age." *New Left Review* 212: 68–93.

Friedman, Edward. 1995. *National Identity and Democratic Prospects in Socialist China*. Armonk, N.Y.: M. E. Sharpe.

Friedman, Edward, Paul G. Pickowicz, and Mark Selden. 1991. *Chinese Village, Socialist State*. New Haven and London: Yale University Press.

Fu Lehuan. 1955. "Guanyu Dahuer de Minzu Chengfeng Shibie Wenti." *Zhongguo Minzu Wenti Yanjiu Jikan (Guanyu Dahuer de Laiyuan)* 1: 1–32.

Geertz, Clifford. 1980. *Negara: The Theatre State in Nineteenth Century Bali.* Princeton: Princeton University Press.

Gellner, Ernest. 1983. *Nations and Nationalism.* Oxford: Blackwell.

Gerould, Daniel. 1994. "Melodrama and Revolution." Pp. 185–98, in *Melodrama: Stage, Picture, Screen,* ed. Jacky Bratton, Jim Cook, and Christine Gledhill. London: British Film Institute.

Gladney, Dru C. 1991. *Muslim Chinese: Ethnic Nationalism in the People's Republic.* Cambridge, Mass.: Harvard University Press.

———. 1994. "Representing Nationality in China: Refiguring Majority/Minority Identities." *Journal of Asian Studies* 53(1): 92–123.

Gleason, Gregory. 1991. "Fealty and Loyalty: Informal Authority Structures in Soviet Asia." *Soviet Studies* 43(4): 613–28.

Golan, Daphna. 1997. "Between Universalism and Particularism: The 'Border' in Israel Discourse." Pp. 75–93, in *Nations, Identities, Cultures,* ed. V. Y. Mudimbe. Durham, N.C., and London: Duke University Press.

Goode, William J. 1978. *The Celebration of Heroes: Prestige of a Social Control System.* Berkeley: University of California Press.

Gu Jianhua. 1992. "Qingchao Shiqi de 'Qinghai Yamen' jiqi dui Zhongda Xingshi Anjian de Shengpan." *Qinghai Shehui Kexue* 4: 106–12.

Guha, Ranajit. 1997. *Dominance without Hegemony: History and Power in Colonial India.* Cambridge, Mass., and London: Harvard University Press.

Guo Daofu. 1924. *Menggu Wenti.* (Publisher unknown).

Guo Kexing. 1987. *Heilongjiang Xiangtu Lu.* Harbin: Heilongjiang Chubanshe.

Guo Mingsheng. 1989. "Zai Gulai Xiansheng Shenbian Gongzuo Shinian zhong de Jijian Shi." *Dawuer Zu Zizhiqi Wenshi* 1: 126–68.

Guo Moruo. 1959. *Cai Wenji (wumu lishi xiju).* Beijing: Zhongguo Xiju Chubanshe.

———. 1982. "Wang Zhaojun." Pp. 122–88, in *Guo Moruo Juzuo Quanji,* vol. 1. Beijing: Zhongguo Xiju Chubanshe.

Guo Yingjie and Baogang He. 1999. "Reimagining the Chinese Nation: The 'Zeng Guofan Phenomenon.'" *Modern China* 25(2): 142–70.

Gupta, A., and J. Ferguson. 1992. "Beyond 'Culture': Space, Identity, and the Politics of Difference." *Cultural Anthropology* 17(1): 6–23.

Halliday, Fred. 1999. *Revolution and World Politics: The Rise and Fall of the Sixth Great Power.* Durham, N.C.: Duke University Press.

Handsuren, Tsendiin. 1997. *Tsend Gun ba Mongolin Nuuts Tovchoo.* Ulaanbaatar: MHAUT-iin Hariaa Hevleliin Gazar.

Hanguan Quejia. (n.d.). "Jianshu Qinghai zhi Jihai yu Huimeng." *Qinghai Minzu Yanjiu* 2: 94–106.

Hansen, Valerie. 1990. *Changing Gods in Medieval China, 1127–1276.* Princeton, N.J.: Princeton University Press.

Hao Weimin, ed. 1991. *Nei Menggu Zizhiqu Shi.* Huhehaote: Nei Menggu Daxue Chubanshe.

———. ed. 1997. *Nei Menggu Geming Shi.* Huhehaote: Nei Menggu Daxue Chubanshe.

Hao Yufeng. 1997. *Wulanfu yu Weiren de Jiaowang he Youyi.* Beijing: Zhonggong Dangshi Chubanshe.

Hao Yufeng and He Limin, eds. 1997. *Wulanfu yu Sanqian Gu'er*. Beijing: Zhonggong Dangshi Chubanshe.

Harrell, Stevan, ed. 1995a. *Cultural Encounters on China's Ethnic Frontiers*. Seattle and London: University of Washington Press.

———. 1995b. "Introduction: Civilizing Projects and the Reaction to Them." Pp. 3–36, in *Cultural Encounters on China's Ethnic Frontiers*, ed. Stevan Harrell. Seattle and London: University of Washington Press.

———. 1995c. "The History of the History of the Yi." Pp. 63–91, in *Cultural Encounters on China's Ethnic Frontiers*, ed. Stevan Harrell. Seattle and London: University of Washington Press.

———. 1999. "The Role of the Periphery in Chinese Nationalism." Pp. 133–60, in *Imagining China: Regional Division and National Unity*, ed. Shu-min Huang and Cheng-Kuang Hsu. Taipei: Institute of Ethnology, Academia Sinica.

He Jihong. 1996. *Xiyu Lungao*. Ulumuqi: Xinjiang Renmin Chubanshe.

Hechter, Michael. 1975. *Internal Colonialism: The Celtic Fringe in British National Development, 1536–1966*. Berkeley: University of California Press.

Hein, Laura, and Mark Selden, eds. 2000. *Censoring History: Citizenship and Memory in Japan, Germany, and the United States*. Armonk, N.Y.: M.E. Sharpe.

Herberer, Thomas. 1989. *China and Its National Minorities: Autonomy or Assimilation?* Armonk, N.Y.: M. E. Sharpe.

Hershatter, Gail. 1993. "The Subalterns Talks Back: Reflections on Subaltern Theory and Chinese History." *Positions* 1(1): 103–30.

Herzfeld, Michael. 1997. *Cultural Intimacy: Social Poetics in the Nation-State*. New York and London: Routledge.

———. 2001. *Anthropology: Theoretical Practice in Culture and Society*. Malden, Mass.: Blackwell.

Heuschert, Dorothea. 1998. "Legal Pluralism in the Qing Empire: Manchu Legislation for the Mongols." *The International History Review* 20(2): 310–24.

Hevia, James L. 1994. "Sovereignty and Subject: Constituting Relations of Power in Qing Guest Ritual." Pp. 188–200, in *Body, Subjectivity, and Power in China*, ed. Angela Zito and Tani E. Barlow. Chicago: University of Chicago Press.

———. 1995. *Cherishing Men from Afar: Qing Guest Ritual and the Macartney Embassy of 1793*. Durham, N.C., and London: Duke University Press.

Hinton, Harold C., ed. 1980. *The People's Republic of China: A Documentary Survey*, vol. 1. Wilmington, Del.: Scholarly Resources.

Hirsch, Francine. 2000. "Toward an Empire of Nations: Border-Making and the Formation of Soviet National Identities." *The Russian Review* 59: 201–26.

Hirschman, Albert O. 1970. *Exit, Voice, Loyalty: Responses to Decline in Firms, Organizations and States*. Cambridge, Mass.: Harvard University Press.

———. 1991. *The Rhetoric of Reaction: Perversity, Futility, Jeopardy*. Cambridge, Mass.: Belknap Press of Harvard University Press.

Ho Pin and Gao Xin. 1992. *Zhonggong 'Taizidang.'* Toronto: Canada Mirror.

Ho Ping-ti. 1998. "In Defense of Sinicization: A Rebuttal of Evelyn Rawski's 'Reenvisioning the Qing.' " *Journal of Asian Studies* 71(1): 123–55.

Hobsbawm, Eric J. 1990. *Nations and Nationalism since 1780: Programme, Myth, Reality*. Cambridge: Cambridge University Press.

Honig, Emily. 1996. "Native Place and the Making of Chinese Ethnicity." Pp. 143–55, in *Remapping China: Fissures in Historical Terrain*, ed. Gail Hershatter, Emily Honig, Jonathan N. Lipman, and Randall Stross. Stanford, Calif.: Stanford University Press.

Hsiung, Ann-Marie H. K. 1996. "Examining Wang Zhaojun in *Hangong Qiu* as Fiction of Woman." *Asian Culture (Asia-Pacific Culture) Quarterly* 14(3): 61–70.

Huang Guangxue, ed. 1995. *Zhongguo de Minzu Shibie*. Beijing: Minzu Chubanshe.

Huang, Philip C. 1995. "Rural Class Struggle in the Chinese Revolution: Representational and Objective Realities from the Land Reform to the Cultural Revolution." *Modern China* 21(1): 105–43.

Humphrey, Caroline. 1992. "Women and Ideology in Hierarchical Societies in East Asia." Pp. 173–92, in *Persons and Powers of Women in Diverse Cultures*, ed. Shirley Ardener. Oxford: Berg.

———. 1997. "Exemplars and Rules: Aspects of the Discourse of Moralities in Mongolia." Pp. 25–47, in *The Ethnography of Moralities*, ed. Signe Howell. London: Routledge.

Humphrey, Caroline, with Urgunge Onon. 1996. *Shamans and Elders: Experience, Knowledge, and Power among the Daur Mongols*. Oxford: Clarendon.

Hung Chang-tai. 1985. *Going to the People: Chinese Intellectuals and Folk Literature 1918–1937*. Cambridge, Mass., and London: Harvard University Press.

Ikeshiri, N. 1982. *Dawuer Zu*, translated from Japanese to Chinese by Odongowa. Huhehaote: Dawuer Lishi, Yuyan, Wenxue Xiehui.

Jagchid, Sechin. 1999. *The Last Mongol Prince: The Life and Times of Demchugdongrob, 1902–1966*. Bellingham, Wash.: Center for East Asian Studies, Western Washington University.

Jankowiak, William R. 1993. *Sex, Death, and Hierarchy in a Chinese City: An Anthropological Account*. New York and Oxford: Columbia University Press.

Jian Bozan. 1980a. "Wencheng Gongzhu Shu le Hua." Pp. 457–64, in his *Jian Bozan Lishi Lunwen Xuanji*. Beijing: Renmin Chubanshe.

———. 1980b. "Gei Wencheng Gongzhu Yingyou de Lishi Diwei." Pp. 645–74, in his *Jian Bozan Lishi Lunwen Xuanji*. Beijing: Renmin Chubanshe.

———. 1980c. "Cong Xi Han de Heqin Zhengce shuodao Zhaojun Chusai." Pp. 475–89, in his *Jian Bozan Lishi Lunwen Xuanji*. Beijing: Renmin Chubanshe.

———. 1982. "Wang Zhaojun Jiashi, Nianpu ji youguan shixing." *Beijing Daxue Xuebao* 6: 29–35.

Jiang Ping. 1995. "Weida de Minzu Lingxiu Wulanfu Yongcui Buxiu." Pp. 169–70, in his *Minzu Zongjiao Wenti Lunwen Ji*. Beijing: Zhonggong Dangshi Chubanshe.

Jiang Xiaowang. 1995. *Xing Zhangli Xia de Zhongguo Ren*. Shanghai: Shanghai Renmin Chubanshe.

Jiansheju "Dongfanghong" Liandui. 1967. "Jiechuan Wulanfu, Chen Bingyu zhiliu Xiujian Zhaojunfen yinmu." *Weidong Zhanbao* (November 8).

Kang Xijun. 1989. "Mianhuai Mengguzu Wang Benba Tongzhi." *Qinghai Wenshi Ziliao Xuanji* 18: 154–59.

Kaup, Katherine Palmer. 2000. *Creating the Zhuang: Ethnic Politics in China*. Boulder, Colo.: Lynne Rienner.

Kertzer, David I. 1988. *Ritual, Politics and Power*. New Haven, Conn., and London: Yale University Press.

Keyes, Charles. 1981. "The Dialectic of Ethnic Change." Pp. 124–71, in *Ethnic Change*, ed. S. Giner and M. Archer. London: Routledge & Kegan Paul.

Ko, Dorothy. 1997. "The Body as Attire: The Shifting Meanings of Footbinding in Seventeenth-Century China." *Journal of Women's History* 8(4): 8–27.

Kuang Qinghuan (Kwong Hing Foon). 1990. "Xiandai Minjian Chuanshuo de Wang Zhaojun." *Hanxue Yanjiu* 8(1): 461–87.

Kymlicka, Will. 1995. *Multicultural Citizenship*. Oxford: Clarendon.

Kymlicka, Will, and Wayne Norman, eds. 2000. *Citizenship in Diverse Societies*. Oxford: Oxford University Press.

Lattimore, Owen. 1969. *The Mongols of Manchuria: Their Tribal Divisions, Geographical Distribution, Historical Relations with Manchus, and Chinese and Present Political Problems*. New York: Howard Fertig.

Lee, Robert H. G. 1979. "Frontier Politics in Southwestern Sino-Tibetan Borderlands during the Ch'ing Dynasty." Pp. 35–68, in *Perspectives on a Changing China: Essays in Honor of Professor C. Martin Wilbur on the Occasion of His Retirement*, ed. Joshua A. Fogel and William T. Rowe. Boulder, Colo.: Westview.

Li Gui. 1966. *Li Gui Fandong Yanlun Zhaibian*. Huhehaote: Nei Menggu Zizhiqu Wenhua Gemin Bangongshi Ziliaozu.

Li Shijun. 1987. "Feng Yuxiang yu 'Lei-Ma Shijian.' " *Gansu Wenshi Ziliao* 4: 82–96.

Li Xiguang. 1996. *Zhaohui Zhongguo Zuori Huihuang*. Beijing: Guoji Wenhua Chuban Gongsi.

Lin Gan. 1979. *Zhaojun yu Zhaojun Mu*. Huhehaote: Nei Menggu Renmin Chubanshe.

Lin Gan, and Ma Yi. 1994. *Minzu Youhao Shizhe—Wang Zhaojun*. Huhehaote: Nei Menggu Renmin Chubanshe.

Lin Gan, Wang Xiong, and Bailadugeqi. 1995. *Nei Menggu Minzu Tuanjie Shi*. Huhehaote: Yuanfang Chubanshe.

Link, Perry. 2000. *The Uses of Literature: Life in the Socialist Chinese Literary System*. Princeton, N.J.: Princeton University Press.

Lipman, Jonathan N. 1984. "Ethnicity and Politics in Republican China: The Ma Family Warlords of Gansu." *Modern China* 10(3): 285–316.

———. 1996. "Hyphenated Chinese: Sino-Muslim Identity in Modern China." Pp. 97–112, in *Remapping China: Fissures in Historical Terrain*, ed. Gail Hershatter, Emily Honig, Jonathan N. Lipman, and Randall Stross. Stanford, Calif.: Stanford University Press.

———. 1997. *Familiar Strangers: A History of Muslims in Northwest China*. Seattle: University of Washington Press.

Litzinger, Ralph A. 2000, *Other Chinas: The Yao and the Politics of National Belonging*. Durham, N.C., and London: Duke University Press.

Liu Chun. 1989. "Nei Menggu Gongzuo de Huiyi." *Nei Menggu Dangshi Ziliao* 2: 69–112.

———. 1993. "Minzhu Geming Shiqi Nei Menggu Muye Qu de Minzhu Gaige." *Xing'an Dangshi Wenji* 2: 127–44.

Liu Jung-en, trans. 1972. *Six Yuan Plays*. Harmondsworth: Penguin.

Liu, Lydia. 1994. "The Female Body and Nationalist Discourse: *The Field of Life and Death* Revisited." Pp. 37–62, in *Scattered Hegemonies: Postmodernity and Transnational Feminist Practices*, ed. Inderpal Grewal and Caren Kaplan. Minneapolis and London: University of Minnesota Press.

Lockwood, Christopher. 1998. "How Mao's Soldier Is Inspiring New China." *Daily Telegraph* (London) (March 10).

Longmei and Yurong. 1990. "Mianhuai Wulanfu Yeye dui Women de Qinqie Guanhuai." Pp. 348–54, in *Wulanfu Jinian Wenji*, vol. 1, compiled by Wulanfu Geming Shiliao Bianyanshi. Huhehaote: Nei Menggu Renmin Chubanshe.

Lu Xun. 1981. "Suibian Fanfan." Pp. 630–32 in his *Lu Xun Quanji*, vol. 2. Beijing: Renmin Wenxue Chubanshe.

Lu Yan. 1987. "Lishi de Jueze." *Liao Wang* (July 20): 17–19.

Ludden, David. 1996. "Introduction. Ayodhya: A Window on the World." Pp. 1–23, in *Contesting the Nation: Religion, Community, and the Politics of Democracy in India*, ed. David Ludden. Philadelphia: University of Pennsylvania Press.

Ma Hetian. 1932. "Qinghai Shicha Ji." *Xin Yaxiya* 3(6): 143–51.

———. 1949. [Ma Ho-t'ien] *Chinese Agent in Mongolia*, translated by John De Francis. Baltimore: Johns Hopkins.

Ma Li. 1997. *Sanqian Gu'er he Caoyuan Muqin*. Huhehaote: Nei Menggu Jiaoyu Chubanshe.

Ma Rong and Zhou Xin. 1999. *Zhonghua Minzu Ningjuli Xingcheng yu Fazhan*. Beijing: Beijing Daxue Chubanshe.

Ma Ruheng and Dazheng Ma. 1994. *Qingdai de Bianjiang Zhengce*. Beijing: Zhongguo Shehui Kexue Chubanshe.

Mackerras, Colin. 1994. *China's Minorities: Integration and Modernization in the Twentieth Century*. Oxford: Oxford University Press.

Malkki, Liisa. 1995. *Purity and Exile: Violence, Memory, and National Cosmology among Hutu Refugees in Tanzania*. Chicago and London: University of Chicago Press.

Manduertu. 1995. "Minzu Minzhu Gemin de Doushi—Guo Daofu Shengping Shulue." *Dawuer Zu Yanjiu* 5: 34–40.

Mao Zedong. 1977. "On the Correct Handling of Contradictions among the People." Pp. 384–421, in *Selected Works of Mao Tse-tung*, vol. V. Peking: Foreign Languages Press.

McLaren, Anne. 1994. "Desire and Conquest: The Politics of Eroticism and Repression in the Construction of Chinese Identity." Pp. 42–65, in *Modernity and Identity: Asian Illustration*, ed. Alberto Gomes. Bundoora: La Trope University Press.

Meisner, Maurice. 1967. *Li Ta-chao and the Origins of Chinese Marxism*. Cambridge, Mass.: Harvard University Press.

Meng Yue. 1993. "Female Images and National Myth." Pp. 118–36, in *Gender Politics in Modern China*, ed. Tani E. Barlow. Durham, N.C., and London: Duke University Press.

Meng Zhidong. 1995. *Yunnan Qidan Houyi Yanjiu*. Beijing: Zhongguo Shehui Kexue Chubanshe.

Menghe. 1996. "Mianhuai Jiechu de Guo Daofu Xiansheng." *Dawuer Zu Yanjiu* 5: 41–49.

Mi Yizhi, ed. 1993. *Qinghai Menggu Zu Lishi Jianbian*. Xining: Qinghai Renmin Chubanshe.

Millward, A. James. 1994. "A Uyghur Muslim in Qianlong's Court: The Meanings of the Fragrant Concubine." *The Journal of Asian Studies* 53(2): 427–58.

———. 1998. *Beyond the Pass: Economy, Ethnicity, and Empire in Qing Central Asia, 1759–1864*. Stanford, Calif.: Stanford University Press.

Mountcastle, Amy. 1997. "The Construction of a Tibetan Identity: Women's Practices and Global Process." *Inner Asia: Occasional Papers* 2(1): 128–42.

Mu Shouqi. 1970 reprint. *Gan Ning Qing shilue*. Taibei: Guangwen Shuju, vol. 8.

Mudimbe, V. Y. 1997. "Introduction." Pp. 1–6, in *Nations, Identities, Cultures*, ed. V. Y. Mudimbe. Durham, N.C., and London: Duke University Press.

Munohoi (Mao Aohai). 1995a. "Shilun Jichu Minzu Lishi Ju de Sixiang Qingxiang: Ping Guo Moruo, Cao Yu, Yu Boyuan san Tongzhi de Muxie Zuoping." Pp. 112–22, in his *Minzu Wenti Lilun Yanjiu Tansuoji*. Shanghai: Shanghai Sanlian Shudian.

———. 1995b. "Guanyu Minzu Wenti de Shizhi Shifu Jieji Douzheng Wenti." Pp. 11–16, in his *Minzu Wenti Lilun Tansuo Ji*. Shanghai: Shanghai Sanlian Shudian.

Nagudanfu. 1985. "Guo Gaofu Lüezhuan." *Hulunbeier Shizhi Ziliao* 1: 95–103.

Nei Menggu Dangwei Zhengce Yanjiushi and Nei Menggu Zizhiqu Nongye Weiyuanhui, eds. 1987. *Nei Menggu Xumuye Wenxian Ziliao Xuanbian 2*. Huhehaote (internal publication).

Nei Menggu Geming Shi Bianji Weiyuanhui. 1978. *Nei Menggu Geming Shi*. Huhehaote: Nei Menggu Geming Shi Bianweihui Bangongshi.

Nei Menggu Gongchandang (Nei Menggu Gongchandang Gongzuo Weiyuanhui Xing'anmeng Zhongxinqi). 1993. "Nei Menggu Gongchandang Gongzuo Weiyuanhui Xing'anmeng Zhongxinqi dui Xiaomian Fengjian zhong Qunzhong Douzheng de Jidian Yijian, 1947, 12, 21." *Xing'an Dangshi Wenji* 2: 28–41.

Nei Menggu Zizhiqu Bianjizu. 1985. *Dawuer Zu Shehui Lishi Diaocha*. Huhehaote: Nei Menggu Renmin Chubanshe.

Nei Menggu Zizhiqu Dang'an'guan, compiler. 1989. *Nei Menggu Zizhi Yundong Lianhehui: Dang'an Shiliao Xuanbian*. Beijing: Dang'an Chubanshe.

Nugent, David. 1997. *Modernity at the Edge of Empire: State, Individual, and Nation in the Northern Peruvian Andes, 1885–1935*. Stanford: Stanford University Press.

Odongowa. 1996. "Guanyu Guo Daofu jizhong Chenghu de Buzheng he Guanyu Ta de Jieju." *Dawuer Zu Yanjiu* 5: 165–69.

Olivier, Bernard Vincent. 1993. *The Implementation of China's Nationality Policy in the Northeastern Provinces*. San Francisco: Mellen Research University Press.

Onon, Urgunge, trans. and annot. 1990. *The History and the Life of Chinggis Khan (The Secret History of the Mongols)*. Leiden: Brill.

———, trans. and intro. 1993. *Chinggis Khan: The Golden History of the Mongols* (revised by Sue Bradbury). London: Folio Society.

Orchilon. 1993. *Nei Menggu Minzu Wenti yu Tansuo*. Huhehaote: Nei Menggu Jiaoyu Chubanshe.

Ortner, Sherry B. 1995. "Resistance and the Problem of Ethnographic Refusal." *Comparative Study of Society and History* 37: 173–93.

Ostrovsky, Nikolai. 1959. *How Steel Was Tempered*. Moscow: Foreign Languages Publishing House.

Ounan Wuzhuer. 1995. "Guanyu Dawuer Zu Zucheng yu Zuyuan Wenti." *Nei Menggu Shehui Kexue* 3: 51–56.

Peng Wenbin. 2000. "Recalling the Vanished: Provincial and Ethnic Narratives in the Former Xikang Province." Paper presented at the annual meeting of the Association for Asian Studies, San Diego (March).

Perdue, Peter. 1998. "Boundaries, Maps, Movement: Chinese, Russian, and Mongolian Empires in Early Modern Central Eurasia." *The International History Review* 20(2): 263–86.

Perry, Elizabeth J. 1994. "Casting a Chinese 'Democracy' Movement: The Roles of Students, Workers, and Entrepreneurs." Pp. 74–92, in *Popular Protest and Political Culture in Modern China: Learning from 1989*, ed. Jeffrey N. Wasserstrom and Elizabeth J. Perry. Boulder, Colo.: Westview.

Polosmak, Natalya. 1994. "A Mummy Unearthed from the Pastures of Heaven." *National Geographic* (October): 80–103.

Pomeranz, Kenneth. 1997. "Ritual Imitation and Political Identity in North China: The Late Imperial Legacy and the Chinese State Revisited." *Twentieth-Century China* 23(1): 1–30.

Poppe, Nicolas. 1930. *Dagurskoe Narechie*. Leningrad: Izd-vo Akademii Nauk SSSR.

———. 1983. *Reminiscences*, ed. Henry Schwarz. Bellingham, Wash.: Western Washington University Press.

Pye, Lucian W. 1996. "The State and the Individual: An Overview Interpretation." Pp. 16–42, in *The Individual and the State in China*, ed. Brian Hook. Oxford: Oxford University Press.

Pye, Lucian W., with Mary W. Pye. 1985. *Asian Power and Politics: The Cultural Dimensions of Authority*. Cambridge, Mass.: Harvard University Press.

Qiao Shi. 1996. "Weiji Cui Qingshi, Jingshen Zhao Houren: Jinian Wulanfu Tongzhi Dancheng 90 Zhounian." *Renmin Ribao* (December 23).

Qinghai (Qinghai Shengzhi Biancuan Weiyuanhui). 1987. *Qinghai Lishi Jiyao*. Xining: Qinghai Renmin Chubanshe.

Qiqige. 1993. "Gongxun Zai Shice, Yeji Liu Houren: Wulanfu Tongzhi Jinianguan Neirong Jianjie ji Chouzhan Gongzuo Jishihi." *Wulanfu Yanjiu* 2: 47–48.

Rawski, Evelyn S. 1991. "Qing Imperial Marriage and Problems of Rulership." Pp. 170–203, in *Marriage and Inequality in Chinese Society*, ed. Rubie S. Watson and Patricia Buckley Ebrey. Berkeley: University of California Press.

———. 1996. "Presidential Address: Reenvisioning the Qing: The Significance of the Qing Period in Chinese History." *Journal of Asian Studies* 55(4): 829–50.

———. 1998. *The Last Emperors: A Social History of Qing Imperial Institutions*. Berkeley, Los Angeles, and London: University of California Press.

Ren Hai. 1996. "Taiwan and the Impossibility of the Chinese." Pp. 75–97, in *Negotiating Ethnicities in China and Taiwan*, ed. Melissa J. Brown. Berkeley: Institute of East Asian Studies, University of California, Berkeley: Center for Chinese Studies.

Richardson, H. E. 1984. *Tibet and Its History* (rev. 2nd ed.). Boston and London: Shambhala.

Rodgers, Daniel T. 1987. *Contested Truths: Keywords in American Politics since Independence*. New York: Basic.

Rosaldo, Renato. 1993. *Culture & Truth: The Remaking of Social Analysis*. Boston: Beacon.

Roseberry, William. 1996. "Hegemony, Power, and Languages of Contention." Pp. 71–84, in *The Politics of Difference: Ethnic Premises in a World of Power*, ed. Edwin N. Wilmsen and Patrick McAllister. Chicago: University of Chicago Press.

Said, Edward. 1978. *Orientalism*. London: Routledge & Kegan Paul.

———. 1979. *The Question of Palestine*. New York: Times Books.

———. 1997. "Zionism from the Standpoint of Its Victims." Pp. 15–38, in *Dangerous Liaisons: Gender, Nation, & Postcolonial Perspectives*, ed. Anne McClintock, Aamire Mufti, and Ella Shohat. Minneapolis and London: University of Minnesota Press.

Saussy, Haun. 1997. "Women's Writing before and within the 'Hong Lou Meng.'" Pp. 285–305, in *Writing Women in Late Imperial China*, ed. Ellen Widmer and Kang-I Sun Chang. Stanford, Calif.: Stanford University Press.

Schein, Louisa. 2000. *Minority Rules: The Miao and the Feminine in China's Cultural Politics*. Durham, N.C., and London: Duke University Press.

Schram, Stuart, trans. 1999. *Mao's Road to Power: Revolutionary Writings 1912–1949: Toward the Second United Front January 1935–July 1937*. Armonk, N.Y.: M. E. Sharpe.

Schwarcz, Vera. 1994. "Strangers No More: Personal Memory in the Interstices of Public Commemoration." Pp. 45–64, in *Memory, History, and Opposition under State Socialism,* ed. Rubie S. Watson. Santa Fe: School of American Research Press.

Scott, James. 1990. *Domination and the Arts of Resistance: Hidden Transcripts.* New Haven, Conn.: Yale University Press.

Selden, Mark. 1971. *The Yenan Way in Revolutionary China.* Cambridge, Mass.: Harvard University Press.

———. 1979. *The People's Republic of China: A Documentary History of Revolutionary Change.* New York and London: Monthly Review Press.

Serruys, Henry. 1959. *The Mongols in China during the Hung-Wu Period (1368–1398).* Bruges: Imprimerie Sainte-Catherine.

Seymour, James D. 2000. "Xinjiang's Production and Construction Corps, and the Sinification of Eastern Turkestan." *Inner Asia* 2(2): 171–94.

Shen Sung-chiao. 1997. "The Myth of Huang-ti (the Yellow Emperor) and the Construction of Chinese Nationhood in Late Qing." *Taiwan Shehui Yanjiu Jikan* 28: 1–70.

Shenamjil. 1990. "Wulanfu Tongzhi yu Menggu Yuwen Gongzuo." Pp. 279–87, in *Wulanfu Jinian Wenji,* vol. 2, compiled by Wulanfu Geming Shiliao Bian yanshi. Huhehaote: Nei Menggu Renmin Chubanshe.

Sheng Binhua and Gao Jiangang. 1998. *Zhonggo Dawuerzu Renkou.* Huhehaote: Nei Menggu Daxue Chubanshe.

Sheridan, Mary. 1968. "The Emulation of Heroes." *The China Quarterly* 33: 47–72.

Shnirelman, Victor A. 1996. *Who Gets the Past? Competition for Ancestors among Non-Russian Intellectuals in Russia.* Washington, D.C.: Woodrow Wilson Center Press; Baltimore, Md.: Johns Hopkins University Press.

Shryock, Andrew. 1997. *Nationalism and Genealogical Imagination: Oral History and Textual Authority in Tribal Jordan.* Berkeley: University of California Press.

Slezkine, Yuri. 1996. "The USSR as a Communal Apartment, or How a Socialist State Promoted Ethnic Particularism." Pp. 203–38, in *Becoming National: A Reader,* ed. Geoff Eley and Ronald Grigor Suny. New York and Oxford: Oxford University Press.

Sommer, Doris. 1990. "Irresistible Romance: The Foundational Fictions of Latin America." Pp. 71–98, in *Nation and Narration,* ed. Homi K. Bhabha. London and New York: Routledge.

———. 1991. *Foundational Fictions: The National Romances of Latin America.* Berkeley: University of California Press.

Song Naigong, ed. 1987. *Zhongguo Renkou: Nei Menggu Fence.* Beijing: Zhongguo Caizheng Jingji Chubanshe.

Song Zhending. 1993. "Song Zhending Tongzhi Baogao Xing'an Meng Gongzuo." *Xing'an Dangshi Wenji* 2: 42–55.

Spivak, Gayatri Chakravorty. 1988. "Can the Subaltern Speak?" Pp. 271–313, in *Marxism and the Interpretation of Cultures,* ed. Cary Nelson and Lawrence Grossberg. Urbana: University of Illinois Press.

Steinberg, Stephen. 1995. *Turning Back: The Retreat from Racial Justice in American Thought and Policy.* Boston: Beacon.

Stoler, Ann Laura. 1989. "Rethinking Colonial Categories: European Communities and the Boundaries of Rule." *Comparative Study of Society and History* 13(1): 136–37.

———. 1995. *Race and the Education of Desire: Foucault's History of Sexuality and the Colonial Order of Things.* Durham, N.C., and London: Duke University Press.

Stranahan, Patricia. 1983. "Labour Heroines of Yan'an." *Modern China* 9(2): 228–52.

Stuart, Kevin. 1997. *Mongols in Western/American Consciousness.* Lewiston, Queenston, and Lampeter: Edwin Mellen.

Sun Jiazhen. 1993. "Wulanmaodu Muqu Minzhu Gaige Qingkuang." *Xing'an Dangshi Wenji* 2: 154–57.

Su Keqing and Zhang Xin. 1989. "Suiyuan Mengqi Tudi Gaige Jilüe." *Nei Menggu Dangshi Ziliao* 2: 113–28.

Tambiah, Stanley J. 1976. *World Conqueror and World Renouncer.* London, New York, and Melbourne: Cambridge University Press.

Tao, Jing-shen. 1988. *Two Sons of Heaven: Studies in Sung-Liao Relations.* Tucson: University of Arizona Press.

Taussig, Michael. 1997. *The Magic of the State.* New York and London: Routledge.

Taylor, Charles. 1994. *Multiculturalism: Examining the Politics of Recognition* (ed. and intro. by Amy Gutmann). Princeton, N.J.: Princeton University Press.

Tegusi. 1993. "Nei Menggu Zizhiqu Chengli 10 Zhounian Qianhou de Xi yu Bei." *Nei Menggu Dang'an Shiliao* 3: 54–58.

Teng, Emma Jinhua. 1998. "An Island of Women: The Discourse of Gender in Qing Travel Writing about Taiwan." *The International History Review* 20(2): 353–70.

Tishkov, Valery. 1997. *Ethnicity, Nationalism and Conflict in and after the Soviet Union: The Mind Aflame.* London: Sage.

Thongchai, Winichakul. 1994. *Siam Mapped: A History of the Geo-Body of a Nation.* Honolulu: University of Hawaii Press.

———. 1996. "Maps and the Formation of the Geo-Body of Siam." Pp. 67–92, in *Asian Forms of the Nation*, ed. Stein Tonnesson and Hans Antlöv. Surrey: Curzon.

Tumen and Zhu Dongli. 1995. *Kangsheng yu Neirendang Yuanan.* Beijing: Zhonggong Zhongyang Dangxiao Chubanshe.

Tumote (Tumote Zuoqi "Tumote Zhi" Biancuan Weiyuanhui). 1987. *Tumote Zhi.* H/Huhehaote: Nei Menggu Renmin Chubanshe.

Turner, John A., trans. 1976. *A Golden Treasury of Chinese Poetry: 121 Classic Poems.* Hong Kong: Chinese University of Hong Kong.

Turner, Victor. 1969. *The Ritual Process.* Chicago: Aldine.

Ulanhu. 1967 [1947]. "1947 Nian 7 Yue 23 Ri zai Ganbu Hui shang de Baogao." In *Du Cao Ji: Wulanfu Fangeming Yanlun Xuanbian*, vol. 1: 25–29.

———. 1967 [1957]. "Zai Nei Menggu Danwei Zhaokai de Xuanchuan Gongzuo Huiyi shang de Jianghua." In *Du Cao Ji: Wulanfu Fangeming Yanlun Xuanbian*, vol. 2: 9–24.

———. 1967 [1965]. "Wulanfu zai Qingzhu Ershi Zhounian Chouweihui Zhaokai de Zuotanhui shang de Jianghua (Yuanshi Jilugao), 1965 Nian 12 Yue 21 Ri Shangwu." In *Du Cao Ji: Wulanfu Fangeming Yanlun Xuanbian*, vol. 3: 11–19.

———. 1967a. "Wulanfu zai Tuqi Siqing Pianhui shang de Jianghua ji Chahua (Yuanshi Jilugao)." *Du Cao Ji: Wulanfu Fangeming Yanlun Xuanbian*, vol. 3: 52–63.

———. 1967b. "Wulanfu zai Tuqi Siqing Gongzuotuan Duiyuan Zhengxun Dahui shang de Jianghua." *Du Cao Ji: Wulanfu Fangeming Yanlun Xuanbian*, vol. 3: 67–78.

———. 1987a. "Minzu Quyu Zizhi de Guanghui Licheng." Pp. 1–21 in *Minzu Wenti Lilun Lunwen Ji*, ed. Yan Kexun et al. Xining: Qinghai Renmin Chubanshe.

———. 1987b. "Wulanfu Tongzhi zai Nei Menggu Ganbu Huiyi shang Zongjie Baogao Tigang" (7/30/1948). Pp. 10–18, in *Nei Menggu Xumuye Wenxian Ziliao Xuanbian*, ed. Su Qifa. Huhehaote (internal publication) vol. 2, pt. 1.

———. 1989. *Wulanfu Huiyilu.* Beijing: Zhonggong Dangshi Ziliao Chubanshe.

———. 1990. *Wulanfu Lun Muqu Gongzuo.* Huhehaote: Nei Menggu Remin Chubanshe.

———. 1991. "Yun Ze Guanyu Nei Meng Tudi he Zizhi Wenti gei Zhongyang de Baogao." Pp. 1057–58, in *Minzu Wenti Wenxian Huibian, 1921, 7–1949,* 9, compiled by Zhonggong Zhongyang Tongzhanbu. Beijing: Zhonggong Zhongyang Dangxiao Chubanshe.

———. 1999. *Wulanfu Wenxuan.* 2 vols. Beijing: Zhongyang Wenxian Chubanshe.

van der Sprenkel, Sybille. 1962. *Legal Institutions in Manchu China: A Sociological Analysis.* London: Athlone.

van Grasdorff, Gilles. 1999. *Hostage of Beijing: The Abduction of the Panchen Lama.* Straftesbury, Boston, and Melbourne: Element.

Verdery, Katherine. 1991. *National Ideology under Socialism: Identity and Cultural Politics in Ceausescu's Romania.* Berkeley, Los Angeles, and London: University of California Press.

———. 1994. "From Parent-State to Family Patriarchs: Gender and Nation in Contemporary Eastern Europe." *Eastern European Politics and Societies* 8: 225–55.

Wagner, Rudolf G. 1990. *The Contemporary Chinese Historical Drama: Four Studies.* Berkeley, Los Angeles, and Oxford: University of California Press.

Waldron, Arthur. 1990. *The Great Wall of China: From History to Myth.* Cambridge: Cambridge University Press.

Wang Donghai. 1992. "Qinghai Hu Lidai Fenghao yu 'Lingxian Qinghai Zhi Shen' Bei Suotan." *Qinghai Shehui Kexue* 2: 81–84.

Wang Duo. 1992. *Wushi Chunqiu: Wo Zuo Minzu Gongzuo de Jingli.* Huhehaote: Nei Menggu Renmin Chubanshe.

Wang Feng. 1958. "Guanyu zai Shaoshu Minzu zhong Jinxing Zhengfeng he Shehui Zhuyi Jiaoyu Wenti de Baogao." Pp. 413–50, in *Minzu Gongzuo Shiyong Fagui Shouce.* Beijing: Falü Chubanshe.

Wang Tonglin. 1993. "Han Tang zhi Heqin Zhengce." Pp. 41–50, in *Zhongguo Funü Shi Lunji,* vol. 3, ed. Bao Jialin. Taibei: Daoxiang Chubanshe.

Wang Yuhai. 2000. *Fazhan yu Biange: Qingdai Nei Menggu Dongbu yu Mu xiang Nong de Zhuanxing.* Huhehaote: Nei Menggu Daxue Chubanshe.

Watson, Burton, trans. 1961. *Records of the Grand Historian of China.* New York: Columbia University Press.

Watson, James L. 1982. "Chinese Kinship Reconsidered: Anthropological Perspectives on Historical Research." *The China Quarterly* 92 (December): 589–622.

———. 1985. "Standardizing the Gods: The Promotion of T'ien Hou ('Empress of Heaven') along the South China Coast, 960–1960." Pp. 292–324, in *Popular Culture in Late Imperial China,* ed. David Johnson, Andrew J. Nathan, and Evelyn S. Rawski. Berkeley: University of California Press.

———. 1992. "The Regeneration of Chinese Cultural Identity in the Post-Mao Era." Pp. 67–84, in *Popular Protest and Political Culture in Modern China: Learning from 1989,* ed. Jeffrey N. Wasserstrom and Elizabeth J. Perry. Boulder, Colo.: Westview.

———. 1993. "Rites or Beliefs? The Construction of a Unified Culture in Late Imperial China." Pp. 80–103, in *China's Quest for National Identity,* ed. Lowell Dittmer and Samuel S. Kim. Ithaca and London: Cornell University Press.

Watson, Rubie S., ed. 1994a. *Memory, History, and Opposition under State Socialism.* Santa Fe: School of American Research Press.

———. 1994b. "Making Secret Histories: Memory and Mourning in Post-Mao China." Pp. 65–85, in *Memory, History, and Opposition under State Socialism*, ed. Rubie S. Watson. Santa Fe: School of American Research Press.

Wei, Yuan. 1965. *Sheng Wu Ji*. Preface 1842. Repr., *Jondai Zhongguo Shiliao Congkan*, vol. 102. Taipei: Wenhai.

Williams, Brackette F. 1989. "A Class Act: Anthropology and the Race to Nation across Ethnic Terrain." *Annual Review of Anthropology* 18: 401–44.

———. 1995. "Classification Systems Revisited: Kinship, Caste, Race, and Nationality as the Flow of Blood and the Spread of Rights." Pp. 201–36, in *Naturalizing Power: Essays in Feminist Cultural Analysis*, ed. Sylvia Yanagisako and Carol Delaney. London and New York: Routledge.

Willis, Paul. 1997. "TIES: Theoretically Informed Ethnographic Study." Pp. 182–92, in *Anthropology and Cultural Studies*, ed. Stephen Nugent and Cris Shore. London: Pluto Press.

Wittfogel, Karl August. 1957. *Oriental Despotism: A Comparative Study of Total Power*. New Haven, Conn.: Yale University Press.

Wolf, Eric. 1982. *Europe and the People without History*. Berkeley: University of California Press.

Wong, R. Bin. 1997. *China Transformed: Historical Change and the Limits of European Experience*. Ithaca and London: Cornell University Press.

Woody, W. 1993. *The Cultural Revolution in Inner Mongolia: Extracts from an Unpublished History*, ed. and trans. Michael Schoenhals. Stockholm: Center for Pacific Asia Studies at Stockholm University.

Wulisi Wurong. 1987. *Qiqihaer Dawuer Shilüe*. Qiqihaer: Qiqihaer Shi Shehui Kexue Yanjiusue.

———. 1993. "Wei Man Longjiang xian Woniutu Dawuer zu shenghuo gaikuang." Pp. 643–45, in *Weiman Shehui*, ed. Song Bang et al. Changchun: Jilin Renmin Chubanshe.

Wurijitu, ed. 1997. *Nei Menggu Dashiji*. Huhehaote: Nei Menggu Renmin Chubanshe.

Xining Fu Xuzhi. 1985. Xining: Qinghai Renmin Chubanshe.

Xue Song. 1992. "Zhaojun Chusai Gushi de Yanbian." *Suiyuan Wenxian* 16: 89–95.

Xue Wenbo. 1943. "Jihai Ji." *Bianzheng Gonglun* 2(11–12): 51–54.

Yanagisako, Sylvia, and Carol Delaney, eds. 1995. *Naturalizing Power: Essays in Feminist Cultural Analysis*. London and New York: Routledge.

Yang, C. K. 1961. *Religion in Chinese Society: A Study of Contemporary Social Functions of Religion and Some of Their Historical Factors*. Berkeley and Los Angeles: University of California Press.

Yang Shuhui. 1998. *Appropriation and Representation: Feng Menglong and the Chinese Vernacular Story*. Ann Arbor: Center for Chinese Studies, the University of Michigan.

Yang Zhongmei. 1988. *Hu Yao Bang: A Chinese Biography*, trans. William A. Wycoff; ed. Timothy Cheek; with a foreword by Rudolf G. Wagner. Armonk, N.Y.: M. E. Sharpe.

Yenjing Qinghua Beida 1951. Nian Shuqi Nei Menggu Gongzuo Diaochatuan. 1997. *Nei Menggu Huna Meng Minzu Diaocha Baogao*. Huhehaote: Nei Menggu Renmin Chubanshe.

Yi Ming. 1996. "Qianxi Guo Daofu Xiansheng de Zhengzhi Sixiang—Jinian Guo Xiansheng 100 Zhounian." *Dawuer Zu Yanjiu* 5: 79–91.

Yi Si. 1990. "Yue Zhongqi yu Zangqu." *Zangxue Yanjiu* 6: 222–27.

Yuan Shengpo. 1991. *Kang Yong Qian Jingying yu Kaifa Beijiang*. Beijing: Zhongguo Shehui Kexue Chubanshe.

Zamcarano, C. 1934. *Darhad Köbsögöl Nagur-un Uriyanghai, Dörbed, Hotong, Bayad, Ögeled, Minggad, Jahachin, Torgud, Hoshud, Chahar, Darigangga, Altai-yin Uriyanghai, Hasag, Hamnigan-nar-un Garul ündüsü bayidal-un ügülel*. Ulaanbaatar: Bügüde Nayiramdahu Monggol Arad Ulus-un Sinjlehüi Uhagan-u Hüriyeleng.

———. 1955. *The Mongol Chronicles of the Seventeenth Century* (trans. Rudolf Loewenthal). Wiesbaden: Otto Harrassowitz.

Zhang Bo and Yao Xiuchuan. 1984. "Jiefang chu Qinghai ge Zu Renmin Lianyihui Shengkuang Jishu." *Qinghai Wenshi Ziliao Xuanji* 12: 50–62.

Zhang Fuling. 1990. *Hanjian Miwenlu*. Changchun: Jilin Jiaoyu Chubanshe.

Zhang Hequan. 1993. *Zhoudai Jisi Yanjiu*. Taibei: Wenjin Chubanshe.

Zhang, Jie. 1997. *Manmeng Lianyin: Qingdai Gongting Hunsu*. Shenyang: Liaohai Chubanshe.

Zhang Yingjin. 1997. "From 'Minority Film' to 'Minority Discourse': Questions of Nationhood and Ethnicity in Chinese Cinema." Pp. 81–104, in *Transnational Chinese Cinemas: Identity, Nationhood, Gender*, ed. Sheldon Hsiao-peng Lu. Honolulu: University of Hawaii Press.

Zhao Yuntian. 1994. "Qing Zhengfu dui Menggu, Dongbei Fengjing Zhengce de Bianhua." *Zhongguo Bianjiang Shidi Yanjiu* 3: 20–27.

Zhao Yuting. 1990. "Gongcui Shice, Yinmin Bixou—Dao Wulanfu Tongzhi." Pp. 137–42, in *Wulanfu Jinian Wenji*, vol. 2, compiled by Wulanfu Geming Shiliao Bian yanshi. Huhehaote: Nei Menggu Renmin Chubanshe.

Zhao Zhenbei. 1990. "Guanghui de Bangyang, Buxiu de Yeji." Pp. 93–109, in *Wulanfu Jinian Wenji*, vol. 2, compiled by Wulanfu Geming Shiliao Bian yanshi. Huhehaote: Nei Menggu Renmin Chubanshe.

———. 1998. "A New Appraisal of Democratic Reform in the Pastoral Zone of Inner Mongolia in the 1940s." (trans. U. E. Bulag) *Central Asian Survey* 17(1): 109–37.

Zhecang Cairang, ed. 1994. *Qingdai Qinghai Mengguzu Dang'an Shiliao Jibian*. Xining: Qinghai Renmin Chubanshe.

Zheng Yongnian. 1999. *Discovering Chinese Nationalism in China: Modernization, Identity, and International Relations*. Cambridge: Cambridge University Press.

Zhou Kaiqing. 1968. *Xibei Jianying*. Taibei: Taiwan Shangwu Yingshuguan.

Zhu Shikui, et al., eds. 1994. *Qinghai Fengshu Jianzhu*. Xining: Qinghai Renmin Chubanshe.

Zito, Angela Rose. 1984. "Re-Presenting Sacrifice: Cosmology and the Editing of Texts." *Ch'ing-Shih Wen-T'i* 5(2): 47–78.

———. 1997. *Of Body & Brush: Grand Sacrifice as Text/Performance in Eighteenth-Century China*. Chicago: University of Chicago Press.

Index

263

About the Author

Uradyn E. Bulag is associate professor of anthropology at Hunter College and the Graduate Center of the City University of New York. He is the author of *Nationalism and Hybridity in Mongolia* and coeditor of *Inner Asia*. A specialist on Mongolia and China, his current research centers on Chinese, Japanese, and Mongol deification of the world conqueror Chinggis Khan and its implications for racial/national configurations in modern and contemporary Asia.